PERVERSION FOR PROFIT

WHITNEY STRUB

PERVERSION
FOR
PROFIT

The Politics of

Pornography

and the Rise of the

New Right

Columbia University Press

A portion of chapter 1 was published in *American Quarterly* (2008), and sections of chapters 3 and 4 appeared in the *Journal of the History of Sexuality* (2006).

COLUMBIA UNIVERSITY PRESS
Publishers Since 1893
New York   Chichester, West Sussex

Library of Congress Cataloging-in-Publication Data
Strub, Whitney.
Perversion for profit : the politics of pornography and the rise of the New Right /
Whitney Strub.
p. cm.
Includes bibliographical references and index.
ISBN 978-0-231-14886-3 (cloth : alk. paper)—ISBN 978-0-231-14887-0 (pbk. : alk. paper)—
ISBN 978-0-231-52015-7 (e-book)
1. Pornography—United States—History—20th century.   2. Pornography—Political
aspects—United States.   3. Conservatism—United States   I. Title.
HQ472.U6S77 2010
363.4'70973—dc22
2010025009

Columbia University Press books are printed on permanent and durable acid-free paper.
This book is printed on paper with recycled content.
Printed in the United States of America

c 10 9 8 7 6 5 4 3 2 1
p 10 9 8 7 6 5 4 3 2

Cover design: Martin Hinze   Cover image: AP Images/Dave Pickoff

Contents

PERVERSION FOR PROFIT

INTRODUCTION

PORNOGRAPHY HAS GENERATED AT LEAST as many words as it has orgasms, and the words have arguably been more intense. From the breathless denunciations of Anthony Comstock and Andrea Dworkin to the equally spirited defenses of Annie Sprinkle and Patrick Califia, pornography is a topic guaranteed to inspire heated passions.

Those passions have affected American politics in profound ways in the past half-century, helping shape the public face of the conservative ascendance that constitutes the most important national political movement of the era. Yet for all that has been written on matters of porn and its legal complement, obscenity, the full history of the social, cultural, and sexual contestations that have structured the modern politics of pornography and obscenity remains unwritten. Nothing comparable to Andrea Friedman's excellent *Prurient Interests*, which situates obscenity battles of early-twentieth-century New York City in local gender and political conflicts, has been undertaken for the postwar United States. Many of the most important works on recent porn-related struggles have been polemical rather than scholarly in nature, and outstanding scholarly efforts often hone in on highly specific topics, such as Donald Alexander Downs's *The New Politics of Pornography*, which examines 1980s battles in Minneapolis and Indianapolis.[1]

In *Perversion for Profit* I seek to write the larger national history of postwar American struggles over pornography and obscenity. Particular emphasis falls on the discovery and deployment of the political capital of moralism by the burgeoning New Right in the late 1960s. While the postwar liberal consensus that shaped the American mainstream in the 1950s popularized opposition to censorship, liberals hesitated to follow their free-speech convictions to their logical corollaries and instead allowed a First Amendment exception to be made for "obscenity," a class of material defined as "utterly without redeeming social value." Though the fundamental intellectual incoherence of the liberal position remained successfully obscured for several years, new rhetorical strategies allowing conservatives to frame repressive policies as secular and reasonable put liberals in an untenable position regarding pornography by the 1960s. Unwillingly, they ceded social authority on the matter to the nascent New Right.

The Right's commitment to suppressing porn began as a nominal one. Conservative politicians displayed more interest in attracting voters with pronouncements of their piety than in following through with substantive policy, damning rather than damming the "floodtide of filth" allegedly engulfing the nation, and eagerly adopting moralism as a discursive displacement of the increasingly obsolete conservative tropes of racism and anticommunism. But as the 1970s witnessed the surprising political awakening of evangelical Christians, sexual politics quickly became a key conservative platform item in assuring that those new voters flocked en masse to the Republican Party. The result was a startling new level of government obeisance to normative evangelical sexuality, seen in the Reagan administration's Meese Commission and, most recently, in the overtly religious rhetoric and policies of the George W. Bush years.

Pornography played dual roles in this trajectory from liberal to conservative national politics, both as an indicator of social and political trends in the treatment it received and as a causal agent in alerting the New Right to the tremendous political capital of moralism and sanctimony. Here I trace the politics of obscenity and pornography from the comic-book moral panic that ultimately reintroduced porn as a matter of national concern in the 1950s through the fiercely regressive policies of the Bush II administration a half-century later. I weave together a disparate set of topics—comic books, the Supreme Court, grassroots antiporn efforts, national and local politics, cultural history, and feminism, among others—to show as thoroughly as possible the many ways in which porn debates reflected and influenced postwar America. Though each chapter contains its own analytical argument, my overall case is that pornography and its neglected relationship to free speech provided a fatal flaw in the ideology of the postwar liberal consensus, an Achilles' heel the New Right has stabbed at to great effect since the late 1960s. Social, political, and juridical constructions of "obscenity" and "pornography" have also reinforced normative standards and continue to bear heavy consequences for queer and otherwise noncompliant sexual expression.

In this my project differs from the immense amount of works dedicated to the highly marketable topic of pornography. An endless series of popular books has approached the topic with varying levels of reportorial depth and prurience, foregrounding biographical elements of industry figures and framing politics as a vague backdrop that occasionally intervenes in the form of an arrest.[2] Meanwhile, a legion of scholars has written the history of pornography and obscenity—often portrayed as a joint subset of the larger category "censorship"—as a legalistic one, moving from episode to episode anecdotally rather than analytically in terms of the historical context.[3] My intention is not to reject this body of work but rather to expand on it, drawing from its leads to present a deeper, richer depiction of pornography's convoluted dialectic with American history. I mean for the "politics" of my subtitle to be read broadly, not simply in traditional terms of legislation and elections but also in terms of social, cultural, gender, and sexual politics.

To be sure, several precedents exist for what I am trying to achieve here. Recent work on censorship has attended to the complex ways historical context informs the process, and this scholarship also pays heed to such factors as gender and sexual politics in the decision-making processes behind suppression.[4] Scholars have also been particularly sensitive to the regulation of obscenity in late-nineteenth- and early-twentieth-century America. Paul Boyer, Nicola Beisel, Leigh Ann Wheeler, and Andrea Friedman, among others, have examined the ways in which urbanization, immigration, and the social construction of gender shaped reactions to obscenity.[5] That several of the arguments made by these scholars roughly anticipate (and inform) my own perhaps reinforces Matthew Lasar's claim that porn debates occur cyclically across time.[6]

Of course, semantics come into play immediately with this topic, as the definitions of *obscenity* and *pornography* are often site-specific. The meanings of the terms are entirely contingent on the historical moment in which they are being examined. Pornography is never *simply* a political battleground but rather a discursive site onto which varied social tensions are mapped out. As Joan DeJean notes, "obscenity" took on its modern sexualized meaning only in the seventeenth century in France, when *obscenus* and *obscenitas* recovered their original Latinate meanings after centuries of vague translation as "infamous" and "infamy."[7] Meanwhile, *pornography* entered the English lexicon only in 1857, and then only in its original Greek definition as "a description of prostitutes or prostitution."

Tracing the historical evolution of the term, Walter Kendrick observes that "pornography" properly describes "not a thing but a concept, a thought structure." Kendrick emphasizes the artificiality of the concept—essentially a repository for the culturally verboten at any given time—by bracketing it with quotation marks, but having called attention to my acquiescence in his analysis here, I prefer for stylistic reasons not to follow his example. In this I am in good company; Matthew Frye Jacobson, for instance, makes a similar decision regarding "race" in his *Whiteness of a Different Color*, and Rickie Solinger prefaces her study of single pregnancy by noting her plan to use terms such as *bastard* and *illegitimate* as dictated by the public record of her time of study. Language in this book is intended to be read as always immersed in historically bound contestations over meaning.[8]

In the chapters that follow, then, *obscenity* denotes a legal term, first fully codified by the Supreme Court in 1957, which describes material excluded from the protections of the First Amendment on grounds of sexual explicitness. *Pornography*, however, merely refers to anything deemed pornographic by a given authority at a given moment. Like Solinger I have opted to utilize a full set of synonyms in the interest of avoiding monotony, so I sometimes mention smut, filth, and dirty magazines. My intention in using these terms is never normative; the derogatory light cast by them reflects the public perception of the time, not my own critical judgment.

"If the human capacity for pornography is universal," argues Richard Randall in a psychoanalytic treatise, "the human interest in censoring it is not less so." Most historians would find this claim profoundly ahistorical. Joan DeJean's study of early modern France, for instance, shows the urge to censor pornography emerging only when technological developments in print media brought it to a mass and non-elite audience for the first time. Other works associate what one anthology calls *The Invention of Pornography* with the onset of modernity; Margaret Jacob finds surprising ideological affinities between the "privatized, atomized and individuated" bodies of pornographic writing and the controversial materialist philosophy of such luminaries as Spinoza and Hobbes in the seventeenth century, while Lynn Hunt argues that pornography served a class-based political agenda in revolutionary France, attacking the elite (and especially Marie Antoinette) as debauched, debased, and decaying. Iain McCalman, too, shows the fluid boundaries between radical politics and pornography in nineteenth-century England, where dissident pamphleteers often used pornography as both a source of income and a mode of protest. Even in early America obscene literature served as a forum for criticizing the clergy.[9]

This brief survey suggests some of the reasons pornography became such a focal point of state regulation in the modern era: by harnessing the volatile charge of sexuality to unpredictable ends, it represented a potentially destabilizing social force. Carolyn Dean has noted that as the metaphor of the "body politic" shifted in meaning from a divinely ordained hierarchy to a medical model of social organization, nations perceived themselves in organic terms and sought regulation against contamination or infection. Sexual deviance was seen as a key source of social infections, with pornography as one of its main conduits.[10] The imagined link between pornography and deviance figures as a recurring motif in this book, in several regards, but most notably in the ways obscenity charges were routinely used to stigmatize and suppress queer sexual expression in postwar America.

As technology advanced, pornography rapidly followed, from print media to photography to cinema to the Internet.[11] Rigorous regulation accompanied it, in what Jay Gertzman considers a symbiotic relationship: proscription perpetuated porn's illicit allure, while the existence of smut helped sustain entire bureaucracies dedicated to the preservation of decency. Certainly pornography was not alone in receiving this hostile attention. As Alan Hunt suggests in his study of the late-nineteenth-century British masturbation panic, it was joined by everything from homosexuality to masturbation, which were perceived as traits and practices that weakened the highly gendered masculine project of national empire. American cold war normativity followed in the quaking footsteps of these fears, likewise viewing pornography as a corrupter of both virile American youth and national security.[12]

Such examples preclude any claim for American exceptionalism, yet it is nonetheless possible to discern a uniquely American character in the perpetual oscillations between prudery and brazenness that mark the course of U.S. history. From the use of sexual domination in the conquest period through what Stephen Nissenbaum called the "new chastity of the 1830s" that developed in the face of the market revolution, and from that "passionless" period to the early-twentieth-century sexual revolution that redefined sexuality as a site of not just reproduction but also pleasure, a peculiar ambivalence regarding sex and sexuality marks American history.[13] Oscillating between repression and indulgence as various configurations of power form and dissolve, this American ambivalence toward sexuality made pornography a salient issue for politicians; as we will see, the American people often showed relatively little concern on the matter when left to themselves, but they were also predisposed to respond to moral entrepreneurs who promoted pornography as a source of social consternation.

This study begins with a social transition, as the relative laxity of wartime society gave way to the more rigorous strictures of cold war culture. In this framework free speech attained a new place of social centrality as a key feature that distinguished American freedom from communist totalitarianism. Chapters 1 and 2 examine cold war liberalism. The first chapter shows how a moral panic regarding comic books morphed into one concerning pornography and how cold war sexual politics structured that panic. Privileged standards of "normalcy," threatened by the specter of unchecked libidos and the diversion of sexual energy from the ideal of the heterosexual nuclear family, resulted in a reassertion of normative standards. A community study of postwar Los Angeles reveals the heteronormative contours of normalcy, as queer sexual expression was systematically targeted as obscene.

Such seemingly conservative efforts were undertaken with the complicity of postwar liberals, and chapter 2 follows the liberal response to ongoing worries about pornography. Using the American Civil Liberties Union and the Warren Court as exemplars of postwar liberalism, I argue that liberals relied on endless circumlocution and convolution to avoid accommodating porn into the ostensibly categorical protection of the First Amendment. Despite raging battles over sexuality on the cold war's domestic front, liberalism studiously avoided acknowledging the existence of sexual politics, preferring to simply articulate certain sexual regimes as natural. The result of this was the emergence of the modern obscenity doctrine, in which obscenity joined such categories as libel and "fighting words" in proscription, despite lacking the tangible consequences that justified those exceptions, on the grounds that its "prurience" rendered it without social value and implicitly apolitical.

As this transpired, grassroots activities laid the groundwork for regime change. It took many years for the New Right to oust the postwar liberal consensus, but one significant and overlooked source of that transition was Citizens for Decent Literature (CDL). In chapter 3 I argue that

CDL played an important role in redefining antiporn activism. Whereas such Catholic organizations as the Legion of Decency and the National Organization for Decent Literature had lost mainstream credibility in the face of "book-burner" charges that compared them to communists, CDL presented a new rhetorical face for suppression. The language of sin gave way to that of social science and expert authority, and the untenable term *censorship* was replaced by the dry legalisms of *obscenity*. This nominally secular framework found great acceptance in the 1960s, and CDL rapidly expanded from its Cincinnati base to establish a formidable national empire over the course of the decade.

The influence of CDL was on ample display as the decade closed. The organization played prominent roles in both the derailing of President Lyndon Johnson's attempt to elevate the liberal justice Abe Fortas to chief justice of the Supreme Court and the preemptive souring of public opinion on the 1970 report of the Presidential Commission on Obscenity and Pornography, which advocated the repeal of adult obscenity laws. Chapter 4 depicts the nascent New Right's growing awareness of the political capital of moralism, by which it sought to paint liberals as equivalent to the radicals who permeated the counterculture, much to the disgust of the "silent majority." In the Fortas episode, and several others, New Right politicians recognized the viability of antiporn sentiments, which quickly replaced the standard and increasingly irrelevant conservative tropes of racism and anticommunism in New Right rhetoric. Pornography helped set the stage for the broader "family values" platform of opposition to feminism, gay rights, and abortion access to come.

If chapter 4 represents the key turning point in this narrative, chapter 5 builds up to the final victory of the New Right. In one more swing of the American sexual pendulum, the early 1970s witnessed a surprising cultural acceptance of pornography, as the sexual revolution generated a "porno chic" moment that saw urbane couples and celebrities proudly attending the newly visible hardcore film genre. Not even a Nixon-stacked Supreme Court could stem the rising tide of smut, and in local wars on porn cities abandoned attempts at annihilation and moved toward more conciliatory policies of containment. Liberals, still reluctant to risk identification with libertinism, gave subtle support to such freedom-preserving modes of regulation, but the ultimate benefactor of this "permissive society" was the New Right.

Chapter 6 shows why: as porn became commonplace, evangelical Christians suddenly entered the public sphere with a vengeance. Distraught over pornography, as well as parallel progress in gay rights and legal access to abortion, evangelicals mobilized into the Christian Right, the most visible and vocal component of the New Right. This faction's power could be seen on many fronts in the Reagan years of the 1980s, and the Attorney General's Commission on Pornography was one of the most prominent examples. Distorting and exploiting new developments in social science, feminist analysis, and public awareness of child pornography, the Meese Commission openly catered to the stringent moralism and intolerance of the Christian Right. Though the commission's 1986 report found little favor in the mainstream press, its suggestions informed federal policy and resulted in resurgent repression in the late 1980s.

Chapter 7 backtracks to observe in greater detail the development of contemporary feminism. In contrast to the later claims of antiporn feminists, it shows how an antiporn analysis was far from preordained at the outset of the women's liberation movement. Moving into the 1980s, pornography possessed a unique ability to cut across ideological lines, as some radical feminists found themselves preferring the company of right-wing figures over that of the free-speech left. The resultant internecine warfare certainly damaged any attempts to present a unified feminist front in the face of devastating Reaganite retrenchment; at the same time, the content-neutral arguments favored by groups such as the ACLU reflected the persistent liberal ambivalence about the politics of pleasure.

Finally, chapter 8 pulls together these diverse trails to map the current outcomes of the porn battles across the social spectrum. After finding little solace anywhere in the debates, "sex-positive" feminist and gay male validations of porn's special role in queer history finally found a positive reception in academia in the 1990s, though this reached the mass media only in the watered-down form of "postfeminism," an intellectually empty endorsement of pleasure without the accompanying politics necessary to challenge the status quo. Meanwhile, liberalism retreated to an increasingly marginal place as militant Christian organizing narrowed the parameters of political debate regarding pornography. The Clinton administration exemplified this trend, consistently fleeing from controversy by acquiescing to its opponents while publicly claiming victory, as the Christian Right effectively revived a dormant moral panic involving pornographic menaces to children.

Later, the George W. Bush administration reinjected Christian Right policies into the porn wars, as the federal government instigated a purposefully quiet crackdown on numerous forms of counternormative sexual expression under the rubric of obscenity law. The administration defined itself by the use of this and other moralistic policies intended to maintain evangelical support and conceal the undeniable unpopularity of its economic and foreign policies. Bush reinstituted a vanilla hegemony that reluctantly accommodated the normalization of conventional porn in mainstream culture even as it vigorously renegotiated and policed twenty-first-century notions of normalcy, literally imprisoning those who fell outside its province.

This book attempts to show how pornography acquired its massive political use-value in shoring up public support while effacing issues of more tangible importance. It shows how *obscenity* and *pornography* have served as powerful tropes, capable of demonizing texts, ideas, and identities, and how the resonances of those tropes have been efficiently harnessed for political gain. In the final analysis "perversion" has proved profitable indeed to modern conservatism.

1. THE REDISCOVERY OF PORNOGRAPHY
Emergence of a Cold War Moral Panic

JOHN SAXTON SUMNER finally got his wish in 1946, when New York City's Miami Theatre was closed for screening the "obscene and immoral" film *Guilty Parents*. Sumner, head of the New York Society for the Suppression of Vice (NYSSV), had doggedly pursued the Miami—which had "long observed a policy of showing films that stress sex themes"—for nearly a decade but to little effect. When Sumner complained to the police, they merely issued repeated warnings to the theater between 1942 and 1945 but took no other action. When he sent a report on the Miami to the New York Motion Picture Division, the state's official censorship body, detailing the naked "native women" onscreen in the film *Isle of Desire*, the "flesh color wax models of the infected parts of the anatomy due to sexual diseases" on display in the lobby, and the *Encyclopedia of Sex* that sold for fifty cents after the show to the exclusively male audience, the censors responded by acknowledging that the Miami "has been the subject of consideration for some time past" but did nothing. Sumner must have found cause for celebration, then, when the authorities finally moved against the Miami by closing it, an action that had not been used in three decades.[1]

Victory proved fleeting, however, and Sumner had little time to bask in his glory before local prosecutors "lost" their evidence against the Miami's owner under circumstances so suspicious the presiding judge called the prosecution a "nice fix." The NYSSV fared even worse than the case against the Miami. Though the organization had achieved great national prominence fighting obscene material for seven decades, by the 1940s its profile and reputation had declined tremendously. In 1947 it abandoned its well-known moniker in response to hostile media coverage, replacing it with the bland Society to Maintain Public Decency (SMPD). The shift from aggressive "suppression" to defensive "maintenance" signified the declining potency of the organization. While Sumner's infamous vice-crusader predecessor, Anthony Comstock, had done legal battle with significant works such as Ezra Heywood's 1876 free-love manifesto *Cupid's Yokes*, by 1948 Sumner was reduced to reading "sex instruction" articles in *Better Homes and Gardens* and finding them "not actionable"; while Comstock had taken on such significant figures as Victoria Woodhull and Margaret Sanger, Sumner found himself investigating a nearly anonymous newsstand operator known as "Blind Harry."[2]

By early 1951 the SMPD announced its death throes in a letter to its members. Calling its recent fund-raising campaign a "complete failure," the organization acknowledged, "It is apparent that, for whatever reason, the society has lost its appeal for public support." The SMPD went on "inactive status," and when a reporter called it in 1955, he learned the Society "consisted merely of a telephone," which a volunteer staff of one answered only to refer calls elsewhere. In a final indignity, the retired John Saxton Sumner's autobiographical manuscript was repeatedly rejected by publishing firms; longtime NYSSV opponent Random House declined to make Sumner even a cursory offer, citing with presumable satisfaction the lack of public interest in his story.[3]

In many ways the decline and fall of the NYSSV emblematizes the fate of obscenity and its regulators in post–World War II America. Though social control under Comstock and others had flourished early in the century, it waned in the face of developing urban amusement cultures and the sexual revolution of the 1920s. Historian Samuel Walker reflects a historiographical consensus in noting that by the 1930s "the tide was running against censorship." This trend continued through the 1940s, as the American public insisted on its right to make its own decisions regarding the propriety of its media consumption, forging what Andrea Friedman calls a "democratic moral authority" that reclaimed the levers of social control from authoritarian despots like Comstock. In the face of economic depression and war, obscene material seemed a trivial matter. Though censors sometimes won, as when the Massachusetts Supreme Court upheld a ruling finding Lillian Smith's critically respected novel *Strange Fruit* obscene in 1945, the response was often scorn and ridicule; "Boston Is Afraid of Books," scoffed the *Saturday Review of Literature* on the book's suppression. By the mid-1950s, *censorship* was practically a dirty word in America, and none less than the Republican president Dwight Eisenhower exhorted citizens not to "join the book burners."[4]

Like poverty, though, pornography possesses the capacity to be "discovered" on a periodic basis. And just as Michael Harrington discovered poverty in the 1960s, seven decades after Jacob Riis had done the same, pornography reentered American public consciousness in the mid-1950s, eighty years after Anthony Comstock had first made it a significant political issue. Also like poverty, pornography never actually disappeared, but its spikes in the public consciousness coincided with sociopolitical matrices into which it fit as a link between otherwise disparate cells. During the Comstock era, as Nicola Beisel has shown, antiporn efforts fit into a larger nativist framework. In the case of its 1950s reemergence this matrix was the cold war.[5]

Waged both at home and abroad, the cold war took dual and interweaving forms. Abroad it strove for the spread of democracy and capitalism, in an effort to stabilize and expand American markets, particularly in the politically volatile postcolonial nations classified at the time as the "Third World." Domestically, in addition to the political suppression of the Left, the cold war consisted of programs to normalize and reproduce atomized nuclear families—predicated on heterosexual marriages in which wives avoided the workplace—in an effort to sustain the consumer culture that had begun to replace industry as the heart of the American economy.[6] These twin projects relied on distinct discourses—one of "liberty" and "freedom" from communism, the other of "normalcy" and "family" as opposed to deviance—but the two discourses often melted together despite the ostensible coldness of the war. Thus, foreign policy relied on a phallic model of masculinized nationalism. The diplomat and theorist George Kennan used sexual metaphors of "penetration" to formulate a national body-politic always imagined as male and heterosexual—to penetrate, not to be penetrated, as the public stance of President John F. Kennedy would reflect. Meanwhile, the inward-tending domestic front of the cold war taught girls to practice "containment on the homefront" by fending off their boyfriends' advances, and the family kitchen was utilized by Richard Nixon as a "weapon" against the Russians in proving American superiority.[7]

Sexuality took on political hues in this convoluted but tightly organized framework, as the cold war family was linked to the national project. "Powerful erections in the marriage bed," Jessamyn Neuhas writes of the perceived links between "normal" sexuality and the highly gendered discourse of foreign relations, "comprised a strong front against the peril of perversion facing the United States." If communism embodied the great-

est political perversion, homosexuality played its internal, domestic counterpart. A multitude of mechanisms were instituted to regulate American
sexuality, from the hetero-oriented G.I. Bill to more obvious sodomy laws,
and obscenity law also fit alongside these strictures. Used to stigmatize and
suppress queer texts, it helped shore up the boundaries of normalcy, reifying
heteronormative assumptions about the perversity and prurience of dissident sexualities in cold war America.[8]

This deployment can be best illustrated through a close community
study of postwar Los Angeles, where "obscenity" served as a battleground
in an unacknowledged war over sexual legitimacy. The queer-obliterating
intent of obscenity charges, however, transpired within a larger national
moral panic over pornography, one less specifically attached to any particular "deviation" than to the more abstract notion of deviance itself. This sudden emergence of pornography into the national consciousness relied on
related tropes of normalcy and owed much to the political engineering of
Tennessee senator Estes Kefauver, who publicized the pornographic menace most effectively. Kefauver's leadership role in shaping public response
to pornography illuminates the critical contributions of liberals in the development of cold war policies and politics; not just complicit, but in fact
quite active in the drawing of social boundaries, liberals may have differed
from conservatives on matters of the welfare state and civil rights, but the
two groups coalesced harmoniously in forging an anticommunist, heteronormative national political imaginary. Before the implications for freedom
of speech were fully understood, liberals could thus join conservatives in fo-
menting outrage over pornographic intrusions into the realm of American
families—though without, as chapter 2 will show, actively acknowledging
the political components of sexuality.

Before the moral panic over pornography developed, however, a national outcry over comic books anticipated it in many ways, establishing
an analytic framework that would shape responses to pornography. Once
pornography took center stage, around 1954, it was quickly integrated into
the cold war matrix; this chapter traces that emergence and then looks at
its consequences in postwar Los Angeles. The events of this chapter set the
stage for the developments discussed in subsequent chapters, as first liberals, then conservatives, and finally religious activists would control and mediate the terms of discussion on pornography and obscenity.

The Ink and the Stain

Comics had grown into a large and lucrative industry during the 1930s and early 1940s, but only after World War II did they become a pop-culture phenomenon worthy of public attention. When that attention came, few were pleased to note the abundance of sex, violence, and crime ubiquitous in the medium. Though historians have examined the comics debates, few connections have been drawn between them and the subsequent pornography debates.[9] Understanding the latter, though, requires an understanding of the way the basic argumentative framework took shape in the comics debate, as well as the means of conduction by which the heat of social controversy moved from one to the other. Certainly comics were not the first imagined threat to American youth: dance, drink, movies, marijuana, and a multitude of other corrupters had long served to explain counternormative behavior among the young.[10] The comics uproar did, however, seize on the rhetoric and trappings of social and medical science, while forsaking the substantive methodologies of those fields, in ways that directly informed public responses to pornography for decades to come.

With a frightening portrayal of a boy and a girl "jabb[ing] another boy with a fountain pen 'like a hypodermic'" to catch the reader's eye, the 1948 *Collier's* article "Horror in the Nursery" effectively utilized the sensational techniques of comic books, which by then sold an estimated sixty million copies each month. But it directed these techniques *against* the comics, as the subject of the article, psychiatrist Fredric Wertham, offered examples of children beating, stabbing, and killing after reading violent comics. Wertham also suggested other consequences of exposure to the pervasive conflation of sex and violence in comics, particularly "sexual perversion" and sadism in boys and "frigidity" in girls. These effects were especially anathema, undermining as they did the cold war gender norms that supported American nuclear families. Calling for legislation to remove comics from newsstands and candy stores, Wertham explained that comics did not "automatically cause delinquency in every child reader," but they constituted a "distinct influencing factor" in "every single delinquent or disturbed child we studied." He also argued that even nondelinquents were adversely impacted by comics, in terms of "the weakening of [their] moral codes and ethical concepts."[11]

Wertham immediately attained semicelebrity status, and he went on to reiterate his arguments repeatedly over the next several years. To the *Saturday Review of Literature* he offered more vivid anecdotes, telling of a group of boys who hit, beat with guns, and tied up a four-year-old girl before "pull[ing] off her panties to torture her," as well as a tale of two twelve-year-old boys shooting a random man with semiautomatic weapons, all after reading comics. "You cannot understand present-day juvenile delinquency," he wrote, "if you do not take into account the pathogenic and pathoplastic influence of the comic books."[12]

Timing played an important role in Wertham's rise to prominence. Concerns over juvenile delinquency had emerged during the war, as incidents like Los Angeles' so-called "Zoot Suit Riots" created an image of unruly youth, often drawing on pervasive racial and class-based stereotypes. Perceptions of delinquency spreading beyond urban slums to the rapidly suburbanizing middle classes fostered a transition from Progressive Era structural analyses of delinquency, which emphasized poor housing and the geographic concentration of poverty, to new cultural analyses predicated more on personal alienation and disaffection, a framework with much appeal to conservative critics of the New Deal welfare state.[13] Popular culture ratified this shift, with James Dean driven to delinquency not by poverty but rather a weak father and overbearing mother in the 1955 film *Rebel Without a Cause*; as Frankie Lymon sang the next year in "I'm Not a Juvenile Delinquent," "Life is what you make of it / It all depends on you."[14]

Wertham's emphasis on comics spoke directly to this privatization of delinquency. But another social shift was perhaps even more instrumental in elevating his stature: the rise of the expert. During and immediately after the war, social scientists had reached new heights of prominence, as economists formulated the Keynesian principles by which the government regulated the economy and sociologists explained the patterns of group behavior according to which society organized itself in the course of renormalization. Psychiatrists, too, partook of this elevated status; for instance, the wartime medicalization of homosexuality, earlier perceived as a criminal character trait, reflected the expanding power of the profession over new social terrain. By 1948 "experts" had co-opted the central advisory position on a wide range of subjects, from dating to motherhood, and Wertham benefited from this.[15] His articles never failed to include the "M.D." after his name, and they often mentioned his impressive professional credentials, from chief resident psychiatrist at Johns Hopkins University to director of psychiatric service at Queens General Hospital. The gratuitous use of jargon such as "pathoplastic" (explained as how comics "determine the form that trouble takes") also helped confer an Olympian image of expertise on the doctor.[16]

This expert status made Wertham a persuasive figure to many. Letters to the *Saturday Review* praised Wertham for uncovering comics as the "marijuana of parents as well as their offspring" and agreed with him that they had "a most corrupting effect upon the youngsters." In December 1948 the National Congress of Parents and Teachers adopted Wertham's analysis, declaring fantasy good but warning, "Fantasy rooted in evil will bear an evil harvest." The organization also claimed legislation "may be inevitable" if the comics industry failed to self-regulate. Indeed, governmental response to Wertham's crusade was already under way. Several cities, from Los Angeles to St. Cloud, Minnesota, passed ordinances banning crime and horror comics in the late 1940s, and New York established a state commission to investigate them.[17]

Although Wertham's anticomics campaign held sway over many parents and politicians, other experts took him to task on his methodology. The *Journal of Educational Sociology* devoted its December 1949 issue to the topic of comics, and its opening editorial laid the groundwork for the articles to follow, claiming that "there is cause for alarm" in "the setting up of scapegoats" to explain juvenile delinquency. Frederic Thrasher, an education professor at New York University and member of the attorney general's Commission on Juvenile Delinquency, offered a scathing critique of Wertham, repeatedly emphasizing that his comics-delinquency causal analysis "is not substantiated by any valid research" and comparing Wertham's post hoc, ergo propter hoc logic to that of obsolete criminological theories that claimed people with cleft palates, low foreheads, or large ears were likely criminals. Noting that Wertham's methodology consisted of nothing more than interviews with juvenile delinquents, most of whom had read comics, Thrasher observed that, by the same reasoning, delinquency could be traced back to virtually any commonly recurring habit or media. His conclusion offered a hint about why Wertham's attack on comics had proven so successful: by creating a satisfactory "whipping boy," Thrasher wrote, "we fail to face and accept our responsibility as parents and as citizens for providing our children with more healthful family and community living." Blaming comics thus served to divert blame from parents or social structures.[18]

Similar refutation of Wertham came from an unlikely source. Recently elected Tennessee senator Estes Kefauver, a liberal with high political aspirations (and one of only three southern senators not to sign the 1956 "Southern Manifesto" repudiating the Supreme Court's *Brown v. Board of Education* school desegregation decision), had recognized public concern over crime as a useful issue by which to gain national attention. In early 1950 he formed a senatorial committee to investigate crime. While contemplating approaches to the issue, Kefauver considered focusing on the effect of comics on juvenile delinquency and commissioned a compilation of information on the topic, expecting it to confirm public suspicions of the deleterious effect of comics. During the interim, he settled his focus on gambling and organized crime instead, but when the comics report came in, it indicated an overwhelming consensus among public officials, publishers, and child-guidance experts that comics held little or no connection to juvenile delinquency. Even Federal Bureau of Investigation head J. Edgar Hoover, a consistent advocate of suppressing subversive, sexually explicit, and violent media, conceded it was "doubtful" delinquency would subside if comics were banned.[19]

Despite such contestation, the attack on comics continued in the early 1950s. State and local legislation proliferated, coinciding with the delivery of Wertham's 1954 magnum opus, *Seduction of the Innocent*. Again reasoning from anecdotes rather than rigorous scientific methods, Wertham spent four hundred pages on the various depravities of comics. Blaming comics for everything from delinquency to murder to drug addiction ("All child drug addicts . . . were inveterate comic-book readers," Wertham noted), *Seduction of the Innocent* ran the gamut from crackpot theorizing to progressive politics. Among Wertham's stories were child killers, sexually traumatized teens, and a young boy who, when asked what he wanted to be when he grew up, gave the instant and enthusiastic reply, "I want to be a sex maniac!" Wertham reasoned that the freedom to publish comics "has nothing to do with civil liberties. It is a perversion of the very idea of civil liberties." In advocating the suppression of comics, he lingered on their sexual effects. For instance, the "special emphasis" given to women's buttocks in comics "leads to rigid fetichistic [*sic*] tendencies," which "may have a relationship also to early homosexual attitudes." Dwelling on this theme, Wertham called Batman "psychologically homosexual" and put telling quotation marks around his companion Robin's real name, "Dick" Grayson.[20]

Between unfocused condemnations of comics that conflated delinquency, murder, and homosexuality, as if all emerged from some monocausal process of "deviation," Wertham did go to extensive lengths to distance himself from puritans, prudes, and censors. His proposals for legislation exempted adults, regulating only children's reading, and he insisted on a difference between mere depictions of sex—which he found acceptable for adults and harmless for children—and those of sex mixed with violence, which he blamed for sadism in boys and frigidity in girls. Wertham even called masturbation "harmless enough," adding that only when accompanied by "sado-masochistic fantasies" did it lead to maladjustment. Noting the pervasive racism by which nonwhites were portrayed as "the inferior people," Wertham also accused comics of planting the "seeds of prejudice" in impressionable minds. As something of a tangent, the author discussed the importance of desegregating schools to offset the institutionalized racism of American society.[21]

Wertham concluded *Seduction of the Innocent* with an anecdote that validated one of Frederic Thrasher's 1949 criticisms. Describing a mother who brought her delinquent son in to see Wertham, the psychiatrist described her parting words. "Tell me again," she pleaded; "Tell me again it isn't my fault." The final sentence of the book—set off as a separate paragraph for emphasis—read simply, "And I did."[22] Unwittingly or not, Wertham staked the appeal of his analysis on an exoneration of worried parents from culpability for their children's problems.

The ploy worked. *Seduction of the Innocent* further expanded Wertham's public profile and drew great attention. Though social scientists remained unconvinced, with the *Science News Letter* approvingly citing two psychologists who described comics as holding "insignificant importance" in the causation of juvenile delinquency, even the urbane *New Yorker* called *Seduction* "a formidable indictment."[23] The renewed attention on comics also pulled back into the fray Senator Estes Kefauver, who began a Senate investigation of the link between comics and juvenile delinquency in 1954, despite his own 1950 compilation of data that explicitly rejected any such connection.

Kefauver had made good use of the new medium of television to attract a national audience to his televised organized crime hearings. The senator had hoped to parlay this fame into a presidential nomination in 1952, but his hopes were thwarted when Adlai Stevenson beat him in the primaries. When Kefauver reconvened his Senate committee in 1954, at least one journalist accused him of "prospecting for publicity" with his eye on the 1956 nomination. The commission invited Wertham to testify, and it also drew publicity for a fiery confrontation between Kefauver and the horror-comics publisher William Gaines.[24]

When Kefauver released his report in 1955, though, it reflected a profound ambivalence over the nature of comic books' relation to juvenile delinquency. Calling delinquency "the product of many related causal factors," the report opened by also claiming, "It can scarcely be questioned that the impact of these media does constitute a significant factor in the total problem." After surveying the consensus of various experts, the report admitted Wertham's was a minority perspective and that most social scientists believed comics were unlikely to cause delinquency in a "well-adjusted and normally law-abiding child," though they might "give support and sanction to already existing antisocial tendencies" in maladjusted children.[25]

This hardly constituted a ringing endorsement of Wertham's analysis. But Kefauver's hesitant report failed to undermine the pervasive anticomics sentiment visible throughout the nation. Bans on horror comics continued emerging in 1955 from Alaska to Kentucky, without a single negative state-legislature vote in the latter case, and when the Florida city of St. Petersburg banned crime comics, it persisted in calling them a "contributing factor" to juvenile delinquency.[26]

The absence of evidence to connect comics to delinquency was difficult to ignore, and legislators dealt with it in various ways. A 1956 Massachusetts state commission to investigate links between comics and delinquency openly confessed that "no completely scientific study has yet been called to our attention," but reasoned, nonetheless, "despite this fact . . . we do feel that these same publications contribute to the 'anti-social' behavior of certain juveniles deemed 'delinquent.'"[27] The political pressure to reach such a conclusion was powerful, as a nuanced stand on the complexities of delinquency ran the risk of mischaracterization as a lack of concern for the nation's young. During a 1957 Idaho debate over an anti-comics bill, state representative Perry Swisher spoke against it, saying it would ban *Crime and Punishment* and Brothers Grimm fairy tales. As an observer wrote, however, Swisher "said the members would not have courage enough to vote against the bill and demonstrated this by voting for it himself!"[28]

Since reason alone could not stop the mounting comics panic, the Comics Magazine Association of America decided to deflate the crusade by reining in its own excesses. A voluntary code adopted by the Association in October 1954 mandated new standards of comic publishing. The code emphasized crime, insisting that no sympathy or glory be bestowed on criminals, but it also responded to Wertham's other points, proscribing ridicule of racial or religious groups as well as "suggestive and salacious illustration or suggestive posture." Romance stories now had to "emphasize the value of the home and the sanctity of marriage" instead of perverse or illicit sexuality, thus aligning comics with the national cold war project.[29]

By mid-1955 Wertham had modified his analysis, retreating to the curious position that "the most important harm done by comic books is in the field of *reading*." Because of the design and layout of comics, Wertham alleged, comics interfered with the acquisition of basic left-to-right perceptual mechanisms.[30] This criticism, while perhaps more scientifically grounded than his earlier claims, was hardly the sort of topic to inspire outrage. And, indeed, it did not. Though residual outrage carried anticomics campaigns through a few more years in some areas, by 1955 the national panic had begun its decline.[31] It had no reason to continue existing, having successfully tamed the wild comic beast; meanwhile, its premises, analyses, conclusions, and attendant outrage had all been transferred to a new concept, "pornography."

The Mechanics of Rediscovery

Before the tropes of moral panic could stick, pornography had to become a source of sustainable outrage. Despite occasional cries of alarm, this failed to occur until the comics panic subsided; when it did, the liberal Kefauver led the way. As the New York Society for the Suppression of Vice sank into obsolescence in the 1940s, pornography showed little capacity for arousing public concern. In 1945 the Southern California suburb of Lynwood displayed its lack of interest in the topic, when a local youth welfare group investigated pornography sales. "No action was taken as the report indicated no flagrant offenses," read the entirety of the group's summary, relegated to the fifteenth page of a seventeen-page, single-spaced description of the year's activities.[32]

When *Woman's Home Companion* ran an article titled "The Smut Peddler Is After Your Child" in 1951, author Albert Maisel noted that the "smut racket" had grown into a multimillion-dollar endeavor whose effects were widespread. For instance, "mass outbreaks of sexual promiscuity" were discovered among students at "the exclusive suburban Evanston High School" outside Chicago. Investigating police attributed this otherwise inexplicable promiscuity to "obscene books or pictures in their possession." By emphasizing the affluence of the families, Maisel clearly hoped to reach influential members of a public that "has not yet realized how vast and menacing the smut trade's operations have become." His effort failed. When the largely inactive Salacious Literature Committee of the Los Angeles Federation of Coordinating Councils read the article, instead of registering alarm or gratitude, the committee responded with a curt letter informing the magazine that the article "was not based on fact." Though Maisel had called Los Angeles "the largest single center of smut traffic today in the entire country," the committee said police had done a good job of cleaning smut out of L.A., and it was a minor problem at most. A local inspector found smut unalarming, shrugging, "This problem is not a new one. . . . It has been occurring for years and probably always will." Despite the magazine's best efforts, widespread outrage would have to wait.[33]

Only as the comics panic receded did pornography rise in public profile to replace it. The transition began in 1954, even before Wertham's *Seduction* and the adoption of the Comics Code. In New York a set of 1953 bills targeting "obscene and other objectionable comics" failed; when virtually identical bills passed in 1954, the media characterized them as "bills on obscene books," emphasizing pornographic magazines over comics.[34] That same year in Hackensack, New Jersey, a local newsdealer told an ACLU member that a "strong wave" of juvenile delinquency had inspired vocal groups to protest comics and initiate a cleanup drive; once the drive had successfully removed offending crime and horror comics from the town, "it spread to other publications as well." Magazines such as *Art Photography*, *Modern Man*, and *Pix*, most carrying photographs of attractive women topless, were seized by the police.[35]

The Hackensack case showed clearly the direct transference of outrage from comics to "filthy magazines" or "smut." The legislative infrastructure of the anticomics campaigns also facilitated attacks on obscene literature. In St. Petersburg, Florida, the 1955 comics ban also included "obscene publications" among its provisions, while similar wording in the 1950 St. Cloud, Minnesota, comics ban had allowed the city to ban more than three hundred books and magazines by 1953, when the town finally reconsidered its ordinance.[36]

Another important factor was the evolving smut market, which expanded rapidly over the course of the late 1940s and early 1950s. Historian Jay Gertzman describes an "unprecedented amount of erotica" generated in the 1920s; social change and new printing technology meant once-expensive erotic novels could be sold in affordable versions.[37] Many of these works contained drawings or pictures of naked bodies and sexual imagery. Paperback books also became increasingly available, creating a market for pulp fiction that often relied on sexy covers and content.[38] By the 1930s nudist magazines such as *Sunshine and Health*, available mostly by subscription but on many newsstands as well, also entered the market. Sometimes these magazines drew the wrath of the post office, but often they circulated freely; the May-June 1947 issue of *Naturel Herald*, featuring full-frontal nude photographs of variously aged people of both genders, was withheld by postal inspectors but then cleared for delivery after further consideration.[39]

While nudist magazines earned a certain modicum of social acceptance by refraining from overt appeals to eroticism in their depictions of naked men and women, other magazines began staking out more lurid territory; at one level, respectable publications like *Esquire* offered "cheesecake" pictures of scantily clad women, while lower on the cultural hierarchy cheaply produced magazines such as *Wink, Whisper*, and *Cutie* flourished during and after World War II, presenting more seductive photos of women in various stages of undress.[40]

Erotic film reels also reached a new prominence in the late 1940s. Though a cinematic market revolving around unsimulated sex acts has been documented back to the very birth of the cinema, this "hardcore" material remained underground for a quarter-century after the war, while less-explicit short films proliferated.[41] The Baltimore-based Benefit Corporation sold 8- and 16-millimeter films, which its catalog claimed were intended "only and expressly for the use of STUDENTS OF ART, CINEMATOGRAPHY, and ALLIED ARTS, who wish to study figure, lighting and composition through the medium of the motion picture." It then listed several medical films on childbirth, tumor removal, and lung removal, before finally offering its key wares: "Hollywoods," "Co-eds Will Be Girls," "Naughty Co-eds," and other 8-mm reels of naked young women frolicking. R. J. Ross of North Hollywood presented no such legitimizing subterfuges in its 1950 catalog, selling nude movies, color slides, three-dimensional pictures, and photographs. For $3 ($10 for full color) a consumer could order from a varied selection of film reels that included a globe's worth of racial and ethnic fetishizations: *Fiesta of Love*, *Ming Toi*, and *Congo Drums* each catered to a specific interest. Other vendors, such as William H. Door, focused more exclusively on conventional American notions of beauty, offering forty nude photographs of "Hollywood's Best Figure Models"—all nonethnically white and contorted to conceal their genitals—for $2.[42]

The single most significant addition to the erotic market was *Playboy*, founded by Hugh Hefner in late 1953. Its first issue promised, "If you're a man between the ages of 18 and 80, *Playboy* is meant for you," and its rapid sales supported the claim. With pictures of a naked Marilyn Monroe as its "Sweetheart of the Month" (soon to be Playmate), *Playboy* softened its prurient appeal with articles that strove for sophistication; Hefner famously imagined the magazine's typical reader as a man who enjoyed cocktails and hors d'oeuvres, "a little mood music," and "inviting in a female acquaintance for a quiet discussion on Picasso, Nietzsche, jazz, sex." *Playboy*'s success spawned a series of imitators that ignored the first three topics to focus on the last. By 1957 *Time* counted more than forty "stag mags" on news racks, surely a conservative estimate. While *Playboy* would later feature writings by literary luminaries from Norman Mailer to Studs Terkel, its imitators took a more lowbrow approach. A typical 1955 issue of one such magazine, *Modern Man*, featured a topless pictorial of well-known stripper Lili St. Cyr, full-frontal nude pictures of other women with the crotches airbrushed into blurs, and juvenile articles on the Pony Express and movie special effects.[43]

This juvenile appeal did not go unnoticed, and it proved critical in the emergence of pornography as an American crisis. Still reeling from the impact of the 1948 and 1953 Kinsey reports, which shattered reigning cultural myths by exposing the vast discrepancy between normative standards of sexuality and the actual lived behavior of Americans, the nation overwhelmingly preferred myths of idyllic childhood innocence to the verities of empirical data. The mass media would contrast pornography to the image of the pure, asexual youth for years to come. *Newsweek* reported on the ominous "spread of smut" in 1959, claiming the market was "now being directed at the nation's youth—the impressionable teenager." Two years later, *Good Housekeeping* called pornography "the poison that preys on our children," explaining that "youth's mind is clean," at least until corrupted by pornography.[44] Though this construct of childhood innocence had been dispelled repeatedly, first by Freud, then by Kinsey, who revealed American youth of both genders as sex-curious, heavily masturbating entities, it fit hand-in-glove with the image disseminated by such television shows as *Leave It to Beaver* and perfectly buttressed the cold war ideal of the American family. Rather than being ascribed to inherent curiosities and unruly desires of American youth, whatever aberrant sexual behavior might transpire could now be attributed to pornography. Much as comic books had provided explanations for juvenile delinquency that conveniently avoided either social inequities or parental accountability, pornography thus fell into a belief structure in need of an explanatory variable.

Exploiting this newfound link, the Kefauver Committee moved beyond comics in May 1955, holding hearings on "obscene and pornographic" literature and its relation to juvenile delinquency that summer. Kefauver himself had learned from his excursion into comics and delinquency. Whereas that investigation had produced ambiguous results that proved difficult to capitalize on politically, Kefauver went into the pornography hearings predisposed to find a connection, and unsurprisingly, he did. The early hearings in May 1955 were largely stacked with friendly witnesses: religious leaders, educators, and psychologists all willing to vouch for a link between pornography and delinquency. Kefauver felt no need to await further evidence before endorsing their conclusions; "Smut Held Cause of Delinquency," reported the *New York Times* in June 1955, quoting Kefauver as calling pornography a "definite factor" in the ruination of youth.[45]

The impact was instantaneous; New York's Joint Legislative Committee on Comic Books suddenly reinvented itself as the Joint Legislative Committee on Obscene Material, while the Catholic magazine *America* abruptly shifted gears from comics to pornography. In March 1955, after a lengthy series of anticomics articles, it declared a "comic-books cease-fire" to allow the industry to police itself with the new code. By June *America* had discovered the "pornography racket," declaring pornography peddlers "as dangerous to society as dope peddlers," and the new topic sustained several angry articles in subsequent months.[46]

The Kefauver Committee's next set of hearings, in June 1955, examined the pornography industry by subpoenaing a number of prominent figures from its semiunderground market. Many, such as Abraham Rubin and Edward Mishkin, pled the Fifth Amendment in refusing to answer any questions. This allowed Kefauver to intensify his antagonism; when Irving Klaw—famous for his bondage pictures and films of pin-up queen Betty Page—took the Fifth, Kefauver ordered him to speak under threat of contempt charges. "We are not asking any quarter and we are not giving any quarter, Mr. Klaw," the senator caustically declared. When Samuel Roth, a dealer of pictures, books, and magazines, whose own obscenity case would soon reach the Supreme Court and set a lasting precedent, agreed to talk, Kefauver walked him into a trap. After Roth claimed that his mailing lists carefully precluded the possibility of children obtaining his wares, Kefauver waved before him several letters from parents whose children had received unsolicited catalogs from Roth. The humbled publisher's only response was that he bought his mailing lists from reputable companies that assured him no minors were included.[47]

Other members of the committee joined Kefauver in his attack. Republican William Langer of North Dakota, for instance, brought his home state's attorney general to the hearings and asked him whether the fact that North Dakota had not had a single murder in three years could be traced to the absence of smut in the state. "I think that is generally true," replied the attorney general.[48] But Kefauver left no doubt that the hearings were his show, and he tailored the committee's report to generate maximum emotional impact. By positing pornography as a "$500-million-a-year-racket" run by "loathsome and lecherous purveyors," Kefauver helped construct a new national menace against which he happened to stand as the nation's foremost opponent; though "little attention has been given" to pornography, Kefauver planned to change that.[49]

Kefauver's report downplayed juvenile delinquency as a general concept and instead dwelled specifically on sex crimes. A "very large percentage" of the pornography market "reaches the hands of juveniles," the report claimed, and "the impulses which spur people to sex crimes unquestionably are intensified by reading and seeing pornographic materials."[50] Once again, as with the comics, an absolute lack of evidence confronted Kefauver in his efforts to establish the pornography–sex crime connection. This time, instead of grappling with this obstacle in the text of his report, he banished it to the margins: a brief note buried in the report's bibliography—presented in smaller print type than the report's body—observed, "There are no studies on the relationship of pornographic literature to sexual offense." This was the only note of uncertainty struck in the seventy-some pages of the report. The bibliography itself included several pages of annotated citations to works discussing various facets of sexual deviance, obscenity law, and teenage development; the sole work that actually focused on pornography and its relationship to delinquency or sex crimes was an article from the *Science News Letter* called "Psychiatrists Say Sexy Books Don't Cause Crimes." The article began with the categorical statement, "Pornographic literature does not lead to sex crimes, does not create juvenile delinquents," describing that stance as "the opinion of most leading psychiatrists and psychoanalysts." In its commentary on the article, Kefauver's bibliography dismissed it as a "very short article" with "no names, sources, studies, statistics, or other data given to back up this statement," a curious criticism, given that it could clearly be applied to Kefauver's own conclusions.[51]

Reflecting his liberal bent, Kefauver avoided legislative suggestions that would anger civil libertarians. Instead of giving the postmaster general blanket powers over dubious mailings, the Kefauver Committee suggested procedural safeguards ensuring due process in such circumstances. It also focused on new laws to confiscate vehicles used to transport pornography and, most emphatically, to authorize obscenity prosecutions at the delivery point of pornography rather than the mailing point. The providing of adequate sex education for teens to counteract the negative effects of pornography was a final suggestion, clearly added to distinguish the Kefauver Committee from puritanical groups that opposed both pornography and sex itself. Modernizing attitudes toward sex coincided with the drawing of boundaries around permissible sexuality.

The Kefauver Committee in effect institutionalized opposition to pornography, creating an image of it as a massive industry run by murky characters who, whether by design or lack of concern, targeted children and sexually corrupted them. This vision of a pornographic menace was perpetuated in various forums, from government committees to popular media.

Among public officials other than Kefauver, none took a more prominent role than J. Edgar Hoover. Though the FBI chief's attention had focused on communists and other subversives during most of his career, a disdain for sexually explicit material also consistently permeated his rhetoric. As far back as 1925 Hoover had begun compiling obscene material in a private FBI file, and in 1940 he had linked "smutty magazines" and "salacious literature" to sex crimes, telling the *Reader's Digest*, "This trash must go!" Inspired by Kefauver's conclusions, Hoover grew more vocal about pornography. "Not so long ago," he wrote in a 1957 essay intended for the public, "this problem existed as a serious juvenile hazard largely in the hard-to-control underprivileged areas of our big cities." But the FBI chief noted with alarm, "Today it has spread to the green-landscaped schoolyards of our best suburbs," again invoking the dangers posed to the middle class. Hoover concurred in Kefauver's analysis, again proclaiming pornography a "major cause of sex violence." Though his only evidence for this conclusion was a slight rise in sex crimes per capita during the 1950s, Hoover presented his belief as an axiomatic fact, alluding in 1960 to "the knowledge that sex crimes and obscene and vulgar literature often go hand in hand."[52]

Hoover's voice lent great authority to the supposed pornography-deviance connection, and it allowed journalists to state the connection as fact rather than theory. *Better Homes and Gardens* declared in 1957, "Experts agree that [pornography] undoubtedly contributes to juvenile delinquency." Redefining *expert*—which now referred not to social scientists and psychologists but to such authority figures as Hoover, Kefauver, and Detroit policeman Herbert Case, who said, "There hasn't been a sex murder in the history of our department in which the killer wasn't an avid reader of lewd magazines and books"—allowed the magazine to sidestep the lack of empirical support for the "fact." The article, titled "Newsstand Filth," exemplified the quick discursive slide from pornography to deviance when it leapt from a paragraph in which some "man about town" magazines "even describe sexual intercourse in detail," without transition, to an adjacent paragraph claiming, "Homosexuality, nymphomania, Lesbianism, fetishism, and bestiality are common subjects," never explaining why any men about town interested in pictures of naked women and descriptions of heterosexual sex would take an interest in bestiality.[53]

With public interest piqued, more politicians rushed to "investigate" the issue. A California legislative subcommittee on pornography unintentionally revealed the invisible pressures to conform to the Kefauver-Hoover party line on pornography. In its 1958 preliminary report the subcommittee concluded, "There appears to be no substantial evidence that there is a positive correlation" between pornography and sex crimes. By the time of its final 1959 report, however—an interval during which no research breakthroughs on the topic had been announced—the subcommittee had modified its position: "There appears to be substantial conflicting evidence of a positive correlation between obscene literature and sex crimes." Predictably, the subcommittee recommended stronger obscenity laws and more rigid enforcement. A New Jersey pornography commission reached similar conclusions in 1962, after hearings at which the "evidence" of pornography's effects came from Legion of Decency members who cited J. Edgar Hoover.[54]

Though Georgia had established a state literature commission to monitor newsstands in 1953, only after Kefauver's 1955 report did such bodies proliferate. Oklahoma created a literature commission in 1957, Massachusetts in 1958, and Washington in 1961. These commissions were generally mere advisory bodies without any real power—the Oklahoma commission was not even funded, existing mostly as a conceptual entity—but they reflected the widespread concern about pornography. Protecting children often provided the motivation behind the formation of these groups, such as the Rhode Island Commission to Encourage Morality in Youth, formed in 1956, and the Salt Lake City Youth Protection Committee, formed in 1958, both of which focused their efforts on shielding youngsters from pornography.[55]

At the national level Pennsylvania representative Kathryn Granahan's Subcommittee on Postal Operations turned pornography into a governmental juggernaut, holding repeated hearings on the topic in the late 1950s and early 1960s. Beginning with the proposition—explicitly attributed to Hoover—that pornography made an "undoubted contribution" to the "growth of juvenile delinquency," Granahan's hearings consisted almost entirely of sympathetic witnesses who validated her premise. With very little to add to the ongoing discourse on pornography beyond a repetitive display of outrage, Granahan seemed content to pander to her home-state voting constituency, bringing at least five Pennsylvanians to repeat testimony before her subcommittee in 1961 nearly identical to that which they had already offered it in 1959.[56] The rapidly expanding antiporn bandwagon also included Postmaster General Arthur Summerfield, who spoke out against the dangers of pornography and even instituted a new stamp on postage reading, "Report Obscene Mail to Your Postmaster" in 1960.[57]

At times the seriousness of these efforts was undermined when lapses by leaders were made public. For instance, James Bobo, Estes Kefauver's chief counsel during the Senate investigations of pornography, shortly thereafter privately screened pornographic films in his native Memphis. When the local press revealed this, Bobo explained that his "primary purpose was educational." Confronted with allegations that his screening, apparently of leftover evidence from committee hearings, took place at a Memphis State University fraternity rush party, Bobo conceded, "Perhaps it got a little out of line and was not strictly educational." Though Bobo had admitted to a criminal act of exhibiting obscene material, no charges resulted, and the matter quickly passed.[58] Such infractions suggested the disjuncture between what politicians considered expedient and their private perspectives, but they did little to silence the outcries against pornography. By 1960 a full-fledged moral panic was under way, framed as part and parcel of the normative sexual politics of the cold war.

Seeing Red in Blue: The Com-Porn Conspiracy

The Granahan Committee most aggressively forced pornography into the cold war, moving beyond its alleged effects and into the motives behind it. Kefauver had simply attributed the pornography market to the profit motives of the pornographers, but Granahan seized on a decades-old theory of a communist conspiracy to demoralize America. Though the theory held little apparent credibility, Granahan used her position to legitimize it. Her 1959 Subcommittee on Postal Operations report cited an alleged 1919 communist document titled "Rules for Bringing About Revolution," which instructed revolutionary vanguard cadres to "corrupt the young, get them away from religion, get them interested in sex." The subcommittee itself did "not believe it unreasonable to suspect that there is a connection between pornographic literature and subversive elements in this country."[59]

This theory had been used before. John Saxton Sumner had endorsed similar charges during the Red Scare of 1919, framing smut as an implicitly Soviet "foreign invasion."[60] A 1956 Senate subcommittee investigating Soviet activity in the United States attempted to establish ties between the radical historian Philip Foner's alleged communist activities and his work as the publisher of books such as *Casanova's Homecoming* and *The Power of Sex*. An interrogation of Foner, however, yielded no useful connections, and the mainstream media shied away from the topic.[61] Granahan's revitalization of the communist-pornography connection also failed to attract the popular media, but it assisted the anticommunist Right in wrenching an effective cold war trope from the free-speech advocates who had been capitalizing on communist censorship for years.

Eisenhower's 1953 speech against book burners, for instance, directly juxtaposed American liberties against Russian repressiveness, and a typical editorial (from the *Christian Science Monitor*) agreed, calling censorship "exactly what the Communists would do." When the Norwich, Connecticut, American Legion planned to burn comic books in early 1955, an ACLU press release called their plan "an imitation of totalitarian dictatorship that is wholly contrary to the American way of life," and the burning was canceled.[62] By the mid-1950s, free speech advocates had learned to harness the rhetorical power of the cold war to their own ends; in this sense the cold war served an inadvertently progressive end analogous to the effect Mary Dudziak has shown it had on civil rights, imposing freedoms that reluctant cold warriors had to accept in the name of keeping sharp the contrast between the United States and its enemies.[63]

As with civil rights, the cold war could be a double-edged sword—the coded white-supremacist phrase "outside agitators" being a case in point, invoking communism to discredit civil rights activists.[64] The 1959 Granahan report sharpened the other blade, inspiring a rash of allegations regarding the communist influence on the porn industry. A 1960 *American Mercury* article called pornography "a political weapon" and claimed "obscenity and communism often go hand in hand." That same year in Georgia, a member of the state literature commission announced a "strange tie-up in names" between pornography publishers and "leftwingers," concluding "this was a deliberate sabotage of the morals of our youth by Communist effort."[65]

To support their arguments, proponents of this perspective often gave narrative explanations of the conspiracy. A typical example came from the Chicago columnist Jack Mabley, who charged communist agents with extracting "hundreds of sex criminals, perverts and prostitutes" from Russian and Polish prisons and turning them loose in a small Polish town. For ten days "there was an incredible orgy," photographed by the agents, who then returned the deviants to jail and shipped the pictures to Mobile, Alabama. From there "literally millions of reproductions" were made and distributed, which "are poisoning the minds of countless young Americans." Mabley admitted the "story sounds fantastic" but argued that the evidence—of which he presented none—"is too solid to be shrugged off."[66]

If theories of comics causing delinquency and pornography causing sexual deviance found fairly widespread acceptance despite their resolute absence of evidence, stories as far-fetched as Mabley's found much less public favor. Kathryn Granahan continued to support the theory; when antipornography activist Dr. William Riley called the smut market "part and parcel of the Communist movement to destroy the United States" during testimony before her subcommittee, and even referenced the case of Philip Foner, Granahan interrupted to offer a friendly, "I agree with you, Doctor." Much of the com-porn theory's perpetuation came from what was becoming known as the "radical Right." In Southern California, a hotbed of right-wing activity, the theory flourished; Garden Grove activists publicized the red menace of blue movies, while the Los Angeles American Legion and Elks Club both endorsed the analysis in 1961.[67] That same year Oklahoma City policeman Weldon Davis investigated pornography, unintentionally revealing the extreme elasticity of cold war rhetoric by stating that "anything un-Christian can be called Communistic." Another law enforcer, W. Cleon Skousen of Salt Lake City, listed the promotion of pornography among "current communist goals" in his book *The Naked Communist*, which was widely read by the radical Right.[68]

These conspiracy theorists had little impact on public policy. When a House of Representatives committee held hearings on "protecting postal patrons from obscene and obnoxious mail and communist propaganda" in 1963, the connection was only one of similarly invasive and unwanted mail, and no attempt was made to link the two categories.[69] By the mid-1960s the ridiculous aspects of the communist theory of pornography had risen to the surface; an Omaha judge's claim that "the communists want us to get to the point where sex is the way to live" struck an amusingly ill-phrased note, while the judge's description of teenagers mooning him as "sex perversion" reflected a worldview far from the popular consensus. Likewise, an Indianapolis woman's attempt to show the com-porn connection by observing that the sex-drenched novel *Candy* was written by Terry Southern, who also scripted the film *Dr. Strangelove*, a "bitter attack on the dedicated men of our Strategic Air Command," could inspire only laughter among the moviegoing public who had made *Dr. Strangelove* a hit.[70]

Despite their seeming irrelevance, the com-porn conspiracy theorists effectively muddied the rhetorical waters of the pornography debate at precisely the point where it bled into the issue of free speech by reclaiming the cold war for those who most actively supported it. Minimal policy impact notwithstanding, these efforts helped shape the parameters of the publicly acceptable by further demonizing pornography, a trend that would never leave the consciousness of the liberals eager to prove their own anticommunist credentials. Though the postwar liberal consensus dominated federal policy until the late 1960s, it operated within clear social constraints that led to convolutions on the part of liberals regarding obscene material. Already it was clear that factual evidence could pale in the face of unified, albeit unfounded, theories of social threats and ills for many Americans.

The com-porn theory was a blunt rhetorical weapon in the hands of deeply conservative parties trying desperately to claim the power of definition over Americanness. Cold war discourse more smoothly, and with the support of both conservatives and liberals, integrated antiporn sentiment into its model of sexual normativity, against which "perversions" were easily contrasted and conflated amongst themselves. A brief look at postwar Los Angeles shows how easily authorities could deploy obscenity charges against homosexual "deviants," thus using obscenity as part of the greater cold war repressive apparatus.

Clearly Obscene or Queerly Obscene? Demonization in the City of Angels

Awareness that "the number of 'queers' and degenerates are increasing in this city" was noted by an LAPD vice squad officer in 1943, and the numbers continued to bear out his observation into the postwar years: arrests for sodomy jumped from nineteen in 1940 to ninety in 1947, while "sex perversion" arrests accelerated even more rapidly, leaping from 22 to 437 in the same period.[71] World War II, with its homosocial army settings and relaxed home-front mores attributable to social instability, had functioned as a catalyst for thousands of gay men and women to recognize their sexual identities and structure their lifestyles around them. These newly self-identified homosexuals often opted for city life rather than a return to their hometowns after the war, and like the rest of urban America Los Angeles saw a dramatic increase in the visibility of their presence.[72] Gay enclaves such as Silver Lake and cruising grounds such as Pershing Square and Griffith Park were well known, and by the end of 1950 the city was home to the nation's first homophile activist group, the Mattachine Society, which vocally called for gay legal rights.[73]

Predictably, postwar visibility was met with repression from local authorities. Civic leaders eagerly enlisted in the antigay crusade, as the city council adopted a resolution in 1947 imploring the LAPD to use "every latitude in its power" to close gay bars and even threatened to criminalize casual handshakes "in order to reach these homosexuals." New chief of police William Parker, who took charge in 1950 and helped institutionalize the "war on crime" framework, eagerly complied, assuring the council that the LAPD "will continue its impressive activities against this type of offense" in 1951. Meanwhile, the local media fostered moral panic with its sensationalist coverage of homosexuality; the *Daily News*, for instance, alerted readers to the "alarming increase in sex crimes" in 1948, using the phrase as a thinly coded reference to homosexuality. For readers incapable of decoding the allusions, the paper also provided headlines such as "Hunt Pervert Who Lured Two Boys." In this, Los Angeles reflected national trends; as David Johnson notes in his history of cold war–era antigay governmental activity, "many politicians, journalists, and citizens thought that homosexuals posed more of a threat to national security" than communists.[74]

Antigay local sentiment would be sustained across the years; from the "mentally twisted sexual perverts" described in 1952 by Councilman Ed Davenport—fondly remembered by historians as "the darling of the neo-fascists"—to the "cancer-like spread of vice" depicted by the *Los Angeles Times* a decade later, the prevailing image of gay men was as venereal-disease-spreading sexual psychopaths intent on making L.A. a "mecca for queers," as another local paper put it. One Angeleno woman responded to that article with a letter in 1962, describing her "nausea and anger" over gay public visibility and proposing to "mak[e] it impossible for them to exist here." The authorities agreed, and while sodomy laws and police violence were favored methods of establishing those conditions, obscenity laws also aided in the attempted restoration of traditional heterosexual hegemony.[75]

When it came to the branding of gay-themed media as obscene, the most recurrent pattern was initial courtroom convictions followed by subsequent reversals exonerating the defendants. These ultimate vindications came at great cost, both in the literal financial sense and in the less tangible but no less real sense of perpetuating the discursive conflation of the queer and the obscene. The travails of Bob Mizer, an early victim of these efforts who had cofounded the Athletic Model Guild in 1945, serve as a case in point. By selling black-and-white photographs of barely clad men, often in erotic but ambiguous scenarios such as wrestling matches, AMG quickly attracted a constituency. When Mizer encountered trouble placing advertisements in resistant men's magazines, he simply bound sets of his photographs and began publishing them as a magazine, *Physique Pictorial*. Debuting in 1951, it found a global subscription list by the next year, and its influence extended far enough to directly inform the paintings of the famous L.A. artist David Hockney.[76]

Physique Pictorial also found a vocal public opponent in the *Los Angeles Mirror* columnist Paul Coates, who had repeatedly used his position to denounce homosexuality. After a condemnation of the Mattachine Society in 1953 and the presentation of "an unpleasant fact—the fact of homosexuality in Los Angeles" on his television program *Confidential File* in early 1954, Coates next targeted Mizer's publication. Warning that "sooner or later, almost every teen-age kid will have some contact with the homosexual," Coates listed possible contact locations as movie theaters, public restrooms, and parks—or, he added, "maybe the homosexual will be the man who stops his car to offer your boy a ride home from school." Coates then singled out *Physique Pictorial*, calling it "a kind of *Esquire* for men who wish they weren't" and "thinly veiled pornography." Adding rhetorical sparks to his incendiary framework, he also claimed that "it finds its largest audience among the most brutal, horrifying sex criminal—the sadist."[77]

When Coates returned to *Physique* two weeks later, he reiterated that the magazine's appeal, "whether intended or not, is really to the sick, half-world of homosexuals, sadists, and masochists." Disingenuously suggesting that "perhaps the harm wouldn't be too great, if perverts limited their practice to their own small circle," Coates immediately followed with a staccato rejoinder: "But they don't." Coates's column inspired action, and the next morning, May 19, 1954, the *Mirror*'s front page announced the arrest of Bob Mizer on charges of "possession and sale of indecent literature."[78]

Meanwhile, the local sale of such straight men's magazines as *Playboy*, chock-full of pictures of naked women, continued unabated.

At trial the prosecution's case rested on one witness (the arresting officer) and nine photographs, several portraying fully naked men but unrelated to *Physique* and neither photographed by nor even possessed by Mizer. A conviction nonetheless ensued. Although Mizer managed to win his appeal in Los Angeles Superior Court in 1955, as the city abandoned the mysterious nudes and arguments descended into competing analyses of "uncovered rumps," the impact of his victory was quite muted. Local newspapers ignored the reversal, and because it was a local case, it set no viable precedent. Furthermore, the consequences of the obscenity charges outlived their short legal life; Mizer himself took a self-described "timid" approach to publishing after the case; while gay male magazines grew steadily more explicit over the course of the 1960s, Mizer restricted *Physique Pictorial*'s imagery out of a direct concern for his freedom. "I didn't want to spend my whole life in jail," he later explained.[79] The stigmatization of Los Angeles' queer community via obscenity law thus began without legal validation but nonetheless served its purpose, imposing a chilling effect on queer expression and stunting the growth of the mail-order community to which Mizer had contributed.

These purposes were even more apparent in the next major effort to suppress queer media, when Los Angeles postmaster Otto Oleson initiated a vendetta against the homophile magazine *ONE*. Unlike *Physique Pictorial* and its racy photographs, *ONE*—created by activists with Mattachine backgrounds—took a more staid approach toward gay rights issues, addressing police entrapment, psychiatric homophobia, and other pertinent matters. Oleson commenced activity against *ONE* shortly after its inception in 1953, detaining the August issue from the mail. Forced to let it circulate after the solicitor general in Washington found no grounds for withholding, Oleson struck again when the October 1954 edition featured a short lesbian story and a mildly ribald gay ballad. Considering their challenge to Oleson's edict strong, the publishers of *ONE* were quickly disappointed by the federal district court, which upheld Oleson's ruling. On appeal, the Ninth Circuit Court affirmed in a vitriolic decision lambasting *ONE* as "obscene and filthy"; the short story, "Sappho Remembered," which featured nothing more explicit than a kiss, was described as "cheap pornography calculated to promote lesbianism," while the poem "Lord

Samuel and Lord Montagu," whose most overt lines mentioned "ins and outs with various Scouts," earned scorn as "dirty, vulgar, and offensive to the moral sense."[80]

An incensed *ONE* asserted that "homosexual literary themes, compared to heterosexual, are not judged with nearly an equal degree of candor and realism" in the judicial realm. Its legal briefs also made the point repeatedly, first arguing before the district court that lesbian kisses were no more salacious than heterosexual ones and then declaring that the court "repeatedly begged the question by assuming, without argument, discussion, or any explanation of any kind whatsoever, that the mere depiction of homosexuals or homosexual problems in literature is 'lustful' or 'stimulating' in such a manner as to render the literary work 'obscene.'"[81] In 1957 these arguments failed to persuade even the American Civil Liberties Union (which at that point refused to challenge the constitutionality of "laws aimed at the suppression or elimination of homosexuals") to join the case on *ONE*'s behalf; while an ACLU representative promised *ONE*'s editor to give "serious consideration" to the case, the union ultimately decided against involvement.[82] The notion that homosexuality was inherently obscene remained so deeply institutionalized that even America's most aggressive civil libertarians passively accepted it.

Despite such adversity, *ONE* maintained its resistance, finally appealing to the Supreme Court in 1957. Circumstances gave the homophile magazine hope: after decades of inaction on the issue of obscenity, the Court that year finally codified rigorous standards for the suppression of expression, as will be discussed in the next chapter. These standards portended hope for *ONE*, and indeed, in January 1958 the Court reversed the obscenity ruling, exonerating *ONE* and clearing it for mailing.[83]

Yet, as with the Mizer case, a landmark decision went largely unheeded. The Supreme Court issued its ruling per curiam, without a written decision, and the media followed suit. In the *New York Times* a reporter devoted sixteen paragraphs to a companion decision regarding nudist magazines delivered alongside *ONE*, only cursorily acknowledging that "in another brief order the court today reversed a post office ban on a magazine, one which deals with homosexuality," in an article titled "Nudist Magazines Win Mail Rights."[84] Back in Los Angeles, the local press gave even less attention, covering everything from antics at a Bing Crosby golf tournament to a fire that threatened John Wayne's baby but ignoring the case.

ONE continued to rail against the antigay bias of obscenity law, but to no discernibly increasing audience outside the homophile community. Indeed, by the time of *ONE*'s much-delayed exoneration, Los Angeles officials had expressed their overt intent to continue the persecution of queer texts through obscenity charges.[85]

As the *ONE* case percolated up through the court system, the LAPD found a new target. The Coronet Theater, on La Cienega Boulevard in West Hollywood, served as a gay male social hub, frequently screening art films with queer overtones, such as the avant-garde biblical short *Lot in Sodom* (1933), Leni Riefenstahl's propagandistic but male-physique-centered *Olympiad* (1936), and Jean Cocteau's surreal *Blood of a Poet* (1930). "Even when they were showing Buster Keaton," gay archivist Jim Kepner would later recall, "two-thirds of the audience would be gays."[86] An October 1957 bill featured four films: *Plague Summer, Closed Vision, Voices,* and *Fireworks.* The last one, made by Kenneth Anger in 1947 and shown often across the nation during the intervening decade, stood as perhaps the most aggressively queer film of its era, brimming over with homoerotic signs and symbols, from sailors to public bathrooms to phallic imagery. On seeing *Fireworks,* the LAPD vice squad leveled an obscenity charge at Coronet operator Richard Rohauer—and, more broadly, at the Coronet itself as a site of gay community formation.[87]

Prosecutor William Doran made clear that the Coronet was the true target of the legal attack, calling forth a series of male teenage theater patrons as witnesses and asking them the sole question of their ages, which ranged from sixteen to nineteen. When defense attorney Stanley Fleishman objected to the witnesses as immaterial, the judge overruled him; however, when Fleishman cross-examined one sixteen-year-old, sustained objections prevented the young man from speaking to questions such as "Did any film in the program corrupt or deprave you?" and "Did any film in the program arouse lascivious thoughts or lustful desires on your part?" LAPD vice officer Donald Shaidell, who confessed to finding *Fireworks* "sickening," likewise reflected the emphasis on the Coronet rather than the films when he described "the many known homosexuals whom I recognized in the audience of this theater" and "many others who [*sic*] I had seen in homosexual bars in the Hollywood area." Indeed, Shaidell testified that he had asked Rohauer whether the theater operator knew that "there was a lot of homosexuals in the audience tonight." The vice officer also made a telling comment when he was pressed to define obscenity; after complaining that "I don't have my dictionary with me," he reluctantly explained, "Obscene is something that isn't general practice by the public."[88]

Prosecutor Doran also zeroed in on the film's queer symbolism, calling specific attention to one scene with a lit firecracker protruding from a man's pants. "Somebody set fire to his penis, is that right?" Doran asked one witness. Though the witness responded, "Well, it wasn't his penis," Doran nonetheless persisted in later referring to "the penis scene." Midway through the trial, an exasperated Fleishman complained to Judge Harold Shepherd that, procedurally, the trial was "a travesty of the worst kind." When he called for a dismissal, Shepherd acknowledged, "I think you have a good argument, counsel," but denied the request. None of Fleishman's objections, nor the defense's impressive roster of witnesses (ranging from a psychoanalyst to a Guggenheim-winning poet), could sway the case from its inevitable conclusion.[89]

Doran's tactics of parading teenage boys before the court and collapsing the distinction between literal nudity and phallic symbolism proved effective, and Rohauer was found guilty of exhibiting obscene material. Yet again, the conviction failed to withstand appellate review, and the Los Angeles Superior Court reversed, citing the *ONE* case (decided by the time of the appeal in 1959) and definitively declaring that while homosexuality "may be regarded as a cruel trick which nature has played on its victims" and "is not a condition to be approved," it was nonetheless not obscene, in and of itself. Dissenting judge Leon David, however, reflected prevailing cold war cultural beliefs, describing *Fireworks* as "abnormal stimuli" for the "lascivious thoughts, lustful desires and sadistic satisfactions" of "sexual psychopaths." In covering the decision, the *Los Angeles Times* conspicuously failed to note the unequivocal declaration that homosexuality was not inherently obscene.[90]

The legal disentangling of homosexuality from obscenity, then, carried little impact, in part owing to media influence. While newspapers continuously downplayed any information divorcing the two concepts, they vociferously reinforced the notion of the two concepts' mutually constitutive nature. "Smut can change a perfectly normal boy or girl into a homosexual," asserted the *Herald and Express* in 1956, and two years later an extended "Report on Pornography" by the *Daily Journal* would refine and develop the thesis. "Pornography as a subject is hard to divorce from sex deviation, strip teasing, nude exhibitions, juvenile delinquency," and other matters, claimed reporter Edsel Newton, giving the first category the most pressing attention. Creating his own taxonomy, Newton softened his references to heterosexually oriented "unwholesome literature," described as "harmless," while reserving "hard core" pornography for gay media, which would inspire an animal breeder to "look around for new stock if he observed among his herds such deviations," a metaphor that emphasized the base depravity of homosexuality. Effacing the overwhelming predominance of heterosexually oriented erotic materials, Newton explained that "the publications, photographs and films in this particular hard core category cater to the 200,000 homosexuals that are said to exist in the Los Angeles area and to morbidly curious youths and adults."[91]

Such tropes made manifest the unspoken but evident belief structure of the antigay obscenity charges: homosexuals, particularly gay men, were disproportionately attracted to sexual materials; the worst and most threatening form of erotic expression was the queer variety; and queer texts were inherently obscene. By conflating homosexuality and obscenity, L.A. authorities discursively reconfigured the relationship of the terms, embedding the former within the latter, and legal rulings alone showed little capacity to break the link. Not even the Supreme Court's overt 1962 declaration that homosexual publications were subject to the same standards of obscenity as heterosexual ones (always read in terms of naked females depicted for straight male audiences), which finally decreed what the 1959 *ONE* case had already seemingly established, carried much immediate impact in Los Angeles, as the 1964 trial of Michael Aaron Getz indicated.[92]

Arrested for exhibiting the film *Scorpio Rising*, Getz found himself in an uncannily precise repeat of the earlier *Fireworks* trial. Like that film, *Scorpio* was made by the avant-garde filmmaker Kenneth Anger, who won a prestigious Ford Foundation grant only a week after Getz's arrest. The film itself, again like *Fireworks*, privileged connotative imagery over linear narrative, featuring a biker gang whose homoerotic endeavors are refracted against images of James Dean, Marlon Brando, and Jesus Christ. Anger's project of queering iconic masculinity culminated in a transgressive party, featuring imagery that would be hotly contested at trial. Prosecutor Warren Wolfe followed precedent in framing the film in the context of its queer-friendly setting, this time the Cinema Theatre in Westwood, near UCLA. Asking a witness, "Were most of the patrons in the theatre that evening male?" Wolfe clearly announced his strategy; later in the trial, when another witness professed not to know the term *queen* but to live in Westwood, Wolfe quipped, "Evidently not near the Cinema Theatre."[93]

Because of the Supreme Court, Wolfe was unable to simply contend that *Scorpio Rising*'s homosexual content constituted a priori evidence of obscenity. Rhetorical circumlocutions abounded as he attempted to maintain the substantive linkage while adhering to the letter of the law. "The people's position is this: the problem is not the idea of homosexuality . . . but it is the depiction of the idea which is the problem, not the idea," Wolfe explained at trial. When this analysis seemed vulnerable, Wolfe resorted to visceral antigay slurs. "Do you believe artistic ability is an excuse for degeneracy?" he asked one film-critic witness. Though an objection by defense attorney Stanley Fleishman—a repeat party from the *Fireworks* trial—was sustained, Wolfe persisted in his language. The next day he again described "depiction of certain degenerate activity." In another sustained objection Fleishman attempted to defuse the term of its charge by mentioning that "degenerate is a very vague word and kind of emotionally-laden," but despite the repeated objections Wolfe went on to continue using the term before the jury.[94]

The parallels to the *Fireworks* trial ran deep: again, Fleishman delivered a stirring speech calling for a mistrial, to which the judge, Bernard Selber, acknowledged that the "people's case at this point I will say is very weak," before denying the plea. Amazingly, the trial *again* boiled down to disputes over an alleged penis, in a shot from the climactic party scene occupying mere frames of film. The shot was so brief—described by one witness as "subliminal"—that consensus on its content was impossible. "I cannot even identify it as a penis by magnification," testified one witness; "I see a blob of something there," which he suggested "might be a potato." As with *Fireworks*' phallic firecracker, though, Wolfe peppered his speech with reference to exposed penises. And again, it worked: *Scorpio Rising* was found obscene and Getz convicted. Because the case so openly flouted obvious precedent, it came as little surprise when an appellate court reversed the decision six months later. That it even came to trial in 1964 shows how persistently cultural convictions superseded legal doctrine in cold war Los Angeles.[95]

The systematic persecution of queer Los Angeles through obscenity laws represented not the excesses but the intended design of the domestic cold war project: "deviant" sexuality was stigmatized and suppressed through whatever means available, to better maintain the cherished normalcy on which social ideals of "Americanness" were predicated. It is important to note, however, that this project remained under the control of the postwar liberal consensus, and many early antiporn leaders represented liberalism. Fredric Wertham, for instance, vigorously supported civil rights and rejected Victorian sexual mores, and in the political sphere Estes Kefauver resisted the temptation to overstate the threat of pornography beyond certain limits that would invite unbridled suppression. After cosponsoring legislation allowing individual states to regulate obscenity without federal interference, Kefauver, on reflection, withdrew his support, explaining that the legislation "might be too broad in the standards of prohibition it would establish," permitting the suppression of literature deemed "indecent or immoral" rather than legally obscene. The senator also refused to stretch his crusade beyond reasonable limits; in a 1960 speech he claimed pornography was "not as momentous as the U-2 incidence [sic], the Summit meeting, defense appropriations, and a number of other domestic and international problems." Reflecting the cold war framework that shaped American responses to pornography, Kefauver's comment also showed his liberalism coexisting, uneasily, with the moral panic he helped engineer.[96]

Even the liberal upstart Hubert H. Humphrey joined the action in Congress, inserting a St. Paul, Minnesota, antiobscenity ordinance into the *Congressional Record* in 1954.[97] If there seemed a strange incongruity in liberal politicians supporting moral panics deployed to conservative ends, this had much to do with the muddy waters of liberal stances toward pornography and obscenity law. Chapter 2 turns to those convoluted contemplations, as liberals failed to adequately address the issues and thus left an opening for conservatives to later reclaim the moral high ground.

2. AMBIVALENT LIBERALS
Theorizing Obscenity Under Consensus Constraints

SUPREME COURT JUSTICE WILLIAM O. DOUGLAS remains best known as a free speech absolutist, reading the First Amendment literally as barring any restrictions whatsoever on expression. In 1951, though, his speech doctrine had yet to emerge. "The freedom to speak is not absolute," Douglas contended. "The teaching of methods of terror and other seditious conduct should be beyond the pale," he continued, adding as an afterthought, "along with obscenity and immorality."[1]

Douglas was dissenting from a decision to allow the prosecution of communist advocates even in the absence of any actual insurrectionary plans, demanding more expansive freedoms than the Court majority was willing to grant in 1951. Even so, to encounter his words in light of his later, well-earned absolutist reputation can be jarring. To encounter his argument in 1951, however, would shock no one; virtually no recognized voices, at least within the mainstream American political consensus, doubted that obscenity was "beyond the pale" or that its suppression posed no threat to freedom of expression.

Although even Republican president Dwight Eisenhower exhorted citizens not to "join the book burners," a narrative of declining censorship and developing public antipathy toward it obscures the profound ambivalence at the heart of the American freedom-of-speech consensus.[2] As chapter 1 showed, Americans in the 1950s were quite susceptible to claims that pornography constituted a social menace. Immediately after Ike told Americans, "Don't be afraid to go into your library and read every book," he qualified his comment with, "as long as any document does not offend our own ideas of decency." Such items were labeled "obscene," and the almost universal corollary of anticensorship statements in the first two decades after World War II was that obscenity was not included in free speech; it *deserved* to be censored. As *Redbook* put it in 1951, after comparing censorship to Nazi book burnings, "No one, of course, objects to the censorship of obscenity for obscenity's sake."[3]

Within these parameters postwar liberalism staked its claim to social authority. Condemning censorship while condoning obscenity law, liberals facilitated the regulatory mechanisms of a normative sexual regime that would, decades later, help dismantle their political reign that ran from the New Deal through the Great Society. The "family values" framework that would emerge in the 1970s found its bedrock in the cold war notions of Americanness predicated on various forms of exclusion: racial, religious, ideological, and sexual. By shoring up the lines of the socially acceptable to exclude "prurient" obscene material—a category that could be read quite widely, as we have seen—postwar liberals proved complicit in their own downfall, setting in motion a social trajectory with ultimately conservative implications.

None of this appeared obvious at the time. The American Civil Liberties Union and the Supreme Court under Chief Justice Earl Warren constitute the two iconic institutional faces of postwar liberalism, and while both of them grappled with questions of obscenity at great length, rarely did either reflect on the unspoken sexual politics they endorsed. For that matter postwar liberalism generally failed to acknowledge sexuality as political in the first place, even as liberals participated in its very politicization. A tacit sexual exceptionalism permeated the interstices of cold war era liberal discourse. Economics, philosophy, religion—these were understood as political matters. So naturalized, though, were the normative sexual standards of heterosexual, procreative marital sexuality that challenges to them were seen not as political but as merely perverted—criminal, perhaps, as in the case of homosexual activity or, in the case of "prurient" materials, obscene.

As such, this fit smoothly into the prevailing liberal historical consciousness, which remained steadfastly oblivious to its own historicity. In 1950 Lionel Trilling called liberalism "the sole intellectual tradition" in America, effectively effacing the various radical (and conservative) movements whose boisterous contestations of the status quo throughout American history had helped forge the norms taken as axiomatic in the postwar era.[4] Those norms, more than anything else, defined liberalism. Like its predecessor progressivism, liberalism resists encapsulating definitions, and even its two leading historians struggle with the term; Alonzo Hamby calls it "somewhat slippery," while Alan Brinkley concedes that "there are probably no satisfactory answers" to the question of definition.[5] Examined as a set of interlocking beliefs and constituencies, postwar liberalism manifested itself in a general acceptance of capitalism, along with an active federal government that provided a basic social-welfare safety net to mitigate the market's worst ravages, a belief that social conflict could be solved through economic progress, internationalism in foreign policy, support for civil rights and cultural pluralism, anticommunism, and a general preference for personal choice over governmental intrusion in matters of culture and morality. These ideas found their constituencies in labor unions, African Americans, religious believers in the social gospel, civil libertarians, intellectuals, and the majority of the voting public until the late 1960s.

Underlying its forward-looking faith in progress was liberalism's acceptance of certain key social institutions—the market, the nation-state, the family—as givens, not to be interrogated. Liberalism, in short, was not radicalism, and its boundaries were often rigid. As Alan Brinkley shows, a brief flirtation with class-conscious radicalism exhibited by the Second New Deal was already in remission by 1937, and at war's end the program's critique of capitalism was replaced by a more business-friendly liberalism that merely hoped to compensate for capitalism's shortcomings. Conservative resistance failed to overturn the New Deal, but it successfully halted its expansion and began to encroach on it; a would-be Full Employment Act in 1946 was reduced to a mere statement of goodwill rather than government mandate, and the 1947 Taft-Hartley Act reversed the advances of organized labor. Cold war anticommunist rhetoric forced liberals to scale back their ambitions, as President Harry Truman's proposed federal health insurance program disintegrated in the hands of the American Medical Association lobby's endless reiteration of the phrase "socialized medicine." The liberal Truman even capitulated to anticommunist loyalty programs that anticipated the subsequent McCarthyist purges in the vague name of national security.[6]

The ACLU and the Warren Court would generally operate within the boundaries of this liberal framework. Thus as the ACLU "joined the liberal mainstream," it shifted away from its radical pacifist and labor-oriented roots and proved "more willing to compromise for the sake of influence and popularity," historian Judy Kutulas writes. Some of these compromises would include a purge of communist board members beginning in 1940 and extending across the cold war era, and even praise for and collaboration with the repressive FBI, as well as taking a less than aggressive stance toward the civil-liberties travesties of the World War II Japanese internment.

Accepting the validity of obscenity laws into the 1960s fit well into this pattern of fighting for rights *within* prevailing norms. As a group passionately committed to defending free speech, the ACLU also helped define *speech* to exclude such ostensibly valueless and apolitical forms of expression as pornography. The group would gradually adopt a more expansive vision of free speech over the course of the 1960s, but because it launched no powerful defense of free sexual expression and cultivated no widespread support for its integration into the liberal free-speech agenda, the ACLU's gradual transition to a more libertarian position would carry minimal social influence.[7]

Likewise, the Warren Court too embodied the ambivalence of postwar liberalism. Historians now challenge as "not entirely accurate" the public memory of the Warren Court as a force for revolutionary change, but the Court clearly partook of and helped define postwar liberalism.[8] While the undeniable net effect of the Court's landmark decisions was to expand rights and liberties for African Americans, political dissidents, those accused of crimes, and other disempowered groups, the actual trajectory toward this end proved quite erratic. In the wake of the 1954 *Brown v. Board of Education* decision that at long last bestowed formal equality on black citizens by ending school segregation, the Court did very little to implement the substantive social equality that would render legal equality meaningful and even deliberately used *desegregate* rather than *integrate* in opinions because it was "a shade less offensive" to segregationists, as Justice William Brennan privately reminded his colleagues.[9]

When the Court did give offense, as in its notorious "Red Monday" cases of 1957, which exonerated communists from state-sponsored persecution, or the string of criminal-procedure cases of the 1960s that scaled back police power, the Court often retreated in the face of public anger. A sharp post-1957 "lurch to the right" helped reinstate the dictates of the national security state for several years, and a 1966 decision allowing police the right to stop and frisk without direct provocation proved "at least as significant a victory" for law enforcement as the Court's liberal decisions had been for the accused. While none of this eliminates the massive significance of the Court's contributions to social justice, it does suggest that the liberal justices operated self-consciously within understood political limits.[10]

On matters of sexual politics, both the ACLU and the Warren Court fully joined in the liberal consensus, implicitly framing sexuality as an anomalous, apolitical social sphere unaffected by civil liberties applicable in all other realms. The historians John D'Emilio and Estelle Freedman observe the emergence of "sexual liberalism" in the early twentieth century, a framework that "detached sexual activity from the instrumental goal of procreation [and] affirmed heterosexual pleasure as a value in itself," but sexual liberalism continued a tacit policing of sexualities and pleasures outside its privileged zone of straight marriage. Thus the ACLU acquiesced to the "lavender scare" that saw gay men and lesbians barred from federal employment for decades after President Eisenhower's 1953 Executive Order 10450, declaring it "not within the province of the Union" to evaluate "laws aimed at the suppression or elimination of homosexuals" and even calling homosexuality "a valid consideration in evaluating the security risk factor in sensitive positions."[11] Supreme Court decisions also revealed the contours of sexual liberalism, repeatedly ratifying unspoken heteronormative boundaries of the legally and socially acceptable. The Court actively endorsed traditional gender roles, explaining in a 1961 opinion that "woman is still regarded as the center of home and family life," in explaining why the excepting of women from jury duty in the absence of their volunteering was constitutional. As Marc Stein shows, other sexuality-related decisions on such matters as birth control often expanded freedoms but only within certain confined realms of socially-sanctioned behavior that continued to privilege marriage and "the family" as a monolithic entity. Under the guise of deregulating sexuality, the Warren Court in fact reinscribed and policed evolving but tradition-based normative borders.[12]

This left "obscene" material without any significant defenders. While such conservative groups as the New York Society for the Suppression of Vice, the Legion of Decency, and the Knights of Columbus had long fought to censor sexually explicit (and otherwise nonconformist) material, postwar liberals concurred in the suppression of that which fell "beyond the pale." Defining the borders of "the pale" proved challenging, but neither the Warren Court nor the ACLU doubted its fundamental linkage to the unquestioned "normalcy" they both upheld. "Prurience"—lewd, salacious sexual interest pursued for the sheer sake of pleasure as an end in itself—fell outside the realm of the normal, its central role in the history of human behavior notwithstanding, and became the linchpin of the obscenity doctrine developed in the 1950s.

En route to that doctrine, the lower courts fashioned an obscenity mishmash mired in confusion and subjectivity. Out of this judicial quagmire emerged an argument for applying the clear and present danger test established by the Supreme Court during World War I to obscenity, a position the ACLU would ultimately endorse. For all its definitional flaws, the test would at least place prurient materials alongside other forms of expression before the law. The Warren Court, though, rejected clear and present danger for a "redeeming social importance" test, a unique burden foisted on no other form of expression. Because liberal notions of normalcy precluded arguments for prurience as itself containing social importance, or for graphic depictions of sexuality as inherently political forms of expression, this left material deemed obscene subject to state-sponsored suppression, even in the absence of any evidence for its harmful effect.

Only in the final years of the 1960s did the Court adopt a near-absolutist stance on the permitting of obscenity into the marketplace of ideas. With pornography so widely reviled and liberals in the untenable position of defending free speech while torturing logic to justify exceptions, a window was opened for conservative backlash. Freedom of sexual expression had never been effectively sutured into Americanness, and the Warren Court's brief flirtation with free speech absolutism would last only a moment before conservative retrenchment began scaling it back.

The Obscenity Framework and Its Discontents

From the start the ACLU detached sexuality from its understanding of politics, as Roger Baldwin and the other founders of the ACLU deliberately marginalized obscenity in devising their banner of "free speech" in the 1920s. The ACLU's most prominent predecessor, the Free Speech League, organized in 1902 by libertarian radical Theodore Schroeder, had explicitly included obscenity among areas protected by the First Amendment. But when ACLU cofounder Zechariah Chafee published the group's first major work on free speech in 1920, he conspicuously failed to mention the Free Speech League. Chafee was not unaware of the League's positions; he even sent Schroeder a letter apologizing for his failure to cite him. Historian David Rabban reads this as a conscious effort to write radicalism out of liberalism, and the narrowing of "speech" to exclude obscenity surely made the ACLU's agenda more palatable to potential members. As Chafee explained, obscene material "do[es] not form an essential part of any exposition of ideas," meaning its "very slight social value" was "clearly outweighed by the social interests in order [and] morality." Its suppression was therefore of little consequence.[13]

Under Baldwin's direction the early ACLU placed a premium on its notion of political speech, arguing for the rights of radicals jailed during the antisubversive sweeps of 1919 and labor organizers silenced by corporate-friendly government officials. When the producers of *The God of Vengeance*, a serious play about prostitution written by Sholom Asch, the premier Yiddish American author of the period, were charged under an obscenity law in New York City in 1923, the ACLU declined to assist the defendants; Baldwin saw no point in "agitating." Even after a suppressive series of bookstore raids by the Boston police later in the decade, the ACLU stuck to its policy, as a union director called obscenity "a phase of free speech which we have kept clear of . . . to avoid complicating our main issues." Though the group occasionally intervened in such matters, defending Mary Ware Dennett's sex-education manual *The Sex Side of Life* on educational grounds in 1928, such participation remained rare. The union often prized free speech primarily as a corollary of freedom of association for the labor movement and other dissenting groups; thus, the 1937 Wagner Act's legitimization of union activity constituted "the most important single step toward the attainment of meaningful freedom of speech which has taken place in modern times," according to the ACLU's 1938 annual report.[14]

Given Baldwin's years living as part of the sexually experimental "Greenwich Village Left" in the 1910s, his own biographer considers his stance on obscenity—which was so conservative as to consider the word *damn* improper when spelled out in full—"paradoxical, at the very least, and arguably hypocritical."[15] It nonetheless established the framework for early ACLU policy, and even the more expletive-friendly members of the union accepted the proscription of obscenity. Morris Ernst, for instance, the celebrated lawyer who successfully defended James Joyce's novel *Ulysses* from obscenity charges in the 1930s, had no qualms about including the word *fuck* in his 1929 anticensorship book *To the Pure*, albeit enclosed within quotation marks. When Ernst returned to the subject of censorship in a 1940 book, *The Censor Marches On*, he unintentionally exposed the intellectual convolutions necessary to defend free speech while excluding obscenity from its province. Complaining that judges relied on circular logic to define obscenity, Ernst listed a series of synonymous phrases often utilized as definitions, such as "excite lustful or lecherous thoughts," "incite dissolute acts," "pander to prurient taste," and "exploit dirt for dirt's sake." Later in the book, though, when he offered suggestions on obscenity legislation, he fell back on precisely one of the phrases he had listed as meaninglessly tautological, writing that obscenity laws "should be amended so as to make it indisputably clear that they are aimed solely against smut—dirt for dirt's sake."[16]

Baldwin never questioned the legitimacy of obscenity as a legal category. In 1947 he even drafted a letter to assist the post office in formulating criteria for determining obscenity. "One of the basic considerations is the motives of the publisher or distributor," Baldwin began, distinguishing "legitimate" purposes such as medical studies, scientific work, and art from presumably less-legitimate aims such as sexual arousal. Other criteria Baldwin discussed included the relation of the intended audience to the work's ostensible purpose and the relation of pictures to accompanying text. A second draft commissioned by Baldwin added that classics of art and literature "which have proven their value or appeal through the ages" should also be exempt from obscenity charges. Although the letter apparently was not sent, it outlined a framework of accepting obscenity prosecutions as congruent with free speech unless they targeted "legitimate" material, which became de facto ACLU policy.[17]

In response to a newspaper reporter's 1949 inquiry, the union's press director, Alan Reitman, wrote, "There can be no objection to punishment for obscenity." Staff counsel Herbert Monte Levy, who performed a solicitor general–like function in advising the union on which cases to pursue, frequently rejected pleas for ACLU assistance in obscenity cases. To a California woman charged with distributing obscenity for selling nude photographs through the mail in early 1951 he denied legal aid, curtly informing her, "I am also not sure whether we would consider the dissemination of nude photographs to be a civil liberty," especially when the purpose was "purely to cater to sexual curiosity or desire." Another case that year involved postcards declared obscene and unmailable by the post office. The postcards contained no photographs, only extremely cartoonish illustrations intended to be humorous; a typical example involved a caricaturized "Chinaman" pointing to a topless (and also heavily caricaturized) African woman while asking her husband, "Ubangi?" Levy informed the distributor that he had discussed the case "with several of my colleagues," and it was agreed that this was "not an appropriate case" for the ACLU to enter.[18]

Though Roger Baldwin had been forcibly retired as executive director of the ACLU by 1950, his conservatism regarding obscenity lived on in Levy. Never raising a priori objections to obscenity prosecutions, Levy instead continued Baldwin's case-by-case approach in which the perceived "legitimacy" of the material in question proved more pertinent than the abstract principle of free expression. "We constantly do take a position on whether or not a particular book or object is obscene," Levy explained in a 1950 letter. "We then aid in attempting to prove non-obscene those books which we think are thus." Levy's conception of the obscene went beyond nude photos and smarmy postcards. When Henry Miller's novel *Tropic of Cancer* was found obscene in a California court in 1953, Levy advised the national office against supporting an appeal, explaining that the book "really is dirt for dirt's sake." As we saw in chapter 1, Levy's attitude filtered down to local ACLU branches, with the Southern California unit declining to support homophile political magazine *ONE* in its challenge to postal suppression.[19]

Levy's extension of Baldwin's philosophy dominated the ACLU during the first half of the 1950s, as the organization frequently went out of its way to proclaim its support for obscenity laws even as it took an otherwise inflexible stand in defense of free expression in all other aspects of American life. The ACLU's 1954 annual report displayed this inconsistency, denouncing censorship: "All censorship laws ever devised appear to rest upon vague definitions or to call for subjective judgments. . . . Censorship law makes thought control possible." In the same paragraph the report also explained that "the ACLU, of course, has no quarrel whatsoever with appropriate laws which punish obscenity."[20]

Prurience and eroticism could be neither political nor thoughtful within this framework, carrying no value whatsoever when not equipped with properly highbrow aesthetic accoutrements. A widely cited 1954 article on obscenity authored by the ACLU members and University of Minnesota law professors William Lockhart and Robert McClure exemplified this stance. Calling for stringent restrictions on obscenity prosecutions, Lockhart and McClure did not adopt an absolutist stance of untrammeled free expression. Rather, they simply argued that obscenity should be legally restricted to pornography, "which is, of course, not entitled to constitutional protection." Instead of justifying this claim, the professors merely commented later in the article that "the banning of such books poses no serious threat to freedom of expression in literature."[21] Sexual expression remained in its anomalous sphere, held apart from other forms of expression by the apparent lack of ideational content in the bodily oriented.

Not all ACLU members assented to the organization's obscenity framework. As early as 1944 the historian and *Harper's* columnist Bernard DeVoto categorically wrote, "The right to own and read pornography appears to me unquestionable." But the obscenity framework so pervaded ACLU policy that even Baldwin critics accepted several of its premises. The Connecticut-based playwright Elmer Rice would emerge as one of Baldwin's most vocal critics, telling him in 1948, "Our whole attitude seems to me a hush-hush one, compounded of timidity, prudishness, and opportunism, and designed to persuade or cajole some minor government official to drop a particular proceeding." Yet when Rice's National Council on Freedom from Censorship issued a statement-of-purpose pamphlet calling censorship "a futile and absurd business," it limited its critique to arbitrary suppression at the hands of a government official. Other forms of suppression were more acceptable, and the pamphlet observed, "Laws exist in all the states to deal with commercial pornography. Prosecution in the courts should constitute the only control and with right to trial by jury." As long as juries rather than Comstocks labeled material obscene, the council acquiesced in the ruling.[22]

Rice advocated an "uncompromising stand for freedom of expression, with respect to sexual matters just as we do with respect to political and religious matters." In a seemingly contradictory display of ambivalence, though, he added that "a jury of average citizens"—a group he would never empower to judge religious or political expression—was the appropriate arbiter in determining obscenity.[23] Still immersed in the ACLU habit of tacitly depoliticizing sex, Rice nonetheless chafed against the borders of the obscenity framework. His influence would ultimately guide ACLU policy but only after the unwieldy status of obscenity in the court system deteriorated into complete wreckage, necessitating interventions by both his organization and the Supreme Court.

Confusion in the Courts

Obscenity, argued the state of Ohio before its highest court, "has certainly not become a blurred symbol in 1954."[24] In at least one unintended sense the state was correct: it was blurred long before then. Not since the late nineteenth century had the Supreme Court substantively weighed in on obscenity, leaving state and local courts to improvise a chaotic body of case law with no clear standards or definitions. Out of this legal wilderness emerged little coherent doctrine. Reluctant even to address the issue of obscenity, the Court avoided it until the existing legal discrepancies were too glaring to ignore.

In its 1896 decisions that commenced its half-century of avoidance, the Supreme Court had upheld the 1873 Comstock Act prohibiting obscenity from the mails and ratified the 1868 common-law English precedent *Regina v. Hicklin*, which proscribed as obscene those works that tended to "deprave and corrupt" the most susceptible persons who might encounter them. It also exempted the merely "coarse and vulgar" from the province of obscenity, restricting the category to material "which has relation to sexual impurity," embracing sexual exceptionalism well before Baldwin and the ACLU.[25]

With that, the Court left further clarification to the lower courts. No truly important legal developments followed until 1933, when customs officials refused entry to James Joyce's much-lauded novel *Ulysses*. In a brief decision New York district judge John Woolsey approached the book from a literary perspective, finding much aesthetic value. Without directly engaging the *Hicklin* standard, he replaced it with a new standard-bearer, the "person with average sex instincts." *Hicklin*'s other premise, that isolated parts of a work could render it obscene, also fell before Woolsey's modernist-friendly judicial approach, which held that the work must be evaluated as a whole; though he found parts of *Ulysses* "disgusting," Woolsey found the novel in its entirety to constitute a work of considerable artistic merit. "Nowhere does it tend to be an aphrodisiac," he added.[26]

Upheld on appeal the next year, the *Ulysses* case set an important liberal precedent, delivering a powerful blow to the forces of censorship. Expanding on Judge Woolsey's thoughts, appellate judge Augustus Hand found Molly Bloom's closing monologue in *Ulysses* "pitiful and tragic, rather than lustful." The obvious underpinning of both *Ulysses* decisions was that the book was redeemed by Joyce's unusual artistic mastery, his technical experimentation, and his intent to convey the stream of consciousness of average people as acknowledged in a post-Freudian world. Had the book simply appealed to lustful thoughts or prurience, both decisions suggested, its suppression would be justified. Sexual arousal for the mere sake of its own enjoyment simply held no value or merit. Full-frontal nudity in photographs of men and women might be acceptable in the book *Nudism in Modern Life*, as the Court of Appeals for the District of Columbia ruled in 1940, but only because the book was "an honest, sincere, scientific and educational study," distinguished from sheer lust-inducing exploitation.[27]

Aside from a general consensus on the impermissibility of lust for lust's sake, courts varied widely in their understandings of obscenity. On the one hand, in 1943 the Supreme Court of Arkansas upheld an obscenity conviction based on the nudist magazine *Sunshine and Health*, defining obscenity as "something offensive to modesty or decency." On the other hand, a Cincinnati court a few years later exonerated the magazine, along with twelve striptease photographs, calling obscenity laws "shackles on the brains of men." The *Hicklin* standard survived in Massachusetts, where the state's highest court defined obscenity as that with "a substantial tendency to deprave or corrupt its readers by inciting lascivious thoughts or arousing lustful desires" in upholding the obscenity of Lillian Smith's novel *Strange Fruit*. Though the court acknowledged the book—dealing with southern race relations and including a few brief scenes of a sexual nature—was "a serious work" and a "work of literary merit," those factors were considered "not decisive of the issue before us." All of these cases were final, showing clearly the lack of a uniform legal definition of obscenity.[28]

One seemingly possible resolution to this intellectual and juridical morass at the time was the clear and present danger test. First articulated by Supreme Court justice Oliver Wendell Holmes in 1919, the test had initially been used to uphold restrictive World War I curtailments of the right to dissent. After a dormant period in the 1930s, though, it reemerged in the 1940s as the commonly accepted barometer of free expression, excluding only direct incitements to lawbreaking or fields of speech that caused tangible harms, such as libel. While liberal stalwarts like Zechariah Chafee endorsed a watered-down "clear and probable danger" test for obscenity that would incorporate abstract moral dangers, other more aggressive civil libertarians began to push for a consistent application of free-speech standards.[29]

By the late 1940s, some of the more progressive members of the legal community began the attempt to subsume obscenity under the clear and present danger standard. The recently appointed appellate judge Jerome Frank, who held an iconoclastic reputation for his scholarly work, protested the withholding of publisher Samuel Roth's *Waggish Tales of the Czechs* from the mails in 1949. Noting that censorship "is compatible with the ideologies of Hitler, the Czars and Commissars," Frank found in the ninety-six ribald stories of the *Waggish Tales* nothing more obscene than Balzac's *Droll Stories*. Warning of the chilling effect the book's suppression might have on other authors, Frank argued for the application of the clear and present danger test to obscenity, adding, "I think that no sane man thinks socially dangerous the arousing of normal sexual desires."[30]

The Philadelphia city judge Curtis Bok made a similar case just one month later. Local police had raided several bookstores in late 1948, rounding up books by James Farrell and William Faulkner alongside several less-distinguished works, and the case reached Bok's court in March 1949. Finding none of the books obscene, Bok delivered a scorching condemnation of contemporary obscenity law. Dismantling one of the most common arguments for regulation, Bok mused, "It will be asked whether one would care to have one's young daughter read these books." Answering his own question, the judge declared, "I should prefer that my own three daughters meet the facts of life" in the library rather "than behind a neighbor's barn." Moving on to doctrinal matters, Bok acknowledged prurient and pornographic content to be a precursor to an obscenity conviction but found such qualities merely necessary, not sufficient. Instead, he adopted a literal version of the clear and present danger test, ruling that a book, "however sexually impure and pornographic," could not be a present danger "unless the reader closes it, lays it aside, and transmutes its erotic allure into overt action." Only then, if the action were criminal, could a book be suppressed on grounds of obscenity.[31]

Neither Bok's nor Frank's perspectives prevailed. Bok's opinion was invalidated when the Pennsylvania Supreme Court nullified its content.[32] Amazingly, despite his bold rhetoric, Frank was actually *concurring* in the withholding of the waggish Czech stories, which he sheepishly attempted to explain as a result of his "judicial inexperience in this field," creating an unwillingness to challenge his more experienced colleagues (one of whom personally agreed with Frank but wrote in a memo, "I doubt if we should upset the Postmaster"). "I concur," Frank concluded, "but with bewilderment." The malleability of the clear and present danger test did it no favors, either. While civil libertarians like Bok and Frank might apply it with a restrictively tangible notion of "danger," the open-endedness of the test allowed for competing interpretations, such as that of the Supreme Judicial Court of Massachusetts, which cited the test in holding *Strange Fruit* obscene in 1945 but declared that the "danger of corruption of the public mind is a sufficient danger." The Supreme Court rendered the test even more elastic in 1951, upholding the anticommunist Smith Act on the grounds that the mere existence of the Communist Party constituted a clear and present danger because of its revolutionary doctrine, even in the absence of any concrete plans to overthrow the government. Freedom of speech, Chief Justice Fred Vinson explained, "is not an unlimited, unqualified right" but rather one that must, "on occasion, be subordinated to other values and considerations."[33]

While that case involved national security rather than obscenity, it clearly boded poorly for the more literal readings of the clear and present danger test. Consequently, the state of obscenity case law remained one of disarray, often defined by judges less liberal than Frank or Bok. The Ninth Circuit Court of Appeals in Northern California upheld an obscenity conviction regarding Henry Miller's novels *Tropic of Cancer* and *Tropic of Capricorn* in 1953, noting the "sticky slime" of the books but declining to attempt a definition of obscenity beyond a footnote to a dictionary. The court obliquely addressed the clear and present danger test by mentioning that "salacious print in the hands of adults . . . may well incite to disgusting practices and to hideous crime." No more specificity was forthcoming, but the ruling stood. That same year in Georgia the state legislature defined obscenity as "any literature offensive to the chastity or modesty, expressing or presenting to the mind something that purity and decency forbids to be exposed."[34]

Nowhere did this judicial disarray so precipitate a crisis as in the case of the nudist magazine *Sunshine and Health*, whose tumultuous legal history had already included both obscenity convictions and exonerations, both withholdings from the mails and postal victories. At the ACLU Herbert Levy considered *Sunshine and Health* an ideal test case because it avoided the erotic enticements he so devalued: "the women pictured therein are almost uniformly ugly, and would have difficulty arousing even a frustrated male." His one caveat was that "it features bodies of nude males with quite frank views of their genitals."[35]

If Levy's letter reflected the extent to which the heteronormative masculine sexuality of the day and its attendant insecurities helped structure notions of the obscene, its psychosexual implications paled in comparison to those of the decision written by the District of Columbia federal judge James Kirkland in 1955 after the postmaster general withheld *Sunshine and Health* from the mails. The judge listed a painstaking set of criteria for determining obscenity, including the angle and distance of photography, the age of the subject, the subtleties of pictures revealing breasts (depiction alone was not obscene, though "its accentuation, its distortion, or its grossness" could change that), and effect of shadows on the genital areas. He then proceeded to evaluate every picture in the withheld issue at length, to make "particular findings of fact." The result was a bizarre, obsessively detailed opinion. The front cover, for instance, showed a young woman in her twenties; while her genitals were obscured by the angle, she did possess "a bosom quite larger by far than normal," shot "as to elongate and make quite massive the breast as distinguished from the very small nipple." This picture, Kirkland decided, was not obscene. Nor was the picture of a young girl on page seven; "while the labia major are shown, they are diminutive and juvenile. One would have to be prudish" to hold the picture obscene. Less to Kirkland's liking was a shot of a man standing by a pool. Though a shadow covered the man's pubic area, his "male organ" was "prominently shown": "the corona of the penis is clearly discernable; in fact even a casual observation of it indicates the man is circumcised." This picture was deemed obscene.[36]

On and on went Kirkland's decision, past a woman with "matted varicose veins that cause her to be grotesque," past a woman with "large, elephantine breasts that hang from her shoulder to her waist," and past even an entire paragraph devoted to deliberation over a blurry spot on a woman that could have been either pubic hair or a shadow (Kirkland settled on the former) to finally reach an inevitable ruling that the magazine was obscene. *Sunshine and Health* responded in its July 1955 editorial, explaining that nudists "are dealing not with the logic of mature minds, but with the illogic of people blindly depending upon unchallenged tradition. Thus our genitals, our pubic hair, and our mammary glands have become . . . lewd things." The magazine, which had unabashedly displayed full frontal nude pictures for its two decades of existence, reluctantly began airbrushing the genitals of its nudists or putting them in contorted poses to avoid genital exposure. The result, ironically, was to bring the magazine's content closer to the fetishization of the body that marked *Playboy* and its ilk, with their carefully posed photographs that balanced the revealing of flesh against its concealment.[37]

This brand of judicial aesthetic criticism, it grew increasingly evident, could not abide. It was too subjective, too unwieldy, and too unpredictable. With these and other complaints in mind, appellate judge Jerome Frank wrote another stirring opinion, again in a case involving publisher Samuel Roth. Roth had been found guilty on four counts of mailing obscenity, and the New York–based Court of Appeals for the Second Circuit upheld the conviction, writing in its lead opinion that "we are hardly justified in rejecting out of hand the strongly held views of those with competence in the premises as to the very direct connection of this traffic with the development of juvenile delinquency." Frank explicitly rejected that connection, as well as its relevance to Roth's conviction, and called the federal obscenity law "exquisitely vague." Returning to clear and present danger, he argued that freedom of speech could be denied only when discourse was "likely to incite to a breach of the peace, or with sufficient probability tend either to the overthrow of the government by illegal means or to some other overt anti-social conduct." None of these consequences, Frank insisted, could reliably be traced to obscene material. Wondering why sexual speech was held to different standards from religious or political speech, Frank cited John Milton, Thomas Jefferson, James Madison, and John Stuart Mill in rejecting "any paternalistic guardianship by government," which he accused of fostering immaturity and a "Papa knows best" attitude in the citizenry.[38]

His bark remaining stronger than his bite, however, Frank again reluctantly concurred in upholding Roth's conviction. As a lower court justice Frank felt bound by the Supreme Court's words. Though the Court had not ruled on obscenity in the twentieth century, it had suggested its exclusion from First Amendment protection in several obiter dicta, such as a passing 1942 mention of "certain well-defined and narrowly limited classes of speech, the prevention and punishment of which have never been thought to raise any Constitutional problem." Among these classes were "the lewd and obscene, the profane, the libelous, and the insulting or 'fighting' words."[39] Considering himself bound by such comments, Frank nonetheless attached a lengthy appendix to his concurrence critically examining and systematically dismantling the logic of obscenity laws, hoping to force the Supreme Court into finally acknowledging and resolving the lower-court confusion it had so long allowed.

Reading Frank's opinion, Elmer Rice was elated. By 1956 the National Council for Freedom from Censorship had evolved into the ACLU Censorship Panel, and at the group's next meeting Rice brought Frank's decision along. ACLU executive director Patrick Murphy Malin, in attendance at the meeting, conceded that the union had long held obscenity to a standard separate from religious or political speech. Faced with the discrepancy exposed so plainly in Frank's opinion, Malin urged "full consistency" in ACLU standards. The panel agreed, voting nine to one in favor of a statement that "the constitutional guarantees of free speech and press apply to all expression, and there is no special category of obscenity or pornography to which different constitutional tests apply." That uniform test, the panel also agreed, was establishing "beyond any reasonable doubt that the material represents a clear and present danger of normally inducing behavior which validly has been made criminal by statute."[40] The ACLU board adopted the censorship panel's recommendations, and when Samuel Roth appealed his case to the Supreme Court in 1957, the ACLU assisted with an amicus curiae brief proposing the clear and present danger test be applied to obscenity. If Frank's opinion helped galvanize the ACLU into a more aggressive stance, though, it found less favor in a conflicted Court uneager to confront the legal rot it had let spread.[41]

Codifying Ambivalence

While avoiding obscenity for six decades, the Supreme Court did send occasional signals of its positions. A general free-speech orientation was evident even before Earl Warren joined the bench in 1953. When the postmaster general stripped *Esquire* magazine of its second-class mailing privileges, the Court restricted postal power to regulate mail content in 1946. It also hastened the demise of film censorship by belatedly bestowing First Amendment protections on motion pictures in 1952, four decades after a more conservative Court had denied that films constituted expression. At the same time, a number of offhand obiter dicta over the years made clear that the Court accepted the proscription of obscene materials as axiomatic.[42]

This tension, between free-speech proclivities and an unwillingness to pursue their implications, would mark the Warren Court's obscenity doctrine. Intending to bring much-needed lucidity into the murky debate, the Court instead publicly aired its own internal ambivalence over the course of the subsequent decade, failing to consistently satisfy either the censorious or the libertarian or even to maintain a steady trajectory in its own rulings. Expanding free speech protections while condoning the suppression of "prurient" sexual expression as obscene and thus illegitimate, the Warren Court embodied the postwar liberal marginalization of counternormative sexuality.

The Court's attempt to render cohesive the unruly patchwork of local, state, and federal laws on which officials relied began tentatively, with a case lacking broad applicability. In the 1957 *Butler* decision the Court unanimously voided a Michigan law outlawing the sale of any book with obscene language "tending to the corruption of the morals of youth." "Surely, this is to burn the house to roast the pig," Justice Felix Frankfurter wrote, since the effect of the law was to "reduce the adult population of Michigan to reading only what is fit for children." Frankfurter carefully avoided direct comment on obscenity per se, which allowed for the undivided Court.[43]

Any hope of preserving the unified front dissipated four months later when the Court ruled on Samuel Roth's conviction, combined with a parallel California case. While *Roth* reached the Court because Jerome Frank's impassioned opinion had essentially forced its hand, Justice William Brennan's lead opinion quickly vanquished the hopes of free-speech absolutists. After a very brief overview of laws from the early republic banning libel, blasphemy, and profanity Brennan concluded, "it is apparent that the unconditional phrasing of the First Amendment was not intended to protect every utterance." Looking at the series of obiter dicta tangentially issued by the Court in other cases Brennan also decided "this Court has always assumed that obscenity is not protected by the freedoms of speech and press." Finally, he fused the two arguments together to rule that "implicit in the history of the First Amendment is the rejection of obscenity as utterly without redeeming social importance." Without so much as a substantive engagement with the idea Brennan also curtly dismissed the clear and present danger test with a brief citation to a 1952 obiter dictum aimed at libel, thus foreclosing once and for all the integration of sexual expression into the general field of speech acts.[44]

Brennan, however, epitomized postwar liberalism, and he went to great lengths to avoid serving the interests of censors or book burners.

"Sex and obscenity are not synonymous," he insisted, providing a test to determine obscenity: "whether to the average person, applying contemporary community standards, the dominant theme of the material taken as a whole appeals to prurient interest." This ratified the *Ulysses* decisions two decades after they entered the common law and finalized their rejection of the *Hicklin* standard of "depraving and corrupting." It also meant "all ideas having even the slightest redeeming social importance—unorthodox ideas, controversial ideas, even ideas hateful to the prevailing climate of opinion—have the full protection" of the First Amendment. Buried in the interstices of this ostensibly progressive opinion, however, lay an unstated endorsement of the sexual politics that structured prevailing notions of "average" personhood and community standards—a heteronormative status quo still deeply suspicious of prurience for the sheer sake of pleasure, which failed to qualify as an "idea" in and of itself.[45]

The decision, which affirmed the convictions of Samuel Roth and David Alberts but placed stringent restrictions on the application of obscenity law, failed to generate a unified Court, with a 7–2 split for *Alberts* and a 6–3 for *Roth*. Chief Justice Earl Warren concurred on both but on grounds different from those of Brennan. "It is not the book that is on trial; it is the person," he wrote, arguing that "the conduct of the defendant is the central issue, not the obscenity of a book." In Warren's view it was the "willful and lewd" manner in which the defendants marketed their publications that justified their convictions; in other contexts the same works might be protected. John Marshall Harlan offered another approach, based on state over federal regulation. Voting to uphold Alberts's conviction since it happened in a California state court, Harlan dissented on Roth's case because it was federal. The "dangers of federal censorship" Harlan found "far greater" than any state legislation; the justice saw nothing significant in a state banning *Lady Chatterley's Lover*, "so long as there is no uniform nation-wide suppression of the book."

Finally, William O. Douglas and Hugo Black, New Deal–era appointees generally on the left flank of the Court, dissented on both cases. Noting that "the arousal of sexual thoughts and desires happens every day in normal life in dozens of ways," Douglas wondered why the "common conscience of the community" was allowed to govern literature relating to sex when it was kept from deciding the acceptability of works on religion, economics, politics, or philosophy. He rejected Brennan's historical analysis and found no credence for the case that the First Amendment was intended to exclude obscenity. Instead, Douglas supported a rigorous variation of the clear and present danger test: expression could be suppressed, he wrote, only when "it is so closely brigaded with illegal action as to be an integral part of it."[46]

Roth was delivered only a week after the Supreme Court's "Red Monday," on which several opinions friendly to communists persecuted by repressive laws were handed down. One case, *Yates v. U.S.*, revisited the 1951 Smith Act decision to rather awkwardly reinterpret it as distinguishing "advocacy of abstract doctrine" from "advocacy directed at promoting unlawful action"; the Court consigned its one mention of the clear and present danger test to the footnotes, finding it "unnecessary to consider," without further comment. While the test remained implicit in the opinion, it clearly held little overt sway.[47]

The publicity from the Red Monday cases overshadowed the obscenity case; *Time*, for instance, gave the Supreme Court's "new direction" a lengthy cover story after the political decisions on July 1, 1957, but gave only passing coverage to the obscenity cases the next week. At the Catholic *America*, editors quickly recognized *Roth*'s importance, as Harold Gardiner enthusiastically wrote that the rulings "will be welcomed by those who favor some forms of censorship." Liberals paid heed more slowly. A Connecticut ACLU member wrote to the *Nation* in September that *Roth* facilitated censorship and threatened to usher in a "new wave of puritanical moralism" that could "reach the proportions that prohibition or McCarthyism had in their impact on freedom." By December the ACLU had "observed a definite rise" in local drives against smut and a "new emphasis on local police and prosecutory action," tracing them back to *Roth*. Indeed, the decision directly shaped the rhetorical strategies of the nascent Citizens for Decent Literature, as the next chapter will show.[48]

The ACLU observation made a persuasive case, citing numerous examples of recent obscenity prosecutions against magazines such as *Gent* and *Playboy*. Film censorship boards also saw *Roth* as a means to legitimize their efforts. In New York the state censor board had long used the terms *indecent* and *immoral* to ban films. When it used such logic to ban the nudist film *Garden of Eden* in 1957, the film's distributors went to court. Just one week after *Roth* a state court directed a license to be granted, holding that "indecent" as a term "standing alone and read literally, is much too broad and vague" to justify banning the film. The censors saw this not as a loss but as a clarification; their elimination sheets began using *obscene* instead of the old terms, reflecting a terminological but not a substantive shift in policy.[49]

Not oblivious to these misuses of *Roth*, the Supreme Court indicated its disapproval in a series of late-1950s decisions. When Chicago censors banned the French film *The Game of Love* in early 1957, the Illinois Supreme Court ruled in their favor. A federal appellate court affirmed, agreeing that the film's "dominant effect is substantially to arouse sexual desires" and that "this effect is so great as to outweigh whatever artistic or other merits the film may possess." Acknowledging those merits was a mistake; Brennan's *Roth* opinion clearly sanctioned any work with "redeeming social importance," not a balancing test between prurient aspects and artistic merit. The Supreme Court unceremoniously reversed the decision in a November 1957 per curiam decision. It also overturned or vacated other obscenity rulings, including the nonpictorial homophile magazine *ONE* and the long-suffering *Sunshine and Health*.[50]

The tendency of the New York censors to simply replace other terms with "obscene" also did not escape the Court's gaze. When the censors banned a film version of *Lady Chatterley's Lover*, a state court upheld the ban, explaining that obscenity included "that form of immorality which has relation to sexual impurity," a reference to the film's approval of adultery. To cover itself, the state court misleadingly noted, "Our conclusion, therefore, is the same as that of the United States Supreme Court in the *Roth* case." The Supreme Court was not convinced by the ruse and reversed the ruling, explicitly declaring "sexual immorality" an idea, thus protected. The Court concluded this run by reversing the obscenity conviction of a Los Angeles book dealer on the grounds that the statute under which he was tried lacked a *scienter* clause, a requirement that the defendant had knowledge of the content of his merchandise.[51]

While these rulings made clear that a majority of the Court would not tolerate the suppression of material with any claim to social importance, they made equally clear that the Court would not reconsider its exemption of obscenity from First Amendment protection. Only Black and Douglas espoused that position, and not even the string of obscenity reversals placated them. As a frustrated Black wrote of the First Amendment, "I read 'no law . . . abridging' to mean no law abridging." Even the post-*Roth* free-speech orientation of the Court proved fragile; Justice Tom Clark, for-

mer attorney general under Harry Truman and the Court member most
hostile to sexual expression, mustered up a bare five-justice majority to uphold Chicago's film censorship law in early 1961, basing his ruling on Chicago's "duty to protect its people against the dangers of obscenity." Elicit-
ing angry howls of dissent from Warren, Brennan, Black, and Douglas, the
decision revealed the profound ambivalence of the Court on the obscenity
issue. Later that year the Court denied certiorari to a Wisconsin obscenity
case in which the appellant based his argument on the clear and present
danger test.[52]

The ACLU consensus on the clear and present danger test had been
fragile to begin with, and with that standard so explicitly rejected, the organization floundered. Strategic limitations on sexual expression found the
most vocal support. "We should attempt to define 'hard core' pornography,"
Herbert Levy argued in 1958, "and should expressly state that we disapprove
of its dissemination." In a 1959 memorandum press director Alan Reitman
hinted at one reason for supporting the obscenity framework: the ACLU's
public image. "We should make clearer that we do not support obscenity
per se," Reitman wrote, concerned that the ACLU could be characterized
by its opponents as a friend to pornographers.[53]

Proponents of obscenity restrictions failed to amass a unified majority in the censorship panel, as did free-speech absolutists who would place
no restrictions on speech without evidence of tangible harms. One member, George Soll, admitted the absence of evidence to link pornography to
illegal conduct in 1960 but proposed supporting obscenity laws nonetheless, arguing that "since it offends such a great number of people it stands
in a special position." To this Soll's fellow panelist Harriet Pilpel quickly
retorted, "Communism offends a great number of people also." Soll had
no response. Dan Lacy, director of the American Book Publishers Council, vigorously supported the obscenity framework, telling Congress in 1960
his organization's stance on obscenity law: "We heartily favor its relentless enforcement against the pornographer." His proposal in a censorship
panel meeting later that year to amend the ACLU's stance of defending
"all expression" to defending "any material having the slightest redeeming
importance"—fitting his phrasing to the Supreme Court's own—failed, as
did most other proposals, as the ACLU sank into an obscenity deadlock.[54]

A March 1961 censorship committee meeting reflected the standstill:
a motion to resolve that the ACLU oppose "all prosecutions or restrictions

of obscenity"—a direct rejection of the obscenity framework—lost four to five. Immediately following came a motion to amend ACLU policy to defend "all expressions of ideas," with the explicit stipulation that "hard-core pornography does not involve such an expression of ideas" as to bring it within the protection of the First Amendment. It lost by the same count.[55]

At the dawn of the 1960s the Warren Court's obscenity rulings fell so short of delivering a clear mandate that state and local courts easily evaded their intent, as when a Rhode Island statute banning as obscene any book whose content or cover was "principally made up of descriptions of illicit sex or sexual immorality" was upheld by the state's Supreme Court in late 1959 as congruent with *Roth*. Perhaps the most ambiguous phrase in *Roth*, and most susceptible to co-optation, was "contemporary community standards." A concerned ACLU had considered "most unfortunate" the possibility that the phrase would necessitate "a geographical atlas of the United States indicating 'obscenity sensitivity,' something along the lines of the annual rainfall index." It had reason to worry. In 1958 Congress, following a Kefauver suggestion, passed a law allowing for the prosecution of obscene matter sent through the mails at either the point of departure or that of receipt. This modified the existing policy that allowed prosecution only at departure points—mostly California and New York—and opened the door to charges in what a California legislative committee on pornography smugly called "less sophisticated" locales.[56]

The case of Sanford Aday reflected the most egregious abuse of this new policy. A publisher of lurid dime-store novels based out of Fresno, California, Aday had been tried on federal obscenity charges in his hometown in 1958. When the jury failed to return any convictions on eleven different books, the federal government indicted him again in 1960, first in Phoenix, then Grand Rapids, Michigan, and again in Honolulu. The cases were consolidated to one trial, held in Grand Rapids—presumably the most conservative of the bunch. When Aday moved for a transfer to California, citing health problems and travel costs, the Michigan court denied the motion, explaining, "It is obvious that a jury drawn from the southern district of California would not have knowledge of the community standards in this western district of Michigan." The Grand Rapids jury subsequently found Aday guilty on several obscenity charges, resulting in a sentence of twenty-five years imprisonment and a $25,000 fine. His appeals process would occupy the next half-decade.[57]

Localized community standards remained dominant between 1958 and 1964. The Kansas state censor body won in court on a ban against *Garden of Eden* with a brief explaining that the standards of "the average person residing in the Midwest are different from the contemporary community standards of an average person living in Massachusetts or New York." Abilene, Texas, created a Citizens Review Board to monitor obscenity in 1961, using "present day standards in Abilene" as its barometer. Henry Miller's highly sexual novel *Tropic of Cancer* exemplified the trend. Grove Press's decision to finally publish the novel in 1961 generated nearly one hundred separate trials. When the journalist Anthony Lewis surveyed national bookstores in 1962, he found the novel for sale in New York City, Washington, San Francisco, and Minneapolis but banned or held obscene in Los Angeles, Chicago, Atlanta, and Phoenix. As the Marin County district attorney in Northern California said while trying the novel, "pornography is a matter of geography."[58]

Unable to clarify this legal mess because of its own lack of internal cohesion, the Supreme Court continued to plod along without creating effective precedent. The 1962 *Manual Enterprises* case showed once again that very little suppression would be deemed constitutional but also failed again to deliver a unified opinion that might lead to an actual cessation of obscenity prosecutions. Herman Lynn Womack was a philosophy professor who began publishing homoerotic physique magazines in the 1950s. The *Roth* decision and the Court's subsequent reversals had comforted him; "I am now more than ever convinced that the [post office] is going to do nothing to us," he wrote to a friend in 1959. Womack was wrong: postal authorities labeled his magazines, which frequently showed naked men in poses that concealed any genital exposure, obscene and unmailable in 1960. The case reached the Supreme Court in 1962, and though reversal followed on a firm 6–1 split, the varying arguments offered by the justices merely perpetuated the confusion surrounding obscenity.[59]

Justice Harlan's lead opinion, joined only by Potter Stewart, found the magazines "dismally unpleasant, uncouth, and tawdry" but not legally obscene. Harlan also explained "community" as "a national standard of decency." Brennan's concurring opinion, however, outnumbered Harlan, with Warren and Douglas signed on to reverse the case on procedural grounds of limited postal authority. Tom Clark issued a gruff dissent, complaining that the ruling required the post office to become "the world's largest disseminator of smut." Not only did *Manual Enterprises* resolve nothing; it also had the misfortune of falling on the same day as the Court's ruling against mandatory prayer in public schools. The juxtaposition outraged the religious press, particularly Catholic media. "Prayer, No; Obscenity, Yes, Supreme Court Decrees," printed the *Chicago New World. America* bemoaned the "promise of preferential treatment" given to homosexuals by the Court, despite the fact that Harlan had gone out of his way to hold Womack's physique magazines to the same standards as straight fare like *Playboy*.[60]

A 1963 decision holding unconstitutional a Rhode Island commission to regulate youth consumption of literature did little to ease the Court out of its rut, and a plethora of approaches to obscenity persisted across the nation. Asked to define obscenity in early 1964, the head of Virginia's state film censorship board replied, "what offends me." Next asked whether she followed court decisions, she explained, "I try not to confuse myself with anything like that." In light of such arbitrary policies, the Supreme Court had little choice but to continue revisiting the obscenity debacle.[61]

Opportunity arose when the Ohio Supreme Court upheld the obscenity of *The Lovers*, a film directed by French New Wave leader Louis Malle. Though the film garnered global critical acclaim, the Ohio court described it as "87 minutes of boredom induced by the vapid drivel appearing on the screen and three minutes of complete revulsion during the showing of an act of perverted obscenity," a love scene with the very briefly bared breasts of actress Jeanne Moreau and vaguely implied cunnilingus.[62] The Supreme Court took the case, *Jacobellis v. Ohio*, in 1963, heard arguments but could reach no conclusion and had the case reargued in 1964. Its decision of reversal, written by main obscenity-doctrine architect Brennan, sought to restore order to the topic of obscenity. Predictably enough, it failed.

Brennan's lead opinion, joined only by recent Kennedy appointee Arthur Goldberg, reiterated the *Roth* test and addressed the issue of contemporary community standards. Observing the many assertions of local standards, Brennan called these "an incorrect reading of *Roth*." With discernable weariness he reiterated Harlan's earlier assertion that the relevant standards were national; "It is, after all, a national Constitution we are expounding," he added. In this, Brennan's opinion paralleled his landmark *New York Times v. Sullivan* opinion, delivered earlier in 1964 and insuring freedom of the press by protecting media from libel suits in the absence of "actual malice"; both opinions protected expression from the dictates of provincial interlocutors (in the newspaper case, specifically from Alabama public officials attempting to obstruct reporting on the civil rights movement and the atrocities being committed against its members). The major difference, of course, was that unlike libel, obscenity lacked an actual victim, even as mendacious a one as the ostensibly wronged law-keepers of Alabama.[63]

A typically absolutist concurrence came from Black and Douglas, but the surprise of *Jacobellis* was Potter Stewart's concurring opinion. Appointed by Eisenhower after *Roth*, Stewart had been a minor figure in obscenity decisions to this point. But in a brief paragraph he elaborated a doctrine containing the aphorism for which he would become best known. Concluding that obscenity law was "limited to hard-core pornography," Stewart attempted to avoid the Court's ongoing problems of definition, since "perhaps I could never succeed in intelligibly" defining his term. "But I know it when I see it," he quipped, "and the motion picture involved in this case is not that."[64]

While Stewart's stance came as close to the absolutism of Black and Douglas as one could go without unproscribing obscenity, it was balanced at the other end by Warren, Clark, and Harlan, all of whom dissented and placed standards in the hands of states rather than the federal government. The same day *Jacobellis* was read, the Court also issued a per curiam reversal of a Florida obscenity conviction based on *Tropic of Cancer*, reflecting the deadlock, each justice signified his reasoning as stemming from his respective *Jacobellis* stance.[65]

In its disunity the Court functioned as a microcosm of American society in the early to mid-1960s. For every angry woman writing to the ACLU asking it to stop defending *Tropic of Cancer* because "hundreds of men will go out and attack and rape women after reading this book," there was a supporter of John F. Kennedy, who casually pocket-vetoed a Washington, D.C., obscenity bill in late 1962. For every leader like the Nation of Islam's Elijah Muhammad, who charged white America with plotting the destruction of black America by "parading their own bold, half-nude women and girls before the public along with some of the most filthy and indecent acts known to man," there was a Mayor Jerome Cavanagh of Detroit, who favored a "campaign for the classics" over pursuing obscenity prosecutions. When the Nassau County, New York, district attorney made intrusive "lightning raids" on nineteen "middle-income bracket" homes in 1963, he discovered obscene pictures in fourteen of them; that same year the city prosecutor in Dayton, Ohio, recommended that "the city take no legal action in fighting obscene literature," describing it as a problem for individual homes to deal with. And while New York City mayor Robert Wagner headed an antipornography city committee and New York governor Nelson Rockefeller signed antiobscenity legislation in 1965, a Wisconsin state senator that year voted against similar legislation, telling a reporter, "You're going to have these old biddies saying that any sex education in school is obscene."[66]

Meanwhile, obscenity prosecutions proceeded apace, devoid of any consistency. Henry Miller had taken a mere five pages to arrive at "I am fucking you, Tania" in *Tropic of Cancer* and spent the next three hundred pages elaborating in far more graphic and vulgar detail, and the book had been protected by the Supreme Court. Meanwhile, Sanford Aday saw his twenty-five-year prison sentence upheld in a federal appellate court in 1966, entirely on the basis of the book *Sex Life of a Cop*. The Sixth Circuit Court of Appeals in Ohio found the book "by any standard obscene," even paraphrasing Potter Stewart to claim, "we know hard core pornography when we see it, and *Sex Life of a Cop* is just that." Yet the book was standard dime-store pulp fiction, devoid of Miller's four-letter words and blunt descriptions of sex organs; its most titillating prose ran along the purplish lines of, "Running the tip of his tongue around the nipple, he started working it like a small boy sucking juice out of a luscious orange." Another victim of the 1958 venue-modification law, the Los Angeles–based publisher Milton Luros, was similarly arraigned and convicted in Sioux City, Iowa, in 1966 for several nudist magazines and lesbian pulp novels, after he was exonerated by a local judge back in Los Angeles.[67]

The ACLU remained conflicted over these developments. The position it adopted in 1962 would guide it through the decade, a reiteration of the clear and present danger test, requiring for prosecution "proof that the material would cause, in a normal adult, behavior which has validly been made criminal by statute." That such behavior might include not only rape or murder, but also still-criminalized acts like masturbation or sodomy, went unmentioned. Still concerned with public image, some members considered it "a wise and proper concession" to make an exception in the policy to protect children, as "an aid to winning some of the doubters." While the longtime free-speech advocate Elmer Rice disagreed vigorously, the cautious approach carried the day, with a "special exception" in the ACLU position if "the target of the allegedly obscene material were children." In such instances, the ACLU went on, the proper test would be "whether its effect on children would lead to behavior that would violate a criminal statute."[68]

While the ACLU policy carried a seemingly insurmountable burden of proof for prosecutors in the continuing absence of evidence connecting pornography to crime, its exception for children privileged public relations over reason or analysis, implicitly invoking the very juvenile-delinquency arguments that had drawn pornography back into the political arena in the 1950s. The policy reflected ambivalence, confusion, trepidation, and an intellectual incoherency that distinguished between sex and such other social fields as religion and politics without a clear explanation for why. In this sense it perfectly paralleled developments in the Supreme Court.

Redrupping Obscenity Law

As the 1960s continued, the obscenity debacle dragged on interminably. Displaying its weariness and frustration, the Supreme Court confronted the issue again, disastrously, in a trilogy of 1966 decisions, beginning a series of abrupt shifts that marked its trajectory for the rest of the decade. By 1970 the Court would have a clear disposition but no discernible doctrine, supporting free sexual expression when consumed by adults with minimal intrusion onto the public sphere but nowhere clearly articulating this, leaving it instead scattered across numerous decisions. This left a feeble precedent when personnel changes in the Court moved in a more conservative direction in the 1970s.

In its three 1966 decisions the Supreme Court attempted to mitigate the rampant provincialism of obscenity prosecutions, and the result was the Court's most colossal failure yet, a dramatic curtailment of free expression that left few but the censorious pleased. All three decisions, announced on March 21, were split, for a total of fourteen opinions in the three cases, though Brennan wrote the lead opinion for each. Taken as a trio, the decisions represented a glaring lack of cohesive doctrine from the justices.

The first case, *Memoirs v. Massachusetts*, involved the eighteenth-century novel *Memoirs of a Woman of Pleasure*, commonly known as *Fanny Hill*. The Massachusetts Supreme Judicial Court had held the book obscene, despite acknowledging "some minimal literary value," on the grounds that the redeeming social importance test of *Roth* did not necessitate a book being "unqualifiedly worthless before it can be deemed obscene." Brennan rejected this position, ruling that "a book cannot be proscribed unless it is found to be utterly without redeeming social value. This is so even though the book is found to possess the requisite prurient appeal and to be patently offensive." Brennan's opinion was followed by a predictably absolutist concurrence by Douglas, as well as an angry dissent from Clark, who wrote of having "stomached" obscenity cases for ten years without complaint. The justice now let loose with a graphic summary of *Memoirs* to properly convey the novel's obscenity, a bit of description that caused him "much embarrassment." Clark also cited J. Edgar Hoover and other police officials in an attempt to revive the connection between pornography and "violence, degeneracy and sexual misconduct," which had hardly been voiced by the mainstream media in several years.[69]

Superficially, *Memoirs* portended an expansion of freedom of expression, tacitly adopting the Stewart formula that only the most worthless pornography could be suppressed. But an important aside hinted at other implications; "it does not necessarily follow" from the decision, Brennan mentioned in conclusion, that finding *Memoirs* obscene "would be improper under all circumstances." In fact, the "circumstances of production, sale, and publicity are relevant in determining whether or not the publication of the book is constitutionally protected."[70] This abrupt non sequitur was in fact the linchpin on which the *Memoirs* decision hung. Brennan himself had seemed ready to uphold its obscenity when recent Lyndon Johnson appointee Abe Fortas reminded him of the doctrine Chief Justice Warren had espoused since *Roth*, that bookseller conduct trumped content as the determinant of obscenity, in an effort to form a majority in favor of *Memoirs*. Brennan agreed to give *Memoirs* First Amendment protection, but at a cost: Fortas's vote in affirming the conviction of the publisher Ralph Ginzburg in the second 1966 obscenity case.[71]

On its face Ginzburg's conviction seemed destined for reversal. The publisher had begun his career in 1961, sending out three million mailings advertising *EROS*, a magazine that "handles the subjects of Love and Sex with complete candor." As the mailing explained, *EROS* was occasioned by "recent court decisions ruling that a literary piece or painting, though explicitly sexual in content, has a right to be published if it is a genuine piece of art."[72] The magazine sold well, with twenty-five thousand copies of its first issue in 1962, seventy-five thousand of its second, and eighty-six thousand of its third ordered.[73] Its content included essays on polygamy, contraception, the clitoris, and President Warren Harding's love life, alongside photos of erotic Hindu sculptures, Marilyn Monroe in see-through tops, and nineteenth-century French postcards, though none with explicit shots of genitals or sex acts.

Despite his success, Ginzburg's *EROS* mailings aroused much anger among their recipients, and he collected ten thousand response cards sent in with messages rather than subscription orders. These ranged from religious ("God did not make sex for a toy") to anti-Semitic ("You dirty pornographic Jews!") to a plainspoken entreaty to "Keep your Eros out of Tulsa." One angry citizen even somehow returned a solicitation smeared in feces, which Ginzburg dutifully filed in his records. In the second issue of *EROS* he called the responses "a candid view of present-day Puritanism in the United States" and wryly noted that most were sent several months before *EROS* had even been published.[74]

The loud protests against *EROS* alerted the federal government to the magazine, and Justice Department investigators dutifully inspected each of *EROS*'s four issues, writing lengthy descriptions but concluding in each case that the magazine fell short of obscenity. Also closely monitored was Ginzburg's newsletter *Liaison*, which contained bawdy jokes and stories; again, the officials advised against prosecution.[75] Ginzburg's third literary contribution was a book by Rey Anthony titled *The Housewife's Handbook on Selective Promiscuity*, the sexual autobiography of a middle-aged housewife. The book dealt frankly with masturbation, pregnancy, venereal disease, anal sex, and the frustration of trying for vaginal orgasms. Though it sometimes used the work *fuck*, the *Handbook* was generally clinical, never erotic, and often sexually progressive. A typical passage read:

> I liked the feeling when he was having intercourse with me. After the third or fourth time, I told him I hadn't come. I said I would like to.
> "What's the matter with what I'm doing?"
> "I like to have the clitoris rubbed gently." . . .
> He ground his teeth together. "It's not normal. It makes me feel like I'm not a *real* man if I can't use my peter."
> "You can use it. But, for me, use your hand."

The book's introduction, by psychologist Albert Ellis, called *Handbook* an "honest, courageous, valuable" book and claimed several therapists had suggested it to patients with sexual problems. Justice Department inspectors again found the book not obscene.[76]

Despite the repeated clearing of Ginzburg's works by Criminal Division investigators, an administrative assistant ignored their detailed reports and suggested prosecution to Attorney General Robert Kennedy in December 1962, mentioning that "politically, I would not see a net loss" in prosecuting. Ginzburg was quickly arrested and tried in an eastern Pennsylvania federal court. Noting that Ginzburg had sought to mail his works from Blue Ball and Intercourse, Pennsylvania, before settling on Middlesex, New Jersey, the court found him guilty of mailing obscene publications, including *EROS*, *Liaison*, and the *Housewife's Handbook*. The decision left several openings for reversal. The trial judge admitted he had not read the *Handbook* at the time of the trial, calling it "boring, disgusting, and shocking" and describing his eventual consumption as "a fast reading, skipping the obviously repetitive phrases and descriptions." He admitted the "entertainment value" of *Liaison*, and he found redeeming value in several *EROS* articles but singled out the "obscene portions." Finally, the judge mentioned "children of all ages, psychotics, feeble-minded and other susceptible elements" as part of the community, despite *Roth*'s straightforward insistence on the "average person" as the barometer of obscenity.[77]

Douglas, Black, Stewart, and Harlan urged reversal of Ginzburg's conviction, but the free-speech-friendly Fortas had pledged his vote for Brennan's reversal in *Memoirs*. Though Fortas would later admit to Douglas he made a mistake, he cast his crucial concurrence with Brennan, Warren, Goldberg and Byron White to affirm the lower court.[78] The logic of Brennan's decision represented a turn away from *Roth*. "Standing alone, the publications themselves might not be obscene," the Justice conceded, but the "context of the circumstances of production, sale, and publicity" were also registered as factors, as Warren had been insisting since 1957. In these factors Brennan saw the "leer of the sensualist"; because Ginzburg's advertisements presented his works as erotically arousing, they "stimulated the reader to accept them as prurient" and thus became obscene. The *Housewife's Handbook* carried therapeutic and educational value, Brennan admitted, but only in a "controlled" environment. Ginzburg's marketing "proclaimed its obscenity," and Brennan accepted the claim at face value. Thus

Ginzburg became the first American since 1957 to have a prison sentence resulting from publishing activities upheld by the Supreme Court, not because the works were intrinsically obscene but because of his "pandering" in their presentation.[79]

The dissents of Black and Douglas echoed familiar refrains, but the normally staid Harlan supplied the most outrage, calling *Ginzburg* "an astonishing piece of judicial improvisation" that veered away from the actual substance of the case in the interest of creating precedent. Stewart also baldly accused the Court of depriving Ginzburg of due process by affirming his conviction on grounds other than the actual charges. Ginzburg "was not charged with 'commercial exploitation'; he was not charged with 'pandering'; he was not charged with 'titillation,'" reminded Stewart.[80] The decision inspired great disappointment at the ACLU, where the Censorship Committee saw it as "cut[ting] into *Roth*," concluding, "We're in a worse position than before." In the *Supreme Court Review* C. Peter McGrath condemned *Ginzburg*, calling obscenity a "constitutional disaster area" as a result of the decision, which added "yet another layer of subjectivity" onto an already subjective legal terrain. A group of prominent cultural figures including Arthur Miller, Otto Preminger, Hugh Hefner, Rex Stout, Kenneth Rexroth, Nat Hentof, the Rev. Howard Moody, and others formed the Committee to Protest Absurd Censorship and purchased space in the *New York Times* condemning the decision; "the sick will celebrate" the repression, they intoned. In what the committee would consider verification, Citizens for Decent Literature applauded *Ginzburg* as "a major defeat to the smut industry."[81]

While *Memoirs* and *Ginzburg* drew the most notice, the final decision of the 1966 trilogy carried the greatest immediate impact. *Mishkin v. New York* dealt with Edward Mishkin, a publisher sentenced to three years in prison for selling fifty books. As Brennan described them, some depicted "relatively normal heterosexual relations," but most dwelled on "such deviations as sado-masochism, fetishism, and homosexuality." Titles like *Mistress of Leather, Cult of the Spankers, The Violated Wrestler*, and *Swish Bottom* accurately represented the bunch. The constitutional question *Mishkin* presented lay in the implications of prurient books not intended to appeal to those regarded as "normal." In a brief decision affirming Mishkin's conviction Brennan "adjust[ed] the prurient-appeal requirement to social realities" by modifying *Roth*: when material was designed to appeal to a "clearly defined deviant group," the prurient-appeal test was met if the dominant theme of the material taken as a whole appealed to the prurient interest of members of the group.[82] The legal stigmatization of queer media seen in chapter 1's examination of Los Angeles now carried the official imprimatur of the Supreme Court.

Mishkin inspired only two written dissents, by Black and Stewart, both of which paled in intensity compared to their fiery bursts in *Memoirs* and *Ginzburg*. It drew little media attention. But it acted as a catalyst for rapid police crackdowns, mostly directed at gay-themed erotic material. Only three days after the decision a Columbus, Ohio, policeman told a reporter that the police "don't concern ourselves with anything but outright pornography in the rawest form," though they "may seize homosexual magazines" for "test purposes." The next day Denver media reported "a crackdown on dealers who traffic in magazines aimed at sex deviates." Two more days later the Oklahoma Literature Commission, entirely inactive since its 1957 inception, suddenly sprang to life and banned fourteen books, most with an obvious gay theme in the title, such as *Night Train to Sodom*, *The Abnormal Ones*, *Man for Hire*, and *Strange Desire*. The next month federal authorities investigated a Minneapolis firm that published *Vagabond* magazine, an issue of which showed one nude man carrying another on its back cover.[83]

While *Memoirs* and *Ginzburg* provided ambiguous precedents at best, *Mishkin* proved easily applicable. A federal judge in Baltimore cited it in dismissing an injunction against customs officials who refused to grant entry to *Hellenic Sun*, a Dutch nudist magazine centered on men. Male nudist magazines had circulated relatively freely since the 1962 *Manual Enterprises* case, but the judge held *Hellenic Sun* obscene in 1966 on the grounds that it appealed to the prurient interest of a "deviant group," male homosexuals. Also that year a California appellate court affirmed a trial court's ruling that Jean Genet's short prison film *Un chant d'amour* was "nothing more than cheap pornography calculated to promote homosexuality, perversion and morbid sex practices." Despite cataloging the artistry of the production, the court cited *Mishkin* in finding the film obscene, since its depictions of masturbation, fellatio, and sodomy were presumed to appeal to gay men.[84]

As 1966 drew to a close, the Supreme Court's only indisputable contribution to the obscenity debate in a decade of effort was to codify the same ambivalence that marked the postwar liberal consensus. The Court had removed obscenity from protected speech but attempted to pare the category down to a bare minimum of unadulterated smut. Though the justices—even Tom Clark—unanimously abhorred censorship, none but Black and Douglas saw the suppression of obscenity as overlapping with that concept. Publishers like Samuel Roth, David Alberts, Ralph Ginzburg, and Edward Mishkin, meanwhile, would have a hard time appreciating the Warren Court's sympathy for free speech from their jail cells. By 1967 sexual discourse remained distinctly separate from economic, political, philosophical, and religious discourse, and the Supreme Court's role was mostly that of a semantic referee who shaped the articulation but not always the substance of the ongoing obscenity debate. Rejecting the clear and present danger test implicitly ratified the unsupported notion that pornography was somehow related to "deviance," no matter how carefully the justices, particularly Brennan, attempted to cloak this in legalistic equations measuring "prurient appeal" or how many lamentations issued from Douglas and Black.

The Court was thus forced to continue its blind groping for a viable precedent. The justices were not, however, unaware of the many prosecutions and convictions contravening the position that, however imperfectly, they had elaborated. Three cases involving pulp novels and adult magazines, consolidated under the heading *Redrup v. New York* in 1967, led to an abrupt clarification that reconfigured the 1966 decisions into a nearly absolutist free-speech stance. In a per curiam decision the Supreme Court— with only Harlan and Clark dissenting—reversed all three convictions. A brief paragraph of explanation gave three reasons for the reversals: in no case did the statutes in question reflect "a specific and limited concern for juveniles"; none involved "an assault upon individual privacy . . . in a manner so obtrusive as to make it impossible for an unwilling individual to avoid exposure to it"; and no case involved "pandering" of the sort involved in *Ginzburg*.[85]

The brief decision masked a Court divided over means of articulating its obscenity doctrine; several written opinion drafts had circulated among the justices for *Redrup*, but when it became clear a majority favored reversals without agreeing on a single explanation, the per curiam format was settled on.[86] To prevent any misunderstanding of its new position, the Court embarked on a spree of reversals, issuing twenty-two per curiam decisions in 1967 and 1968. These included Sanford Aday's twenty-five-year prison sentence for publishing *Sex Life of a Cop* (Clark alone voted to affirm) and the male nudist magazine *Hellenic Sun* that had been convicted in light of *Mishkin*. During this cycle of reversals, however, the Court did uphold one lone obscenity conviction, in the case involving Jean Genet's *Un chant d'amour*. Given how undistinguished and undifferentiated from the mass of other lower-court convictions the decision finding that film obscene was, the Supreme Court affirmation reflected a deeply entrenched aversion to homosexuality among the chief justice and his four allies in the affirmation, which was opposed by Black, Douglas, Fortas, and Stewart. It also showed that the Court had not completely adopted an absolutist stance, although the affirmation received little notice and legal writers began to use "redrupping" as a verb. *Redrup* "has become the password for reversing findings of obscenity," one law article explained, since the per curiam reversals ignored *Roth* to merely cite the new decision as their basis.[87]

Breaking the per curiam trend in 1968, the Court affirmed the conviction of Sam Ginsberg, a New York City luncheonette owner with a newsstand who sold two "girlie" magazines to a sixteen-year-old boy. Brennan's lead decision expanded on the "variable obscenity" concept introduced in *Mishkin* to rule that material may be obscene for minors but not for adults. This drew the expected dissents from Black and Douglas, but only the dissenting Fortas raised the question of defining rather than simply acknowledging obscenity for minors. Though the Court in some ways appeared to have erratically veered from its trajectory in affirming Ginsberg's conviction, in fact the joint result of *Redrup* and *Ginsberg* was to tacitly endorse a new policy that obscenity for heterosexual adults was permissible as long as it did not intrude on public space or involve unwanted, pandering solicitations.[88]

This policy became overt in 1969, as Thurgood Marshall—the civil rights activist who replaced Tom Clark shortly after *Redrup* in 1967—issued his first lead opinion in the obscenity debate. *Stanley v. Georgia* involved a man whose house was searched under a warrant to find evidence of bookmaking activities. When police found 8-mm films in his bedroom, they set up a projector found in his living room, screened the films, and arrested him on obscenity charges. Marshall made his allegiances clear, ruling that "the mere private possession of obscene matter cannot be a crime." Part of Georgia's case was based on pornography's causal effect on "devi-

ant sexual behavior or crimes of sexual violence." Wholeheartedly rejecting that theory, Marshall found "little empirical basis for that assertion"
before pointedly observing that the state could no more prohibit obscenity
on that basis than it could "prohibit possession of chemistry books on the
ground that they may lead to the manufacture of homemade spirits." Not
all of the justices agreed with Marshall's reasoning; a concurrence signed by
Stewart, Brennan, and White preferred to reverse on procedural grounds
related to the warrant's intent. Significantly, though, there were no dissents
in *Stanley*.[89]

The Court had, for the first time, bestowed constitutional protection on obscene material. Even more surprisingly, it had done so via erratic steps that left no single statement of doctrine but no doubt about the
Court's position. This had the effect of retroactively recasting *Ginzburg* not
as a travesty but as the beginning of a slow crawl toward integrating sexual
discourse into a marketplace of ideas with the same rights as other forms
of expression. As did the ACLU (which, as historian Leigh Ann Wheeler
shows, increasingly framed freedom of speech in terms of consumerist
rights *to* that speech), the Warren Court ultimately embraced a stealth defense of sexual expression without ever dismantling or even substantively
discussing the social framework that denied legitimacy to prurience. Hand
in hand with *Stanley*, the Court embraced during the same term and without direct acknowledgment the most rigorous version of the clear and present danger test, reversing the conviction of a hate-spewing Ohio Klansman
under a criminal syndicalism statute; henceforth, only direct "incitement to
imminent lawless action" could be proscribed by law, the per curiam opinion in *Brandenburg v. Ohio* declared.[90]

It was too little, too late. By the time the Court changed course in
the late 1960s, the chance to institutionalize a sustainable new framework
of expansive freedom that made no irrational exclusions of sexuality had
passed. Retrenchment loomed on the horizon, and the mangled, ad hoc
set of scattered obscenity opinions left by the Warren Court utterly failed
to establish a strong or even coherent doctrine. Reversing course would be
quite simple and had to await only a shortly forthcoming change in the
composition of the Court.

The expansion of free-speech rights brought with it a massive pornography industry, ultimately helping to fuel the New Right's engine, which
ran on public outrage and anger. Liberal ambivalence would persist, and this

ambivalence would undermine attempts to mount resistance to the Republican Party's monopolization of outrage. The next chapter, however, follows a group entirely lacking in ambivalence: Citizens for Decent Literature. The Cincinnati-based organization emerged in the 1960s by reconfiguring the terms of public debate on censorship and obscenity, shaping them in new ways that made repression more palatable to a vast range of citizens. By the time of the 1969 *Stanley* decision, Citizens for Decent Literature presented a formidable counterpoint to the Court's liberal tendencies.

3. AROUSING THE PUBLIC

Citizens for Decent Literature and the Emergence of the Modern Antiporn Movement

"THE LIGHTS WENT OUT in the basement amusement room," reported Timothy Hogan of the *St. Louis Globe-Democrat* in May 1963. "A color movie flashed on the screen, showing a man talking. Soon the screen was filled by pictures of nude women and men, fetish illustrations and scenes of sadism. It lasted an hour." Having grabbed his readers' attention, the reporter promptly subverted their expectations: "This was not a stag movie. It was a showing of *Perversion for Profit*," a film produced and distributed by the antiobscenity group Citizens for Decent Literature. Described by its parent organization as a "documentary which focuses on the extent of the pornography racket and the different types of pornography," *Perversion for Profit* also carried the titillating warning, "FOR ADULTS ONLY."[1]

Released in 1963 to a seemingly endless series of American Legions, Elks Lodges, YMCAs, and Catholic groups, *Perversion for Profit* crystallized the philosophy and methodology of Citizens for Decent Literature (CDL), the preeminent antipornography group of the 1960s. Beginning with "outstanding news reporter" George Putnam warning viewers that a "floodtide of filth . . . is threatening to pervert an entire generation" (Figure 1), the film goes on to present a parade of unsubstantiated information: 75 percent to 90 percent of the pornography purchased by adults winds up in the hands of children; pornography is a $2 billion per year industry; the "moral decay" wrought by obscene magazines weakens American resistance to communism; exposure of even a "normal" adult male to male physique magazines can "pervert" him, causing him to become a homosexual, while young boys have even less resistance; one of every twenty births is illegitimate; and venereal disease is on the rise, even among the ten-to-eighteen age bracket.[2]

After overwhelming its audience with this barrage of horrors, *Perversion* reveals the solution: the law. Because the Supreme Court has placed obscenity outside the protection of the First Amendment, the film declares, citizens possess a "constitutional guarantee of protection from obscenity,"

FIGURE 1. The "outstanding news reporter" George Putnam alerts audiences to a "floodtide of filth . . . engulfing our country in the form of newsstand obscenity." Screen capture from *Perversion for Profit* (Citizens for Decent Literature, 1963).

which is best realized by forming a local CDL chapter. To further motivate viewers—in the event that George Putnam's threat of "your daughter, lured into lesbianism" failed to suffice—the film also displays and explains various examples of obscene magazines, with slim red bars covering the "obscene" body parts (Figures 2–4). Thus, a rear shot of a naked woman "appeals to the sodomist," and a picture featuring a naked woman on a farm, with a goat in the distant background, contains "overtones of bestiality." The bars leave little to the imagination; a patch of female pubic hair eludes the red bar on one nudist picture, and midway through the film the naked breasts of a tied woman being whipped receive no bar whatsoever. The prurient charge hinted at by the reporter is never far beneath the surface of *Perversion for Profit*, and for jaded viewers unmoved by the dangers of nudist and male physique magazines, the narrator promises the existence of other material "too obscene" to show at the local newsstands.

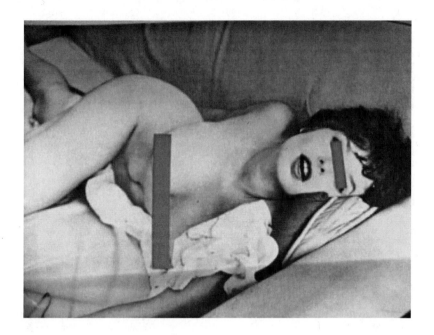

FIGURES 2–4. In *Perversion for Profit* CDL unleashed a barrage of prurient imagery under the guise of "knowing the enemy." Stills from *Perversion for Profit* (Citizens for Decent Literature, 1963).

Seen today, the film has the quaint charm of a camp classic. But CDL meant no joke by it, nor did the film's intended audiences perceive it as such; as late as 1970, an official of the Southern Baptist Convention described *Perversion* as "a pretty good introduction" to the problem of obscenity. Although the film's facts and statistics often held no merit whatsoever— in a rare unguarded moment in 1966, CDL founder Charles Keating admitted the origin of the monetary value placed on the pornography industry: "It came out of my head"—their constant repetition over the course of a decade gave them a public legitimacy based entirely on their ubiquity.[3]

Through the methods shown in *Perversion for Profit*—fabricated facts presented as self-evident truths, appeals to legal recourse against obscenity, and an antisex message articulated in oversexed rhetoric and imagery—Citizens for Decent Literature rose to prominence in the 1960s and reshaped the discourse of antiporn activism. Reaching its pinnacle of influence late in the decade, it repeatedly impacted the operations of the federal government by helping derail Abe Fortas's nomination for chief justice of the Supreme Court and undermining the Presidential Commission on Obscenity and Pornography appointed in 1967. While the group faded into relative obscurity in the 1970s as its founder turned his attention to less-decent innovations in junk-bond financing, CDL helped lay the groundwork for the New Right and its politics of outrage, as we will see in chapter 4. Many techniques pioneered by the group shaped the tactics of activism against feminism, the ERA, and gay rights, as a politicized set of "family values" revealed its immense political worth. CDL's success proved a model in a plethora of ways.

Indeed, CDL proved crucial in carrying procensorship activism past its various 1950s setbacks. While the substantive designs of the group remained very similar to previous Catholic pressure groups, CDL achieved a mainstream success unimaginable to a Catholic group in the 1960s. As Catholic domination of American censorship crumbled in the postwar years, CDL grafted a nominally secular and respectably legalistic rhetoric onto the existing language of sin, damnation, and authoritarianism. In a 1960 pamphlet, CDL asked itself the question, "Do you approach this problem on religious grounds?" Its answer was a resounding "No. Ours is a civic organization."[4] Early critics would tarnish CDL by highlighting its various Catholic connections, not the least of which was the group's obvious titular invocation of the Catholic National Organization for Decent Literature. But more important to CDL's self-presentation was the word *citizen*. Effectively utilizing unspoken cold war assumptions, CDL appealed to Americans not as members of sectarian groups but rather as citizens— citizens determined to defend their nation from threats external *or* internal. In keeping with hegemonic ideas of Americanness, these citizens were framed as middle-class, often suburbanite, implicitly white, and always led by men.

The legal rhetoric of enforcing obscenity laws gave CDL a moderate image and widespread credibility in a period marked by perceived extremism on both sides of the political spectrum. Equally instrumental to the group's success—and equally important in laying the groundwork for the New Right—was the organization's emphasis on grassroots organizing. Founder Charles Keating described CDL in 1962 as "a worldwide network of local autonomous units mothering on the Cincinnati parent for the accumulation and dissemination of information," and the flexibility built into that decentralized structure proved a great asset.[5] While Keating could present a restrained, legalistic face to the national media and ensure CDL's moderate image, local units were free to indulge in less rigorously conceptualized policing of their towns. The fervor inspired by local crusades kept membership high and donations flowing, while the activities that often ran directly counter to stated CDL policy generally remained outside the scope of national media coverage, thus preserving CDL's carefully tailored image.

Another facet of CDL fundamental to understanding the group was its consistent reappropriation of pornography's sexual charge in the service of its conservative cause. The group often insisted on the "importance of an aroused public," supplementing this with calls for the "stimulation of community action."[6] It is not merely playful to locate significance in these word choices or to hear echoes of a lurid dime-store sex novel heroine's heavy breathing in an early Keating missive imploring supporters to recommend him for a congressional appointment. "Don't let me down," Keating begged. "ACT NOW!!!! PLEASE!!!! PLEASE!!!! PLEASE!!!!"[7] Indeed, the deployment of sexual imagery, such as that found in *Perversion for Profit*, was a cornerstone of CDL's methods. While several scholars have followed Michel Foucault's lead in identifying the "perpetual spirals of power and pleasure" inherent in repressive projects, finding "the pleasure of the surveillance of pleasure" in numerous texts, rarely have these mechanisms been as critical to the very functioning of a discourse as in the case of Citizens for Decent Literature.[8] The arousal inspired by its presentations was necessary to create impassioned audiences, whose responses could then be channeled into enthusiastic adoptions of CDL agenda.

These techniques succeeded in drawing an extensive membership in the 1960s. With its secularized legal rhetoric, decentralized structure, and arousing erotic charge, CDL rose to great prominence over the course of the decade. Yet it remains almost entirely overlooked by scholars, its importance in bridging the gap between the Catholic censors, Old Right anticommunists, and New Right moralizers unrecognized.[9] This chapter restores Citizens for Decent Literature to its place of centrality in the sexual and political battles of the 1960s, finding in the group a harbinger of the New Right and an effective precursor to the "family values" campaigns of subsequent decades. The group's rise to prominence is traced here; the fruits of its labors are on ample display within a broader discussion of the nascent New Right in the following chapter.

Creating a New Antiporn Framework

By the time of CDL's formation in the mid-1950s, not only was censorship on the wane in the United States, but it was enmeshed in religious differences. Such earlier efforts to suppress indecent literature as those of

Anthony Comstock or the Women's Christian Temperance Union had been part of a Protestant-spearheaded "moral reconstruction." As motion pictures moved into a place of cultural centrality in the 1920s, though, censorship efforts underwent a transition. Andrea Friedman and others have shown how the maternalism and purity on which female reformers had staked their claims fell out of favor, resulting in a masculinization of leadership. Meanwhile, with motion picture censorship upheld by the Supreme Court in 1915 and the advent of the Hollywood Production Code two decades later, regulating cinema proved particularly feasible, and the public face of that regulation became known as a Catholic one.[10]

Catholics were instrumental behind the scenes in shaping the restrictive Production Code, but public recognition of their importance came with the creation of the Legion of Decency in 1934, the same year the code was implemented. In 1938 the National Organization for Decent Literature (NODL) was formed as a sister group to inspect magazines, books, and comics. The groups exercised great influence for several years, as filmmakers sought to avoid the Legion's dreaded "C" rating, which would prevent dutiful Catholics from attending, and newsstands often dropped publications on the NODL's blacklist for fear of suffering a boycott.[11]

After World War II, though, this Catholic power met serious resistance. The Supreme Court granted motion pictures First Amendment protection in 1952, and as the Production Code gradually relaxed its provisions to allow American films to compete with sexier foreign imports and the growing television market, the Legion of Decency remained intransigent in its repressive policies, bringing it into frequent conflict with Hollywood. Audience demand for the new cinema increasingly emboldened theater owners to run films without the Production Code seal or Legion of Decency approval, and the Legion grew increasingly irrelevant in the process.

Of equal importance, the social and political context of the anti-censorship liberal 1950s challenged Catholic power. Cardinal Spellman, the "American pope" and a devoted supporter of the Legion of Decency, brought little credit to the Catholic cause with his continuing allegiance to Senator Joseph McCarthy even after McCarthy's senatorial censure and public disgrace. Though the Legion and the NODL sought out Protestant and Jewish support, response to the suppressive groups sometimes hearkened back to the lengthy American tradition of anti-Catholic suspicions of papal conspiracies. Blaming "a little band of Catholics" for conducting "a shocking attack on the rights of their fellow citizens," John Fischer accused the NODL of "literary lynching" and compared it to communists in a 1956 *Harper's* essay. The American Civil Liberties Union used less inflammatory rhetoric to make a similar point in a 1956 statement criticizing the NODL for assuming the role of "conscience of the whole country" for its role in limiting non-Catholic access to proscribed material through its threats of boycotts.[12]

As Catholic power crumbled, other groups hoped to capture the mantle once worn by the Legion and the NODL. In New Mexico the Crusaders for Decency in Literature, headed by the Rabbi Moshay Mann, broadcast its tripartite support from Protestants, Jews, and Catholics. The Churchmen's Commission for Decent Publications made a similar effort a few years later. Organized in 1957 with an overtly nondenominational Protestant identity, the Churchmen's Commission's primary goal was "to provide coordination of church, organizational and individual efforts to eliminate the sale and distribution of indecent and obscene material." Though it published a "guide-list," its newsletter made clear that "we do not intend that this cataloging shall be in any sense a 'ban list,'" and the group's constitution emphasized "the enforcement of laws" against obscenity, avoiding the word *censorship* altogether. At its founding conference in Washington, D.C., a strong movement to name the group the Citizens' Commission for Decent Publications emerged, with proponents reminding attendees of the separation of church and state, but the initial name prevailed. Like the Crusaders, the Churchmen's Commission never reached prominence or power.[13]

It did, however, earn some press in Cincinnati, where Charles H. Keating Jr., a thirty-four-year-old corporate lawyer, lived.[14] A Catholic man in a heavily Catholic town, Keating possessed a brilliant mind for organization, a deeply held loathing for smut, and a keen awareness of the significance of public image. As a young man Keating had served as a navy pilot during the final months of World War II, returned home to attend college and excel in competitive swimming, and then moved on to law school. Marriage and procreation quickly followed. His ambitious nature brought Keating success and comfort at a relatively young age, and in the mid-1950s he began to turn his attentions toward the problem of pornography.

Certain facts were apparent. The Legion of Decency and the NODL had fallen in stature for two reasons: their obvious Catholicism and their endorsement of censorship and group pressure tactics, neither of which found favor with the American public. The Crusaders for Decency in Literature and other similar—and similarly ignored—groups made progress in moving beyond a Catholic face but lacked useful or exciting solutions that would inspire members. And though the Churchmen's Commission's innovation in emphasizing law enforcement rather than censorship boded well for that group, its reliance on a "guide-list" conjured up inescapably negative connotations of the NODL and its blacklist tactics.

Intending to avoid all of these pitfalls, Keating established Citizens for Decent Literature in 1955 or 1956—the group's origins remain somewhat vague because Keating insisted on building an informal base of friends from the professional world before reaching for public recognition. Indeed, as CDL began to achieve national prominence, variations in its founding narrative appeared. Testifying before Congress in 1958, Keating explained how "the nucleus of a small group of businessmen" gathered together in the fall of 1955 intending to network with civic, religious, and fraternal organizations to create "an aroused public opinion" and ensure the enforcement of obscenity laws. Another account appeared in the *Catholic Digest* in 1963, describing CDL's formation as taking place "during a Jesuit retreat in 1956." With Keating himself as the article's main source, this account seems equally probable, but more important than the actual point of origin for CDL is the self-awareness Keating displayed in marketing the group differently to different constituencies.[15]

This management of public image would also prove crucial in CDL's emergence. Eager to divert attention from his Catholicism and its attendant implications, Keating repeatedly accentuated his all-American features. A 1960 CDL pamphlet described him as "tall, athletic . . . married . . . no humorless puritan or hot-eyed reformer." His 1946 national swimming championship and service as a navy fighter pilot also became motifs of promotional literature. The combined effect of these descriptions was to create an image of sexually healthy Americanism and thus distance CDL from its dubious and unpopular "humorless puritan" forebears. As another CDL leader would claim, "I don't think I am a prude. I spent over 8 years in the Navy as a Chief Boatswain's Mate and I think sex is great!"[16]

For Keating, simply distinguishing CDL from earlier antiobscenity groups was not enough. He could incessantly insist that "Censorship, Blue Stockingism, Prudism, Holier-Than-Thouism—none of these have any place in CDL" and still remain defined by the failed groups that preceded him.[17] What CDL needed was an entirely new analytical framework through which to approach the issue of pornography, articulated in a fresh lexicon that would remove it from the unhallowed tradition of censorship and recapture public favor. Keating located this framework in the newfound social capital of the "expert" and the emerging legal definition of *obscenity*.

By the mid-1950s an entire roster of experts existed for Keating to cite. As I mentioned in chapter 1, Fredric Wertham lent the authority of psychiatry to a theory that violent comics and pornography could cause deviation in normal children, though the loan was one of authoritative voice alone rather than actual evidence. Law enforcers from J. Edgar Hoover of the FBI to Detroit's vociferous police investigator Herbert Case also supported the link between pornography, violence, delinquency, and sexual deviance. Pitrim Sorokin, a sociologist on the Harvard faculty and a future CDL member, wrote of the "moral decay" engendered by the saturation of society with sex and the resultant "enfeebled society." Keating frequently referenced all of these figures, conferring legitimacy on unproven theories and shifting the terms of debate by concealing moralism beneath a veneer of social science.[18]

Even more effective than the CDL canon of experts, though, was Keating's recourse to law. "Censorship" had acquired distasteful connotations for most Americans by midcentury. But in the June 1957 *Roth* decision the U.S. Supreme Court placed obscenity outside the protection of the First Amendment, thus differentiating its suppression from censorship; obscene material could be legally prosecuted and suppressed without any reliance on or reference to group pressure tactics. The *Roth* decision, as Justice William Douglas noted in his dissent, "gives the censor free range over a vast domain." In Cincinnati Charles Keating eagerly contemplated the parameters of that domain.[19]

Roth quickly became the centerpiece of CDL's policy articulations. When asked during a 1959 interview whether CDL engaged in censorship, Keating thundered "a vehement 'No'" and explained the Court ruling that allowed the proscription of obscenity. Keating used a legalistic vocabulary; "I don't know what smut means, and I don't think anyone else does either," he explained in a 1960 CDL pamphlet. Instead he used *obscenity* and *pornography*, terms "that occur in the law." Though he failed to indicate what actual semantic differences distinguished the apparent synonyms, his implication was obvious: *smut* was used by the old breed of censorious reformers in their crusade to impose prudish standards via group pressure; *obscenity* befit the modern CDL approach, based on expert analysis of pornography's ill effects and due process of law.[20]

Another integral component of Keating's construction of CDL was its membership. As he distanced his organization from Catholic pressure groups by repeatedly proclaiming that "CDL does not employ boycott or pressure mechanisms" such as censorship lists, Keating also emphasized the group's inclusion of a wide swath of society. Because "pornography is a problem for all citizens," CDL contained "a broad representation of civic, business, religious, labor, and medical leaders." A 1959 magazine profile described CDL's founding cohort as "young business and professional men (average age 36)," with careers in law, banking, credit management, and medicine; while the article hinted at the group's shared Catholicism in coded terms—most "are married and have large families"—it refrained from identifying CDL with Catholicism. The letterhead on CDL stationery reveals the effectiveness of this approach; a mailing from 1962 lists such honorary members as the president of the Boy Scouts of America, a member of the AFL-CIO Labor Council, and the mayor of Cincinnati. Nothing in the group's appearance or rhetoric gave any explicit indication of Catholic affiliations.[21]

If CDL singled out one demographic group on which to stake its appeal, that group was the white suburban middle class, whose insecurities were often woven into CDL rhetoric. Historians have shown how cold war fears were often refracted into familial anxieties and how the racial fault lines of nascent suburbanization wrought further tensions. As middle-class white parents fled cities for suburbs, they also hoped to leave behind the urban culture thought responsible for spawning a supposed wave of juvenile delinquency in the 1950s. CDL played into these fears, showing just how precariously the cradle of the middle class rocked. A 1960 mailing by the St. Louis CDL chapter emphasized that obscenity "has largely abandoned its former clandestine character" in recent years, moving "into respectable locations." The examples displayed in *Perversion for Profit* were bought not on skid row, the narrator intoned, but in ordinary drugstores. California's CDL spokesman, Raymond Gauer, elaborated: smut was being sold in "good communities," not just those "across the tracks." Gauer even described pornography as "a more serious threat to our community than dope," since adolescent drug users "are already down the road to crime," while obscenity "corrupts and demoralizes good children and sends them down that road." To CDL, "our community" clearly consisted of relatively privileged citizens whose neighborhoods and families were under siege.[22]

Alongside this specific class appeal, the gendering of antiobscenity labor remained a consistent staple of CDL ideology. Numerically, membership had been heavily female from the start; a Pittsburgh unit acquired when the National Better Magazines Council converted into a CDL branch consisted entirely of women. Yet the CDL leadership remained almost exclusively male. A 1959 article included advice on how to start a CDL chapter. Its first step was to "start with three or four men, attorneys preferably." Next, it advised expanding to "a dozen or more men" representing a variety of fields and backgrounds. Only when it reached the fourth step did it subtly expand its inclusion: "have many people write letters of thanks and commendations to the police." The unseen, mechanical labor of letter writing could be handled by women, once men had established an organizational infrastructure.[23]

The gendered leadership of CDL was reflected in its letterhead, which in the early 1960s carried the names of only three women among the forty-six eminent members listed. One was "Youth Directress" Carol Trauth, and another was "Women's Committee" director "Mrs. Daniel McKinney." Both were typographically set off from the rest of the list, leaving only "Mrs. James Gunning" in a relatively nonmarginalized position (albeit still stripped of her given name) among the CDL leadership. As CDL expanded and picked up the support of numerous judges and politicians, the youth and women's committees dropped off entirely. A pamphlet sent to interested parties in the mid-1960s continued to suggest finding "six to ten persons (preferably men) besides yourself" in forming a CDL chapter. The logic of this gendering was obvious: in the traditional, conservative social attitudes of the CDL demographic, it followed that men carried greater weight in the legal, political, and scientific spheres in which CDL sought to ingratiate itself.[24]

Men were thus seen as leadership material, whereas women served as the faceless moral infantry units. Like the Republican women activists of the 1950s, relegated to what historian Catherine Rymph calls "the housework of government," female CDL members were given menial tasks such as letter writing and were often called on simply to use their physical presence as a form of moral suasion. The CDL Women's Committee received almost no press, but its function was apparent in a 1961 Cincinnati newspaper article on a city council obscenity debate. A picture of the council chambers showed the room entirely filled with high school girls and women mobilized by CDL. With their presence a constant reminder of feminine "purity," as one young woman phrased it before the council, it came as no surprise when the council passed a new antismut ordinance. Packing courtrooms with women during obscenity trials was another official CDL tactic. As the group's legal counsel James Clancy wrote in 1963, this would serve to "impress on the jury panel that this is a serious matter." With an empty courtroom, Clancy explained, jurors might "break the monotony by wisecracks and inject into the proceedings humor which is better kept outside." The stern faces of observers would prevent this. It went unwritten but clearly implied that these faces would be female—trials, after all, occurred during weekdays, when men would be working. A 1968 photo

Pictured at the new law offices of "Keating, Meuthing & Klekamp" in Cincinnati recently are the "brains" of CDL - Ray Gauer, Jim Clancy and Charlie Keating - with the "beauty" of CDL - Miss Marti Lang.

FIGURE 5. CDL's gender politics embodied in a caption. This photo appeared in the *National Decency Reporter* (March-April 1968, 15).

caption in CDL's official publication symbolized the group's gender politics: calling Keating and two other men standing behind a seated female secretary the "brains of CDL," the caption went on to name the attractive young woman the "beauty" (Figure 5).[25]

This basic framework—the disavowal of censorship and a pseudoscientific rather than moralistic condemnation of obscenity, predicated on a nonsectarian membership led by middle-class men—would remain firmly in place over the course of CDL's existence, and its widespread success gave Keating no reason to modify it. Indeed, the organization's rapid expansion from a behind-the-scenes Cincinnati advocacy group to the premier national organization dedicated to the eradication of obscenity transpired at a breathtaking pace. By the dawn of the 1960s CDL had attained national prominence, and it spent the entire decade as the nation's foremost organization in its field.

Building a Base

Cincinnati proved fertile ground on which to build a moral empire. CDL began quietly, amassing local support and influence before making its public debut. Once emergent, it promptly drew national attention, and local CDL units began proliferating around the country even before the group had formally organized itself. As Keating institutionalized CDL at a national level, he cultivated the favor of the political right wing, while carefully avoiding public association of CDL with the "extremism" that worried many political observers of the early 1960s. CDL's façade of moderation thus made it the perfect vehicle for transporting remnants of the Old Right into the New Right.

Before Keating had conceived of CDL, Cincinnati already evinced attitudes conducive to nurturing its growth. On the geographic margin of Ohio, the city resided at the political center of Taft Country—it had given birth, both literally and figuratively, to Robert Taft, the senator who represented the conservative wing of the Republican Party in the 1940s until his death in 1953. Dominated by social conservatives, and with visible Catholic prominence, Cincinnati was hostile terrain for smut. The 1940s saw several cleanup campaigns, beginning with a 1941 increase in the penalty for possessing or selling obscene literature from $50 to $500. When that ultimately failed to stem the rising tide of postwar lasciviousness, periodic police crackdowns continued into the 1950s.[26]

Keating and his small but growing vanguard cadre made an early appearance at a 1957 obscenity trial. The group may have yet lacked a proper name, since it remained absent from newspaper accounts, but its imprint was felt in the courtroom. A *Cincinnati Post* article noted the presence of more than one hundred activists at the trial and listed Keating first among notable members. As the trial progressed, it had to be moved to a larger courtroom as the crowd grew to 150. When the prosecution presented its case, the spectators drew an admonishment from the judge for applauding in support.[27]

The clerk on trial was convicted, and CDL exploded onto the local scene in 1958, mobilizing Catholic high school girls in the name of decency. Inspired by the girls' pleas, the city council increased the jail sentence for obscenity from sixty days to six months. The group received more press for its controversial sending of hundreds of letters to a local judge in an attempt to persuade him to convict newsstand owners of obscenity. By April CDL's influence could be seen in the Cincinnati suburb of Cheviot, which passed an obscenity ordinance despite its mayor's admission that he could recall no actual instances of "smut cases" in the recent past. Plans for a CDL-affiliated Mother's March on Obscenity were publicized in August, and when the march occurred in November, hundreds of participating women gathered more than seventy thousand signatures of support as they strolled door-to-door throughout greater Cincinnati.[28]

This flurry of activity gained the group much recognition. National coverage appeared rapidly, as the Catholic magazine *America* applauded CDL in April 1958 for its new emphasis on legal retaliation against obscenity rather than censorship. Ohio governor C. William O'Neill established an official state CDL advisory committee to draft legislative recommendations in October and appointed Keating to it. More recognition came in 1959, as Pennsylvania congresswoman Kathryn Granahan called CDL "one of the most successful and encouraging campaigns against obscenity" in the nation. *Cosmopolitan* also covered the group, describing "the kind of people" who supported CDL as "members of women's clubs, unions, PTAs, church clubs and chambers of commerce."[29]

With this burgeoning national reputation came rapid organizational expansion. Indicative of the speed with which the group transformed from a small behind-the-scenes Cincinnati advocacy group to a national force is the fact that Keating neglected to formally incorporate CDL until July 1958, by which point it had been existent at least two years and publicly active for many months. In its articles of incorporation as a nonprofit group, CDL's first listed goal was "to encourage and promote the publication and dissemination of constructive and positive literature, movies, plays, books, magazines, etc." Its only other stated goal was "to encourage the efforts of law enforcement and other prosecutive agencies." By the time it held its first national conference in Cleveland three months later, drawing more than 250 representatives from across the nation, encouraging positive literature had fallen to CDL's secondary purpose, with "creat[ing] public awareness of the nature and scope of the problem of obscene or pornographic literature" replacing it as the group's primary goal. By the group's 1960 conference, the promotion of positive literature had vanished entirely from the official "framework of CDL principles."[30]

At the second CDL national convention, in February 1960, heralded in advance as the birth of America's first national organization of "citizens united in a legal effort" to combat obscenity, four hundred attendees formally adopted a national structure based on eight American regions, each with a vice president, and a ninth region covering the rest of the world. Keating chose the position of chief legal counsel, and Dr. Bernard Donovan, assistant superintendent of the New York City school system, was named president. Donovan explained the regional structure by saying that CDL should be a "grass roots" operation, kept "as local as possible."[31]

Other developments in CDL rhetoric were on display at the conference. In his keynote address Keating expounded a new and central tenet of CDL: the judicial branch of the government "will not realistically appraise the problem" of obscenity, and consequently, the "problem exists because of the inability of judges to recognize obscenity as a crime." Keating singled out prosecutors and police as the heroic parties, responsive to public demands and eager to enforce laws. Postmaster General Arthur Summerfield was scheduled to address the conference at its conclusion, but he fell ill, and his speech was read by proxy. In it Summerfield bemoaned the state of mail-order obscenity and dismissed the "hue and cry" raised about censorship, freedom of the press, and civil liberties as "a smoke screen that is utterly without sense." Additionally, the conference program listed several "basic postulates" of CDL, the first of which stated, "Obscene and pornographic publications are harmful not merely to 'younger' people, but to society generally."[32]

Such rhetoric proved effective, as CDL continued to grow in members and affiliated groups. "We are anxious to have the affiliation of all local organizations whose purposes and methods are similar to ours," a 1962 mailing announced. A separate but parallel group called National Citizens for Decent Literature was swallowed whole and integrated into CDL in the early 1960s, as was the Pittsburgh National Better Magazines Council. Even groups that maintained their institutional autonomy relied on CDL; National ALARM, a New Jersey group whose acronym stood for Action Launched Against Relaxed Morals, recommended appointing a representative to CDL as its first suggestion to other groups.[33]

This relatively sudden national prominence made Keating—the undisputed spokesman of CDL—aware of the delicate negotiations necessary to navigate the choppy political waters of the early 1960s. Far-right groups such as the John Birch Society, though scorned by the mainstream media, made for natural allies with CDL. Finding veiled communist propaganda behind many media fronts, local Birch Society chapters often enforced conservative sexual agendas; the Amarillo, Texas, branch fought against "obscene" works such as Henry Miller's *Tropic of Cancer* and the trashy B-movie *Poor White Trash* in the early 1960s, while later in the decade Louisiana Birchers forced a sex education ban through the state legislature. Winning the favor of such groups could expand CDL's resources and influence by tapping into the right-wing network, but at the same time overt gestures toward such groups could frighten off more moderate citizens alarmed by extremists. Charles Keating thus faced the same dilemma that would later be experienced by Richard Nixon, Barry Goldwater, and Ronald Reagan in the 1960s—that of offering overtures to what academics of the time called "the radical Right" without alienating the mainstream.[34]

Keating showed great facility for walking this ideological tightrope, focusing his efforts on the connections between pornography and communist plots to destabilize America through moral decay often alleged by the anticommunist Right of the period. He sought to placate both believers and skeptics. Mentioning an uprising in Kerala, India, while addressing Congress in 1960, Keating claimed correspondents in India had informed him that communists there "were using obscenity to indoctrinate people in the schools." But quickly hedging, he added, "I had better say parenthetically that I am not blaming obscenity in America on the Communists." The next year in Fort Worth, Texas, Keating explained that 90 percent of smut was produced for profit, not by communists, though the same lawyers tended to defend both. By rejecting the too easily ridiculed paranoia of the extremists, he insulated himself from a mainstream backlash, but by mentioning the lawyers he insinuated the possibility of a communist-pornography association. The implication that 10 percent of pornography was produced for purposes other than profit was left open to interpretation. Keating also solicited the support of extremists by reprinting in a CDL publication allegations by the Chicago journalist Jack Mabley that Russian agents were smuggling pornography into Alabama to corrupt American youth. This allowed CDL to disseminate the argument without directly espousing it.[35]

Testifying before Congress in 1963, Keating offhandedly mentioned that a professor opposed to CDL's mission "recently issued a document accusing us of being rightwingers and Birchites." This piqued the interest of some congressmen; "Are you a member of the John Birch Society?" one asked Keating. When CDL leader answered in the negative, a roused Representative Joel Broyhill of Virginia immediately challenged him: "Do you consider being called a Birchite or rightwinger a denunciation or dirty name or something?" Suddenly cautious, Keating calmly explained, "I believe I made very clear in my comments that I spoke neither with approbation nor disapproval," which effectively defused the tension and restored CDL to its intentionally vague position.[36]

Not all CDL leaders were so circumspect. William Riley, a physician who headed the New York State CDL, told a congressional committee in 1961 that obscenity "is part and parcel of the Communist movement to destroy the United States." Noting that media critics often derided antiporn activism as "a new McCarthyism," Riley added, "I am all for the late Senator McCarthy. I don't care what anybody says about that." On the other coast the chairman of the Southern California CDL issued a statement reminding the public that "we cannot overlook the communist international conspiracy. . . . There is little question that communist party activity is involved in publication, distribution, and defense of pornography."[37] Rather than damaging it, these outbursts actually contributed to CDL's cause. Because they were spoken by minor figures of no national importance, these claims received no significant mainstream news coverage. But extremists heard the claims, which helped foment CDL support from the Far Right. In Southern California, a noted hotbed of radical right-wing activity, such claims endeared CDL to extremists; as the *Hollywood Citizen-News* editorialized, "Such suggestions as these are always ridiculed by the leftists among us but we do not ridicule them." The claims also attracted the attention of

W. Cleon Skousen, the Salt Lake City chief of police, whose book *The Naked Communist*, which linked pornography to covert communist psychological warfare against America, was a veritable textbook for the radical Right. In a 1961 column in his law enforcement magazine *Law & Order* Skousen recommended CDL as the best organizational resource for local police forces.[38]

Despite his great efforts to distance himself from extremism, Keating occasionally succumbed to lapses in his moderation. When Major General Edwin Walker was officially admonished for propagandizing his troops with Birch Society literature while stationed in Germany in 1961, public response was divided. Historian Jonathan Schoenwald calls the Walker case a "fission point for conservative factions," with the radical Right taking up his case while moderate conservatives were eager to let the matter drop quietly. Keating displayed his allegiance to Walker's cause by describing him as a "highly decorated, unquestionably loyal, honorable American military leader" in a letter to the *Cincinnati Enquirer*, in which he also asked why Birch Society literature was removed from military newsstands while *Overseas Weekly*, a "smutty, semi-literate, left-wing tabloid that would rot your socks," remained available.[39]

If the letter came from Keating as a private citizen rather than as the CDL founder and spokesman, it was no less indicative of the political bent of the organization and its members. In 1964 the president of the New York CDL denounced the group's foes as "homegrown leftist individuals." But Keating himself refrained from such commentary, at least in the company of mainstream reporters, and CDL remained generally untarnished by charges of extremism. Under the media radar, however, it successfully cultivated a following among the Birch crowd. When a speaker at the 1969 CDL convention claimed obscenity was a communist plot, she received a round of applause. That same year a leftist watchdog newsletter described CDL as a "right-wing group which cooperates closely with the John Birch Society," detailing several instances of CDL leaders—though not Keating—appearing at Birch-related events. No major media outlet picked up the story.[40]

With its moderate image preserved, CDL amassed an extensive membership. Though no substantive membership records exist, the organization's numerical power can be gleaned anecdotally. While testifying before Congress in 1963 Keating claimed five hundred local CDL groups, and that same year a CDL rally in the small city of Dayton, Ohio, drew the largest crowd ever assembled there, nine hundred people. By 1966 the California state chapter estimated its membership at ten thousand. Membership flourished in all regions of the nation, and evidence suggests CDL achieved its goal of building a middle-class base. A sociologist who attended CDL's 1969 convention verified this, describing the crowd as "quite attractive middle-class, white, middle-aged men and women" who "appeared to be obsessed with and anxious about sex."[41]

Through deft political maneuvering Keating had managed to build strong national CDL support based on both a middle class concerned for its children and communities and a radical Right motivated by conspiratorial beliefs in the red menace posed by obscenity. In the process, however, he unleashed a floodtide of grassroots activism that often took action in the name of CDL far beyond the parameters of law and social science so carefully calibrated by Keating. This success would eventually inspire an organizational centralization that buoyed the group to its ultimate height of national power before sinking it to a profitable invisibility.

Moral Wildcat Strikes

CDL's decentralized structure invited local idiosyncrasies to flourish, and flourish they did. By the end of the 1950s local CDL units had already begun to proliferate, and not always according to the flagship group's mandates. Local CDL activities frequently involved blacklists, group pressure, and boycott tactics, with slight regard for due process of law—exactly the behavior against which Keating had initially framed CDL. At times CDL units belied the ostensibly nonsectarian nature of the organization by revealing overtly Catholic agendas. The net effect of these events—more a consistent pattern than isolated anomalies—was to push CDL toward a centralization that would standardize behavior and maintain the public image of moderation Keating had so carefully crafted.

For instance, in the Chicago suburbs of Elmhurst and Villa Park, a CDL unit proudly wrote to *Playboy* publisher Hugh Hefner to inform him that the group had composed a list of thirty-seven magazines to be removed from local newsstands, but after some discussion had removed *Playboy* from the list. Meanwhile, in San Mateo, California, the local CDL succeeded in having the November 1959 *Playboy* removed from city newsstands and told the police chief it had a list of another 175 magazines and 250 books it would also like to see removed. Insufficiently sophisticated to adhere to Keating's loudly proclaimed reliance on legal obscenity as a governing principle, the San Mateo CDL justified its list on the grounds that its titles "minimize patriotism, flout law and authority, exploit sensational sex, ridicule marriage and the family," and thus "destroy in youth the ideals that will keep America strong." As an outraged editorial in the nearby *San Francisco Chronicle* noted, none of these transgressions constituted legal obscenity, and the group was accused of vigilantism.[42]

Similar CDL branch activity was widespread. In Indianapolis a 1959 list included seventy-one magazines, including *Playboy* and even the satirical *Mad*. When local police arrested nineteen newsstand operators, the local ACLU branch called it "a Gestapo maneuver that puts us to shame." The next year in the small town of Winona, Minnesota, the local CDL leader told the city council, "I'd swear by the censor list we have." The trend continued in 1961, as the Maricopa County CDL in Arizona printed a "list of objectionable magazines." This pattern came to mark the divide between CDL policy and implementation; while the former emanated from Keating in tones of legalistic moderation, the latter often leapt forward like moral wildcat strikes.[43]

In 1960 an Oklahoma CDL leader in Tulsa allegedly advocated boycotts against "those who fail to comply" with CDL directives.[44] Even more serious than such transgressions were incidents that revealed the substantive links between CDL and the National Organization for Decent Literature. Such connections were precisely the reason Keating introduced the secular CDL framework, as a means of distancing his group from the oft-disparaged Catholic organization, but local groups operating outside the view of the national media sometimes showed less concern for the distinction. In Louisville, Kentucky, an Episcopal minister relayed a report on a 1959 CDL meeting to the national ACLU. Estimating the crowd as at least 90 percent Catholic, the minister wrote, "It was undoubtedly the old NODL with a new title designed to attract non–Roman Catholics and to try to avoid the charge of being a censoring group." A year later, the Augusta, Georgia, CDL did not even try to avoid that charge, writing to a local magazine distributor, "We employ every legal means to put to an end" the distribution of "those magazines listed by the NODL as objectionable." The local CDL head of Middlesex County, New Jersey, was quoted as saying his plan was "to implement the purpose and goal" of the NODL in order to "standardize" the fight against pornography. Around the same time, the Dayton, Ohio, CDL was "marshalling forces" with the Council of Catholic Men. An ACLU observer in Illinois even claimed to have identified the group Americans for Moral Decency as an unofficial clearinghouse for facilitating the transformation of NODL branches into CDL units. Americans for Moral Decency, he wrote, was "avowedly an arm of the NODL in an organizational sense"; when a unit succeeded in attracting an interfaith membership, "the group then becomes a unit of [CDL] and forgets its NODL designation."[45]

Even Keating himself occasionally threw caution to the wind when addressing his hometown Cincinnati CDL branch and adopted an inflammatory rhetoric of the sort he avoided when speaking before Congress or the national media. A particularly telling example of this occurred in a 1962 skirmish with the Cincinnati chapter of the ACLU. CDL and the ACLU had, of course, been antagonists from CDL's inception. The ACLU monitored CDL activities fervently, and it frequently opposed CDL measures, engaging in a protracted struggle with CDL over Cincinnati's obscenity ordinance. When CDL spearheaded an effort to pass a new ordinance in 1961, the local ACLU branch sent a strongly worded letter to city council members arguing that state law preempted city law, making a new ordinance redundant. The letter continued by describing local laws as "proven by experience to exist solely as a mode for propagating the views on obscenity of certain organized vocal groups."[46]

Though the revised Cincinnati ordinance passed, the ACLU opposition embittered Keating, and in September 1962 he launched a scathing jeremiad against the ACLU in a one-page essay sent out to Cincinnati CDL members. Lambasting "these anarchist architects of chaos" for their defense of "sin, ROT, corruption," and other "agents of moral decay," Keating professed, "I for one choose NOT [to] be enslaved by their dictatorship of chaos, controversy, and confusion." Framing the debate as a holy crusade, he then charged CDL members with a duty to "destroy the filth merchants and their fellow-travelers." The last phrase again hinted at communist ties to obscenity, but the dominant tone of the essay was moral outrage. In case the over-the-top rhetoric failed to properly convey the religious origins of Keating's argument, the attached cover letter ended, "God is Good! Pray!"[47]

Clearly, this mailing shattered the façade of moderation Keating had striven to bring CDL, and the Cincinnati ACLU seized the opportunity to expose Keating's hypocrisy. From the start CDL had capitalized on the names on its letterhead to "give testimony to the fact that a significant number of prominent citizens" supported the group, as a 1960 mailing explained. With the blessings of the national ACLU, the Cincinnati chapter sought to undermine this "testimony" by sending Keating's comments on the ACLU to several local leaders identified on CDL's letterhead and asking whether they stood behind CDL's position.[48]

The results were potentially devastating to CDL. The superintendent of the Cincinnati Public School District notified the local ACLU that he had been unaware of the statement and disagreed with it. Roger Blanchard, the bishop coadjutor of the diocese of Southern Ohio sent Keating a letter informing him that "your categorization is not true" and asking to have his name removed if such statements continued to appear without prior consultation. Blanchard's colleague David Thornberry, archdeacon of the diocese, took an even stronger stand, apologizing to the ACLU and writing that Keating's essay "was uncalled for and exhibits a spirit that I deplore." Thornberry also sent Keating a letter describing himself as "in full accord with the fundamental purpose and policies" of the ACLU. He told Keating of his "considerable embarrassment" at the mailing, blamed him for "not being very responsible," and also demanded either the removal of his name or prior consultation before future mailings.[49]

This groundswell of dissent from within CDL's ranks was limited to Cincinnati. It went unnoticed nationally, and the local press—unanimously sympathetic to CDL—declined to cover the story. Consequently, CDL's image went unchallenged in any substantive sense, and the ACLU was unable to capitalize on the controversy. As the early 1960s progressed, CDL literature and speeches articulated and reiterated the group's moderate public stance endlessly, helping to cover such gaffes as Keating's ACLU letter. This material also obscured the frequent deviations from the CDL framework by local units. Regional concerns sometimes shone through in these local efforts, as when the New Orleans unit reflected southern racial ideology in calling for obscenity charges against James Baldwin's *Another Country*, which contained interracial and gay sex, in 1963. Meanwhile, the Southern California CDL displayed Orange County priorities when, in connecting venereal disease and illegitimate births to pornography, it wrote, "THINK OF THE TAXES TO TAKE CARE OF THESE TWO ITEMS—not to mention the human misery and suffering." In Georgia the Savannah CDL employed extralegal pressure methods not sanctioned by Keating to have *Catcher in the Rye* removed from all county schools.[50]

In a sense CDL headquarters predisposed local units toward such actions. One 1963 mailing listing the "musts for any local CDL unit" included an admonition to "choos[e] people who have the interest (even though not the full share of talent)" when forming a unit. Still, at times local activity went sufficiently beyond the boundaries of CDL behavior as to bother Keating. When Milwaukee CDL members began "requesting" that store owners remove publications in 1965, Keating told the *Milwaukee Journal* he did not support the actions. "He concedes, however," the paper reported, "that headquarters has little control over the activity of local chapters." Only when a suburban Maryland CDL unit began using NODL lists to pressure merchants into removing magazines did the national CDL step in; Indiana CDL cochair Ralph Blume urged the Maryland unit to stay within the law, calling the use of lists "illegal as well as impractical." He also advised against boycotts or picketing, suggesting letter writing and speaking before civic groups as a more viable alternative.[51]

These frequent incidents took their toll on Keating's patience. By middecade he had undergone a shift in thinking, deciding, "We don't need an aroused public that's going to wipe out all the sin that's evident to them." As he candidly added to an interviewer, "The masses just aren't competent to determine what should be on the racks." Fortunately for Keating, by the time he reached this conclusion, CDL had already established three mechanisms useful as means of weaning the organization away from dependence on grassroots activism and further standardizing the organization's discourse: a national magazine, the *National Decency Reporter*; a trilogy of films conveying the CDL framework; and a series of amicus curiae—"friend of the court"—briefs in the Supreme Court, which put CDL squarely in the legal sphere its rhetoric had claimed all along. These devices eased CDL's discursive centralization into place during the mid-1960s, helping it reclaim any authority that had been eroded by local vigilante units, maintain its prominence in the obscenity field by taking its battle to the highest court in the nation, and replace the speeches of local leaders with preprogrammed celluloid speakers.[52]

CDL headquarters in Cincinnati had begun issuing stapled, mimeographed reports in 1960 to discuss court cases and disseminate essays condemning obscenity. These reports sometimes seemed intended as correctives to misdirected local CDL efforts. When the Missouri CDL realized in 1960 that the state legislature had downgraded obscenity from a felony to a misdemeanor with no fanfare in 1957, it publicly endorsed a proposal to restore "smut peddling" to felony status. But a national CDL report later that year argued that obscenity violations should remain misdemeanors, since juries were more reluctant to convict in obscenity cases when felony-level punishment was at stake, and felonies were prosecuted by state rather than local officials. Misdemeanors, as the province of local authorities, were more subject to local standards.[53]

These stapled reports, however, looked more like internal bureaucratic documents than enticing newsletters or magazines, and in September 1963 CDL introduced the *National Decency Reporter* (*NDR*), a biweekly newspaper, complete with invitingly professional design and layout, that began its first issue by announcing "a definite need, indeed, an essential need" for a periodical "which has as its purpose the promulgation of decency." For a $5 annual subscription readers could keep abreast of the latest developments in obscenity law; *NDR* gave impressively thorough coverage of arrests, trials, and judicial rulings across the nation. It also delivered an endless and repetitive succession of editorials denouncing smut, often written by respectable experts such as medical doctors or J. Edgar Hoover.[54]

Even more useful for instructing local branches on the etiquette and analytical framework of CDL, however, was the group's foray into filmmaking, which resulted in three much-screened short films in the mid-1960s. *Pages of Death* came first, filmed in 1962 with funding from the Catholic Third Order of St. Francis. Described by CDL as depicting "the rape-slaying of an 11-year-old girl by a young man stimulated to his crime by obscene magazines," the film was recommended for "all age groups of eighth-grade level and above." Next came *Perversion for Profit*, discussed above, and in 1965 *Printed Poison*, which followed the efforts of a district attorney to prosecute pornographers. Both of these films were recommended for adults only. Quantifying the number of people who saw these half-hour films is impossible, but they were screened widely throughout the nation, generally sponsored by friendly organizations rather than exhibited in any commercial capacity. CDL offered the films for rental or purchase, and they remained in print for many years, proving invaluable in spreading the CDL doctrine.[55] The combined effect of the *NDR* and CDL's films was to take the discursive reins from local units and facilitate their transformation from active grassroots firebrands to passive emulators of standardized models of discourse and behavior. This trend would be exacerbated by CDL policy in the 1970s, but as it began to take hold in the 1960s, the organization focused on its most significant innovation, the amicus curiae brief, another centralizing device that positioned CDL's legal team as definitive national experts on obscenity.

CDL's first amicus effort, in the 1963 *Jacobellis v. Ohio* case (decided in 1964), fell flat. In its brief CDL argued that the "contemporary community standards" invoked by *Roth* referred to specific local standards, as befit jury trials, and that obscenity was not limited to mere hardcore pornography. The Court split 6–3 against CDL's position, reversing the conviction. Justice Brennan's opinion explicitly declared the local standards argument "an incorrect reading of *Roth*," while Potter Stewart's concurring opinion made only one point, that obscenity *was* limited to hardcore pornography. An angry Keating bemoaned "incompetence in the judiciary" in a letter to the *Cincinnati Enquirer*, a theme that would recur frequently.[56]

CDL rarely found the Warren Court sympathetic to the arguments advanced in its briefs, even when decisions upheld obscenity convictions. In the 1966 *Memoirs v. Massachusetts* case the Court directly rejected CDL's central legal contention that "slight social importance does not exculpate where the predominant appeal is to prurient interest." Justice Brennan denied CDL's position, writing that "a book cannot be proscribed unless it is found to be utterly without redeeming social value. This is so even though the book is found to possess the requisite prurient appeal and to be patently offensive."[57]

With that the Court tired of the obscenity debate and set about on its series of 1967–68 *Redrup* reversals. CDL remained defiant in the face of these reversals; as the *Cincinnati Enquirer* reported in early 1968, "23 reversals might seem to be the death knell of the CDL," but the group "still refuses to die." Indeed, headquarters, which moved from Cincinnati to Los Angeles in 1967, still counted more than three hundred CDL units in the nation, and the new executive director, Raymond Gauer, explained there was "still hope," since the Court had not reversed the *Roth* decision that placed obscenity outside the First Amendment. Knowing that the liberal Warren Court was unlikely to endorse its views, though, CDL grew increasingly militant and dogmatic in its court briefs. Arguing for affirmation in a 1968 obscenity case, for instance, CDL's brief lectured the Court, claiming its recent reversals were "wrongly decided" and responsible for opening the "sluice gates on a new deluge of pornography." Such an approach clearly carried slim chances of persuading the justices, but even in losing, CDL's credibility was buttressed by its involvement in Supreme Court cases. Amicus participation by interest groups in noncommercial Supreme Court cases remained a relatively rare phenomenon in the early 1960s, and it conferred an image of legal expertise and leadership on CDL.[58]

CDL also sought other, more direct avenues to legal power, sometimes finding a warm reception from law enforcement officials. CDL's legal counsel, James Clancy, attained official status in Los Angeles as a special assistant district attorney in 1964, inspiring a rash of prosecutions that summer. When ten of the twelve cases initiated by Clancy resulted in acquittals, incoming district attorney Evelle Younger moved to terminate Clancy's employment. In a strongly worded statement Younger called Clancy's original appointment a "political move" and explained that his own policy would be not to "waste the taxpayers' money in merely staging shows" by filing charges "for their publicity values," when any resulting convictions were sure to be overturned. Clancy lost further credibility soon after Younger's victory when a local judge threatened him with contempt of court for making statements to the press about a pending criminal case.[59]

Nonetheless, CDL retained prestige among law enforcers and enjoyed a growing reputation as a supplier of legal experts. In Milwaukee the local CDL drew negative press at the start of 1965 for its vigilante pressure toward newsstand owners. But by the end of that year Clancy was nonetheless invited to help draft a county obscenity measure. Maryland state legislators, too, adopted a CDL model obscenity law in 1966. Other times CDL imposed its "assistance"; the same year in Indianapolis three hundred CDL members crowded a city council hearing, "drowned out" a motion to table an obscenity ordinance, and succeeded in pressuring the council into passing the ordinance. Welcomed or not, CDL was able to effect substantive legal changes in various locales. By the mid-1960s, then, CDL had expanded its operations through various centralizing mechanisms to reinforce its legalistic framework. By consolidating its various local units into a somewhat more unified voice, CDL was able to attain new stature. This voice revealed a central CDL technique by speaking in an undeviating monologue that offered no opportunity for real debate.[60]

The Erotic Monologue of Decency

From its inception CDL had drawn detractors who saw it as perpetuating a censorious trend that ran unbroken from Anthony Comstock through the NODL and finally to CDL. The ACLU called attention to CDL in its 1960 annual report, as did the American Book Publishers Council in its

Censorship Bulletin that same year. A 1961 article in *The Californian* called CDL "only a front group" for the NODL, and in 1963 Hugh Hefner reiterated the charge in *Playboy*, also describing Charles Keating as a neurotic suffering from "pornophilia," defined as "the obsessive and excessive interest in pornographic materials."[61]

The CDL response to these charges was telling; in essence it responded by refusing to acknowledge them, preferring to dismiss the sources as being in cahoots with pornographers, as seen in Keating's wild 1962 letter calling the ACLU "fellow travelers" of "filth merchants" and "anarchist architects of chaos." Sometimes this technique failed, however, and CDL was forced into actual substantive debate. In these situations the group and its representatives tended to fare poorly. But more often than not CDL was able to insulate itself by avoiding such confrontations and preaching an uninterrupted monologue to its constituency. A major component of this monologue, seen in everything from the group's films to its mailings, was a vivid depiction of sexuality, often in its "deviant" forms. An early CDL flier declared it "a well known fact" that "it is very difficult to arouse public opinion" regarding obscenity, and the burdens of explaining the *Roth* decision and the differences between felonies and misdemeanors clearly made for less-than-enthralling rhetoric. By reappropriating pornography's sexual charge under the heading of "decency," though, CDL was able to arouse its constituency by appealing to their prurient interests and offering the tacit compensation of smut in the name of morality.[62]

One example of CDL's evasion methods occurred in mid-1960s St. Louis, where an official county Decent Literature Commission had turned into a battleground between opposing factions, led by CDL member Ray Dreher and ACLU member William Landau. Landau opposed the very existence of the commission but joined it to prevent the local CDL from co-opting the commission's official status entirely. Meanwhile, as Landau and his allies continuously applied the brakes to other commissioners' efforts to transform the commission's function from public awareness to advocacy and enforcement, the St. Louis CDL objected to the "'do-nothing' attitude" of the group and demanded more action. When Dreher moved for the commission to sponsor a screening of *Perversion for Profit*, Landau delivered a rebuttal that encompassed most points of opposition to the film and CDL.[63]

Beginning by calling *Perversion* "thoroughly unsuitable for sponsorship by any Governmental body," Landau adumbrated his attack with alliterative adjectives: "improper, inane, and inaccurate." He then launched into specifics, first regarding the $2 billion annual figure placed on the pornography industry. This figure, Landau observed, exceeded the entire sales of the book publishing industry, and amounted to $50 for each American family. The estimate that 75 percent to 90 percent of pornography ended up in the hands of children, Landau argued, was impossible to document via data collection, and the film's causal connection between smut and homosexuality flew in the face of psychiatric consensus. Landau made a similar case against the film's allegations of a connection between pornography and venereal disease and illegitimacy. He admitted that many sex criminals read obscene literature, but he added that to adduce causality from that would necessitate proscribing the Bible, which was also read by a large portion of criminals. Finally, he found "the apogee of emotional silliness" in the film's claim of ancient civilizations collapsing because of smut. Landau said *Perversion* was "appropriate for an evangelistic tent show" but not for the commission to sponsor, except as a "good example of Big Lie propaganda."[64]

After Landau's critique Dreher's motion to sponsor *Perversion* failed for lack of a second. Instead of responding to Landau's savaging of the film, Dreher, acting secretary for the St. Louis commission, simply omitted Landau's comments from the commission's minutes. Dreher denied intentionally omitting the speech and blamed it on lack of duplicating equipment. Landau next invited Dr. James McClure to address the commission and explain the absence of evidence for a causal relationship between pornography and sex crimes. On this occasion a local CDL leader, Joseph Badaracco, responded with a letter to the local newspaper. "Are his views relevant?" Badaracco first asked of McClure. Next, he asked, "Assuming they are relevant, are they accurate?" Finally, in a display of CDL's remarkable capacity to shift from logical argument to emotional appeal, he asked, "Assuming that Dr. McClure's views are relevant and also accurate, should pornography be held acceptable and encouraged in St. Louis County—or anywhere?" In true monologue form, Badaracco's letter could be persuasive only to someone already converted to the cause. Neither Dreher nor Badaracco at any point substantively engaged with or refuted Landau's critiques of CDL.[65]

Oklahoma CDL president Al Kavanaugh offered another display of CDL's monologic tactics. In 1966 he debated two university professors while running an unsuccessful gubernatorial campaign. After Kavanaugh parroted the usual CDL party line, the professors tore his argument apart to the applause of the University of Oklahoma crowd, accusing CDL of "offering simple answers for a complex problem" and wanting "no book published that is not fit for a five-year-old." One professor warned that "Big Brother Decency is watching us," leaving Kavanaugh with no response except to admit to reporters he had learned much during the debate and had now "relented slightly in his hitherto intransigent attitude toward so-called pornography." The relenting was temporary, however; the next year Kavanaugh advocated prosecuting Hugh Hefner for obscenity, claiming, with presumably unintentional irony, "it would be bigger than the Darwin trial." In 1968, having returned comfortably to his unchallenged monologue, Kavanaugh defined as obscene "any publication that creates a desire to commit an illegal sex act" and listed as examples works by the Marquis de Sade, Henry Miller, and James Baldwin, as well as Betty Friedan's *Feminine Mystique*.[66]

Perhaps the best example of CDL's monologue foundering on the rocky shores of debate comes from the group's 1969 national conference. As free-speech lawyers Stanley Fleishman and Irl Baris debated Keating and James Clancy, the challengers had sharp responses to each CDL point. When Keating mentioned the corrosive moral effects of smut on the American Judeo-Christian heritage, Fleishman reminded him that the Bible, "for better or worse, is not a part of our constitution." Fleishman also turned Keating's rhetoric on itself when the CDL founder linked the Supreme Court's decisions to "moral anarchy" by noting, "We should respect and abide by the decisions of the Court . . . unless we want anarchy." Baris leveled the sharpest blow, against Clancy's claim that pornography wrecked individual morality. "Have you been corrupted, or are you a superman?" Baris challenged Clancy. After a clumsy attempt to evade the question, Clancy admitted, "I'm steeled against this stuff, but yes, it has . . . lowered my morals." In a snappy follow-up, Baris wondered, "Then why don't you stop collecting it?" Clancy offered no response, but the crowd sided with him regardless; "you make me want to puke," one member shouted at Fleishman, while another attendee drew laughter by referring to Baris as "Mr. Bare Ass." In its coverage of the conference's "huge success," the *National Decency Reporter* mentioned the "smugness of Fleishman and Baris" but refrained from discussing the specifics of the debate.[67]

Meanwhile, the unbridled sexuality of CDL discourse did not go unnoticed by critics. In 1965 the *Nation* quoted one publisher complaining of *Perversion for Profit* that "hundreds of little old ladies in gym shoes have gotten their first sexual kicks in years from this film." The article went on to note that when Henry Miller's *Tropic of Cancer* was on trial in 1962 CDL had distributed a pamphlet featuring "the nineteen dirtiest passages from the book"; thus, "CDL had actually created a piece of pornography." Like its predecessor *Perversion for Profit*, the 1965 CDL film *Printed Poison* lingered on montages of the "soul-sucking bacteria of a new disease," displaying various books and magazines and featuring a narrator graphically summarizing one story of public sex and masturbation as he addressed the camera, "C'mere, I want you to hear this." When asked about this facet of the film, Keating "sheepishly" admitted, "I think this is a little pornographic itself." Keating's disingenuousness aside, the admission acknowledged prurience as a vivid and significant facet of CDL material.[68]

The films' imagery was far from an isolated incident. Even a brochure advertising *Perversion for Profit* embedded salaciousness in its very format. "Take a close look . . ." the cover instructed, its ellipses heightening the thrill of discovery by deferring resolution (Figure 6). Catharsis was effected with the unfolding of the brochure, as its interior roared, "at the rack!" Pictured was a book rack with titles such as *Man Alive, Bikini, Stud*, and *Hotel Girl* (Figure 7). The inside text went on to describe this "flood of filth"

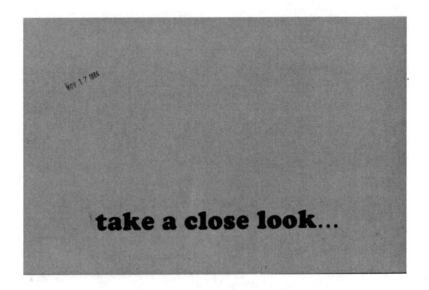

FIGURES 6, 7. Salaciousness was infused into the very format of this brochure. Citizens for Decent Literature brochure (1964). Kinsey Institute for Research in Sex, Gender, and Reproduction, vertical files.

at the rack!

as "detailed courses in sex perversion" and promised further enlightenment at the film. In every detail, the brochure matched the advertising techniques of the midcentury exploitation films that traveled small-town America promising illicit thrills under the radars of censors.[69]

Further supporting the analogy, CDL speakers often seemed to take their cues from the professional-looking lecturers who opened exploitation films like *Mom and Dad* or *Because of Eve*. For instance, the former film was often introduced by a live actor posing as "eminent hygiene commentator Elliot Forbes," who gave a brief presentation explaining that the film about to be shown was not made for sleazy purposes but rather for education. In the exact same manner, Keating explained in a typical CDL speech after showing several pornographic pictures, "Again, I repeat, Ladies and Gentlemen, that the purpose of showing these pictures and quoting from this material is not to shock you—it is to inform you of what is available on your newsstands, and what, very possibly, your children are reading." Similarly, CDL speaker Raymond Gauer told his audience, "I don't do this just to make this talk sensational or to try to shock some of you people," citing a "very serious ignorance of the serious nature of this material" as "the only reason" for his various displays and quoted passages. Such comments performed an important legitimizing function, framing the audience's curiosity in the obscene material as "decent" rather than prurient and making CDL speakers educators instead of showmen, although after reading from *Sex Jungle* Gauer promised, "We will get public opinion aroused as we never have before."[70]

CDL presentations did differ from exploitation films in one way: they delivered the goods. Whereas lurid exploitation posters often promised explicit content that the films failed to supply, CDL reliably provided graphic depictions of sexuality. At its 1965 national conference in New York City's Waldorf-Astoria Hotel, a display behind an "Adults Only" door included examples of the latest magazines dealing with traditional nudism, as well as "flagellation, bestiality, incest, lesbianism, fetishism and other perversions." As one reporter noted with laconic humor, "The display had many visitors yesterday." Indeed, the display brought national attention to the CDL conference, as the *Washington Post* covered its contents, while the *Louisville Courier-Journal* marveled in detail at the s/m magazine *Dominate*. In 1966, with the caption, "Pictured above are front and back views of the nudist magazines and paperback books found obscene by the jury in Sioux City,

NUDIST MAGAZINES AND PAPERBACK BOOKS ADJUDGED OBSCENE

Pictured above are front and back views of the nudist magazines and paperback
books found obscene by the jury in Sioux City, Iowa, on January 14, 1966.

FIGURE 8. Embedding prurience in the discourse of decency. *National Decency Reporter*, March 1966, 14.

Iowa," the *National Decency Reporter* ran a half-page spread that included at least ten pairs of visible female breasts, as well as several naked backsides (Figure 8). The CDL magazine offered no editorial commentary explaining why the pictures were obscene in Iowa but acceptable within its pages.[71]

At times CDL discourse amounted to a sort of sexual safari, exposing various exotic sexual kinks to its audience. Homosexuality provided CDL's greatest shocker, appearing ubiquitously in the group's warnings. *Perversion for Profit* displayed numerous physique magazines of nude men and claimed that "today's conquest is tomorrow's competition" was a gay "slogan" that "betrays the evil of the breed." The film also gave a lengthy close-up to the homophile magazine *ONE* as it profiled gay obscenity—an odd choice for such a legalistic group, since the Supreme Court had overturned obscenity charges against *ONE* in 1958. When the Court ruled subsequently in 1962 that male nudist magazines could not be held to a more stringent standard of obscenity than those depicting women, Keating rationalized the decision away by misleadingly calling it "a widely split affair where it was impossible to tell whether or not a majority really existed" and continued parading gay porn as evidence of obscenity's apocalyptic impact.[72]

In 1965 a Georgia newspaper pictured Keating holding up an issue of
Manimal magazine, with a naked man on its cover. Keating's stock speech,
meanwhile, warned of "the lesbian, the cunalinguist [*sic*], the homosexual"
in tones so ominous that even listeners oblivious to the meaning of cunnilingus could discern its perverse nature. While these excursions could
simply reinforce preexisting homophobia, they were often so lavish in their
descriptions and representations of homosexuality that they could also offer a walk on the wild side for citizens too timid to pursue their curiosity
about the "perversion." Other perversions abounded in CDL discourse, all
described in exquisite detail. In a 1965 speech one member discussed a book
in which the main character "is famed for her specialty of spending night
after night performing fellatio—drawing the seed of life from men, who
wait in long lines for their turn." Seeking to raise the bar of perversion a
notch in the early 1970s, a widely distributed CDL mailing asked, "Did you
know that in [whichever city was targeted by the mailing] there are theaters
that show movies of men and women having sexual intercourse?" In case
that failed to rouse the recipient, the letter went on to describe depictions
of "women having sexual intercourse with animals and other sexual activities too unbelievable to mention."[73]

CDL material could so easily serve as de facto smut that the group
suggested certain cautions. Not only did the presence of so much pornography in the CDL coffers reinforce the already rigid gender lines of the
organization, keeping women "safe" from the heavy exposure meted out to
group leaders, but instructions on forming CDL units hinted at the need
for a sanctioned sexual outlet among members with its first, boldfaced criterion for recruiting members: "Married, with children." Even dedicated
single men could be considered suspect in the face of such powerful smut.
Clearly the power of the erotic monologue was as much understood as it
was unstated.[74]

That power would soon be reflected in the nascent New Right's exploitation of the pornography debate. Enterprising conservative politicians
would use pornography as a discursive displacement of other political issues more complex than the simple set of dualisms that aligned liberalism
with libertinism. As this shift transpired, CDL remained at the forefront
of national sexual politics, playing a prominent role in both the derailing
of Lyndon Johnson's nomination of Abe Fortas to the chief justiceship of

the Supreme Court and, shortly thereafter, the burying of the liberal Presidential Commission on Obscenity and Pornography. CDL's fortunes would waver after 1970, as we will see in later chapters, but in the remaining years of the 1960s power remained in the group's hands, as "decency" began its lengthy tenure in partisan rhetoric.

4. DAMNING THE FLOODTIDE OF FILTH
The Rise of the New Right
and the Political Capital of Moralism

IN MAKING HIS CASE that "America is in serious trouble" in his 1964 book
None Dare Call It Treason, the right-wing author John Stormer cited numerous examples of the "conspiratorial plan to destroy the United States."
Eisenhower had given money to "the communist enemy" in Poland and
Yugoslavia and stood idle as Russia trampled freedom fighters in Hungary.
Kennedy had created "a sanctuary for the communists in Cuba" by backing down in the face of Khrushchev's missile threats. And devious interna-
tionalists at the United Nations plotted excessive foreign aid as a means of
creating inflation, undermining confidence in free markets, and using the
resulting "national emergency" "as a justification for abolishing the constitutional processes and establishing a totalitarian, socialistic government."[1]

It was a daunting, nightmarish, and paranoid vision, but it was not to
last. When Stormer surveyed the American scene again four years later, in
1968, he saw new threats that far surpassed the old ones. The communists
still clung to their evil designs, but they had refined their techniques; instead
of tanks rolling through Eastern European streets, Stormer emphasized in
The Death of a Nation's first paragraph that "filthy books, dirty movies, and
burned draft cards are weapons in the communist war to corrupt America's
youth." He spent the next 180 pages too fixated on this moral decay to give
even Fidel Castro himself more than a passing mention.[2]

Other conservatives agreed on the magnitude of this moral crisis. In
Georgia the Baptist minister and state literature commissioner James Pickett Wesberry called pornography "an enemy worse than communism" in a
1965 speech. "The undermining of moral foundations" from within, he intoned, would bring social collapse "far sooner [than] invading armies" from
without.[3] This shift from an externally focused siege mentality predicated
on fears of communist conquest to an internal siege mentality based on
reactionary cultural and sexual politics constituted much of the "new" component of the New Right.

Historians have sought the origins of the New Right in diverse locations. Certainly white antipathy to the civil rights movement played a criti-

cal role; while the political empowerment of African Americans rendered untenable the overtly racist segregationist rhetoric of many politicians, that discourse was often reconstituted in ostensibly race-neutral areas that substantively perpetuated racially motivated agendas: white ethnic "backlash" against the Great Society; opposition to school busing programs, welfare programs, and taxes; and the coded language of "law and order," among others. This deliberate "color blindness" was assisted by the white suburban middle class, eager to abstract suburbanization from its racialized realities and reimagine it as the natural market-based outcome of hard work, something seen as absent from the inner-city ghettoes that suffered in the wake of government-subsidized "white flight." Even the Equal Rights Amendment debates of the 1970s would be tainted by none-too-vestigial traces of race, as white southern opponents cued up memories of federal impositions with tropes like "desexegration." Beyond race, the easing of cold war fears also figured prominently, as Americans shifted their gaze from the external threat of the Soviet Union to the enemy within—an expansive, malleable entity that would over time include feminists, antiwar protestors, homosexuals, secular humanists, drug users, and other "deviants."[4]

Behind these political shifts lay the abrupt disintegration of the postwar liberal consensus. In the face of massive social unrest, punctuated by urban riots, campus radicalism, political assassinations, and a confusing and seemingly futile war in Vietnam, liberals appeared to straddle a fence that was quickly becoming a wall. Supporting both peace *and* military escalation in Southeast Asia, civil rights *and* law and order, freedom of speech *and* obscenity laws, liberal leaders like Lyndon Johnson and Hubert Humphrey seemed caught in the crosscurrents of history, trapped in nuances that soured into mixed messages. "All this moral anarchy: all of it felt linked," Rick Perlstein writes of the chaotic late 1960s. While liberals attempted to disentangle those linked threads, conservatives mobilized around a much simpler principle of bluntly opposing the various manifestations of moral anarchy that plagued the nation.[5]

Morality assumed a place of centrality in New Right rhetoric, acting both as a replacement for the fading discourses of racism and anticommunism and as a discursive displacement of the complex politics of race and class brought into play by the liberal Great Society programs of the 1960s. While those programs raised questions, New Right politicians preferred to deliver answers, and moral issues provided effectively polarizing and simplistic venues for this; in contrast to matters like institutionalized racial inequalities, the cornerstone social issues of the New Right lent themselves to straightforward "for" or "against" positioning. Sociologist Jerome Himmelstein argues that "the most striking characteristic of the New Right was its continuity" with the Old Right of opposition to the New Deal, communism, and social change, and he is accurate in regard to the substantive goals of New Right politicians, which generally followed well-established conservative trajectories of scaling back social welfare programs and promoting corporate freedom.[6] The moral emphasis grafted onto this agenda, though, while hardly new to American politics, took on new partisan contours in the late 1960s.

From the Puritans to Progressivism, moral regulation had proved a steady motif in American history, one as apt to come from the Left as the Right. But building off the constructs of Citizens for Decent Literature and often following the group's lead, the New Right discovered the political capital of moralism. Janice Irvine has shown how sex education figured into this process, as New Right leaders took a program with wide public support and used polarizing rhetoric to demonize it in such a way that supportive politicians felt intimidated from voicing their positions for fear of having them conflated with fabricated examples of extreme pedagogical practices, but for the most part historians have yet to fully explore the sexual politics of the New Right's emergence.[7] The broader constellation of New Right social issues would grow to include opposition to feminism, reproductive rights, gay rights, and drug use; pornography helped lead the way, establishing a style of simplified, polarized rhetoric that set the framework for the political staging of these subsequent issues.

By the late 1960s the Republican Party had begun to claim a monopoly on such evocative phrases as "decency," "moral order," and ultimately "family values." That this focus was initially more symbolic than substantive will be shown in several of the examples discussed in this chapter; the movement was not yet dominated by the religious elements that would later transubstantiate that rhetoric into meaningful policy. The New Right needed an opportunity to distinguish itself from the "me-too" Republicanism that found the party often in consensus with Democratic leaders, and it found the key in social issues, particularly those pertaining to sexuality. One of the New Right's major innovations, then, was the conservative cooptation of morality in politics, equating liberalism with libertinism at every available opportunity.

While such earlier antiporn leaders as Estes Kefauver had often been liberals, by the mid-1960s liberal support for free speech had fairly immobilized such efforts. The leaders of the New Right eagerly took to the field on this front, adopting a new posture of moralism that superseded increasingly obsolete conservative platforms. In this framework pornography could operate as a substitute to divert public attention from more complicated issues. For example, Orval Faubus, the former integration-blocking Arkansas governor, attempted to generate concern over porn in 1966 as part of an effort to develop industry in his state without the nuisances of government oversight or regulation. As he bluntly put his case to the press, it was more important to protect children from "pollution of the mind" than "from accidents and injuries on highways and in industrial jobs."[8]

Faubus's attempt to shift public focus was rather transparent, but practiced somewhat more subtly and on a mass scale by the New Right in the late 1960s, such tactics proved enormously effective. That a discursive political displacement was consciously orchestrated by leaders of the New Right is undeniable, best exemplified by the Nixon administration, which historian Robert Mason describes as obsessed with public relations, to the point of attaching "more importance to the *communication* of policy than to policy itself." As Nixon advisers framed it internally, in reference to the election of 1972, "The real issues of the election are the ones like patriotism, morality, religion—not the material issues. If the issues were prices and taxes, they'd be for McGovern." Pornography would help Nixon and other conservatives reconfigure the national political landscape to make conservatism more palatable to a wide swath of Americans, exploiting social issues to downgrade the significance of material ones.[9]

As the Warren Court continued to scale back the province of obscenity laws, conservatives continuously lamented the "floodtide of filth" engulfing the nation. In the late 1960s, though, the nascent New Right realized a simple fact that would provide a fundamental organizing principle: damning the floodtide carried more political salience than damming it. For were pornography to suddenly cease, one source of the outrage that energized conservative voters would dry up; but as long as it and other antagonizing agents persevered, conservative politicians could turn the tide without stopping it by reconfiguring the debate. Their strategy left liberals fighting the current to explain the permissiveness generated by their own policies. The New Right grasped all this in the late 1960s; they would have to wait another decade to fully institutionalize it, but the organizational, rhetorical, and political principles took shape as conservatives grasped for a viable platform in a decade still defined by postwar liberalism.

Here I examine several such examples of the early New Right's discovery of the political capital of moralism. In the congressional battle over Lyndon Johnson's nomination of Abe Fortas to chief justice of the Supreme Court; the response to the Johnson-appointed Presidential Commission on Obscenity and Pornography; and the increasingly moralistic rhetoric of Ronald Reagan, Richard Nixon, and other New Right luminaries can be seen the beginning of a massive political shift, as social issues predicated on polarizing outrage began to displace the more traditional policy orientations of postwar liberalism.

Harbingers of Reaction

The journalist M. Stanton Evans was one of the first to use the phrase *New Right*, in his 1968 book *The Future of Conservatism*. Juxtaposing it against the New Left of student revolutionaries and civil rights militants, Evans argued that this new conservative movement could "halt the devolution of our system into a consolidated welfare state and foster a new era of decentralization, constitutional restraint of power, and reaffirmation of individual freedom." While that lofty and abstract formula emphasized freedom in its conclusion, more telling was the articulation of another book coauthored by Evans that same year: in *The Lawbreakers: America's Number One Domestic Problem* Evans and Margaret Moore deplored the "new liberties" created by the Supreme Court, which ranged from procedural rights for defendants to "abortion, homosexuality, narcotics, pornography, alcoholism."[10] Here was the New Right platform in concrete terms: a normative, regulatory state endorsing individual freedom only insofar as behavior remained within the strictures of traditionally accepted moral behavior. Rational Economic Man was entitled to pursue his whims in the market, but not in the bedroom.

The New Right's desire to expand "freedom," while maintaining state surveillance and control over private individual action, contained a contradiction every bit as evident as the one plaguing liberals who defended free speech but excluded obscenity from its grasp. Unlike the self-criticizing liberals, who debated the topic endlessly, the New Right was content to gloss over this paradox with a simple formula: private morality impacts the public good. Thus, when "standards must unceasingly be changed to accommodate the latest exoticisms, standards become meaningless." Stanton Evans and Margaret Moore contended that permissiveness undermined the entire foundation of social order. "If a homosexual is to be forgiven his perversion," they argued, with hot rhetoric intended to press over any flaws in the metal of their logic, "why, then, so is a rapist."[11]

Evans and Moore's book *The Lawbreakers* displayed many other central features of the New Right. A belief that the "new morality" explained rising crime rates better than environmental or educational factors supported attacks on the premises of Lyndon Johnson's New Deal–inspired Great Society, while further justifying state intrusion into the private sphere. The emphasis on law and order reiterated themes already articulated by conservatives and portended the shape of the Nixon campaign. Blaming the Supreme Court for coddling criminals would be a frequent theme in the years to come. By the time of the book's publication in 1968 these themes had already been put into play, as what historian Mary Brennan calls "the conservative capture of the GOP" took shape. The 1964 Republican presidential nomination of Barry Goldwater marked one landmark in this process. Though his disastrous defeat seemingly boded poorly for the conservative wing of the party, the 1966 elections verified the New Right's staying power, as the GOP picked up forty-seven seats in the House and three in the Senate, fueled largely by grassroots conservatism. Conservatives surged forward at the state level also, as nine of ten western states elected Republican governors that year. The most notable of these was California's Ronald Reagan, who amply displayed the early New Right's exploitation of pornography and other social issues, as well as its lack of firm commitment to substantive policies related to them.[12]

A Modest Proposition

Liberal Democrat Edmund "Pat" Brown, elected governor of California in 1958, showed more interest in advancing civil rights than in regulating morality. The state's existing obscenity laws were "strict enough," Brown declared repeatedly in 1959, dismissing efforts to strengthen them. Meanwhile, the governor lent his most strenuous efforts to civil rights legislation guaranteeing equal access to housing. The 1963 Rumford Fair Housing Act signaled the crowning achievement of Brown-era liberalism, outlawing racial discrimination in the real estate market.[13]

The Rumford Act also marked the commencement of the so-called white backlash to the civil rights movement in California. This paralleled other developments across the nation; for instance, working-class ethnic white voters in Wisconsin and Indiana, alienated by what they saw as the unfair advantages of Great Society entitlement programs for African Americans, responded vigorously to the overtures of the segregationist Alabama governor George Wallace in the 1964 Democratic primaries. In California that backlash took the form of Proposition 14, a popular referendum to repeal the Rumford Act. Speaking with a frankness his press secretary repeatedly warned him against, Governor Brown referred to the supporters of Prop 14 as "bigots." Unfortunately for the governor and fair housing, Prop 14 passed with more than 60 percent of the vote in 1964.[14]

While Prop 14 awaited court battle, Ronald Reagan emerged as a contender for the 1966 gubernatorial election. A longtime Democrat who looked up to Franklin Roosevelt, Reagan had established conservative bona fides as a Hollywood anticommunist during the cold war. Switching to the GOP in the early 1960s added to his credibility, but a rousing speech in support of Goldwater in 1964 cemented his reputation as a conservative upstart. Early in 1966, while campaigning for the Republican nomination, Reagan attempted to straddle the housing debate by opposing both the Rumford Act and Proposition 14. Later, campaigning against Brown, he made his true sympathies clear, telling a group of realtors the Rumford Act had created "a big brother sitting in Sacramento" and explaining that bigotry motivated only a small proportion of Prop 14 supporters; most simply opposed government "invading a constitutional right," that of the owner disposing of his or her property as he or she saw fit. Real estate organizations had a lengthy history of profiting off white racism, and the California Real Estate Association clearly understood Reagan's endorsement of its anti–fair housing stance. By the time Reagan finished, the realtors began chanting, "We want Ronnie."[15]

Ratifying a white supremacist status quo was no political innovation, as both liberals and conservatives had done so to some extent or another for decades. Reagan's true innovation was to strip away complex issues in an attempt to boil the election down to a simple set of core agenda items. Reagan's public-relations firm, Spencer-Roberts, believed simplicity was the key to victory; "You can't get through more than two or three issues," they explained.[16] Issues of race and housing, with their complex interplay of property rights and social justice, could prove confusing in a number of ways, so instead Reagan—having already suggested his stance in no unclear terms—generally downplayed the Prop 14 controversy. A campaign pamphlet listed his platform priorities: taxes were the number-one issue, with crime at number two. Reagan's notion of crime was expansive, including everything from disruptive student protestors to the Watts rebellion of 1965. It also prominently included pornography. Promising to "end the flood of smut and pornography," Reagan entered the obscenity debate without ambivalence.[17]

Another proposition already on the ballot afforded easy access to this debate. A new group called CLEAN—California League to Enlist Action Now, a name used only to justify the acronym—gathered enough signatures to put Proposition 16 (largely written by Citizens for Decent Literature legal counsel James Clancy) on the ballot in 1966. As the ACLU explained, Prop 16 aimed to strip California's obscenity law of the "contemporary community standards" by which alleged obscenity was judged, thus allowing towns and cities to set their own standards. It also removed the national "utterly without redeeming social importance" clause so often cited to justify sexually themed works, and it imposed a jury trial for obscenity cases unless the jury was waived by both the prosecution and defense, as well as the judge. Another provision required district attorneys to "vigorously" enforce obscenity laws and allowed for civil action from citizens when they believed a DA was failing to act.[18]

Governor Brown had little to say about Proposition 16. Calling it "unconstitutional on its face," he vaguely proposed more moderate laws protecting minors from pornography, never lingering on the topic in his campaign. Official consensus favored Brown's stance; even law enforcers such as Los Angeles County sheriff Peter Pitchess and the California District Attorney's Association went on record opposing the proposition. The *Los Angeles Times*—conservative enough to endorse Goldwater in 1964—called for its defeat in an editorial. A reporter for the *Nation* called CLEAN's founders and executive committee a "'Who's Who' of California's extreme right," linking it to the John Birch Society. Even Republican lieutenant governor nominee Robert Finch called Prop 16 a "radical" law that "plunges us into the murky waters of censorship."[19]

Nonetheless, Reagan repeatedly endorsed it. "Constitutional or not, if this measure is voted down, my opponent might take it to mean that the people of California are not opposed to pornography," Reagan explained, blurring the distinction between public opinion polls and constitutional amendments. Later he added that, even if the proposition were declared unconstitutional, "at least it would have been an expression of the people's views, a clear mandate."[20] This cavalier attitude toward rule of law coexisted curiously alongside Reagan's law-and-order stances on student radicals in Berkeley and black participants in the 1965 Watts uprising, but it clearly spoke to many California voters; Reagan was elected in a landslide. Brown, too, had opposed student radicals at Berkeley but only after presiding over a massive expansion of higher education in California; he, too, had opposed the rioting in Watts but only after pushing for the unpopular fair housing law. Certainly he opposed pornography, but why not then support Prop 16? In contrast to Reagan's smiling clarity, Brown seemed to offer liberal convolution.

Proposition 16 failed at the ballot, though it did win nearly five million votes—more than 40 percent—despite its self-evident radicalism and unconstitutionality, recognized by nearly every major public figure except Reagan. Political scientists examining the election found significant correlations between Prop 16 supporters and Reagan voters, Goldwater supporters, and anti–fair housing Prop 14 supporters.[21] This suggested a somewhat cohesive New Right, as well as a social-issue voting bloc very responsive to antiporn measures. Had the proposition been less extremist, it might have been quite viable.

As it was, 1966 signaled the California Republican Party's embrace of the antiporn cause and other social issues. When the League of Women Voters submitted a questionnaire to all candidates for state office before the party primaries, one question asked for "the most pressing problems facing Americans today." Democratic responses revolved around a set of issues including slums, smog, Vietnam, farmworkers, and racial discrimination. Republican responses, to the contrary, avoided most of those topics. Instead, one of Reagan's competitors, George Christopher, demanded a "restoration of morality," while Warren Dorn promised to "reduce crime and clean up smut." Lieutenant governor hopeful Norman Davis opposed "license for filth, sex, and degradation." Meanwhile, the GOP attorney general candidate Spencer Williams campaigned for stronger laws "aimed at stopping dope peddlers, rapists, [and] purveyors of smut pornography." Though Williams lost, the 1966 California election was otherwise a sweep for the GOP. Reagan himself implicitly aligned student radicals with the sexual perversions of pornography, describing a dance held at Berkeley as "something in the nature of an orgy."[22]

Once in office, Reagan continued to speak strongly against pornography, at the same time revealing his deregulatory corporate sympathies by calling exposure to porn "even more harmful" to children than alcohol or tobacco. In 1967 he took a relatively moderate suggestion from Lieutenant Governor Finch and proposed new laws to shield minors from obscenity, leaving unspoken the fact that Brown had proposed the exact same measure in opposing Prop 16. It took two years to pass the measure, as a recalcitrant Democratic Legislature held it up until Republicans gained a majority in 1969, during which time Reagan continued to vocalize about smut. He never again mentioned anything vaguely resembling Prop 16 for the simple reason that a moderate minors law served as a functional equivalent to an extremist initiative: both gave him a platform from which he could moralize. The actual substance of that platform was less relevant than the public pronouncement of sanctimony it facilitated. The increasingly partisan nature of the pornography debate was evident in 1969, when the Democratic Assembly member John Burton proposed an amendment defining war toys as obscene to illustrate the hypocrisy of Republican moralism (it was voted down, largely along party lines).[23]

Meanwhile, Reagan did nothing to acknowledge the structural racism addressed by the fair housing law, and his response to the politicized University of California was to push budget cuts and the first-ever tuition requirements, intended to dismantle university power. Reagan would ultimately prove more moderate as governor than those who feared right-wing extremism had predicted. His efforts, however, and those of the California GOP in 1966, to neutralize and efface the contentious politics of race and replace them with more simplistic platforms of moral outrage anticipated national trends as the New Right took shape.[24]

The Fortas Fiasco

When President Lyndon Johnson moved to name Abe Fortas chief justice of the Supreme Court on the impending retirement of Earl Warren in June

1968, the burgeoning New Right reacted with passionate denunciations. Fortas—already appointed to the Court in 1965—had long been despised as overly liberal, both for his associations with the Democratic New Deal and for his courtroom decisions. South Carolina senator Strom Thurmond, a crucial figure for the New Right who helped instigate the political realignment of the South by defecting (a second time) from the Democratic Party to join the 1964 Goldwater campaign, led the charge against Fortas. In June 1968 Thurmond issued a strong statement, claiming that "there was collusion between President Johnson and Chief Justice Warren to prevent the next president from appointing the next chief justice." When this failed to rouse public sentiment, Thurmond upped the rhetorical ante in July, characterizing Fortas as procommunist, soft on crime, and for "open housing."[25]

Other Fortas opponents voiced similar complaints. Louisiana senator Russell Long cited Fortas's record of protecting the rights of accused criminals, while the far-right Liberty Lobby issued an "emergency letter" calling Fortas a "convinced revolutionary" in cahoots with the Communist Party.[26] Republicans also began framing their opposition in terms of "cronyism," given Johnson's and Fortas's long and close relationship. A *New York Times* report at the end of June described these charges as "a broadening of the Republicans' attack," since initially they had "based their opposition solely on the issue of a lame duck President making such appointment." Despite these persistent attempts to undermine the nomination, the damage inflicted by critics fell short of paralyzing; at the end of June Fortas had sufficient mainstream approval to garner the endorsement of the AFL-CIO, which "strongly support[ed]" his nomination. A vote count by a Johnson aide at the end of June suggested that Fortas had enough Senate support to win the nomination.[27]

In July, however, CDL legal counsel James Clancy entered the debate, bringing a new perspective on Fortas: the justice had consistently voted to overturn lower-court obscenity convictions. The Fortas nomination provided CDL with an opportunity to seek revenge for the recent obscenity reversals, and the group played a primary role in introducing pornography into the hearings and ultimately sabotaging Fortas's chance at receiving congressional approval. Revelations of financial improprieties surrounding a set of lectures Fortas delivered at American University ultimately nailed the coffin shut on his nomination but only after CDL supplied woodwork and hammer. In the process it led the nascent New Right to a recognition of the political capital of moralism, showing how social issues such as pornography could prove more viable than anticommunism, which had simply failed to spark public interest when used against Fortas.[28]

Appearing alongside Charles Keating before the Senate's hearings, Clancy fused obscenity decisions to previous Fortas criticisms by calling the many recent summary reversals of obscenity convictions the "common denominators" that explained "what is happening in the U.S. Supreme Court in other areas of the law." Clancy framed the per curiam nature of the decisions as a substitution of personal philosophy for constitutional principles. This analysis won immediate favor. Thurmond expressed gratitude to CDL and helped Clancy frame his attack. "Other than being ashamed of the decisions, and ashamed to write in detail their reasoning," he asked Clancy, could there be any reason for the per curiam nature of the reversals? Naturally, Clancy answered in the negative.[29]

Clancy delivered his coup de grace by bringing to the Senate hearings a film whose California obscenity conviction Fortas had concurred in overturning, an untitled short marked as O-7. He screened it for interested senators and press in late July, with explosive results. The film reel showed "a girl in a bra, garter belt, and sheer transparent panties gradually stripping herself naked, mostly while writhing on a couch," as one journalist wrote, and Fortas opponents quickly mobilized around it. Citing the film, Thurmond reported that "the effect of the Fortas decisions has been to unleash a floodtide of pornography across the country," obscuring the fact that Supreme Court decisions require a five-person majority by labeling Fortas the crucial "swing vote." The new line of opposition quickly took hold. Conservative newspaper columnists circulated news of Fortas's alleged pornographic sympathies, as William Buckley insisted, "Obscenity Ruling Needs Explaining" and James Kilpatrick suggested, "Let a Movie Decide Fortas' Fate." The new approach proved effective, as reflected in letters to Johnson. "Until two days ago I was with you," a California man wrote to the president, explaining that his perspective had been changed by hearing about Fortas's obscenity stands. A Connecticut couple found themselves "very troubled" by the obscenity issue. "His liberal stand on pornography is obvious," they wrote, "and our nation is wracked enough by libertinism."[30]

By early September the terms of the Fortas debate had shifted so thoroughly to obscenity that in Mobile, Alabama, a newspaper editorial called the porn critique "well and good" but forgetfully argued that "the battle should be broadened" to include already tried and discarded attacks on Fortas's "leniency toward communism and the criminal elements." When the Senate returned from a brief recess, the situation looked dire, and a second set of hearings in mid-September focused almost exclusively on porn. "Thurmond tastes blood now," a Johnson aide wrote in a memo, explaining that the cronyism charge "has fallen of its own weight." Recent revelations of a $15,000 lecturing fee for a summer seminar at American University paid by questionable sources, though "hurtful," were a "secondary issue." "The movies were what the opposition needed to make their positions gel," the memo explained.[31]

The Johnson administration fought back as best it could, issuing a memorandum that positioned Fortas as a moderate in the obscenity debate. Closer to the center than the free-speech absolutists William Douglas and Hugo Black, it argued, Fortas "provided the crucial fifth vote" when the Court "for the first time in nearly a decade upheld a conviction in the obscenity area," in the 1966 *Ginzburg* decision. The defense was to little avail, and support for Fortas declined over the month of September. While it was no surprise to see such Republicans as North Dakota senator Milton Young or CDL member Jack Miller of Iowa blame their opposition to the nomination on Fortas's obscenity stance, even Democrats utilized the argument. In September North Carolina senator Benjamin Everett Jordan notified the White House that he would vote against Fortas's confirmation because his state Democratic Party had threatened him with exclusion from local rallies. His foremost reason was "Fortas' position on pornography."[32]

At the beginning of October, recognizing futility, a bitter Fortas asked Johnson to withdraw his nomination. A jubilant CDL published a self-congratulatory article in the *National Decency Reporter*, proudly proclaiming "the greatest victory for the forces for decency that this country has ever seen" and emphasizing that "CDL played a key role in shaping the future direction of this nation." "There is no question but that the Fortas involvement in obscenity decisions," it continued, "was the key issue that turned the tide against his confirmation as Chief Justice."[33] Indeed, CDL participation had reconfigured the attack on Fortas, changing its language from narrow charges that appealed to a small cadre of right-wing extremists and into terms more palatable to a mainstream constituency.

Led by Strom Thurmond, the members of the New Right recognized the significance of this discursive shift toward moral outrage and quickly adopted the new rhetoric. On the House floor Wisconsin Republican Henry Schadeberg bemoaned "the floodtide of obscenity engulfing the mailboxes and minds of our youth." Even Barry Goldwater joined the crusade. In his 1960 manifesto *The Conscience of a Conservative* Goldwater had devoutly described the Constitution as "an instrument, above all, for *limiting* the functions of government," which he abhorred for its putting of "power in the hands of some men to control and regulate the lives of other men." Taking this philosophy to its logical limit, Goldwater thus argued the document "does *not* require the United States to maintain racially mixed schools." In what can only be described as an about-face, however, in 1969 Goldwater supported federal antiporn legislation, warning of the "attack of knee-jerk civil libertarians" who opposed bills to safeguard children from smut, which apparently threatened them more than school segregation. Conceding that definitions of obscenity differed, Goldwater made Potter Stewart's oft-mocked subjectivism appear a model of Kantian rigor by explaining, "As a father and a grandfather, I know, by golly, what is obscene and what isn't." Early in the decade Goldwater had told fellow Republicans to "go hunting where the ducks are," meaning not to pursue civil rights when their voting base was so clearly white. By the end of the 1960s, the ducks clearly flew in skies overcast with smut.[34]

The Report That Shocked a Nation

The Presidential Commission on Obscenity and Pornography gave the New Right a chance to open fire. Appointed by President Johnson in 1967 and releasing its report in 1970, the commission (discussed at more length in chapter 5) adopted a libertarian perspective calling for the repeal of all adult obscenity laws and declaring pornography harmless. Led again by Charles Keating and CDL, the New Right reacted to the report with the type of moral grandstanding it was quickly perfecting, showing how rapidly the politics of outrage were coalescing.

Though the Johnson administration had declined to appoint Keating to the commission, hope returned to CDL with the election of Richard Nixon. Naming another commission member ambassador to India, Nixon created an open slot for CDL's founder in June 1969. "I shall serve on the commission with the objective of seeing these criminals jailed," Keating said of pornographers upon his appointment. This clearly conflicted with the commission's established social-scientific approach. Nonetheless, the University of Minnesota legal scholar and commission chairman William Lockhart welcomed Keating to the "warm and congenial group" with the expectation that "you will bring insights that will be helpful to the Commission."[35]

Lockhart wrote from formality rather than conviction, but he was surely unprepared for the rapidity with which Keating assumed an obstructionist position within the commission, promptly defying a preexisting unanimous agreement that no commissioner would act privately in his or her capacity as a commission member by writing to Attorney General John Mitchell to recommend CDL-approved Clement Haynesworth for the Supreme Court. In September Keating demanded to serve as "a Commission member-at-large entitled to attend and participate with any or all of the panels in their meetings and deliberations" rather than accepting assignment to one panel. That same month CDL launched a series of letters warning congressmen of the free-speech "direction in which the Presidential Commission appears to be moving." The letters resulted in inquiries from concerned congressmen, which the commission head answered with elusive promises to "make recommendations only after thorough study." With the commission put on the defensive, Keating continued by attempting to coax executive director W. Cody Wilson into verifying CDL's charges. "I am given to assume you are advocating a position," Keating wrote the director; "Is this correct?"[36]

October saw Keating propose a study to the effects panel on the relation between pornography and sex crimes, to be based on criminal case histories provided by law enforcement officials. The panel, already alienated by Keating's attempts to undermine the commission, minced no words in unanimously rejecting Keating's proposal. Informing him that his methodology "would not withstand the critical review of social scientists," the effects panel chairman, Otto Larsen, went on to clarify: "The leading questions which you proposed putting to the police simply do not meet the cannons [sic] of scientific objectivity." An angry Keating got his revenge later that month when the commission met to discuss confidentiality regarding the progress of the ongoing panels. A motion to preserve confidentiality passed 15–1, with Keating the lone dissenter. After the vote Keating "stated that he does not feel himself bound by this action of the Commission."[37]

Keating's stance greatly concerned chairman Lockhart, who worried that media leaks would predispose public opinion against the commission by framing it as an ACLU pet project. Until Keating's appointment, Catholic priest and Operation Yorkville (later Morality in Media) founder Morton Hill had been the most vocal dissident on the commission. In his separate remarks to the commission's July 1969 progress report to Congress Hill advocated for public hearings and accused the body of "becoming an 'effects' commission" rather than paying heed to prevailing moral sentiment. But Hill took no stand on the confidentiality vote, and Keating quickly moved to the forefront of Lockhart's attention. In a November letter Lockhart implored Keating to abide by the decision, since premature reporting of research "would jeopardize the successful and accurate completion of our difficult research project."[38]

This, of course, was Keating's precise intent, and the rogue commissioner sent a cold reply beginning with the observation, "We are in basic conflict." Lockhart's approach, Keating accused, was to study and philosophize in a detached manner, whereas his own belief was that the commission should focus on helping law enforcers arrest and convict pornographers. "Accordingly," he concluded, "I continue to decline adherence to confidentiality policy." To preempt any action against himself, Keating reminded the chairman that he served "during the pleasure" of the president and could not be removed except by Nixon's orders.[39]

A distressed Lockhart appealed to New Jersey congressman and CDL honorary board member Dominick Daniels, who had sponsored the legislation creating the commission. Daniels "agreed completely with the necessity for confidentiality," but he declined to intervene unless Keating came to him. Meanwhile, the standoff between Keating and Lockhart continued, as the CDL founder asked permission in January 1970 to send "personal representatives" to sit in on panel sessions. The chairman, finally able to exercise authority, tersely denied permission. Keating responded by simply attending no meetings, informing executive director Wilson in March that the panels were inherently unproductive by virtue of their philosophy, and that "the experts you have chosen—you should have saved the Government's money."[40]

As the commission approached completion of its work several months later, Keating launched his final assault. In anticipation Lockhart urged all members except Keating, Hill, and fellow dissenter and Methodist minister Winfrey Link to attend the final commission meetings, explaining, "We need full attendance to overcome any efforts [Keating] may make to hamper completion of our work." But Keating's next efforts occurred outside the commission. News stories began circulating in early August that the commission's report would call for the repeal of all obscenity laws, and the Nixon White House quickly distanced itself, with the president's press secretary, Ron Ziegler, reminding reporters that Nixon "had nothing to do with appointing the commission." At a commission meeting it was observed, to the surprise of none, that some newspaper reporters had privately identified the source of the leaks as Keating. Since Keating was absent from the meeting, the commissioners contemplated withholding further drafts from him or issuing public statements communicating his refusal to abide by commission policy, but both measures were rejected.[41]

Days later a new story broke, as reporters published letters from Keating to the president calling on him to fire most commission members. Again, Ziegler explained, "This is not a Nixon commission," though the president took no action against any commissioners. Near the end of August, Keating finally attended a commission meeting, opening it with a motion against publishing the forthcoming report. Not even Morton Hill supported Keating, and the motion died for want of a second. Keating then moved to extend the commission by twelve months "in light of the dramatically changed situation," which also found no second. When Keating asked Lockhart for thirty days after the report's completion to write a dissenting report, Lockhart lambasted him for not attending earlier meetings at which he could have obtained report drafts; any lack of awareness of the report's contents "was the result of your own choice not to participate in those deliberations," the chairman wrote, denying the request. Keating then moved to federal court to seek a restraining order halting publication of the report until he finished his dissent. Lockhart won this round, and publication was scheduled for September 30.[42]

The final report, encompassing seven hundred pages, argued that massive public demand sustained the growing pornography industry and suggested that the most effective positive response to pornography was sex education, which would undermine the appeal of smut by demystifying sex. As promised by the news leaks, it also called for the repeal of all laws regarding obscenity for adults, maintaining that no evidence showed a causal connection between pornography and juvenile delinquency, sex crimes, or sexual deviance. The report contained dissents, such as Hill's and Winfrey's charge that the majority report "is a Magna Carta for the pornographer." Keating, however, had the last word, and his chief objection was to the report's philosophy, summarized when it declared, "The Commission believes that interest in sex is normal, healthy, good." Saturated with exclamation marks—"Such presumption! Such moral anarchy! . . . Such a bold advocacy of a libertine philosophy!"—Keating's dissent described a "runaway commission" slavishly devoted to an extremist ACLU perspective. He charged Lockhart with withholding information from him and called for a congressional investigation into the commission's misuse of power and government money. To refute the report's conclusions, Keating offered anecdotes such as the story of migrant Puerto Rican farmworkers who "changed from rather manly, decent people to rapists being obsessed with sex, including many deviations," when they were suddenly exposed to pornography. His outrage knew no limits; recalling the commission's rejection of his request to allow the press into panel deliberations, Keating could but marvel, "Amazing! Incredible! Beyond belief!"[43]

Few involved were surprised by Keating's dissent, but Lockhart seemed caught off-guard by the wave of public backlash directed at the report. When Keating accused the chairman of assisting President Johnson in hand-picking a sympathetic commission, Lockhart categorically denied it; headlines read, "Smut Probe Head Accuses Keating of Lying." Lockhart dictated a scathing statement calling Keating's comments "insult borne of desperation," "a figment of Mr. Keating's imagination," and "a completely irresponsible and baseless statement." He decided against issuing it, perhaps because he recognized anger would play into Keating's hand by creating a diversionary public feud. Lockhart's interest lay in relying on the substance of the report itself, but the document remained largely unread and negatively prejudged. Before the report was even published, for example, the *Nashville Banner* carried an editorial arguing, "Aside from the fact that pornography DOES encourage antisocial conduct among many people," the amount of smut in America "is an accurate barometer of the nation's moral health." Without having read it, the *Fort Wayne News-Sentinel* called the report "an unscientific piece of tripe." So effective was Keating at preemptively structuring the response to the report that even sympathetic newspapers focused on the controversy rather than the substance of the commission's recommendations.[44]

As the report went to press, members of the New Right escalated their rhetoric. Vice President Spiro Agnew lashed out at "these radical-liberals who work themselves into a lather over an alleged shortage of nutriments in a child's box of Wheaties—but who cannot get exercised at all over the same child's constant exposure to a flood of hard-core pornography that could warp his moral outlook for a lifetime." Meanwhile, denunciations rang through the halls of Congress; in the Senate, Kansas Republican Robert Dole demanded an investigation of the commission, while Ohio Republican William Harsha echoed this in the House, rejecting the commission's "libertine recommendations." California representative Don Clausen called the report "absolutely unbelievable," while Michigan Republican Robert Griffin hoped the report would "if anything, spur Congress on to the enactment of more legislation in this field."[45]

The New Right had yet to invest itself in one party, and socially conservative southern Democrats lambasted the report in equally harsh terms. West Virginia senator Robert Byrd expressed "indignation" over the "disgusting" report, and Georgia's John McClellan used Agnewesque alliteration in denouncing its "pervasive posture of permissiveness."[46] This antagonism from southern Democrats was emblematic of the shift then taking place in national politics, reflecting their need to appease constituencies that would shortly convert to Republicanism. Moral indignation proved one effective tactic by which to retain voter support.

Ultimately the Senate voted 60–5 to reject the commission's report, citing inadequate research and "unscientific testing." In the House outrage continued as Utah Republican Laurence Burton called the report "an affront to intelligent, decent, concerned Americans" and Tennessee Republican John Duncan wondered of the commissioners, "Are they blind?" President Nixon, too, entered the fray, "categorically reject[ing]" the "morally bankrupt conclusions" of the report. Charles Keating continued to shape public memory in the aftermath, writing "The Report That Shocked the Nation" for *Reader's Digest* in 1971, an article that distorted the commission report by reframing it as "the panel majority's bizarre proposal for handling the pornography problem." Commission leaders remained active in attempting to draw attention to their analysis, but for naught. Tellingly, while

Keating wrote for the mass-circulation *Reader's Digest*, a typical defense by W. Cody Wilson appeared in *Annals of the American Academy of Political and Social Science.*[47]

Nowhere in any of the condemnation was a substantive discussion of the report's assumptions or arguments. Instead, the flurry of knee-jerk reactions revealed a New Right gaining mastery over the mechanics of engineering outrage. The American public generally found pornography a relatively insignificant issue; for instance, a 1965 Gallup poll indicated that only 3 percent of the population considered "moral problems" the most important issue facing the nation, compared to 27 percent who chose civil rights and 19 percent who opted for Vietnam. Yet when asked more specifically whether obscenity laws were sufficiently strict, 58 percent said they were not. Although moral issues remained marginal in terms of national problems in 1969, that year 73 percent of Americans polled found nude pictures in magazines objectionable, and a reported 85 percent favored stricter obscenity laws. As the Kinsey Institute sex researcher Weldon Johnson noted, that figure decreased tremendously if the survey was handled with more nuance, with the question framed as whether citizens ought to have access to erotic materials if such materials had no harmful effects. In that case, support for unfettered access to pornography rose to 51 percent.[48]

Clearly it was in the New Right's interest to exploit American tendencies toward suppression by minimizing the level of nuance and rigor in public discussion. With Charles Keating helping to color public opinion before the commission report even reached publication, conservative politicians grasped that their most beneficial actions consisted of facilitating Keating's demonology, not engaging in debate. As the 1970s took shape, New Right leaders promoted pornography and a moral agenda to the forefront of their platform.

Arming for the Culture Wars

At the dawn of the 1970s conservatives had secured a virtual monopoly on the porn issue, but the New Right had yet to obtain its own domination of the Republican Party. Thus, anomalies like James Buckley's 1970 election occurred, as he ran for the Senate from New York on a Conservative Party platform to the right of either of his major-party opponents. Buckley, brother of the famous William, repeatedly used pornography as a means to distance himself from the establishment candidates. "I don't feel that there is an issue in this race in the classic sense," he noted on October 7, describing instead his "concern over a seeming breakdown in the stability of American institutions in American life." Growing more specific a few days later in a three-way debate, Buckley cited "an avalanche of filth and pornography" as a leading indicator of this breakdown. This paid off in the next debate, when both major-party candidates blandly suggested the family rather than the state should mediate children's access to pornography; Buckley instead argued society was growing "too permissive" and that curtailment of certain civil liberties was an acceptable remedy. Initially considered a marginal candidate, Buckley surprised many in an upset victory, to the delight of incumbent president Richard Nixon, who admired him. Other Republicans could but learn by example.[49]

The other area where the GOP lacked a monopoly on social-issue outrage was the South, which was midway through converting from a solid Democratic bloc to a solid Republican one. Thus, as mentioned above, conservative Democrats also seized on pornography, with Georgia governor Lester Maddox declaring war on smut in 1969. In Alabama politics such proclamations became de rigueur, as George Wallace lambasted the Supreme Court in 1968, calling it "sick" for its "perverted" decisions. Governor Albert Brewer "escalated his personal war on pornography" in 1969, so when Wallace returned home after running for president to compete against Brewer in the 1970 gubernatorial election, he again proclaimed his plan to "rid the state of filthy literature."[50]

This sudden introduction of moralistic outrage over pornography provided southern politicians with an effective means of abandoning their traditional segregationist rhetoric while keeping touch with many of its tropes and appealing to a similar constituency of conservative whites. North Carolina senator Jesse Helms, for example, transposed decades of overt racism onto a new social map of morality, converting himself from Democrat to Republican in the process. Embracing reactionary sexual politics in the late 1960s as his longtime segregationist rhetoric fell out of favor, Helms fought pornography, feminism, gay rights, and reproductive rights, notoriously supporting his first civil rights bill only in the 1980s—for unborn fetuses. Pornography's paving of the road for this New Right moral agenda was nowhere evinced more emblematically than in the cases of South Carolina's Strom Thurmond or Memphis mayor Henry Loeb.[51]

Thurmond built his long career on an undeniable foundation of racism, marked most notably by his 1948 Dixiecrat presidential candidacy and his record-setting twenty-four-hour filibuster against the 1957 Civil Rights Act. During his climb toward power he showed little interest in obscenity. When a concerned constituent wrote him in 1959 to protest "trashy" movies, Thurmond returned a rather stern lecture on the problem of approaching the issue "without compromising the constitutional guarantee of freedom of the press." He called it "extremely difficult" to legislate "such things as morality without empowering the administrator of such a law to infringe unjustifiably on the basic American concept of liberty." As late as the Fortas controversy he published *The Faith We Have Not Kept*, a dry tome detailing the "mortal blows" the Supreme Court had dealt the Constitution since *Brown* in 1954. At great length Thurmond discussed criminal procedure, civil rights, school prayer, communism, and states' rights, but not once did he mention the numerous liberal obscenity decisions of the Warren Court. Only with a boost from Citizens for Decent Literature did Thurmond discover porn as a rhetorical device, after his own attempts to portray Abe Fortas as a criminal-coddling communist sympathizer fell flat.[52]

Once alerted to the political capital of pornography in the Fortas hearings, Thurmond refused to drop the topic. In July 1969 his personal newsletter to voters excoriated pornography as "an attack on the family," and the newsletter returned to the topic in 1970 to call the Presidential Commission's report "a license for filth . . . fundamentally evil in its basic assumptions." Thurmond joined the GOP-led fray against the report in the Senate, calling it "an utter disgrace" that "should go straight into the trashcan." In a letter to Practice and Procedure Subcommittee chair Edward Kennedy, Thurmond asked for an investigation into the commission, listing several charges of "far from proper" behavior by its staff. Again in 1971 he called for laws to "protect our society from the continuation of pornographic filth which is being forced upon us."[53]

As Thurmond discovered pornography, he supported Republican Albert Watson for governor in the 1970 South Carolina race. Utilizing a traditional racist approach, Watson opposed school desegregation and linked his opponent to the NAACP. He lost. According to a well-known story, Thurmond put his arm around Watson on election night and said, "Well, Albert, this proves we can't win elections any more by cussin' Nigras." Twenty years later Thurmond denied making the comment, but apocryphal or not, it suggests his appreciation of the new political framework, in which pornography provided a suitably demonic replacement for integration. From that point on Thurmond escalated his moral rhetoric and downplayed the racism on which he had built his career.[54]

Meanwhile, in Memphis Mayor Henry Loeb made the same discovery nearly simultaneously. Memphis had a long history of censoring images that local leaders found disruptive of the white supremacist status quo.[55] As Warren Court rulings left local censorial powers emaciated, though, Loeb pioneered new tactics that kept race implicated in censorship policies—no longer as the target of the policies but rather as their structuring principle. He provides an ideal example of the discursive shift from racism to moralism that marked the New Right.

Loeb had first been elected mayor of Memphis in 1959 on an openly racist platform. "I am a segregationist," he publicly stated that year, adding, "I don't think any good would come to the city if a negro [*sic*] were elected to the City Commission." This theme continued as he ran for reelection in 1963, promising to "do everything within the law to prevent desegregation."[56] Before the election, though, Loeb withdrew his candidacy to focus on private business matters. When he returned to run again in 1967, he found an entirely new political landscape.

Under subsequent mayor William Ingram, liberal policies had prevailed. Black voters, empowered by the civil rights movement, held increasing political power, and Ingram brought attention to such matters as police brutality toward African Americans rather than sweeping incidents under the rug, as had so often happened in the past. Ingram also devoted little attention to obscenity, even allowing the local censorship board to expire after an adverse court decision in 1965. Campaigning in 1967, Loeb sought to reverse that pattern, pushing the spotlight away from race but engineering moral outrage over social issues like pornography. If he could not return to his now-obsolete segregationist rhetoric, he could at least attempt to render invisible the civil rights movement. With the black vote split between white incumbent Ingram and African American challenger A. W. Willis, Loeb was able to recapture his old mayoral office by attracting a solid white vote.

Once in office, Loeb adhered to his plan, commencing an immediate discursive downsizing of race. When black sanitation workers went on strike in 1968, or when "Black Monday" protests over the failure of the city's schools to desegregate began in 1969, drawing sixty-seven thousand teachers and students, Loeb simply disregarded them. Reminding his white constituents that he was "just as fed up with Black Mondays as you are," Loeb also refused to take seriously public indignation over the use of the term *nigger* by white police officers, blithely assuring upset citizens that "there was no intention of offense." Not even the globally mourned 1968 assassination of Martin Luther King Jr. in Memphis could compel Loeb to acknowledge the persistence of racial inequalities; if his terse statement of "deepest sympathies" spoke loudly as it failed to offer even passing praise of the martyred civil rights hero, his declining to attend a biracial "Memphis Cares" rally four days after the killing announced with even more volume his absolute unwillingness to offer the slightest signal of support to the ongoing black civil rights movement.[57]

Instead of addressing the racial turmoil engulfing Memphis, Loeb sought to divert attention from it by manufacturing obscenity as an issue of great social importance. Demanding the creation of a new censor board in 1968, beginning a crusade against the presence of Philip Roth's sexually graphic novel *Portnoy's Complaint* in 1969, and even sending female police officers to churches and women's clubs to display magazines like *Beaver*, Loeb devoted himself to the arousal of outrage with a zeal worthy of Charles Keating. These efforts served dual ends, both shoring up support among socially conservative voters and filling the space on the city's political map left blank by Loeb's erasure of race as a matter worthy of discussion. Numerous letters implored Loeb for help against the "filthy literature" being sold in "our wonderful city of Memphis," and Loeb responded with promises to "do everything we know how . . . but we need the public's backing and active support."[58]

Loeb railed tirelessly against pornography, stirring the United Methodist Club with a speech titled "The Pollution of Pornography" one week and linking his message to that of Vice President Spiro Agnew the next. Like Ronald Reagan's casual lack of interest in the unconstitutionality of the antiobscenity Proposition 16 in the 1966 California election, Loeb's own dedication to the "law and order" values he often espoused proved selective. "I concede that there's not much law left to support a censor board," he admitted in early 1968, "but I plan to go ahead" regardless. Such bold stances sometimes inspired concerned discussion in the newspaper columns of civil libertarians, but they also generated enthusiastic displays of public support. "I not only sympathize with Mayor Loeb myself," one man wrote to a local newspaper after a typical Loeb jeremiad, "but I admire him more than I ever did."[59]

Lurking within Loeb's rhetoric was a latent secondary language; when the mayor insisted that "this country has to turn back to some kind of morality," the notion of "turning back" carried with it inescapable resonances, summoning imagery of a bygone, "simpler" era with more clearly defined social and racial roles. Other tropes of Loeb and his local antiporn colleagues fleshed out these connotations. Loeb and his ally Robert James, a Goldwaterite city councilman, subtly maintained their antiquated language of segregation in coded terms aimed at morality. The Supreme Court, for instance, which had been a focal point of racist anger since the 1954 *Brown* decision, remained the enemy. Loeb invoked the Court to white citizens irritated by Black Monday marches in 1969, utterly effacing the structural racism that inspired the protests by explaining, "The problem is created by our Supreme Court." Both Loeb and James would also make the Court their bugbear in regard to obscenity. Responding to a citizen's letter, James assured her that he was doing all he could to oppose the "filthy, rotten, depraved sources of pornography and immorality" but that "the Supreme Court has left us very little power in these matters." Growing even more explicit in his grafting of the old rhetoric onto the new situation, James wrote in regard to *Portnoy's Complaint*, "The City shouldn't have to buy it— just for a minority group that is depraved enough to read it." After years of deployment in the racial arena, attacks on the Supreme Court and "minorities" carried their special visceral charge into the battle against obscenity.[60]

Such tropes abounded in the Loeb-led Memphis New Right attack on pornography, both glaringly and subtly. When the mayor's new censor board criticized the Motion Picture Association of America staff responsible for rating movies, it emphasized that "none of them are from our part of the country," recalling the pervasive cries of "outside agitator" so often used to discredit civil rights activists in earlier years. Much more blunt was the local police director, Frank Holloman, who described pornography as "a concerted and planned campaign to destroy the morals of our young people" while appearing alongside Loeb at an antiporn rally in 1969, before claiming that Memphians "don't have to accept the rulings of the Supreme Court," which functionally doubled as an allusion to massive resistance efforts of the past.[61]

Just as Citizens for Decent Literature had acted as a bridge group, transporting remnants of the moribund Old Right into the revitalized New Right, Loeb and his allies offered a superficially reconfigured white supremacist status quo in the new guise of a moral society. By marginalizing racial issues while using coded language to convey their sentiments and generate emotive responses, Loeb and his associates ensured the perpetuation of institutionalized racial inequalities by effacing them with thunderclouds of sanctimony and torrential downpours of outrage. Loeb showed less interest in eradicating porn than he did in denouncing it, explaining in a 1971 letter that "I think the answer is in harassing the purveyors of pornography over, and over, and over again."[62]

To be sure, Loeb—like all New Right politicians—saw porn as one part of a larger social constellation, arguing that "there is a direct connection between so many things like pornography, dope, 'no-win' policy in Vietnam, and other examples of moral decay."[63] In the late 1960s, though, pornography led the way as a particularly effective target for political rhetoric, and Loeb was but one local example of a widespread national trend. Taken on a mass scale, such tactics anticipated and helped set the stage for Richard Nixon's own presidential policy of "benign neglect" toward racial imbalances.

Indeed, Nixon himself utilized moral outrage over pornography in a very similar manner. Unlike Thurmond or Loeb, Nixon had no overtly racist history to escape; his moderate positions on that front had sometimes even brought a limited progressivism to the Republican Party. Nixon had, however, based his earlier career on vigorous anticommunism, and though he continuously reiterated this theme in his approach to the ongoing war in Vietnam, the external threat of the Soviet menace had receded in the American public consciousness. Domestic issues thus took a paramount importance in Nixon's campaigning and rhetoric; while Nixon's primary interests lay in foreign policy, he saw domestic policy as a means of managing public relations. As president, Nixon effectively used social issues to obscure the Republican economic agenda, reaching out to blue-collar workers by using backlash rhetoric of "the forgotten man" and the "silent majority" while downplaying the relevance of unions. He also vetoed 1971 universal day-care legislation that would have extended the reach of the Great Society, citing its "family-weakening implications." Meanwhile, Nixon swerved away from the liberal 1960s policy emphasis on institutionalized racial inequalities, promoting individual initiative over collective social-class approaches to urban decay in the nation's ghettos.[64]

His commitment to domestic policy was often nominal. When the administration proposed a Family Assistance Plan that would serve as a social welfare net, its primary goal was merely to undercut liberals; Nixon "wants to be sure it's killed by Democrats and that we make a big play for it, but don't let it pass, can't afford it," chief of staff H. R. Haldeman secretly wrote in his diary. All for show: pornography fit perfectly into this matrix of social issues and helped ease Nixon from a discourse of exterior communist threats to interior moral ones.[65]

Almost immediately after taking office in 1969, Nixon identified the political value of moralizing about porn. In response to a staff memorandum regarding postal efforts to control juvenile access to obscene materials, Nixon jotted a note highlighting his true interest: "What can we do to get some publicity on this?" One idea was to "go to a play in New York where they take off clothes, and get up and walk out, to dramatize his feeling," as Haldeman recorded. Instead, Nixon sent a message to Congress insisting on legislative measures to prohibit the sending of "offensive sex materials" to minors and "the sending of advertising designed to appeal to a prurient interest in sex" to anyone. While the president acknowledged the importance of the First Amendment, he made clear that his priorities were moral, beginning his message by noting, "American homes are being bombarded with the largest volume of sex-oriented mail in history" and framing his proposals as "added protection from the kind of smut advertising now being mailed, unsolicited, into so many homes." Nixon's language repeatedly emphasized the home, presenting it as a fragile place of private family refuge under lurid assault from salacious smut peddlers—intended as a broader metaphor for how his silent majority felt in the face of the decade's social upheavals.[66]

Congress's failure to act on these suggestions gave Nixon more grist for his social-issues mill; in his 1970 annual message to Congress he mentioned the legislation and curtly added, "None of these bills has reached my desk for signature." Eager to capitalize on the porn issue, administration staffers recommended "very visible raids on the pornography shops" located in the "near vicinity of the White House" in order to "demonstrate an immediate concern on the part of the President," a suggestion carried out in the spring of 1970. Later that year, at a press conference in Denver, Nixon described porn as a "priority," demanding that Congress not "treat this as a business-as-usual matter." As he continued to complain that pornography legislation still awaited action, in yet another 1971 message to Congress he offered five bills "toward a more secure and decent society." They included new police powers and curbs on smut, which Nixon called "essential at a time when the tide of offensive materials seems yet to be rising."[67]

Nixon's most vitriolic comments came in response to the 1970 Commission on Obscenity and Pornography report. After his categorical rejection of the report's conclusions, Nixon professed, "So long as I am in the White House, there will be no relaxation" of antiporn efforts; in addition, smut should not simply be "contained at its present level," he declared; "it should be outlawed in every State." Because pornography contributed to "an atmosphere condoning anarchy in every field," it "would increase the threat to our social order as well as to our moral principles." In conclusion, Nixon warned, "American morality is not to be trifled with." This was strong language for a president who could claim no more substantive progress in his war against porn than he could in his war against Vietnam, and Nixon sent members of his administration out to reaffirm the message. Attorney General John Mitchell vowed to "seek strong measures to curb pornography," regardless of whether or not it held connections to antisocial behavior, while Postmaster General Winton Blount urged, "Let's Put the Smut Merchants Out of Business" in *Nation's Business*.[68]

Despite all of this rhetorical bombast, there can be no doubt the Nixon administration held little interest in actually eliminating pornography, which gave the president something to consistently rail against without much fear of political challenge. The administration kept the porn commission under close surveillance, relying on leaks from both Morton Hill and Charles Keating for access into its workings. Nixon advisers considered the possibility of "remov[ing] the offensive members" of the commission in June but decided that would constitute "bad politics." Instead, "letting the Commission run its course" would "create the issue which we can hammer home in strong moral tones by denouncing any proliferation of smut," knowing that a report "based on the behavioral sciences" would carry less traction in the press than these denunciations.[69]

When in September it briefly looked as if the commission might temper its free-speech conclusions because of negative public reaction, chief of staff and key strategist H. R. Haldeman wrote in a memo, "Obviously we don't want to let them do this—we want to develop the issue and we need to move hard to be sure that this is done." Controversy, not resolution, was the goal. To that end the administration relied on slush funds to help finance Charles Keating's outraged dissenting report, even lending staff member Patrick Buchanan for his ghostwriting skills. This literal underwriting of moralism was done outside the public eye but with a clear intent to upstage the measured tone of the commission report with an angry and misleading diatribe that would keep the issue alive. As adviser John Dean noted, the commission report "provides an excellent opportunity for the Administration to be very vocally placed on the right side of this issue." Nowhere in the flurry of internal administration memoranda was any concern for actually combating pornography on display, merely the pursuit of "excellent opportunity for exploitation of the pornography issue," as a later memorandum presented a 1973 Supreme Court obscenity decision.[70]

This, then, was New Right strategy in its purest form: the cultivation of new modes of outrage, as segregation and anticommunism became offal to fertilize the flowering new moralism. As such, the old discourse lent its tropes, as Henry Loeb, Strom Thurmond, and other southerners railed against a Supreme Court they had long protested, while Nixon, in attacking the commission report, accused pornographers of "deal[ing] a severe blow to the very freedom of expression they profess to serve." He might well have used the same words twenty years earlier to describe ACLU defenses of political dissent.

Very little substance came of any of this outrage, and it is doubtful whether any was ever actually intended. As we will see in chapter 5, the early 1970s represented the peak of pornography in American culture and an unprecedented level of freedom of expression. But in at least one regard Nixon effected substantive change: by overhauling the Warren Court. Though his attempts to place conservative southerners on the bench failed, Nixon managed to appoint four justices during his tenure, thus reshaping the Court. Harry Blackmun and Lewis Powell eventually turned out to be less conservative than anticipated, but Nixon's two major appointments proved more amenable to the New Right. William Rehnquist would ultimately ascend to the chief justiceship, commencing the most openly reactionary Court since the 1920s, but between 1969 and 1986 the position resided with Warren Burger, an appellate judge who replaced Earl Warren after the ill-fated Fortas fiasco. From the start Burger showed his dissatisfaction with the obscenity cases of the late 1960s. Dissenting from such a standard per curiam reversal in 1970, Burger argued, "We should not inflexibly deny to each of the States the power to adopt its own standards as to obscenity and pornographic materials," something he reiterated later that year.[71] This position found little favor in 1970, but as Nixon's appointments reshaped the Court, it would obtain more support, culminating in the 1973 decisions we will examine in the next chapter, decisions that dramatically altered the Court's approach to obscenity.

That support, however, was absent not only from the Court at the dawn of the 1970s but also from society as a whole. Though the tremendous rise of Citizens for Decent Literature in the 1960s showed significant public dissatisfaction with the ubiquity of pornography, no cultural consensus emerged on the topic. While the American Legion's magazine discussed the "Problems of Pornography" at great length in 1969, one measure of how seriously members took it came when two Legionnaires outside Washington, D.C., were arrested that year for possessing obscene materials with intention to exhibit them at a Legion party. *Christianity Today* declared, "Surely this is a time for the Church to be voicing a great outcry against pornography" in 1969; but it was correct in noting that "this is not happening." Indeed, even the Catholic *America* called Nixon's statement on the commission report "an election-campaign ploy" and suggested the response to the report showed the inabilities of many Americans "to cope with the complexities of the sexual evolution taking place in modern society." In the same issue, another article called the report "brave" and chided the dissenters, claiming "Keating's step backwards helps no one."[72]

As the 1960s ended, the New Right had its modus operandi in place and enough appeal to win the presidency. It had forcefully begun the process of displacing the political issues of race and social welfare that had maintained the New Deal's liberal cohesion with a new social politics of moralism. But it lacked both the commitment to follow through on its rhetoric of outrage and the voting base to demand such action. It would find both later in the 1970s with the politicization of evangelical Christians, but it would have to await their awakening by the social developments to which we now turn.

5. THE PERMISSIVE SOCIETY
Porno Chic and the Cultural Aftermath of the Sexual Revolution

ONE PHRASE THAT MEMBERS OF the burgeoning New Right commonly used was "the permissive society." It stood for everything they stood against, from sex to drugs to antiwar protesting. In its most exaggerated form, as seen in the conservative biologist Boris Sokoloff's 1971 book *The Permissive Society*, which described "extreme permissiveness, of an almost pathological nature," this construct existed mostly as a fantasy, outside the experiences of most Americans, who never participated in the orgies, drug binges, or revolutionary plotting of which Sokoloff wrote.[1] But for a brief period in the late 1960s and early 1970s the sexual revolution did bring a more moderate permissive society to life. Government commissions, courts, social scientists, and the general public alike reached a consensus that, if pornography might not be something to celebrate, it nonetheless posed no threat to the perpetuation of the republic, Charles Keating's rhetoric aside. This recognition occurred in the broader context of social changes whose political fallout would shape the politics of the next several decades, as endless retrenchment sought to roll back the progress unleashed in the tumult.

Even before the 1969 Supreme Court *Stanley* decision, which took the Court to the brink of legalizing obscenity, noticeable cultural shifts had indicated greater lenience for sexually explicit media. Competition from cheap exploitation films put pressure on Hollywood from the 1950s onward, and in 1965 *The Pawnbroker* managed to win the Production Code seal of approval despite including multiple scenes with bare female breasts. The scenes were somber and not erotic, even set in Holocaust concentration camps, but the precedent portended further testing of the code's boundaries. Three years later the code was dead, replaced by a new industry rating system that provided greater leeway for filmmakers. By 1968 male and female full-frontal nudity could be glimpsed in the Paramount release *Medium Cool*, and the X-rated *Midnight Cowboy* won the Best Picture Oscar for 1969.[2]

Outside of Hollywood a similar cultural trajectory ensued. "There's a Wave of Pornography/Obscenity/Sexual Expression," read the title of a

1966 *New York Times Magazine* article, pointedly illustrating the lack of semantic rigor clouding the topics. The article's author, Richard Gilman, showed little horror at the wave he covered; D. H. Lawrence "would have censored pornography," Gilman concluded, "and he was wrong." Instead, Gilman proposed, "let us be troubled or enthralled or dismayed or untouched by it, as each of us will." Increasingly, this laissez-faire approach came to dominate American culture. Especially after the Supreme Court began its *Redrup* reversals in 1967, obscenity charges became more difficult to sustain. Even the conservative Maryland Board of Censors reluctantly conceded the inexorability of permissiveness. In early 1967 it passed the softcore sexploitation film *The Love Cult* after deciding a ban "might not withstand court action"; by the end of that year it opened Maryland screens to the "first nudist film to have complete genital exposure." Even more explicit was the Swedish import film *I Am Curious (Yellow)*. Seized by customs as obscene in 1968, the $160,000 film nonetheless earned over $5 million in its first year of release, playing to endless crowds in cities such as New York, Seattle, Portland, Denver, Minneapolis, and Detroit.[3]

This cultural shift regarding sex-themed media transpired in the context of a broader evolution of social mores known as the sexual revolution. As the birth-control pill facilitated easy and reliable contraception and universities abandoned their traditional in loco parentis roles, sexual experimentation was normalized, both in the radical youth culture and beyond. Over the course of the 1960s the dominant trajectory of the youth culture itself shifted from a militant political stance, best exemplified by the New Left campus group Students for a Democratic Society, to a counterculture more defined by its proclivities for sex, drugs, rock music, and rhetorical support for revolution. The New Left leader Todd Gitlin marks a turning point in late 1966, using as an example a protest at which Berkeley antiwar protestors began singing the traditional labor hymn "Solidarity Forever." When few knew the words, the group instead launched into the Beatles' "Yellow Submarine."[4]

While the increasingly old-guard theoretical wing of the radical Left took issue with porn, which Baltimore's *Dragonseed* called "an illegitimate arm of rip-off capitalism," cultural visibility favored those who promoted it as an extension of the sexual revolution. Hippies, invested in the notion of "free love," often worked in pornographic films. Mary Rexroth, a teacher at Stanford and the daughter of the well-known poet Kenneth, appeared in several hardcore films and articulated the affinities between hippies and the pornographic ethos as a shared rebellion against what she called "the incredible amount of conditioning in this society about sex and what's right." Arlene Elster, an activist in the Sexual Freedom League, ran a porn theater in San Francisco as an extension of her sexual politics, and early erotic film festivals strove to create what Elena Gorfinkel calls "the utopian sexual public sphere" by combining expansive visions of pleasure with avant-garde aesthetics.[5]

Outside the countercultural vanguard, pornography would be viewed through neither a utopian nor an anticapitalist lens but rather as one component of an ever more sexualized cultural landscape. Several plays of the late 1960s, from *Hair* to *Che!*, featured nude actors and actresses. More significant than the plays was the media coverage of them. Though sometimes textually opposed to the "Sex Revolution," as *Time* called it in a July 1969 cover story, the media nonetheless presented explicit nudity with the graphic pictures that inevitably joined news articles in several periodicals. A March 1969 *Newsweek* article on "Sex and the Arts" featured a shot from the play *Faustus* in which a woman's bare breasts and backside were clearly visible. The next month, *Life* showed breasts and buttocks alongside a similar article, and the July *Time* story featured full-frontal nudity (with conspicuous shadows over the men's crotches but nothing obscuring a female cast member) from a production of *Hair*. Though a brief interview with Billy Graham, deploring the "dangers of sexuality," was tacked on to the article's end, a much lengthier symposium piece discussed "The Merits of Permissiveness." These articles brought the spectacle of New York City's off-Broadway underground into living rooms across the nation, normalizing and legitimizing the permissive society and pulling it into the cultural mainstream. Network television's increasing immersion in the sexual revolution also further primed the cultural pump for the arrival of "porno chic."[6]

Recognition of these trends extended to even less-likely sources. In Dallas the *Morning-News* waxed positive on the Supreme Court's *Stanley* decision to allow obscenity in the privacy of the home. Rejecting an analogy between pornography and "dope" or whiskey, the paper explained that "their harm is physical . . . [and] the justices pretty well had to rule as they did. Privacy covers a host of virtues as well as sins." Even the Catholic Church—already in retreat from the liberal heyday of its Vatican II reforms, as seen in the draconian anticontraceptive stance of the 1968 papal encyclical *Humanae Vitae*—implicitly acknowledged the new openness; in

1969 its Office of Motion Pictures gave three X-rated films the A-4 rating ("morally unobjectionable for adults, with reservations") and even bestowed a B rather than the prohibitive C on the also-X-rated *Baby Love*, despite the film's "wallow[ing] in all the currently popular screen deviations, from attempted rape to lesbianism, with plenty of nudity," as the *Catholic Film Newsletter* described it. None of this signified a substantive political revaluation of prurience as such, but it did permit a sometimes begrudging absorption of explicit sexuality into "normal" cultural discourse.[7]

With the culture thus disposed, the years between 1969 and 1973 broke new ground in free speech and sexual expression. Even after the turning point of the 1973 Supreme Court *Miller* decision consenting adults could, for the most part, openly produce and consume pornography. The cultural shifts of the sexual revolution made for a society more tolerant of sexual expression in the 1970s, but they proved difficult for liberal politicians to capitalize on, especially in the ongoing absence of a meaningful engagement with sexual rights beyond the cloak of abstracting principles like "privacy." Though pornography would attain a place of cultural centrality in the mid-1970s, it also took a distinct political backseat. Liberals continued to fear public association with porn, while conservatives lost sway with the cultural mainstream on a topic that had seemingly lost its threatening hues. As the permissive society spawned a brief cultural moment of "porno chic," the long-term effect was not continued liberalization but rather confirmation of the dire predictions of New Right naysayers. Soon a powerful backlash would shape the second incarnation of the New Right, which eagerly welcomed evangelical Christians horrified by the national culture of the 1970s. This chapter, then, details the cultural shifts of the 1970s that resisted immediate politicization along partisan contours, and chapter 6 reveals their gradual consequences in the emergence of the Christian Right.

Commissioning Permissiveness

Social and political movements resemble tectonic plate shifts in that seemingly sudden catastrophes actually reflect the net effect of long-term incremental change. Just as the Christian Right would emerge gradually from the perceived decadence of the late 1960s and early 1970s, the permissive society itself grew out of the groundwork laid by postwar liberalism. If a look at the inner workings of the Presidential Commission on Obscenity and

Pornography reveals the precise moment of the permissive society's emergence, an examination of its earlier legislative history reveals social plates shifting. Although the commission's report won mere scorn politically, it proved influential in other fields, from social science to jurisprudence.

Efforts to create a governmental commission on pornography dated back to 1960, when South Dakota senator Karl Mundt, an old-line conservative Republican, introduced a bill to create a Commission on Noxious and Obscene Matters. The combative nature of Mundt's proposed commission was apparent in its very title, and though his bill passed the Senate, it died without even coming to a vote in the House. Five years later Mundt tried again, with a very similar bill intended to create a commission whose first duty was "to explore methods of combating the traffic in obscene matters"; its subsequent five duties all revolved around "the suppression of such traffic." Again the House balked, and concern for civil liberties quickly led to the introduction of a counterpart bill by New Jersey Democrat Dominick Daniels. Instead of presupposing the harmful effects of pornography, the Daniels proposal bestowed four duties on its commission, neutrally renamed the Commission on Obscenity and Pornography: analyzing laws to devise definitions of obscenity and pornography; describing the porn market; studying the effects of pornography on the public, as well as its "relationship to crime and other antisocial behavior"; and recommending legislation to "regulate effectively the flow of such traffic, without in any way interfering with constitutional rights."[8]

At House hearings on the bill Citizens for Decent Literature–affiliated Iowa senator Jack Miller called for a "declaration of policy" for the proposed commission that called pornography "a menace to the moral fiber of the American people" and framed the body's mission as part of a "coordinated national effort to eliminate pornographic materials from our society." But Daniels rejected all such intrusions. Calling himself "disconcerted by the problems of pornography" as he brought the bill to a House vote, Daniels nonetheless asserted, "I will not allow myself to subvert the protections of the first amendment." The rhetoric proved effective, as the House promptly passed the bill. The Senate, cognizant of the futility surrounding efforts to further Mundt's conservative version, acquiesced and passed the legislation. A commission was born.[9]

In 1960, and again in 1965, the ACLU had opposed Mundt's bills, declaring itself in favor of a "properly-selected Commission . . . to make a scientific study" of possible causal relationships between pornography and antisocial behavior. Even when Daniels replaced Mundt's moral approach with a scientific one, the ACLU declined to support the commission; as ACLU representative Lawrence Speiser told Daniels's subcommittee, it was "unlikely that a scientific, that is, objective, study would be undertaken." The American Library Association joined the ACLU in protest, doubting that more than a veneer of social science would be adopted to shroud commission moralism. A headline in *Variety* seemed to confirm these trepidations: "Congress Okays Anti-Pornography Commission," it read. Nowhere was it acknowledged that Daniels's House bill represented a profound philosophical swerve from Mundt's Senate bill, moving Congress for the first time past preconceived notions on pornography such as those on display in the earlier Kefauver and Granahan committees of the 1950s and into the field of actual social science. This was the first time pornography would be addressed with resort to neither the abstracting lens of free speech nor the distorting one of morality.[10]

Even the liberal Johnson administration eyed the commission with suspicion. Before the Daniels bill passed, Lyndon Johnson's aide Jim Gaither predicted a commission, if established, "will probably attack the courts and might make proposals we can't live with on constitutional grounds." Nonetheless, presciently recognizing the political dangers to liberals—and the concomitant boon to Republican conservatives—Gaither warned that active opposition from the White House "would probably be read as pro-pornography." He advocated "stay[ing] out of this" and hoping the bill failed. Another aide proposed using the federal budget to "try quietly to kill" the commission, but inner-circle LBJ aide Ernest Goldstein warned against this, noting that it would limit the amount of actual research the commission could accomplish and pave the way for more ideological and moralistic results. "Congress has saddled us with the Commission," Goldstein lamented, but as long as the body existed, "we ought to avoid turning it into a political liability."[11]

Instead of trying to kill the commission, the Johnson administration attempted to shape it through tactical member selection. Of the seventeen members, most came from academia, representing fields such as law, sociology, and psychology. Atlanta magazine distributor Edward Elson was selected to represent publishing concerns. Johnson recognized the need for some measure of balance and sought out conservative participation as well. Though hundreds of letters recommending Charles Keating poured into the White House, some from governors, judges, and congressmen, Johnson conspicuously declined to appoint the CDL leader. In an internal White House memo, Johnson aide Goldstein informed the president, "The Department of Justice feels that having Mr. Keating on the Commission will be a mistake.... It is certainly my own view." Instead, Johnson chose Operation Yorkville (later Morality in Media) founder Morton Hill and Methodist minister Winfrey Link to ensure a conservative, religious presence on the commission. That Johnson overlooked the much more prominent Keating shows an interest in marginalizing antipornography sentiment; the less vociferous Hill and Link, it was accurately predicted, would prove less troublesome than Keating and less inclined to politicize the commission.[12]

Most important was the commission's chairman, William Lockhart. A University of Minnesota Law School dean and coauthor of the influential 1954 article that had helped shape the Supreme Court's 1957 *Roth* decision, Lockhart embodied perfectly the ambivalences of postwar liberalism. Militantly protective of free speech, Lockhart's canonical article "Literature, the Law of Obscenity, and the Constitution" was described by coauthor Robert McClure as an attempt "to provide some sort of constitutional protection against statutes purporting to regulate 'obscenity.'" But Lockhart and McClure, like their liberal peers, felt the most concern for sexually graphic works with recognized critical pedigrees, such as the novels of Henry Miller or D. H. Lawrence. Of hardcore pornography, they wrote in their 1960 follow-up article, it "is so foul and revolting that few people can contemplate the absence of laws against it—that would be unthinkable." In the wake of the commission's report its many critics would seize on Lockhart's ACLU membership as evidence of his bias, but none would ever acknowledge that such statements put Lockhart closer to moderate liberalism than free-speech absolutism or sex radicalism.[13]

Nonetheless, Lockhart's stance, as well as that of most commission members, clearly tilted toward an extensive embrace of free speech, and this attitude was reflected in the functioning of the commission. All four of the commission's panels (legal, traffic and distribution, effects, positive approaches) displayed some evidence of liberal predispositions even before the ostensibly neutral research got under way. As the legal panel took form in 1968, assisted by commission general counsel (and ACLU member) Paul Bender, its number-one research proposal ended with the question, "Does the fact that material is legally prohibited increase its attractiveness, its disturbing effect upon recipients or the likelihood [of] antisocial or detrimental conduct?" By shifting the burden of proof from pornography to obscenity laws themselves, the panel made clear the critical approach it would take. In the traffic and distribution panel, meanwhile, the contracted researcher John Sampson regularly exchanged friendly and chatty letters with porn distributors.[14]

The effects panel and its social science analysis, however, would prove most controversial, and here, too, some evidence of preconceptions exists. In a 1969 memorandum, for instance, staff member Weldon Johnson suggested commissioning a study on "The Loneliness of the Pornography User." The study, Johnson noted, would "have an academic appeal to a number of behavioral scientists" interested in then-fashionable topics such as alienation, marginalized men, and outsiders; it might also "function to underscore the positive social function" of porn, Johnson added.[15]

More significant than individual member bias, though, was the very existence of the effects panel, which sought to finally investigate the claims of pornography's causal effects on everything from rape to "sexual deviancy." Conservatives such as Morton Hill rejected the very social science framework in which the effects panel operated, preferring to look at porn's unquantifiable debasing effects on culture and civilization. To Hill the nature of a social-scientific approach insured libertarian conclusions, and in his dissent to the commission's July 1969 progress report to Congress Hill lamented that the body was "becoming an 'effects' commission, and this is not what Congress intended." The progress report contained a response to Hill's dissent, estimating the effects panel's budget as 40 percent of the entire commission budget and defensively noting this figure had already been reported to Congress at budgetary hearings. But the progress report, after dismissing Hill's proposal for public hearings as not being "a likely source of accurate data or a wise expenditure of its limited resources," went on to assure its congressional readers that Hill's dire predictions of libertarian results were "not a fair report as to our intent or future actions"; it was "premature" to predict conclusions at this point.[16]

This assurance pacified several legislators, who wrote letters of commendation to executive director W. Cody Wilson. It failed to note, however, that any survey of contemporary social science would indeed suggest a particular direction for the commission and would also explain Hill's resistance to an emphasis on effects. Two psychology professors and a law professor had explored the existing research on pornography in 1962 and found no empirical basis for obscenity laws. The authors leveled criticism at authorities who maintained the existence of links between pornography and ill effects. "While experts in behavior have every right to speak," they wrote, "they do disservice if they confuse personal theory with scientific fact." While repressive leaders such as J. Edgar Hoover continued to insist pornography was "one major cause of sex crimes, sexual aberrations and perversions" well into the late 1960s, such rhetoric was long-obsolete in sex-research circles. A research team from the Kinsey Institute directly refuted such claims in a 1965 monograph on sex offenders. "The possession of pornography does not differentiate sex offenders from nonsex offenders," the team forthrightly stated after extensive quantitative analysis. To clarify further, they added that possession of pornography should be interpreted to mean two—and only two—things: "the individual was probably a male of an age between puberty and senility," and "he probably derived pleasure from thinking about sex. No further inferences are warranted."[17]

This position reflected the social science consensus of the 1960s, and further research on pornography in the decade approached the topic from a physiological perspective, using it to ascertain sexual preferences and orientation; few claims were made for its effects beyond a team that that found more sea imagery and sex in young men's dreams after exposure.[18] In late 1969 the *Journal of Sex Research* reiterated the earlier 1962 assessment that no evidence linked pornography to any negative effects, and a symposium in the journal *Medical Aspects of Human Sexuality* found experts emphasizing the adverse impact of parents instilling shame and repression into children; pornography, explained one child psychiatrist, "has little or no influence on the attitude or behavior of the healthy child." As the presidential commission commenced its work in 1969, *School and Society* reported that 84 percent of psychiatrists and psychologists believed persons exposed to pornography were no more likely to engage in "antisocial sexual acts" than unexposed persons, and 86 percent of the profession believed "people who vigorously try to suppress pornography often are motivated by unresolved sexual problems in their own characters."[19]

Given these conditions, Hill was right to worry that an emphasis on social science portended conclusions at odds with his conservative stance. Social scientists contracted by the commission lost no time in applying their skeptical interrogations. By September 1969, for example, psychiatrist Marshall Katzman of St. Louis University had already reported that his experiments showed the definition of obscenity to vary so dramatically among different demographic groups that it was impossible to offer a consensus definition, making it a suspect legal term.[20] As commission chair, Lockhart sensed ideological opposition from the incoming Nixon administration to such lines of inquiry. When presidential assistant Robert Ellsworth wrote Lockhart in early 1969 asking for "all significant releases" and advance notices on "important events," Lockhart advocated a policy of stonewalling. "Let's not say anything to Ellsworth about the minutes," he wrote in a memo.[21]

Lockhart fervently defended the commission's objectivity. When a dissatisfied Hill and Link held their own privately funded hearings in early 1970 to spotlight "the other side" of the issue, a tight-lipped Lockhart told a reporter for the *Nation*, "There is no other side. . . . We are neutral." When the reluctant commission finally sponsored official hearings in May 1970, effects panelists sought to display objective, scientific detachment. One opportunity arose when a young (and underinformed) radical called the commission "McCarthyesque" before smashing a pie in sociologist Otto Larsen's face. Larsen surprised all by holding his temper and even grinning. "What he wanted was outrage," he later explained. "I've had classroom confrontations with militants before. I try to engage all kinds of people in serious dialogue. These people have something important to tell us." This recognition of validity even in countercultural extremism was intended to symbolize the commission's approach: instead of knee-jerk reaction, it took a measured analysis even of outrageous behavior.[22]

As such, the commission embodied the permissive society in its very demeanor. This embodiment was made even more manifest in its 1970 report. Beginning with the assertion that "discussions of obscenity and pornography in the past have often been devoid of facts," the report went on to call for the repeal of all laws pertaining to consenting adult consumption of pornography—a word the report studiously avoided because of its derogatory connotations ("erotic materials" and "sexually explicit materials" were often substituted).[23]

All four panels contributed to the report's central libertarian conclusion. The traffic and distribution panel noted that 75 percent of American males were exposed to pornography before the age of twenty-one and that the expansive porn market was driven largely by white, middle-class men, while the legal panel emphasized the futility of legislating morality for "consenting adults," a phrase it emphasized. The effects and positive approaches panels proved most ideological in their libertarianism. Noting that various social science surveys and experiments failed to show any causal evidence linking pornography to sex crimes or antisocial behavior, the effects panel even suggested exposure to pornography might benefit society; those with more exposure, it noted, "are more liberal or tolerant than those with less experience to other people's behavior." The positive approaches panel put quotation marks around the "problem" of pornography to highlight its artificiality; the problem, claimed the panel, stemmed from "the inability or reluctance of people in our society to be open and direct in dealing with sexual matters." The panel even verged on pathologizing members of groups such as Citizens for Decent Literature: "the fear of pornography felt by many people is a symptom of this confusion and ambivalence about sexuality." It suggested a "massive sex education effort be launched," based not on orthodoxy but on "a pluralism of values." As the report said, "The Commission believes that interest in sex is normal, healthy, good," and sex education could redirect this interest away from pornography and toward healthy, fulfilling relationships.[24]

These recommendations clearly deserved the label "permissive." They were far more liberal in their attitude toward pornography and sex than were the positions of Hill, Link, or Charles Keating. The commission report, however, avoided radicalism, rejecting free-speech absolutism. The concept of "consenting adults" lay at the heart of the report's policy recommendations. Hence the commission supported laws shielding minors from pornography; though it made no case that children needed such protection, it framed this proposal in terms of parental rights to decide on children's access to such material. "Consent" was as significant as "adult," and the commission also supported laws regulating public exhibition of sexually explicit material and prohibiting unsolicited mailings. These recommendations actually put the final commission report at the center of its own spectrum of opinion. Twelve of the seventeen members signed on to the final report. South Dakota School of Mines and Technology professor Cathryn Spelts and California attorney general Thomas Lynch joined the three dissenters but without concurring in their written dissents or offering written reasons for their own dissent. Meanwhile, two members offered a concurrence that went beyond the commission. Otto Larsen and Marvin Wolfgang wrote that they would repeal *all* laws, even those for children, on the grounds that no logical reason existed to justify such laws.[25]

If the faith in reason and empiricism invoked deeply entrenched liberal values, so too did the report perpetuate the liberal tradition of depoliticizing sexuality. In calling for sex education, the commission claimed this "would provide a sound foundation for our society's basic institutions of marriage and family," thus taking these social institutions as axiomatic rather than worthy of analytical inquiry. As well, the firmly established demographic profile of the average porn consumer as male resulted in virtually no gender analysis whatsoever by the many social scientists under contract with the commission, who seemed to take for granted the naturalness of this fact. Even the notion of "consenting adults," later scrutinized by feminists for its abstraction of often unequal power relations into an imagined vacuum, was simply presented as a self-evident and unproblematic category. While liberalism had moved beyond its cold war complicity in repression, it still swerved away from a meaningful engagement with its own sexual politics, tacitly endorsing a more subtle disciplining of sexuality through unquestioned notions of normalcy.[26]

In the firestorm of controversy that engulfed the commission's report, observers rarely noted that the report was far from an isolated indication of social permissiveness. As reported in a 1969 newspaper article, obscenity arrests in California were "so few as to be almost nonexistent," and of forty-eight statewide convictions in 1968, all but nine of those found guilty were merely put on probation. Even the American Medical Association Council on Mental Health issued a statement in June 1970 declaring a "lack of scientific knowledge which can lend real support to any argument on this topic." Because the default condition of the null hypothesis in any test of statistical significance is one of skepticism, this amounted to a reluctant concurrence, though the AMA council was quick to add that pornography had "not enhanced personal psychological development, inter-personal relations, or adaptive personality skills."[27]

Other commissions joined the Presidential Commission. In New Jersey the Commission to Study Obscenity and Depravity in Public Media issued a report in May 1970, several months before the Presidential Commission. It perfectly anticipated the later report, describing state obscenity laws as "obsolete . . . based on certain unexplained assumptions as to the 'depraving and corrupting' effect" of pornography. Calling the legal concept of obscenity "mischievous" for falsely implying standards "which can scarcely fall within the legitimate province of criminal legislation," the New Jersey commission made the same recommendations as the better-known subsequent report, calling for the repeal of all obscenity laws affecting willing adult consumers. In San Francisco a 1971 Committee on Crime also agreed, noting that "little has been accomplished by the effort to put down pornography by means of the criminal law." The committee called for legalization of obscenity for consenting adults, along with decriminalization of homosexuality and prostitution.[28]

Such recommendations occasionally shaped legislation. In 1970 a federal district court in Oregon struck down the state's obscenity law, citing recent Supreme Court decisions to declare that "a new doctrine of First Amendment protection has evolved." The court ruled that the mere fact of a work's obscenity, "or that it offends either the self-elected or self-appointed guardians of the public morality, no longer justifies suppression by the government." Instead, the circumstances of distribution were read as determinative of obscenity; so long as obscene material was concealed from children and uninterested adults, the court ruled that a truly free market was permissible. Rather than issuing sanctimonious rebukes to the court, the Oregon State Legislature ratified the decision with new legislation placing no prohibitions on selling or distributing obscenity to consenting adults when it convened for its 1971 session.[29]

The commission's major effect, though, was in shaping social science research, as the commission's efforts formed the centerpiece of investigation into pornography's effects in the early 1970s. The September 1970 report contained only summaries of most panel research in its seven hundred pages, but the expansive ten-volume *Technical Report* published in 1971 gave the full version of each project. Several researchers examined imprisoned sex offenders, concluding that pornography was not to blame for their crimes. One group found "very repressive family background" and "fear of sex" to be the major correlates of rapists. Surveys of prisoners in Wisconsin revealed "less frequent and milder exposure" to pornography among sex offenders than the control group; the general consensus of these studies was that seeing and enjoying pornography at a young age was, if anything, an indicator of normalcy rather than deviance. Other research projects looked at legalization of pornography in Denmark, associating it with lowered rates of sex crime, and the responses of college males to repeated exposure, which showed only boredom as a result. In a stinging rebuke to the authority figures who had promoted a link between pornography and juvenile delinquency since the 1950s Kefauver hearings, a research team examining a random sample of 436 juvenile court case records found "absolutely no mention of pornography or erotica in any of the materials." As they emphasized, this did not necessarily disprove a connection, but it certainly undermined claims that actual police officers took the causal role of pornography seriously, since none even mentioned the topic in their reports. Taken as a whole, the *Technical Report* allowed no doubt of a social science consensus that rejected the ominous prognostications of antiporn activists as unfounded.[30]

Social scientists funded by commission contracts continued to dominate the scholarly discourse on pornography for most of the 1970s. Sociologists Louis Zurcher and R. George Kirkpatrick, for instance, expanded their commission research into the 1976 monograph *Citizens for Decency*, which placed antiporn activists into a theoretical framework equating them with earlier temperance crusaders. In both cases "status politics" generated resistance to social changes that threatened to expose or revoke the "over-rewarded status inconsistency" of those people who held social power but felt an underlying sense of unworthiness. Because the structural sources of social change were diffuse, abstract, and difficult to directly resist, "symbolic crusades" resulted against indicators of the changes already under way. Zurcher's and Kirkpatrick's analysis reflected the critical lens through which their contemporaries viewed antiporn activists, and *Contemporary Sociology* called the book "a model of social science research reportage."[31]

Even as the commission report was widely rejected by politicians, its conclusions infiltrated the cultural mainstream. The magazine *Good Housekeeping* provides a vivid example. In 1961 it had called pornography "the poison that preys on our children." By the early 1970s that stance had shifted dramatically. A 1970 "true/false" test posed "Pornography leads to sex crimes" and the suggestion that children found reading pornography should have it taken away without discussion. Both were presented as false. On the former point the magazine cited commission researchers (without mentioning their commission affiliation), and on the latter it suggested "us[ing] the incident as a way of opening discussion" on sex. When a 1972 first-person article described a mother's "horror and disbelief" at finding her thirteen-year-old son's secret pornography stash, it also included her husband's reaction: "You know, dear, wanting to find out about sex is a perfectly normal thing for a youngster. . . . I don't think any boy grows up without seeing or reading something we'd call pornographic." After discussion, the mother agreed, and she concluded, "If his questions aren't answered, or if sex is made out to be something terribly mysterious or 'dirty,' he is going to be even more curious" and thus seek out pornography to explain things. This agreed precisely with the commission's positive approaches panel.[32]

The federal courts paralleled social scientists in their attitudes, veering strikingly toward endorsement of an unregulated marketplace of ideas as they frequently rejected the legal bases of obscenity charges. One major contribution to this movement came from Massachusetts federal judge Bailey Aldrich, who expanded *Stanley*'s protections in a later 1969 case. Whereas the Supreme Court had protected private possession of obscenity in an individual's home, the question posed by Aldrich was, "How far does *Stanley* go?" In the judge's view it extended to adult cinemas that neither pandered in their advertisements nor allowed children in. "If a rich Stanley can view a film, or read a book, in his home," Aldrich mused, "a poorer Stanley should be free to visit a protected theatre or library." In this new reading, "*Roth* remains intact only with respect to public distribution," and as long as that distribution met the consenting adults criterion, anything was allowed.[33]

A plethora of like-minded decisions followed, exonerating defendants of obscenity charges even when it was conceded that the material in question met the legal standards of obscenity. In New York a federal court issued an injunction against customs officials, barring them from confiscating obscene material imported for private use in 1970. That same year a federal appellate court also ruled in favor of a defendant who had sent obscene films through the mails in his correspondence with a group of self-declared swingers, placing personal communications under the provisions of *Stanley*'s "privacy" rather than seeing them as public distribution. The court wrote, "If the only reason for a prosecution is to protect an adult against his own moral standards which do harm to no one else, it cannot be tolerated."[34]

Even as adult material grew increasingly graphic around the turn of the decade, courts continued to defend adult distribution and consumption. When a Minneapolis theater showing the highly graphic documentary *Sexual Freedom in Denmark* was charged with obscenity in 1970, a federal court ruled in favor of the theater on the basis of its exhibition policies (which restricted admission to adults), not even considering the film's sexual content. After customs officials in New York seized the Swedish film *Language of Love*, also depicting "actual insertion," a federal appellate court nonetheless ruled in favor of the film. Perhaps the furthest extension of this libertarian attitude came from a federal district court in Philadelphia, which in 1971 exonerated a man who sold books with hardcore photographs through the mails. Though the court acknowledged that Ronald Stewart had sent unsolicited advertisements for his merchandise, it cited the notice that appeared on his envelopes warning recipients of sexual content as a "great precaution to protect those who might be offended," and thus evidence that Stewart was innocent of pandering.[35]

The Supreme Court initially did fairly little to check these judicial tendencies. With Potter Stewart as the swing vote, the Court in 1971 favored government suppression in only two cases. One prevented importation of obscene material for commercial purposes (Stewart's concurrence explicitly noted the decision did not apply to material for personal use), and the other scaled back the federal courts' extension of *Stanley* by ruling that the right to own obscenity did not include the right to sell or deliver it. That year the Court also deadlocked 4–4 over the Maryland Board of Censors' ban of *I Am Curious (Yellow)*, thus leaving the ban intact, but only because William Douglas—who would have certainly cast the deciding vote to overturn—recused himself because of his ties with the distributor, Grove Press. No written decision resulted, and the case clearly set no precedent. For the most part the Court continued its *Redrup* trajectory of overturning obscenity convictions without written decisions. Thus cases involving magazines and films from Michigan, South Carolina, and Washington were reversed in 1971 and 1972. A war protestor from California convicted of obscenity for wearing a jacket that read "Fuck the Draft" was exonerated, as was a Wisconsin underground paper with nude pictures and a "sex poem." A film described by the Missouri Supreme Court as including "scenes of nude women including close-ups of naked breasts" also won predictable reversal by the justices.[36]

From the 1969 *Stanley* decision to 1973, then, free expression in the sexual realm went largely unregulated as long as the material in question circulated only among consenting adults. Spearheaded by the presidential commission, a virtual movement among social scientists agreed that this hurt no one, thus finally putting the imprimatur of the expert in direct contrast to the dire warnings of such figures as Estes Kefauver and J. Edgar Hoover. These attitudes were often codified into law by federal judges uncompelled to regulate adult morality. Though New Right politicians had already recognized the capacity for coalition-building through moralism, that emerging bloc vote took a backseat to a more urbane social tolerance of sexual expression in the early 1970s.

The Emergence of Porno Chic

Neither the courts nor the commissions showed much visible awareness of the changing American erotica market, but by the early 1970s an indisputable shift had occurred, as dramatically more explicit material rose to prominence. Hardcore pornography—graphic depictions of actual sex acts—apparently infiltrated the photographic mail-order market first, and its onset can be dated with reasonable specificity to 1968; though underground hardcore material had circulated since the advent of photography, that year marked an unprecedented public surfacing of the material.[37] From there it moved quickly into the cinematic sphere, with surprising results: instead of a backlash, the public embraced hardcore, and for a brief moment it earned a sudden cultural legitimacy. The backlash would arrive by the end of the decade, but until then pornography achieved its greatest cultural acceptance at precisely the moment it reached its greatest level of explicitness.

The changing market can be mapped by comparing two works published by Collector's Publications, based in Southern California. *My Name Is Bonnie*, a fifty-page booklet stapled magazine-style, contained pictures of a single young woman in what were called "split beaver shots"—full nudity with an emphasis on splayed genitalia. That work came out in July 1968 and sold for $10. By the end of the year Collector's Publications offered the book-length *Intercourse*, with hardcore shots of an ostensibly married couple having sex. The book justified its explicitness in its introduction: "At first glance you may be shocked," it explained, but "this book cannot be construed as anything else but a marital manual." It offered the "stipulation" that qualified experts had "long known the tremendous value of pictures as a basis for training." This explanation bestowed a nominal measure of redeeming social value on the book in the hopes of avoiding obscenity charges, but *Intercourse*'s $4.95 price tag was more revealing; for prices to drop by half despite increased explicitness and classier binding than *Bonnie* clearly indicated a market glut.[38]

One common thread uniting such works was a belabored attempt to frame them as something more than mere prurient entertainment. The "historical study" *Sex, Censorship and Pornography* offered a seven-page discussion of obscenity law since *Roth* before launching into its hardcore photos. As mail-order films joined the hardcore movement, a 1970 solicitation by Los Angeles distributor Dale Armstrong exemplified this self-justification (Figure 9). Armstrong described his 8-mm films as marital

FIGURE 9. A truly thin veneer of socially redeeming value is all that seemed necessary in 1970. Dale Armstrong mailing (1970). H. Lynn Womack Papers, box 2, folder 70, Human Sexuality Collection, Cornell University.

aids, "FOR EDUCATIONAL PURPOSES ONLY," but quickly added, "Naturally, the genitalia is fully visible." Each reel received its own dubious redemptive aspect. For instance, *Maiden Voyage*: "THEME: Watch a virgin being introduced to sexual intercourse. SOCIALLY REDEEMING VALUE: How to initiate an inexperienced girl into the joys of love-making"; *Scandinavian Extravaganza*: "THEME: Watch far-out technique in action, as used by swinging Swedish couples. SOCIALLY REDEEMING VALUE: Learn how Scandinavians make love. Improve your marital knowledge with what's latest in Europe." This social value was transparently flimsy but enough to protect Armstrong in the generally relaxed legal atmosphere of 1970.[39]

This hardcore revolution went beyond mail order, though. By 1967 peep-show booths in New York City had begun running various permutations of the "beaver" film, featuring solo women. As peep-show magnate Martin Hodas told the *New York Times* in 1969, "As long as there's no auto-erotica or sexual contact, it's all right." By the end of that year, Hodas's claim would seem quaint. Andy Warhol's *Fuck* played in San Francisco and New York City and was described by one reporter as "the first full-length film which includes an instance of clear, plain, unmistakable sexual intercourse." The film—legitimized to some extent by Warhol's avant-garde art-world credentials—played in art-house theaters to audiences "with jackets and ties." It portended immediately imminent trends in less reputable locales, though, as small storefront theaters began to open for the express purpose of screening pornography. The cultural drift of the permissive society and the libertarian nature of the judicial realm clearly structured this development, although as film historian Eric Schaefer notes, the technological emergence of 16-mm film as a mode of theatrical exhibition also played a significant role by lowering the market's cost of entry for entrepreneurial pornographers and exhibitors.[40]

Uncertainty marked the emergence of hardcore films into the public sphere. Leading adult film producers had formed the Adult Film Association of America in 1969, and when the body met in April 1970, it held a discussion on self-regulation. When a vote was held, a motion for self-regulation lost, but only by a tight 6–5 vote. Clearly, profit motives inspired further risk-taking. Like the mail-order companies, the hardcore pioneers shrouded their films in purported social value, framing them as documentaries or marital helpers along the lines of recent popular books by Masters and Johnson. *Sexual Freedom in Denmark*, one of the earliest publically screened films to feature hardcore sex scenes, spent an entire hour examining the sexual sociology of its titular nation, venereal disease, and other tangents before finally depicting an attractive man and woman having sex in various positions for its final "informative" reel. The pseudoscientific hardcore marital aid film *Man and Wife* also screened widely, offering graphic sex in the guise of instruction and education.[41]

A Kansas City judge declared of *Man and Wife* that the "only person it possibly could appeal to is someone with a warped mind." If so, America's mind warped collectively because by mid-1970 hardcore features had permeated several major cities, and not even periodic police raids could stop their spread. The *San Francisco Chronicle* announced "The Pornography Film Boom in S.F.," but not only cities renowned for their decadence housed storefront adult theaters and hardcore pornography. Cincinnati had only one adult bookstore in 1969 but seven the next year; by early 1971 *Man and Wife* had reached the Citizens for Decent Literature birthplace, though not without attracting the vice squad. In North Carolina the city of Durham itself owned a theater described in 1970 as playing "X-type product exclusively." By 1973 even Dodgeville, Iowa (pop. twenty), had a tavern that doubled as a hardcore theater certain nights; indeed, early that year the *New York Times* was able to find plenty of material for a lengthy story on pornography in the Midwest. Meanwhile, although the staunchly conservative Maryland Board of Censors rejected peep-show loops *Harem Orgy* and *Gang Bang Pt. 2* in early 1973, it did allow both *Porno #69* and its numerically insistent sequel, *Porno #69, Part 2*.[42]

Variety regularly reviewed hardcore features in the early 1970s, generally offering lukewarm capsules devoid of either outrage or enthusiasm for such films as *Pornography in Denmark*, *Black Is Beautiful*, and the gay landmark *Boys in the Sand*. The industry magazine showed how lucrative hardcore films were; *Pornography in Denmark* was described as "the highest weekly grosser in San Francisco for the past seven weeks" in April 1970, and the producers of *Black Is Beautiful* purchased a full-page ad that same month to announce their "fascinating scientific study" that showed "the strange and erotic practices which made the Modern Black Man the happiest, best adjusted of all humans." Such advertising also served to legitimize the porn industry through frank public announcement of its presence.[43]

As hardcore porn institutionalized itself across the nation, it acquired a certain newfound respectability, or at least recognition. While *New York Times* film critic Vincent Canby sang "The Blue Movie Blues" in 1970 after a tour of several local theaters, he was distraught not by the explicitness of adult movies but by their "complete lack of humor," a quality shared with "the people who would put them out of business." Two years later film critic Arthur Knight credited the hardcore film *School Girl* with "an eroticism all too rare in American films," while the *Wall Street Journal* ran "A Kind Word or Two About Smut," calling for decriminalization of obscenity and asking, "Why can't we all just mind our own business?"[44]

Several early hardcore films revolved around female lead characters. In *Mona* (1970), often regarded as the first narrative hardcore feature, the title character, played by Fifi Watson, fends off her fiancé's sexual advances but offers to "do that other thing to you," sating his needs with oral sex. The film situated itself in the generational shifts of the sexual revolution, as Mona's mother reminds her, "I was a virgin when I married your father, and he's the only man I ever went to bed with." For Mona sex will not be so simple, and she roams the streets in search of men to fellate as she explores her sexuality, negotiating her accession to retrograde notions of marital "purity" with her own desire to experiment. The film's sexual politics veer inconsistently from an emphasis on female agency (Mona tells one pickup who wants penetrative sex, "I call the shots. I blow you, and that's it, understand?") to the misogynistic conclusion, in which Mona's fiancé discovers her adventures, ties her up, and invites her other partners over for what is presented as an orgy but effectively constitutes a gang rape. Still, the centrality of narrative and the presence of a female star helped legitimize hardcore; the *San Francisco Chronicle* called 1970 "the year when women began going to stag films in great numbers," suggesting a shift in the cultural position of pornography.[45]

That trajectory, once set in motion, culminated in the breakout success of *Deep Throat* in 1973. Shot in Miami and released in late 1972, the film again featured a female lead, Linda Lovelace, ostensibly playing herself. Like *Mona*, *Deep Throat* problematized female sexuality and pleasure, with Linda beginning the film complaining to her best friend that her active sex life leaves her disappointed. "It makes me feel sort of tingly all over," she explains, "and then, nothing." Linda demands more from sex, wanting "bells ringing, dams bursting, bombs going off," to which her friend quips,

"Do you want to get off, or do you want to destroy a city?" A trip to the doctor reveals that Linda suffers from a misplaced clitoris residing in her throat; fortunately for her, the "deep throat" fellatio technique can deliver her belated bells and bombs, and the rest of the film showcases Linda's unleashed talents and her newfound pleasure. As with *Mona*, a surface concern for women's sexuality is belied by the film's rendering it a corollary of male pleasure through oral sex. However glibly, though, the film does again engage with the changing sexual politics of its time, an approach that clearly resonated with the public as *Deep Throat* became an unexpected hit, the accidental catalyst in pornography's cultural transformation from back-alley shame to middle-class phenomenon.[46]

By early 1973 *Deep Throat* had become a cultural *cause célèbre*, capitalizing on its relative verbal and visual wit (at Linda's first climax, director Gerard Damiano shows bells ringing and dams bursting) to embody the newly "liberated" mores inspired by the sexual revolution. Couples attended it in droves, and celebrities did too: media coverage listed Johnny Carson, Jack Nicholson, Sandy Denny, and Truman Capote in attendance, among numerous others. Critics reviewed it everywhere, from the *New York Times* to *Vogue*. Even sociologist Herbert Gans joined the discussion, weighing in on the film in *Social Policy*. Linda Lovelace suddenly became a household name, and the film's title permanently entered the vernacular. As if in revenge for his moralism, the film even lent its title as a pseudonym for the then-secret informant who brought down President Nixon's illegal political tactics and toppled his administration.[47]

The popularity of *Deep Throat* ushered in the new phenomenon of "porno chic." Both the *New York Times Magazine* and *Playboy* devoted lengthy articles to the topic, persuasively arguing that the middle-class fad reflected the changes in sexual mores wrought by the sexual revolution of the 1960s. Attending porn films became a way to display hip sexual sophistication, to declare that one wasn't plagued by "hang-ups." Other hardcore films also drew massive audiences in 1973; *Behind the Green Door* featured former Ivory Snow model Marilyn Chambers in a kidnapping fantasy, while *The Devil in Miss Jones* brought darker, existentialist aesthetics to the porn field. *Film Comment* devoted an issue to cinematic sex, while the prestigious New School for Social Research offered a course called "Pornography Uncovered, Erotica Exposed," featuring a guest appearance by Chambers. Porno chic met continued resistance from prosecutors, but police action alone could not curtail it; by the time a San Bernardino police officer left a theater with a confiscated print of *The Devil in Miss Jones* in late 1973, a new print was already entering the theater. As *Newsweek* concluded, obscenity prosecutions failed to address the basic fact that Americans "seem to want" pornography "just as they wanted alcoholic beverages during prohibition."[48]

Some Americans even romanticized pornographers just as earlier generations had bootleggers. "If their dreams are meretricious, why, then, so were Gatsby's," wrote the Didionesque journalist Carolyn See in her 1974 paean to the industry, *Blue Money*. "I would like to think," she continued, "because I like them all, that they do no more than give America what it wants. They take a tidy profit, but so do the men who make cornflakes." Sometimes this approval clouded See's judgment, as when she wrote glowingly of Linda Lovelace and Lovelace's manager-husband, Chuck Traynor, "I think they might really be in love," despite describing his extremely controlling behavior. Later revelations would show Traynor's violent, abusive side. Kenneth Turan and Stephen Zito also depicted the porn industry favorably in their 1974 book *Sinema*, portraying the filmmakers and stars in positive terms. For instance, they described the actor John C. Holmes as "very candid and well-adjusted . . . a very moral person." He would go on to heavy drug abuse, statutory rape, and the concealment of his contraction of HIV while still working (without condoms) in sex films in the 1980s. If such books were complicit in covering the seedier sides of pornography, from drugs to abuse to mafia involvement, these were aspects the moviegoing public also clearly preferred to overlook.[49]

The Detumescent Repressive Apparatus

As porn underwent its cultural mainstreaming, conservative moralism seemingly lost traction. House Minority Leader Gerald Ford attempted to repeat the Fortas fiasco in late 1969 and 1970 by singling out Supreme Court justice William Douglas for "writing signed articles for notorious publications of a convicted pornographer" (referring to Ralph Ginzburg). Ford even imagined that the title of the *Evergreen Review*, another countercultural publication to which Douglas had contributed, might have some "secret erotic significance" because "otherwise it may be the only clean word in the publication." Not even throwing in allegations of Douglas's unsavory underworld gambling connections could make the charges look like anything but blatant political opportunism, and Ford's moralistic gambit backfired, as no notable anti-Douglas campaign coalesced and the increasingly leftist justice remained on the bench.[50]

Ironically, just as the permissive society reached its apex, the New Right's judicial investments paid off. As president, Richard Nixon had the opportunity to appoint four Supreme Court justices, reshaping the entire philosophy of the Court from Warren-era liberalism to a new conservative demeanor.[51] New members Lewis Powell, Harry Blackmun, William Rehnquist, and Chief Justice Warren Burger had little immediate effect on the obscenity debate, but in one fell swoop, a series of decisions handed down on June 21, 1973, they suddenly reversed the Court's judicial trajectory. The new obscenity doctrine of the Burger Court carried great consequences in the abstract, as it created a far more prosecution-friendly legal environment than the Warren Court had allowed, but at least in the 1970s its tangible effects were fairly minimal, as obscenity cases declined in importance.

Four of the 1973 cases were minor but notable for the new attitude they displayed. In *U.S. v. Orito* a new five-vote majority, consisting of the Nixon quartet plus Byron White, extended the scope of customs jurisdiction to include material slated for private use, a distinct step beyond the Court's recent 1971 decision limiting such jurisdiction to material intended for commercial distribution. Another decision along the same lines ruled that federal obscenity laws covered interstate transportation of obscene matter without regard for distinctions between public and private use, a step back in terms of freedom from the prevailing judicial framework. In a third case, *Paris Adult Theatre I v. Slaton*, the Court "categorically disapprove[d]" the theory that obscene matter was protected when it was exhibited for consenting adults only. Burger's opinion disregarded the ten volumes of studies published by the Commission on Obscenity and Pornography to instead cite Hill, Link, and Keating's dissenting reports, which "indicate that there is at least an arguable correlation between obscene material and crime." Though Burger conceded the lack of "conclusive proof" supporting such a conclusion, he warned that sex could be "debased and distorted by crass commercial exploitation."[52]

Burger took this moral argument to its furthest extent in *Kaplan v. California*, which involved a conviction based on the book *Suite 69*, a book that "has a plain cover and contains no picture." The Burger Court held that the book's extensive verbal descriptions of sex constituted legitimate grounds for an obscenity conviction and that states could "reasonably regard" the book as "capable of encouraging or causing antisocial behavior, especially in its impact on young people." This emphasis on youth disregarded the child-protective variable-obscenity framework already established by the 1968 *Ginsberg* decision, as well as Felix Frankfurter's 1957 comment about "burning the house to roast the pig," describing Michigan's law prohibiting material for adults in order to protect children.[53]

None of these decisions went uncontested, all butting against solid four-justice opposition from Douglas, Marshall, Stewart, and Brennan. As the architect of the Warren Court's obscenity doctrine, Brennan had written most of the important opinions of the previous fifteen years, navigating through his ambivalence to attempt a synthesis of expansive free-speech protection and reasonable obscenity law. Confrontation with the Burger majority radicalized Brennan, especially after Burger circulated a memorandum suggesting "a little 'chill' will do some of the 'pornos' no great harm and it might be good for the country." Angered by the moral rather than juridical foundation of the new decisions, Brennan joined Douglas and the now-retired Hugo Black in free-speech absolutism, renouncing his previous *Roth* and *Memoirs* tests in a long, fiery dissent on *Paris Adult Theatres I*. Even Burger's Nixon-appointed colleagues showed some doubts about the Court's new direction; Lewis Powell was initially poised to vote with the liberals until his first-time exposure to pornography (actually, the softcore Russ Meyer film *Vixen*) left him "shocked and disgusted."[54]

In the most important 1973 case, *Miller v. California*, the Burger Court laid out its new obscenity standards. Gone was the *Memoirs* "utterly without redeeming social value" test, explicitly rejected as "a burden virtually impossible to discharge under our criminal standards of proof." Gone, too, was *Roth*'s protection of all works with "the slightest redeeming social importance." In its place stood a new barometer: "whether the work, taken as a whole, lacks serious literary, artistic, political, or scientific value." No longer would a single quantum of value protect a work. Retrenchment went even deeper, reaching the national community standards established by Brennan in 1964's *Jacobellis* decision. Calling this approach "an exercise in futility," Burger instead allowed states to define the communities that would judge "contemporary community standards." "It is neither realistic nor constitutionally sound," Burger added, "to read the First Amendment as requiring that the people of Maine or Mississippi accept public depiction of conduct found tolerable in Las Vegas, or New York City." The chief justice would have gone further, abandoning the "taken as a whole" clause and thus returning obscenity law to the pre-*Ulysses* days of the 1868 *Hicklin* test, but Blackmun withheld his decisive fifth vote until Burger agreed to retain the standard.[55]

The *Miller* decision was greeted with predictable enthusiasm by prosecutors and antiporn activists. The press described the "delighted" reactions of state attorneys and police officers from Florida to Rhode Island, while Charles Keating wrote an essay calling *Miller* a "green light to combat smut." In the *New York Times* an equally predictable collection of essays by civil libertarians and Hollywood figures protested the decision for having a chilling effect on expression. Filmmakers, including the mainstream Hollywood director Paul Mazursky, the radical black independent director Melvin Van Peebles, and *Deep Throat* auteur Gerard Damiano voiced dissent, as did the actresses Joan Crawford and Shelley Winters. More important than media discussion of *Miller*, though, were its repressive legal effects.[56]

First indications suggested both celebrants and critics were right and that the Court had opened the door for a massive crackdown. In New Orleans the city attorney began padlocking adult theaters within the week after *Miller* was announced. City police in Charlottesville, Virginia, raided two local bookstores with "adults only" sections the same week. Elsewhere in Virginia the city attorney of Hopewell issued a letter to local news dealers threatening, "I will not tolerate" material that he decided had become obscene, including even such mainstream mainstays as *Playboy*. Hugh Hefner's long-running publication also appeared on a similar list sent out by the mayor of Shelbyville, Kentucky, that cited *Miller* and warned, if the magazines were not removed from stands, "Headlines will have to be made."[57]

Not even Hollywood was safe from the deployment of local standards. United Artists' X-rated *Last Tango in Paris* was charged as obscene in Cincinnati immediately after *Miller*, and Warner Brothers found its box-office hit *The Exorcist* in similar straits in Jackson, Mississippi, later in the year. A Georgia man was convicted on obscenity charges for showing the R-rated *Carnal Knowledge*, a conviction upheld by the state's Supreme Court. And the chilling effect feared by *Miller*'s film-industry critics manifested itself promptly, as a planned cinematic adaptation of Hubert Selby's controversial novel *Last Exit to Brooklyn* was dropped. Its producer explained, "We don't want to produce lawsuits, we want to produce pictures."[58]

As a new era of repression appeared to dawn, however, resistance emerged from diverse origins. In Charlottesville a "predominantly middle-aged" grand jury with housewives, a farmer, a real estate broker, and a school board member refused to return an indictment on the two bookstore owners. Federal judges offered an injunction against Jackson officials and a summary judgment against Cincinnati prosecutors. Most important, in 1974 the steely eyed Burger Court blinked, unanimously reversing the conviction of Billy Jenkins, the Georgia man convicted for screening *Carnal Knowledge*.[59]

A concurring Justice Brennan used the case as an opportunity to declare the failure of *Miller*. The majority lead opinion—signed by the same five justices who decided *Miller* and written by William Rehnquist—rejected Brennan's sweeping analysis yet also tacitly balked at *Miller's* wide-ranging implications. Rehnquist scaled back the provisions of *Miller* by qualifying its emphasis on community standards. The Georgia Supreme Court had, in his opinion, improperly applied the law by giving the jury too much autonomy. Through what must have been clenched lips, the Court's most conservative justice declared it a "serious misreading" of *Miller* to "conclude that juries have unbridled discretion in determining what is 'patently offensive.'" Though *Carnal Knowledge* contained several nude scenes, "nudity alone is not enough to make material legally obscene"; only "ultimate sex acts" met the standard. The Burger Court thus made clear its intent to prevent the new *Miller* standards from becoming a Pandora's box unleashing wildly divergent local standards.[60]

The *Jenkins* decision signaled the Court's reluctance to withhold extensive First Amendment protection from anything but hardcore pornography. But even convictions on hardcore material proved elusive in the mid-1970s, and many prosecutors began to view obscenity cases as wasted efforts. By late 1974 the *New York Times* declared the pornography market "flourishing" and efforts against it "lagging" across the nation. When the Maryland Board of Censors delivered a report on a hardcore Baltimore adult theater to the attorney general in late 1975, his assistant noted the small number of patrons and responded, "We feel that strong action at this time would not be feasible." Instead, he patronizingly suggested the censors "inspect the theatre frequently and regularly and submit prompt written reports."[61] Los Angeles city attorney Burt Pines spoke extensively and emphatically to this effect, campaigning for office in 1973 on a platform of de-emphasizing what he called "victimless crimes," such as homosexual activity and adult obscenity. Inventively reconfiguring a standard trope, Pines contrasted obscenity to "hard core crime," arguing that obscenity prosecutions merely served to clog up the courts and deplete the resources of law enforcers, leaving more serious crimes unattended. He won nearly 60 percent of the vote against his traditional porn-busting opponent.[62]

Certainly, the post-*Miller* legal world lacked the unfettered free-speech horizons of the 1969–73 period. The author of a how-to book for aspiring pornographers warned in 1977 of "a real chance of getting busted if you make a porno movie," and high-profile prosecutions targeted *Hustler* publisher Larry Flynt, *Screw* publisher Al Goldstein, and *Deep Throat* star Harry Reems in 1976–77. But "Pornography Is Here to Stay," wrote sociologist Amitai Etzioni in 1977, and though many resented the fact, few doubted it. An extensive study that year by the NYU Obscenity Law Project confirmed this, concluding in a lengthy report that *Miller* ultimately had "little effect on the day-to-day regulation of obscene materials."[63]

Instead of prosecution, cities began turning to zoning laws to regulate pornography in the mid-1970s. Two models quickly developed: dispersal and concentration. Detroit introduced the first approach. The city had begun attempting to hold urban decay at bay in 1962 with anti–skid row ordinances. When its city obscenity ordinance was declared unconstitutional in 1972, Detroit placed adult theaters and bookstores alongside the strip clubs, hotels, pawnshops, pool halls, and dance halls already included in its skid row measures. These zoning laws precluded any new business from the listed fields to be established within one thousand feet of any other two such businesses or within five hundred feet of any residentially zoned area. Though already-existing establishments were grandfathered in, no further additions would be allowed; the goal was attrition and eventual dispersion, in the interest of avoiding concentrated skid row areas.[64]

Meanwhile, Boston settled on the opposite approach of concentrating pornography in limited areas. The city, once notorious for the phrase "banned in Boston," had over the years continued to show alarm over pornography. The city council passed an ordinance in 1969 requiring all proprietors of adult-only bookstores and theaters to register with the city, but Mayor Kevin White vetoed the ordinance, citing its constitutional dangers.

After several years of debate the city finally devised a new plan in 1974: the zoning of its downtown "Combat Zone" (where most of the city's sex-related businesses already resided) as an "adult entertaining district." The goal was containment, and the city even began a shuttle bus service to and from the Zone, clearly hoping the gesture would force outlying adult businesses to relocate or suffer financially. As a city official explained, "If it's exclusively there, people can avoid it. And if it's your fancy, you can go there."[65]

Of the two models, Detroit's dispersal approach proved most popular. Although it bore the risk of resulting in porn shops relatively near residential neighborhoods, many cities feared that creating their own Combat Zones would look too much like an endorsement of pornography. The Boston model, meanwhile, came to be associated with increased crime and lowered property values, critical factors as cities grasped to retain and attract capital and development in the face of a perceived "urban crisis"; one newspaper called it "a liberal civic experiment that failed." Of equal importance, Detroit's zoning rules won the support of the Supreme Court in 1976. The recent Gerald Ford appointee John Paul Stevens wrote the lead opinion, upholding the Detroit ordinance on the grounds that it violated neither the First nor Fourteenth Amendments, as it neither banned sexual speech nor denied due process, since zoning also applied to numerous other industries. In the wake of the decision several cities quickly adopted zoning laws based on the Detroit ordinance. Kansas City; Des Moines and Dubuque, Iowa; New Orleans; Royal Oak, Michigan; Dallas; and Norwalk, California, were among the many. In New York City Mayor Ed Koch at first campaigned for the creation of "adult pleasure zones" along the Boston model, but he also came to embrace Detroit-style zoning.[66]

For the most part American cities in the 1970s clearly accepted the necessity of as peaceful a coexistence with pornography as possible. The permissive society rather than conservative repression overwhelmingly shaped the culture and policy of the decade, even after the Court issued its new *Miller* standards. Whereas Citizens for Decent Literature had risen to power and influence in the 1960s, the 1970s saw the organization sink into irrelevance as a result of financial scandals and the abandonment of its grassroots emphasis.[67]

Liberal values of pluralism, empiricism, and individual liberty had underwritten the permissive society. Despite this, liberal Democrats saw little advantage in overtly embracing its results. Perpetuating the postwar liberal ambivalence surrounding obscenity, they saw their position as a difficult one. They supported free expression, but they distanced themselves from its consequences—often framed by the media as not just floodtides of porno filth but oversexed college students, open homosexuals, and bra-burning feminists, too.

As conservative politicians competed to issue the most scathing denunciation of the Presidential Commission on Obscenity and Pornography in 1970, liberal Minnesota Democrat Walter Mondale was one of five senators to vote against the rejection of the report. Testifying on the floor to the "high quality, commitment, and understanding" the commissioners had brought to the topic, he singled out chairman Lockhart as a "balanced, responsible, and measured man." But when the ACLU sought national figures to openly defend the report, Mondale ducked out of sight; as his press secretary explained, the senator "did not feel a press conference would be of any value in trying to fight back." He remained willing to meet with journalists individually, but he clearly wanted to avoid being linked too publicly and visibly to the report's call for obscenity decriminalization. When twenty-five national organizations—including the National Council of Churches, the National Education Association, and the National Board of the YWCA—issued a joint statement neither endorsing nor condemning the commission report but merely imploring politicians to devote "serious study and debate" to it, no liberal legislators stepped forward to voice support for the suggestion.[68]

Another of the five senators to vote against rejecting the report was the South Dakota Democrat George McGovern. But McGovern had no public comment on the topic, and in his 1972 presidential campaign he let Nixon establish the tone on morality, issuing more an echo than a choice. Though McGovern held a broader conception of morality than Nixon, he shied away from directly confronting the president's moralism. "Setting the moral tone of this nation is the most serious responsibility of the next president," McGovern intoned, without clarification of his meaning. He tried to strip Nixon of his pious veneer, accusing the administration of immorality for its corrupt practices and warmongering. Yet while he sarcastically noted that "when you're running against Richard Nixon, you're not running against Jesus Christ," McGovern offered little substantive challenge to the president's sanctimony.[69]

The "rights of free speech and free political expression" did appear on the 1972 Democratic platform (neither found a single mention on the Republican platform), but McGovern never made free speech a campaign issue, and he avoided any discussion of pornography. That McGovern was more permissive than Nixon was an obvious truth, but the senator found no value in announcing it to the nation. Indeed, one Nixon strategist recommended that McGovern's vote against rejecting the 1970 commission report be "*well publicized*" as a means of linking the senator to pornographic moral decay; in the face of such tactics McGovern saw little gain in tackling the polarizing and easily demonized issue.[70]

This discursive void allowed the New Right to shape political discourse on pornography. In the polarized framework it presented to the public, liberalism collapsed into libertinism; meanwhile, in the absence of a progressive, affirmative liberal sexual politics, smut spoke for it. The commission report's insights were ostensibly extended by such works as Earl Kemp's leering, openly pornographic *Illustrated Report of the Commission on Obscenity and Pornography*, which ironically crystallized the heart of sexual citizenship as tacitly formulated by liberalism in its dedication to "those millions of middle aged, middle class, married men in neat clothes who had rather make their own choices for themselves."[71]

The only Democrat elected president in the 1970s was also hostile to the suppression of speech but wary of appearing to support porn. As governor of Georgia, Jimmy Carter had presided over the demise of the Georgia Literature Commission. Like Mondale and McGovern, though, Carter avoided public association with permissiveness; he agreed with an aide that letting the Literature Commission "die a nice, quiet death" was the best course of action.[72] Carter went beyond that, even establishing a Governor's Commission in late 1972 to advise on ways to "beef up the state's fight" against pornography. At the same time, however, unannounced in official press releases, he stipulated that the commission would expire quickly after its creation. This veiled vacillation enabled Carter to gain public recognition as a smut fighter even as he discreetly dismantled the state's repressive apparatus, closely paralleling his appropriation of coded racist overtures to conceal his actual liberalism and win the Georgia governorship in 1970.[73]

As a presidential candidate Carter implied his position on pornography in a controversial 1976 *Playboy* interview. Best known for Carter's confession of committing "adultery in my heart," the interview also reflected his hands-off approach to moral regulation. As governor, "I didn't run around breaking down people's doors to see if they were fornicating," Carter told interviewer Robert Scheer, and he also noted, "Victimless crimes, in my opinion, should have a very low priority in terms of enforce[ment]." When Scheer asked whether the "permissiveness" of the 1970s was a positive development, Carter responded, "Liberalization of some of the law has been good. You can't legislate morality." Without directly addressing pornography Carter suggested his stance.[74]

Apart from signing a bill against child pornography in early 1978 ("without comment," the *Washington Post* noted), once in office Carter adhered to his position and showed little interest in porn. Without outward declaration his administration subtly indicated its liberal stance through such measures as the appointment of W. Michael Cody as U.S. attorney for the Western District of Tennessee. Under Cody's Nixon-appointed predecessor a rash of obscenity prosecutions had been undertaken; one of them even involved Cody as a defense attorney. Once installed as U.S. attorney, Cody proceeded to quietly dismiss several obscenity cases still pending. In one motion to dismiss he explained a trial would "involve a great deal of cost to the government as well as the defendants," while of another defendant he wrote that the man "has been convicted on two separate previous occasions. . . . Further prosecutions would not be in the interest of justice or judicial economy." The main liberal argument against obscenity prosecutions thus became one of expedience rather than principle. The less said, the better.[75]

Even when the FBI did launch a major porn-distribution sting operation with the undercover MIPORN sweep at the tail end of the decade, it was handled in stark contrast to the Nixonian approach of exploiting porn opposition for its invitation to public moralizing. The president remained silent on the operation, and the Justice Department consistently presented it as a mere component of the fight against the Mafia. "We didn't go out trying to enforce morality," a Justice Department attorney told the press, capturing the flavor of Carter-administration rhetoric; "We were looking for industries controlled by organized crime, and felt pornography was one of them." Debates over free speech and permissiveness had no place even in the largest porn bust in American history.[76]

The permissive society had achieved a semblance of consensus support in the 1970s, as seen in legislative, judicial, and community reactions. But without any vocal supporters in national politics it remained fragile, susceptible to counterattack by conservatives whose apparent numerical inferiority could be masked by the thundering volume of their dissent. It was this organizational principle to which the New Right fastened itself in the late 1970s, and by the end of the decade the permissive society would be on the defensive, without any national political leaders to protect it. Having never articulated a meaningful sexual politics beyond the realm of abstract endorsements of free speech and privacy, mainstream liberalism continued attempting to synthesize its support for the rights of women, gays and lesbians, and sexual expression with its fundamental reliance on the nuclear family as the basic social unit. The emergence of a desecularized "family values" agenda would knock the legs out from under this tenuous stance, leaving liberalism stumbling for solid ground through the end of the century.

magazine came to embody Christian Right dogma. Though diversity would continue to mark Christian approaches to social issues, by the turn of the decade the Christian Right forcibly presented itself as the unified voice of a monolithic Christianity.[7]

When the controversial Presidential Commission report arrived in 1970, the liberal *Christian Century* credited it for "bravely" delivering an "honest scrutiny of the subject" and condemned President Nixon for "mak[ing] demagogic capital out of it." The Catholic magazine *America* went even further, calling Nixon's condemnation "an election-campaign ploy" and describing "the inability of middle America" to "cope with the complexities of the sexual evolution taking place in modern society." The magazine had written one of the first articles bringing Citizens for Decent Literature to national attention in 1958, but in late 1970 it wrote favorably of the commission report and called Charles Keating's sensationalized dissent a "step backward [that] helps no one." However, the staunchly conservative *Christianity Today*, founded in 1956 to counteract a perceived leftward drift in theology by legitimizing conservative evangelism, called the report "a national disgrace."[8]

These two perspectives would compete over the course of the 1970s, with *Christianity Today*'s conservatism clearly victorious, as evangelical Protestantism grew in numbers while mainline denominations shrank. *America*, reflecting related trends in Catholicism, would display an antiporn perspective by the 1980s. In contrast, the long-running *Christian Century* maintained its liberal demeanor, mentioning zoning laws' "potential threat to the right of citizens to see or read pornography" in 1976 and even advising that a pornographic Danish film featuring a bisexual Jesus be considered "as rationally as possible, and preferably in isolation from the emotional outcries of those who would have the sexual element eliminated from every form of art." Meanwhile the fundamentalist audience was actively courted by the competing *Christianity Today*, which recognized no such right and called for no such rational detachment. Declaring in late 1974 that "we now have incontrovertible evidence that pornography can and does cause sexual deviancy in a wide range of subjects," the magazine argued by faith alone, neglecting to substantiate its claim. And instead of calmly discussing the theological problems of pornography like its competitor (which certainly abhorred the bisexual Jesus film), it described pornographic films in 1975 with a Keatingesque eye for the outrageous, listing

6. RESURRECTING MORALISM
The Christian Right and the Porn Debate

AS I NOTED IN CHAPTER 3, the antiporn efforts of the 1960s were often at least nominally secular. Citizens for Decent Literature towered over other like-minded groups, setting the tone. In Chicago, Americans for Moral Decency cited J. Edgar Hoover rather than biblical passages in its literature, and the blacklisting Indiana group Citizens for Happy Family Living included no religious elements in its statement of purpose.[1]

By the early 1970s this secularity had begun to give way to more overt expressions of religious faith and motivation in what historian Robert Fogel calls "the fourth great awakening" and theology scholar Donald Miller calls a "Second Reformation," as postdenominational evangelicalism exploded in popularity.[2] In Alabama, Christian men formed Dads Against Dirt, with the redundant acronym DAD, in 1971, while the Utah County Council for Better Movies and Literature asked, "As true followers of Christ, have we the courage to fight the pornographic literature trade and keep out of our communities the vile publications which seek to seduce our youth?"[3] Across the nation evangelical Christians in the 1970s began to answer affirmatively. It took time for an organized movement to develop, but while the permissive society captured headlines, resurgent religiosity laid the groundwork for retrenchment.

Following CDL's lead, New Right leaders had discovered the political capital of moralism, with pornography acting as a magnet for their moral compasses. For the remnants of the Old Right, morality began superseding communism as an organizing principle, as Billy James Hargis of the McCarthyite Christian Crusade embraced antiporn efforts, listing pornography second (after the banning of school prayer) in his 1973 outrage-based fund-raising mailings. The 1970s provided fertile ground for the cultivation of the nascent "family values" platform. Cold war ideology had posited healthy American families as a critical bulwark against communism, and with America's global position declining in the face of failure in Vietnam, the OPEC oil embargo, and other debacles, shoring up the American family, a once-venerable institution left shaken by the sexual revolution, took on newfound social and political importance for religious conservatives invested in the national character. Seen as both a destabilizing agent and a reflection of changing sexual mores, pornography drew particular condemnation from these circles.[4]

Nonetheless, the New Right experienced a multitude of setbacks in the early 1970s, from social permissiveness to antiwar sentiment to the devastating exposure of the Nixon administration's corruption, most notoriously in the Watergate scandal. The Republican Party sought to recapture power by pinning its hopes on the burgeoning politicization of evangelical Christians, capturing the fundamentalist vote by speaking its language. It worked, as the new Christian Right joined the party en masse. This outcome was hardly preordained; America's first born-again president was the Democrat Jimmy Carter. But as Carter's liberal policies alienated fundamentalists, a Christian Right began to amass politically, assisting Ronald Reagan in his 1980 defeat of Carter. If not all conservative evangelicals adhered to strictly fundamentalist beliefs, it was nonetheless the booming voice of fundamentalism that most audibly defined Christian Right politics.

In office, Reagan offered much rhetorical support to evangelicals but relatively little substantive policy support in what became known as the "culture wars." Issues such as abortion and gay rights dominated the Christian Right's agenda, and although Reagan's lack of involvement on those fronts sometimes played into fundamentalist hands (his silence on the AIDS crisis being a case in point) the president did attempt to mollify his religious supporters by creating a new commission to study pornography with the express intent of overturning the libertarian analysis of the 1970 Presidential Commission report. The so-called Meese Commission would reflect conservative Christian perspectives on pornography and sexuality, using new developments in social science and public awareness of child pornography to cater to fundamentalist goals while co-opting feminist rhetoric to partially disguise its ideological bent.

For a brief window in the 1970s it looked as though evangelical Christians might endorse a politics of pleasure, albeit one contained within the bounds of heterosexual marriage. As conservatives regrouped in the mid-1970s the *National Review* cofounder William Rusher hoped for a new party that "might be *fun* to belong to, and a downright pleasure to vote for." Like a right-wing Emma Goldman dancing to the revolution,

Rusher asked, "Where is the music that once played so large a part i politics?—the pulse-pounding rhythms, the popular tunes that can communicate so much more effectively than words?" Evangelical Ma Morgan emphasized marital sexual pleasure in her 1973 best-seller *The Woman*, while Tim and Beverly LaHaye informed their fellow Chris "God designed our sex organs for our enjoyment" in a 1976 book that so far as to find "no biblical grounds for forbidding" marital oral sex.[5]

This emphasis on pleasure gave way to the stern face of the M Majority as the political institutionalization of the Christian Right place in the late 1970s. Pornography found a prominent place in this ag as did several other features of the sexual revolution. Indicative of the was Ronald Reagan's secretary of the interior James Watt's 1983 banish of the seemingly innocuous Beach Boys from a Fourth of July celebr to avoid "encourag[ing] drug abuse or alcoholism." William Rusher's i ined music would stop, literally as well as figuratively, as pleasure di ished in significance to evangelical leaders and the imposition of a n: Christian sexual normativity became a key goal of fundamentalists. V unsuccessful in obtaining its goals, the Christian Right interjected rel into the porn debate in such a way as to render Charles Keating's c: secularization project of the 1960s unnecessary—as Keating himself, ar numerous others, would note.[6]

Out of the Wilderness

As the Christian Right slowly emerged in the 1970s, disparate Chri efforts against pornography often occurred as isolated, local events. with the development of formal national organizations late in the de would these efforts fuse into a unified front. Although pornograph mained a staple of Christian outrage, other issues, particularly abortion gay rights, would also fuel the formation of these organizations. Befor coalescence of the Christian Right, the public face of religion in politic often been a progressive one, most prominently displayed in the civil r and antiwar movements. While some Christian sources voiced sentin congruent with the permissive society, this liberalism would be drown the torrent of fundamentalist fervor. The liberal *Christian Century* and conservative *Christianity Today* presented two sides to the porn debate, as local struggles became a national movement, the positions of the l "sodomy, bisexuality, *ménages à trois*, group orgies, bestiality, lesbian lust, and all types of male homosexual action" in its survey of San Francisco theaters.[9]

Evangelical Christians everywhere opposed pornography, though for most of the 1970s these efforts remained fragmented and local. In 1972, when Citizens for Decent Literature changed its name to Citizens for Decency Through Law, a local unit in Victoria, Texas, one hundred miles south of Austin, parted ways from the national organization. While CDL still maintained its secular façade, the Victoria unit morphed into Christians for Decency in Media and Literature, and it swelled to 250 members, from housewives to Halliburton engineers, of both Protestant and Catholic faiths. In 1974 it contravened original CDL policy by sending out a list of "offensive" magazines, including *Playboy*, and asking retailers to "entirely remove" them from their stores. Most of the local merchants complied, and the group drew favorable mention in *Christianity Today*. Although the group apparently failed to sustain itself, its leader, Neil Gallagher, went on to write the book *How to Stop the Porno Plague* in 1977. In it he claimed pornographers had threatened his life with explosives, and he showed how to extend the CDL monologue in the face of challenges by suggesting methods of evasion. For instance, his response to the question of what scriptural authority legitimized Christian antiporn activity was to reverse the burden of proof by responding, "No scriptures exonerate Christians from resisting and defeating the pornographic abuse of God's gift of sex."[10]

Meanwhile, the burgeoning Christian Right found success in La Crosse, Wisconsin, a small town of about fifty thousand located along the Mississippi River. When a speaker from Christian Family Renewal gave a speech letting citizens know "Christians could win" against pornography "if they want to" in 1977, the city council was quickly pressured into considering antiporn legislation. In an attempt to deflate the issue, the council's legal committee substituted a bill banning distribution of obscenity to minors—a measure that would have no practical effect but was clearly intended to show concern over the topic. Unsatisfied activists bypassed the council in 1978, gathering signatures to put a more comprehensive antiporn ordinance on the books. The proposed ordinance declared unlawful "any material portraying sado-masochistic abuse, sexual conduct or nudity which is pornographic." This was clearly unconstitutionally vague, as the 1974 *Jenkins v. Georgia* case indicated that not even the Supreme Court's most conservative justice was willing to include mere nudity in the definition of obscenity.[11]

Unfazed by such legal intricacies, agents of decency bombarded La Crosse with *News for Good Neighbors*, a newsletter whose front-page headline declared, "Report Shows Link Between Smut and Rape." Letters poured in to the local newspaper, which endorsed the ordinance in an editorial that distinguished books like *Gang Bang Baby* from *Ulysses*. One journalist summarized the city: "La Crosse has always seemed to have two distinct populations: a larger group of God-fearing citizens, and a relatively smaller, more libertine group of nightlife devotees."[12]

The so-called libertines defended free speech vigorously. The local university paper called the city newspaper's endorsement "particularly appalling" in light of the press's historical need of First Amendment protection. The La Crosse Citizens Against Censorship bought ads with questions and answers; "Are we not a Christian nation?" asked one, responding, "No, we are a free country composed of Christians, Jews, Moslems, Hindus, Buddhists, etc." The group received angry letters from local opponents. As one wrote, "This is the communist Grand Design"; legalizing pornography was simply the initial step in "fostering and legalizing drug useage [*sic*], obscenity in school books, teaching of sex in all it's [*sic*] phases to children, teaching of magic, the black arts, communist ideologies, and what have you." The antiporn perspective numerically outweighed the free-speech one, and the ordinance passed with a resounding 65 percent of the vote, winning in every district but two adjoining the local university. An angry owner of a local adult store explained how evangelicals had set the terms of the debate: a "yes vote meant you were for God, while a no vote meant you were voting for child molesting."[13]

Even with its draconian new obscenity ordinance, La Crosse found it difficult to eliminate smut from its streets. Only three adult stores were located in the town, and when one was charged with obscenity in 1978, a jury acquitted its owner. Not until 1980 was a conviction finally achieved, in a case relying on traditional notions of deviance. Whereas the first store that was exonerated had been cited for two films depicting heterosexual activity, Gary Enea of Pure Pleasure Bookstore was convicted on the basis of films showing "group sex and homosexual activity." As the city prosecutor said, "The people of La Crosse agree that this was not normal, healthy sex."[14]

Similar examples abounded in cities and regions across the nation, but the various efforts lacked any cohesion, occurring in an institutional void.

6. RESURRECTING MORALISM
The Christian Right and the Porn Debate

AS I NOTED IN CHAPTER 3, the antiporn efforts of the 1960s were often at least nominally secular. Citizens for Decent Literature towered over other like-minded groups, setting the tone. In Chicago, Americans for Moral Decency cited J. Edgar Hoover rather than biblical passages in its literature, and the blacklisting Indiana group Citizens for Happy Family Living included no religious elements in its statement of purpose.[1]

By the early 1970s this secularity had begun to give way to more overt expressions of religious faith and motivation in what historian Robert Fogel calls "the fourth great awakening" and theology scholar Donald Miller calls a "Second Reformation," as postdenominational evangelicalism exploded in popularity.[2] In Alabama, Christian men formed Dads Against Dirt, with the redundant acronym DAD, in 1971, while the Utah County Council for Better Movies and Literature asked, "As true followers of Christ, have we the courage to fight the pornographic literature trade and keep out of our communities the vile publications which seek to seduce our youth?"[3] Across the nation evangelical Christians in the 1970s began to answer affirmatively. It took time for an organized movement to develop, but while the permissive society captured headlines, resurgent religiosity laid the groundwork for retrenchment.

Following CDL's lead, New Right leaders had discovered the political capital of moralism, with pornography acting as a magnet for their moral compasses. For the remnants of the Old Right, morality began superseding communism as an organizing principle, as Billy James Hargis of the Mc-Carthyite Christian Crusade embraced antiporn efforts, listing pornography second (after the banning of school prayer) in his 1973 outrage-based fund-raising mailings. The 1970s provided fertile ground for the cultivation of the nascent "family values" platform. Cold war ideology had posited healthy American families as a critical bulwark against communism, and with America's global position declining in the face of failure in Vietnam, the OPEC oil embargo, and other debacles, shoring up the American family, a once-venerable institution left shaken by the sexual revolution, took on newfound social and political importance for religious conservatives invested in the national character. Seen as both a destabilizing agent and a reflection of changing sexual mores, pornography drew particular condemnation from these circles.[4]

Nonetheless, the New Right experienced a multitude of setbacks in the early 1970s, from social permissiveness to antiwar sentiment to the devastating exposure of the Nixon administration's corruption, most notoriously in the Watergate scandal. The Republican Party sought to recapture power by pinning its hopes on the burgeoning politicization of evangelical Christians, capturing the fundamentalist vote by speaking its language. It worked, as the new Christian Right joined the party en masse. This outcome was hardly preordained; America's first born-again president was the Democrat Jimmy Carter. But as Carter's liberal policies alienated fundamentalists, a Christian Right began to amass politically, assisting Ronald Reagan in his 1980 defeat of Carter. If not all conservative evangelicals adhered to strictly fundamentalist beliefs, it was nonetheless the booming voice of fundamentalism that most audibly defined Christian Right politics.

In office, Reagan offered much rhetorical support to evangelicals but relatively little substantive policy support in what became known as the "culture wars." Issues such as abortion and gay rights dominated the Christian Right's agenda, and although Reagan's lack of involvement on those fronts sometimes played into fundamentalist hands (his silence on the AIDS crisis being a case in point) the president did attempt to mollify his religious supporters by creating a new commission to study pornography with the express intent of overturning the libertarian analysis of the 1970 Presidential Commission report. The so-called Meese Commission would reflect conservative Christian perspectives on pornography and sexuality, using new developments in social science and public awareness of child pornography to cater to fundamentalist goals while co-opting feminist rhetoric to partially disguise its ideological bent.

For a brief window in the 1970s it looked as though evangelical Christians might endorse a politics of pleasure, albeit one contained within the bounds of heterosexual marriage. As conservatives regrouped in the mid-1970s the *National Review* cofounder William Rusher hoped for a new party that "might be *fun* to belong to, and a downright pleasure to vote for." Like a right-wing Emma Goldman dancing to the revolution,

Rusher asked, "Where is the music that once played so large a part in our politics?—the pulse-pounding rhythms, the popular tunes that can often communicate so much more effectively than words?" Evangelical Marabel Morgan emphasized marital sexual pleasure in her 1973 best-seller *The Total Woman*, while Tim and Beverly LaHaye informed their fellow Christians, "God designed our sex organs for our enjoyment" in a 1976 book that went so far as to find "no biblical grounds for forbidding" marital oral sex.[5]

This emphasis on pleasure gave way to the stern face of the Moral Majority as the political institutionalization of the Christian Right took place in the late 1970s. Pornography found a prominent place in this agenda, as did several other features of the sexual revolution. Indicative of the shift was Ronald Reagan's secretary of the interior James Watt's 1983 banishment of the seemingly innocuous Beach Boys from a Fourth of July celebration to avoid "encourag[ing] drug abuse or alcoholism." William Rusher's imagined music would stop, literally as well as figuratively, as pleasure diminished in significance to evangelical leaders and the imposition of a narrow Christian sexual normativity became a key goal of fundamentalists. While unsuccessful in obtaining its goals, the Christian Right interjected religion into the porn debate in such a way as to render Charles Keating's careful secularization project of the 1960s unnecessary—as Keating himself, among numerous others, would note.[6]

Out of the Wilderness

As the Christian Right slowly emerged in the 1970s, disparate Christian efforts against pornography often occurred as isolated, local events. Only with the development of formal national organizations late in the decade would these efforts fuse into a unified front. Although pornography remained a staple of Christian outrage, other issues, particularly abortion and gay rights, would also fuel the formation of these organizations. Before the coalescence of the Christian Right, the public face of religion in politics had often been a progressive one, most prominently displayed in the civil rights and antiwar movements. While some Christian sources voiced sentiments congruent with the permissive society, this liberalism would be drowned in the torrent of fundamentalist fervor. The liberal *Christian Century* and the conservative *Christianity Today* presented two sides to the porn debate, and as local struggles became a national movement, the positions of the latter magazine came to embody Christian Right dogma. Though diversity would continue to mark Christian approaches to social issues, by the turn of the decade the Christian Right forcibly presented itself as the unified voice of a monolithic Christianity.[7]

When the controversial Presidential Commission report arrived in 1970, the liberal *Christian Century* credited it for "bravely" delivering an "honest scrutiny of the subject" and condemned President Nixon for "mak[ing] demagogic capital out of it." The Catholic magazine *America* went even further, calling Nixon's condemnation "an election-campaign ploy" and describing "the inability of middle America" to "cope with the complexities of the sexual evolution taking place in modern society." The magazine had written one of the first articles bringing Citizens for Decent Literature to national attention in 1958, but in late 1970 it wrote favorably of the commission report and called Charles Keating's sensationalized dissent a "step backward [that] helps no one." However, the staunchly conservative *Christianity Today*, founded in 1956 to counteract a perceived leftward drift in theology by legitimizing conservative evangelism, called the report "a national disgrace."[8]

These two perspectives would compete over the course of the 1970s, with *Christianity Today*'s conservatism clearly victorious, as evangelical Protestantism grew in numbers while mainline denominations shrunk. *America*, reflecting related trends in Catholicism, would display an antiporn perspective by the 1980s. In contrast, the long-running *Christian Century* maintained its liberal demeanor, mentioning zoning laws' "potential threat to the right of citizens to see or read pornography" in 1976 and even advising that a pornographic Danish film featuring a bisexual Jesus be considered "as rationally as possible, and preferably in isolation from the emotional outcries of those who would have the sexual element eliminated from every form of art." Meanwhile the fundamentalist audience was actively courted by the competing *Christianity Today*, which recognized no such right and called for no such rational detachment. Declaring in late 1974 that "we now have incontrovertible evidence that pornography can and does cause sexual deviancy in a wide range of subjects," the magazine argued by faith alone, neglecting to substantiate its claim. And instead of calmly discussing the theological problems of pornography like its competitor (which certainly abhorred the bisexual Jesus film), it described pornographic films in 1975 with a Keatingesque eye for the outrageous, listing

"sodomy, bisexuality, *ménages à trois*, group orgies, bestiality, lesbian lust, and all types of male homosexual action" in its survey of San Francisco theaters.[9]

Evangelical Christians everywhere opposed pornography, though for most of the 1970s these efforts remained fragmented and local. In 1972, when Citizens for Decent Literature changed its name to Citizens for Decency Through Law, a local unit in Victoria, Texas, one hundred miles south of Austin, parted ways from the national organization. While CDL still maintained its secular façade, the Victoria unit morphed into Christians for Decency in Media and Literature, and it swelled to 250 members, from housewives to Halliburton engineers, of both Protestant and Catholic faiths. In 1974 it contravened original CDL policy by sending out a list of "offensive" magazines, including *Playboy*, and asking retailers to "entirely remove" them from their stores. Most of the local merchants complied, and the group drew favorable mention in *Christianity Today*. Although the group apparently failed to sustain itself, its leader, Neil Gallagher, went on to write the book *How to Stop the Porno Plague* in 1977. In it he claimed pornographers had threatened his life with explosives, and he showed how to extend the CDL monologue in the face of challenges by suggesting methods of evasion. For instance, his response to the question of what scriptural authority legitimized Christian antiporn activity was to reverse the burden of proof by responding, "No scriptures exonerate Christians from resisting and defeating the pornographic abuse of God's gift of sex."[10]

Meanwhile, the burgeoning Christian Right found success in La Crosse, Wisconsin, a small town of about fifty thousand located along the Mississippi River. When a speaker from Christian Family Renewal gave a speech letting citizens know "Christians could win" against pornography "if they want to" in 1977, the city council was quickly pressured into considering antiporn legislation. In an attempt to deflate the issue, the council's legal committee substituted a bill banning distribution of obscenity to minors—a measure that would have no practical effect but was clearly intended to show concern over the topic. Unsatisfied activists bypassed the council in 1978, gathering signatures to put a more comprehensive antiporn ordinance on the books. The proposed ordinance declared unlawful "any material portraying sado-masochistic abuse, sexual conduct or nudity which is pornographic." This was clearly unconstitutionally vague, as the 1974 *Jenkins v. Georgia* case indicated that not even the Supreme Court's

most conservative justice was willing to include mere nudity in the definition of obscenity.[11]

Unfazed by such legal intricacies, agents of decency bombarded La Crosse with *News for Good Neighbors*, a newsletter whose front-page headline declared, "Report Shows Link Between Smut and Rape." Letters poured in to the local newspaper, which endorsed the ordinance in an editorial that distinguished books like *Gang Bang Baby* from *Ulysses*. One journalist summarized the city: "La Crosse has always seemed to have two distinct populations: a larger group of God-fearing citizens, and a relatively smaller, more libertine group of nightlife devotees."[12]

The so-called libertines defended free speech vigorously. The local university paper called the city newspaper's endorsement "particularly appalling" in light of the press's historical need of First Amendment protection. The La Crosse Citizens Against Censorship bought ads with questions and answers; "Are we not a Christian nation?" asked one, responding, "No, we are a free country composed of Christians, Jews, Moslems, Hindus, Buddhists, etc." The group received angry letters from local opponents. As one wrote, "This is the communist Grand Design"; legalizing pornography was simply the initial step in "fostering and legalizing drug useage [*sic*], obscenity in school books, teaching of sex in all it's [*sic*] phases to children, teaching of magic, the black arts, communist ideologies, and what have you." The antiporn perspective numerically outweighed the free-speech one, and the ordinance passed with a resounding 65 percent of the vote, winning in every district but two adjoining the local university. An angry owner of a local adult store explained how evangelicals had set the terms of the debate: a "yes vote meant you were for God, while a no vote meant you were voting for child molesting."[13]

Even with its draconian new obscenity ordinance, La Crosse found it difficult to eliminate smut from its streets. Only three adult stores were located in the town, and when one was charged with obscenity in 1978, a jury acquitted its owner. Not until 1980 was a conviction finally achieved, in a case relying on traditional notions of deviance. Whereas the first store that was exonerated had been cited for two films depicting heterosexual activity, Gary Enea of Pure Pleasure Bookstore was convicted on the basis of films showing "group sex and homosexual activity." As the city prosecutor said, "The people of La Crosse agree that this was not normal, healthy sex."[14]

Similar examples abounded in cities and regions across the nation, but the various efforts lacked any cohesion, occurring in an institutional void.

CDL still existed and even supplied help to local prosecutors, but it lacked the active, on-the-ground presence its local units had provided in the 1960s. Morality in Media had grown since Morton Hill founded it as Operation Yorkville in the mid-1960s, but it, too, remained a national organization whose primary connection to local activists came through its monthly newsletter. In Mississippi the Methodist minister Donald Wildmon's National Federation for Decency emerged in 1977 to quick acclaim among antiporn circles (Morality in Media named Wildmon "Man of the Month" that November), but the group would obtain national influence only with its infamous 7-Eleven boycotts in the 1980s.[15]

Despite the absence of organizational unity, fundamentalists grew more vocally assertive in the late 1970s. When the assistant U.S. attorney Larry Parrish had prosecuted the distributors of *Deep Throat* in Memphis in 1976, he took great pains to distinguish himself from Victorianism or prudery. By 1978, though, Parrish felt bold enough to publicly renounce evolution, explaining that dinosaur fossils did not bother him because "the second law of thermodynamics says that everything is winding down, devolving instead of evolving." At the *Deep Throat* retrial later that year his prosecutorial replacement told the jury in his closing statement, "They tell you to disregard the Bible, but you can't disregard it because it is the views of those people in the community that you also have to plug in." The jury went on to convict. At the same time, apocalyptic rhetoric took greater precedence in evangelical arguments; while the Southern Baptist Convention had carefully instructed its members to "avoid any type of censorship approach which is unconstitutional" in 1967, by 1978 it had dispensed with the secular constitutional framework entirely, declaring pornography "a tool of Satan" and framing opposition as a spiritual crusade.[16]

Into this messy fray stepped Jimmy Carter. While Carter's appeal to evangelicals was obvious—namely, he was one of them—he practiced a form of Christianity more tolerant of pluralism than many of his coreligionists. Certainly his 1976 *Playboy* interview, with its notorious admission of committing "adultery in my heart" and casual use of the word *screw*, alienated many of the devout. Perhaps worse were Carter's words on abortion; "I think abortion is wrong and I will do everything I can as President to minimize the need for abortions," he declared, but added, "the Supreme Court ruling [*Roe v. Wade*] suits me all right." The political awakening of evangelical Christians transpired swiftly under the Carter administration, and much of it can be directly attributed to the president's liberal stance on abortion—and also, as historians Andrew Flint and Joy Porter charge, to the legitimizing of faith in politics Carter's campaign had facilitated.[17]

Though the Supreme Court's 1973 legalization of abortion had brought attention to the issue and expanded activism beyond its traditional Catholic constituency, Southern Baptists latched onto the issue during the Carter years. In 1971 the Southern Baptist Convention had passed a resolution supporting legislation "that will allow the possibility of abortion" in cases of rape, incest, fetal deformity, or the much broader category "damage to the emotional, mental, and physical health of the mother." Even after the *Roe v. Wade* decision the convention reaffirmed the resolution in 1974. But an indication of the new politicization of religion was on display in a 1980 resolution categorically demanding a constitutional amendment "prohibiting abortion on demand." Carter opposed such an amendment.[18]

Carter also drew the wrath of the burgeoning Christian Right on other issues. He supported the Equal Rights Amendment, which had been uncontroversial when passed by Congress in 1972. Even the Republican Party platform of that year voiced support for it. But as feminism and abortion brought gender politics to the national forefront, the ERA became a major component of conservative gender politics. Groups such as Phyllis Schlafly's Stop-ERA warned the world of unisex toilets and women forced into masculinity, framing the ERA as an attack on traditional gender roles. Meanwhile, Carter's support for the 1977 National Women's Conference brought denunciations from religious leaders who saw it as a platform for abortion and lesbianism. When his administration altered the name of the 1978 White House Conference on the American Family to "Families" in the name of pluralism and diversity, angry evangelicals read it as an endorsement of single mothers and homosexual couples.[19]

By the late 1970s homosexuality had also obtained a position of centrality in the Christian Right agenda. Cities such as St. Paul, Wichita, and Eugene, Oregon, repealed civil rights ordinances protecting sexual orientation, while in Florida the singer Anita Bryant led the "Save Our Children" movement against what her autobiography called "the threat of militant homosexuality." In 1978 the Briggs Amendment, a California initiative to bar homosexuals from teaching positions, failed, though it indicated the deep revulsion evangelicals felt toward homosexuality. This homophobia would remain a constant presence in subsequent conservative politics. Carter also opposed discrimination on the basis of sexual orientation, and though he showed personal discomfort with homosexuality, he filled his White House staff with aides sympathetic to gay and lesbian issues, further alienating the Christian Right.[20]

Most explosive in this regard was the IRS's announcement that Christian private schools could lose their tax-exempt status because of the de facto racial segregation of their predominantly white student bodies. According to some leading figures in the movement, this, more than anything else, catalyzed the Christian Right into political opposition to the Democratic Party. As the New Right organizer and direct-mail pioneer Richard Viguerie wrote in 1980, the Carter administration "has actively and aggressively sought to hurt the Christian movement."[21] Jimmy Carter had piety, but the Christian Right wanted policy.

Praying a Path to Power

Finally, in the late 1970s evangelicals began to coalesce. Groups such as Christian Voice and the Religious Roundtable drew national attention, but the most prominent organization by far was the Moral Majority, founded in 1979 by the Reverend Jerry Falwell and associates. Falwell had risen to fame as a televangelist, broadcasting *The Old Time Gospel Hour* from his home base of Lynchburg, Virginia. Like Strom Thurmond and Jesse Helms, Falwell had been an ardent segregationist. In 1958 he asserted that integration would cause the destruction of the white race; in 1964 he called the landmark Civil Rights Act "civil wrongs"; and in 1965 he labeled Martin Luther King Jr. part of a communist plot. But changing times called for changing rhetoric, so Falwell, too, abandoned racism for social issues. His new emphasis was on display in a La Crosse fund-raising ad run in the local paper shortly after the porn-ordinance referendum. Asking for the reader's "vote" (and money), the clip-out ad asked three questions: "Do you approve of known practicing HOMOSEXUALS teaching in public schools?" "Do you approve of the present laws legalizing ABORTION-ON-DEMAND?" "Do you approve of the open display of PORNOGRAPHIC materials on newsstands, TV, and movies?" By checking "no" on all and returning the "ballot," sympathizers earned two free "Jesus First" pins and added one more name to Falwell's direct-mail juggernaut.[22]

These social issues formed the basis for the Moral Majority, as its name suggested. The group blossomed quickly and by its second anniversary could claim chapters in all fifty states, a newsletter with three million readers, and a daily radio broadcast on more than three hundred stations.[23] The Christian Right had finally found a unified voice with a powerful lobby. Though pornography held no monopoly on the movement's outrage, it formed a crucial component of the "family values" agenda, alongside opposition to abortion, gay rights, and feminism. In his 1980 book *Listen, America!* Falwell condemned porn for destroying "the privacy of sex" and fostering an "atmosphere of sexual license," and when he edited the 1981 Moral Majority anthology *How You Can Help Clean Up America*, the issue of pornography occupied three of the ten chapters. Charles Keating contributed one, exemplifying CDL's transition from secularized legalisms to bold Christian soldiering. Significantly, his contribution also sought to obscure the basic fact that American consumer desire played a major role in the porn market's existence. Keating effaced this by explaining there were two reasons pornography existed: those who produce it and "those who allow it to be produced." He added, as a begrudging aside, "Of course, there are also those who read it." Far from his careful days of the 1960s, he suggested boycotting "anyone who sells anything of a pornographic nature."[24]

Another leader of the Christian Right, Tim LaHaye, sat on the Moral Majority's board of directors, and the issue of pornography likewise ran through his works as a recurring motif. In a series of early-1980s books whose titles suggested an apocalyptic millennialism, LaHaye frequently found pornography behind social ills. *The Battle for the Public Schools* equated pornography and sex education, depicting porn as a causal factor of the French Revolution, whose plotters were hated by the Christian Right as forerunners of the contemporary "secular humanists" seeking to remove God from the public sphere. The revolutionaries, LaHaye contended, flooded France with smut to weaken public morals and thus hasten the fall of the government. In *The Battle for the Family* LaHaye blamed pornography for increased rape rates and supplied such anecdotes as the story of a fifteen-year-old girl whose boyfriend discovered some copies of *Playboy*. Together with three other couples, "they all began reading them until they got so worked up that they stripped off their clothes and performed sexual acts in front of each other." Finally, in *The Battle for the Mind* LaHaye also ascribed responsibility for "our skyrocketing divorce rates" and the fact that "our youth seem obsessed with sex" to pornography.[25]

These arguments were clearly intended for the initiated or born-again, who would be less inclined to question the implied constructs of idyllic, asexual childhood or the historical stability of marriage. Complementing Moral Majority discourse but appealing to a more urbane, secular audience, neoconservatism emerged in the 1970s. Led by a group of predominantly Jewish former liberals, the neoconservatives had opposed both communism and McCarthyism. When American culture turned toward what they perceived as various forms of excess in the late 1960s, intellectuals such as Daniel Bell, Seymour Martin Lipset, and Norman Podhoretz recoiled against the permissive society (ironically, many of these figures had earlier pioneered precisely the "status discontent" analysis of McCarthyites that 1970s sociologists would use to explain antiporn activists). As these figures broke with the left, though, they also felt alienated from traditional conservatives, whom they sometimes sarcastically called "paleoconservatives." Historian Murray Friedman explains the difference as a cultural one; conservatives "looked back nostalgically to a pastoral America of small towns and tight communities," while the neoconservatives "felt at home in the modern industrial world."[26]

The neocons, as they came to be called, opposed pornography but used intellectual instead of religious arguments. Irving Kristol, for example, argued, "If you care for the quality of life in America, then you have to be for censorship." Kristol saw the flourishing of pornography as part of a Nietzschean "everything is permitted" social philosophy, with enormous consequences: "What is at stake is civilization and humanity, nothing less." According to Kristol, American democracy had departed from its original principles, which assumed a citizenry with "a fair measure of self-government (i.e., self-discipline) on the part of the individual citizen." Rampant permissiveness proved the absence of this trait, which justified obscenity laws to rein in humanity's baser instincts. This was an important point for Kristol, because the neocons adamantly contended that government could not solve society's problems, especially those in the economic sphere; thus, while Adam Smith's invisible hand remained applicable to the market, its "results are disastrous when extended to the polity as a whole."[27]

Though often academic, neocon literature frequently fell short of rigor. Kristol's claim that "if you believe no one was ever corrupted by a book, you also have to believe that no one was ever improved by a book" remained an aphoristic non sequitur whether voiced by him, Charles Keating, Richard Nixon, or Warren Burger in the *Miller* decision. None of this stopped Kristol from issuing *Two Cheers for Capitalism*, and the New Right eagerly adopted the neocon movement as its intellectual wing. Though it sought a socially conservative, generally religious voting base, the New Right was heavily corporate-sponsored, and such groups as the Committee for Survival of a Free Congress recognized the value of neocon thought in legitimizing their project of deregulating American markets even as they reregulated American morality. This contradiction lay at the heart of New Right thought as much as the simultaneous support for free speech and obscenity laws expressed the ambivalence of postwar liberalism. For instance, in a single page of Richard Viguerie's 1980 manifesto *The New Right: We're Ready to Lead*, the author noted Christians were "disturbed about sex on TV and in movies," while the middle class was "tired of Big Government … telling us what to do and what not to do." Just as sexual politics remained apolitical to postwar liberals, obscenity laws and FCC "indecency" regulations stood apart from "Big Government" to Viguerie and the New Right.[28]

The neocons and the Christian-oriented New Right, then, offered parallel analyses with similar policy recommendations, despite much tension over the pervasive anti-Semitism of various Christian leaders. This complementarity helps explain the otherwise curious logic of seemingly random moments such as Jerry Falwell's endorsement of free-market economist Milton Friedman. "Ownership of property is biblical. Competition in business is biblical," wrote Falwell in 1980. But while corporations pursued profits with noble holy aggression, "pornographers are idolaters. They idolize money and will do anything for material gain." With a neoconservative intellectual framework already justifying both free markets and government involvement in regulating morality, Falwell felt no need to defend his blatant double standard.[29]

Even libertarians shifted gears and joined the New Right. As historian Patrick Allit shows, William Buckley had tacitly endorsed abortion for non-Catholics in 1966 as a response to global overpopulation, but he later became an avid, even categorical, opponent as abortion debates turned more explosive in the 1970s. When it came to pornography, the *National Review* uneasily followed a similar trajectory. A 1971 book review of early-twentieth-century radical libertarian Theodore Schroeder predicted that, ultimately, Schroeder's belief in "an absence of any limitations on obscenity will at last be vindicated." By 1973 a more reticent attitude was on display in the magazine, as a brief article on the Supreme Court's *Miller* decision referred to William Douglas's dissent as "hysterical" without noting that it was, in fact, the libertarian argument. Subsequent articles occasionally grappled with the complexity of obscenity and free speech, but by 1986 the *National Review* called pornographers "nearer to the drug merchants, than to those who use the First Amendment to give us entertainment and learning."[30]

This conflicted transition in the *National Review* reflected an increased effort on the part of social conservatives to cater to libertarianism. Richard Viguerie's *Conservative Digest*, for instance, combined free-market economics with frequent attacks on gay and abortion rights to attract both business and religious readers. Excited to find pornography it could attack on a strictly libertarian basis, the digest dredged up a story in 1978 about artists who won a $5,000 New York state grant to produce the book *Sex Objects*, with photos of strippers and prostitutes. "Government Pays to Publish Porno Book," blared the headline, as the article opposed "socialized smut."[31]

Such overtures proved effective, as the coalescence of these varied strains of conservatism culminated in the 1980 election of Ronald Reagan as president. Liberal Republicanism was "virtually extinct in American presidential politics" after 1976, writes the historian Nicol Rae, and the conservative Reagan strove for and drew the support of the Christian Right. This was ironic for several reasons. While his opponent was a self-professed born-again Christian, Reagan had shown visible befuddlement the first time he was asked if he was born again. He was a divorced man from sinful Hollywood. As governor of California he had signed the state's liberal abortion reform law in 1967, and later he had opposed the 1978 Briggs Amendment, which would have banned homosexuals from teaching in the state's public schools. Also, as the oldest elected president in U.S. history, he stood in rather sharp contrast to the opening salvo of Richard Viguerie's New Right manifesto, which proudly claimed, "The left is old and tired. The New Right is young and vigorous."[32]

As president, Reagan showed more concern for reviving the dormant cold war, deregulating business, and cutting taxes than he did for the moral issues of the New Right. In 1979 the New Right organizer Paul Weyrich had come dangerously close to admitting the movement's emphasis on social issues was a shallow commitment designed to garner evangelical votes while obscuring the substantive procorporate agenda of New Right politicians: "Yes, they're emotional issues, but that's better than talking about capital formation," he said. Certainly the corporate benefactors of the New Right's organizational superstructure valued profits over ideology; Coors, for instance, was headed by a reactionary zealot whose donations largely funded the important Heritage Foundation. But when the company recognized the consumer power of the gay market in 1979, it unhesitatingly ran ads in the gay paper the *Advocate*. Reagan showed a similarly cavalier attitude toward evangelical concerns in his early years, putting their platform on the backburner while pushing his economic agenda. As a sop to disgruntled Christians, Reagan appointed evangelical James Watt secretary of the interior and C. Everett Koop surgeon general. Neither proved satisfying, though, as Watt invited his own downfall by making offensive racist and sexist public comments. Koop, a longtime abortion opponent, found himself so disturbed by the rigidity on both sides of the debate that he publicly took a neutral stance. After he finally broke years of administration silence on the devastating AIDS crisis by recommending condoms for the sexually active in 1986, he quickly became persona non grata to the Right.[33]

Meanwhile, the Christian Right proved savvy in electing members to Congress who escalated the war against pornography. In the ninety-seventh Congress (1981–82) it helped kill a bill to lower penalties for interstate transportation of obscenity. During that Congress the California Republican William Dannemeyer lectured on "Christian ethics and public policy," voicing a standard Christian Right argument that the United States was a fundamentally Christian republic. To Dannemeyer this meant homosexuality, pornography, abortion, and other issues should be regulated according to biblical principles, not the beliefs of "those elitists, those Humanists." Other movement leaders concurred. Jesse Helms applauded a North Carolina prosecutor for "protect[ing]" the people of the state from "the degradation of pornography," and the California Representative Robert Dornan connected pornography to rape and "the venereal disease epidemics." Dornan also articulated the central concern of the Christian Right: "pornography is a direct challenge to the family because it encourages attitudes that are destructive of it."[34]

As their electoral strength increased, empowered evangelicals grew more assertive. Donald Wildmon's National Federation for Decency began a prominent boycott of 7-Eleven for selling dirty magazines in 1984.

With protests at 400 stores in 150 cities, the Federation quickly persuaded the owner of seventy-eight stores to pull such magazines as *Penthouse* and *Playboy*, while the owner of the 7-Eleven in the Christian stronghold of Wheaton, Illinois, simply closed his store. In 1984 Morality in Media also sponsored a National Catholic Conference on the Illegal Sex Industry, dedicated largely to pornography, in New York City.[35]

The argumentative structure of the Christian Right, like Citizens for Decent Literature before it, was founded on a monologue not intended for debate in the secular world. Thus *Christianity Today* ran numerous articles on pornography, with typical observations such as, "The Fascist African despot Idi Amin would order condemned prisoners to 'make love before him' while he sipped wine and enjoyed the spectacle. The implications and parallels are worth reflecting." Those implications remained implicit, though, while the differentiating factor of coercion went missing from the comparison. As noted above, Tim LaHaye rushed to blame social ills like divorce and illegitimacy on pornography, refusing to acknowledge factors such as the Reagan attack on the working class and its concomitant economically generated familial tensions or the underfunding of education. Donald Wildmon provided one of the more egregious examples of this monologic approach when he wrote of his reaction to a "pornographic" television miniseries: "Well, it's finally happened, I thought. *They're going to bring incest into millions of American homes.*" The fact, as feminists had been noting for years, that incest was already endemic to the nuclear family Wildmon effaced completely.[36]

Overblown rhetoric also continued to mark the Christian Right, as when Pastor Jerry Kirk—president of the National Coalition Against Pornography, one of many such groups to emerge in the 1980s—described his layover at Chicago's O'Hare airport as a "descent into hell" because of its smutty newsstands. But the most prevalent aspect of Christian Right discourse was its hazy melting of diverse topics into one unified construct, as all nonmarital/procreative sexual expression was framed as threats to the family. Thus the Memphis antiporn group MAD (Memphians Against Degeneracy) focused on pornography but also found time to take on topless dancing and homosexuality. The most outlandish such group was the Austin, Texas–based Citizens Against Pornography, which devoted at least as much time to homosexuality as it did to porn. Sometimes the themes coincided, as in a story on regulating adult arcades as it related to AIDS transmissions, but other times the group simply focused on gay and lesbian rights marches, and it held a rally in 1987 to "call attention to the open homosexual behavior in our public parks." In the fundamentalist worldview homosexuality itself qualified as pornographic. One lengthy investigational report filed by the group's leader described homosexual activity he observed in Austin's Pease Park; though the article contained no reference whatsoever to pornography, its title was "Pornography and AIDS in Parks of Austin." The heteronormative conflation of queerness and obscenity that liberals had tacitly endorsed in the 1950s now played directly into the hands of the Right.[37]

Reagan recognized the necessity of delivering the Christian Right something of actual substance. Abortion was too divisive a topic, but pornography lacked defenders among politicians, who feared being portrayed as pro-porn. He spoke against pornography often, mentioning it in a 1983 address to the National Association of Evangelicals in which he declared America "in the midst of a spiritual awakening and a moral renewal." He condemned porn again before the same body the next year and announced his grand revelation shortly thereafter. Signing the Child Protection Act of 1984, which strengthened the federal laws governing child pornography, Reagan announced that the attorney general was setting up "a new national commission to study the effects of pornography on our society." Leaving no doubts as to the predisposition of this new commission—generally known as the Meese Commission, after Attorney General Edwin Meese—Reagan mentioned the 1970 Presidential Commission Report disparagingly; "it's time to stop pretending that extreme pornography is a victimless crime," he said. The formation of the Meese Commission would rely on three recent developments: public awareness of child pornography, new social science projects that questioned the effect of violent sexual media on viewers, and developments in feminist analysis of porn. All would be misappropriated in the service of conservative antiporn ideology.[38]

Child Pornography and Advances in Social Science

Child pornography first seized the public consciousness in 1977. Information on the largely undocumented genre remains sparse, but it seems that imported European child porn—involving both simple nude pictures of children, as well as explicit depictions of sexual abuse—had entered the U.S. market in the late 1960s. Only in the mid-1970s, however, did domestic production grow to a noticeable size. As prosecutors at that time began moving against child pornography, they showed a fair amount of rigor in distinguishing it from the mainstream porn market of works involving consenting adults. Statutes "should punish such activity on the grounds of child abuse, rather than on the grounds of obscenity," a San Francisco district attorney told a California State Senate committee in 1977. A Department of Justice official agreed, telling the committee, "Perhaps our priorities have been misplaced in the past by putting too heavy a reliance on the pornographic statutes."[39]

States acted quickly in response to this new threat, and in 1977 alone laws against making and distributing child pornography were passed in Missouri, New Hampshire, Connecticut, Illinois, Arizona, Delaware, Ohio, and Wisconsin, among others, with a federal law following in 1978. Although these laws enjoyed widespread approval, the ACLU opposed them, preferring "vigorous enforcement of the laws regarding sexual abuse of minors" as the "appropriate response to the child pornography problem." Meanwhile, the media ran a barrage of frightening articles with titles such as "Child's Garden of Perversity," though most sources were quick to note that child pornographers were independent, underground merchants with no connection to the mainstream porn industry. *Time* described Jim Mitchell, codirector of *Behind the Green Door*, as "outraged" by child pornography, while *Parents* magazine pointed out that the Adult Film Association of America wholeheartedly supported laws against it.[40]

Not every contributor to the discourse on child pornography showed such clarity. *Redbook* ran an article on "What Pornographers Are Doing to Children," a "shocking report" whose misleading title suggested child abuse was a staple of American pornography. Evangelical Christians eagerly conflated child with adult pornography in their efforts to demonize the latter, as a 1981 *Christianity Today* article in favor of "excis[ing] the pornographic cancer" discussed First Amendment restrictions on adult pornography and the abuse of children as if they were one single issue. The reason for opposition to child pornography could also turn obscure in some hands; a Milwaukee prosecutor, for instance, explained in 1977, "My main concern was keeping this stuff out of the hands of children and adults who don't want it crammed down their throats," plainly failing to comprehend the perceived link between the production of child pornography and sexual abuse.[41]

Numbers, too, were malleable when it came to this unquantifiable black market. Members of the Los Angeles Police Department showed a particular propensity for stating hypotheses as facts. Testifying before a California Senate committee, one LAPD officer counted two hundred reported cases of child sexual assault in 1976 but then claimed another thirty thousand cases had gone unreported. Without any evidence he asserted that "probably 70% of them are homosexual in nature," letting the LAPD's institutionalized homophobia shape public perceptions. Later that year in another set of hearings, an LAPD Juvenile Division officer, Lloyd Martin, testified that the children sexually abused and used in pornography "make up our burglars and dope dealers and our robbers, and so forth." Asked if he had any evidence to support this, Martin responded, "No. I don't." Such unfounded assertions in the guise of official statements facilitated the spread of misinformation. For instance, as evidence of America's moral turpitude, Richard Viguerie claimed thirty thousand children in Los Angeles alone were used in child porn. This ridiculously high number probably came from a California report by the state Attorney General's Office; the report itself took the number from the LAPD officer's imagination, while Viguerie took the report's estimate of child sexual abuse victims and converted them all into porn victims. In fact, the report counted 160 children from the entire state of California as child pornography participants. By 1982 *Homemakers* magazine reported the unlikely claim that one fourth of the annual porn industry's income derived from "kiddy porn."[42]

These obfuscations clouded the public debate, shifting attention away from actual abuse and toward the circulation of texts and images. For instance, the most publicized "child porn" case of the late 1970s involved *Show Me! A Picture Book of Sex for Children and Parents*, published by St. Martin's Press. The book contained frank photographs of nude children, as part of an effort to educate with directness. After prosecutions in Massachusetts, Oklahoma, and New Hampshire its publisher filed a preemptive injunction in New York, which ultimately failed. Another child pornography case reached the Supreme Court in 1982. Paul Ferber had sold films depicting young boys masturbating, and the Court affirmed his conviction. Exempting child pornography from the *Miller* standard, Byron White's opinion found it "intrinsically related to the sexual abuse of children" and concluded a work "need not be 'patently offensive' in order to have required the sexual exploitation of a child for its production." To secure a unanimous court, White did specifically insist that state child pornography laws "be limited to works that visually depict sexual conduct by children," thus preserving the liberty of such books as *Show Me*. The Reagan administration felt free to push the boundaries of this provision, as the president in 1984 signed a "kidporn" bill that included mere nudity of the "lascivious" type, leaving that term vague enough for prosecutors to bring their own interpretations.[43]

As the child pornography threat emerged, social scientists also opened new avenues in the porn debate. The 1970 Presidential Commission report had been scorned by conservatives but only poorly refuted. In a 1971 article Harry Clor noted several shortcomings of the report: its limited longitudinal reach in terms of effects, its overreliance on college students and sex criminals, the limitations of a laboratory setting in gauging responses to porn exposure, and an obvious ideological predisposition toward libertarianism. But neither Clor nor anyone else offered competing evidence that would refute the commission by showing a causal connection between porn and antisocial behavior.[44]

Only at the end of the 1970s did social scientists finally begin to substantively challenge the commission's report. Two psychology professors, Neil Malamuth and Edward Donnerstein, led the charge, and they compiled an overview of the new research in the 1984 anthology *Pornography and Sexual Aggression*. The results challenged both libertarians and conservatives. Separate studies found violent pornography to have tangible effects on perception and behavior in laboratory-controlled settings. Malamuth found that "exposure to aggressive pornography may alter observers' perceptions of rape and rape victims," leading to greater acceptance—especially among male viewers—of the "rape myth" that women wanted, deserved, or enjoyed rape. Donnerstein, meanwhile, found male subjects more likely to inflict violence (in the form of seemingly real electric shocks) on females after exposure to rape-based pornography. "We have now seen that there is a direct causal relationship between exposure to aggressive pornography and violence against women," he wrote.[45]

Before the antiporn brigades could cheer, however, Malamuth and Donnerstein went to great lengths to qualify their assertions. They very carefully explained that it was the violence and not the sex in violent pornography that generated the effects. Controlling each factor, both authors separately concluded that mere sexual explicitness had no discernible effects on male aggression toward women but that even depictions of non-sexual aggression toward women generated results similar to those of violent pornography. Pornography "is not what influences aggression against women," Donnerstein wrote, "but rather how women are depicted in the media." He suggested that "the issue of whether or not pornography is related to aggression against women might best be served by doing away with the term *pornography*." The other essays collected in the anthology gave conflicting evidence on the topic. Two sociologists found that "massive exposure" of male subjects to porn over the course of six weeks "trivialize[d] rape through the portrayal of women as hyperpromiscuous and socially irresponsible [and] increased sex callousness considerably." On the other hand, researchers in Japan noted that that nation contained much more violent porn than the United States but had a much lower rape rate, suggesting any analysis of the two variables required attention to social context to be meaningful. Nothing in the emerging social science studies, then, overturned the prevailing academic consensus on nonviolent pornography's harmlessness, but the new studies on violent porn loaned themselves to facile misinterpretation.[46]

The Meese Commission

The nascent Meese Commission would use the child-porn black market and the social science conclusions about violent pornography indiscriminately, blurring the lines between those categories and consensual adult pornography to cast a shadow over the entire field of adult entertainment. It also adopted feminist rhetoric without any substantive feminist consciousness on display, thus ostensibly distancing itself from its clear Christian Right commitments. The Reagan administration ensured the commission's disposition with its member selection. Of the eleven commission members, seven had taken public stands against pornography prior to appointment. Religious leaders were represented in James Dobson (founder of Focus on the Family) and Father Bruce Ritter (of New York's Covenant House, a shelter for teenage runaways). On the ostensibly secular front were also the Reagan-appointed federal judge Edward Garcia and a Scottsdale, Arizona, city council member, Diane Cusack. The commission's chair, Henry Hudson, and its executive director, Alan Sears, both worked as prosecutors who sought out obscenity cases. Only the CBS vice president and *Woman's Day* editor Ellen Levine and the psychologist Judith Becker represented liberal or feminist perspectives.[47]

Unlike the 1970 Presidential Commission, the Meese Commission emphasized public hearings rather than social science experiments. This methodology was both ideological and expedient; as the commission's report would note, the body received $500,000 and one year to undertake its study, which amounted to half the time and one-sixteenth of the budget (in adjusted dollars) of the earlier commission. While this showed the Reagan administration's preference for superficial gestures designed to placate the Christian Right over substantive policy support, it also limited the commission's resources dramatically in the expensive and time-consuming field of contracted social science. Regardless, the commission clearly preferred public hearings for the same reason the earlier commission avoided them: the hearings could serve as newsworthy, highly emotional flashpoints where porn opponents could voice their arguments. The Meese Commission began its hearings in 1985, and the media was quick to criticize its procedure. As the feminist anthropologist Carole Vance noted in the *Nation*, 68 of 208 witnesses came from vice squads and law-enforcement organizations, and 77 percent of the witnesses took antiporn stances. Besides law enforcers, the hearings prominently featured various "victims" of pornography, from women forced into posing for pictures to men "corrupted" by exposure. In another piece Vance documented one victim, a man who discovered a pack of pornographic playing cards at age twelve. By sixteen he consumed a "steady diet" of adult magazines; in his twenties he began watching pornographic videos; ultimately he went on to have "promiscuous sex" with "two different women." He concluded, "I strongly believe that all that has happened to me can be traced back to the finding of those porno cards. If it weren't for my faith in God and the forgiveness of Jesus Christ, I would now possibly be a pervert, an alcoholic, or dead! I am a victim of pornography." Vance concluded her description by noting in amazement, "The audience sat in attentive silence. No one laughed."[48]

Vance also observed the differing treatment accorded to witnesses depending on their perspectives. When a former *Playboy* bunny testified about drug use, rape, and even murder in the Playboy mansion, no commissioners challenged her or asked for evidence. But when a former *Penthouse* pet testified about her positive experiences as a porn model, male commissioners asked her prying and irrelevant questions about her sex life, such as whether she enjoyed sex in cars and whether she had a vibrator collection. Even more egregiously, in early 1986 the commission sent a letter to several major corporations, including the owners of Waldenbooks and 7-Eleven, asking them to respond to unattributed accusations (actually made by Donald Wildmon of the National Federation for Decency) that they were "distributors of pornography." The letter informed the companies that failure to respond would be interpreted as acceptance of the description, which would be published in the commission's forthcoming report. Such tactics alienated mainstream journalists, whose sentiments were reflected in media coverage. In one issue, *Publishers Weekly* accused the "Meese Commission Vigilantes" of "bring[ing] us back to the darkest days of McCarthyism" with "blackmail" tactics. *Time*, in a lengthy article on the "new moral militancy" of the GOP in the 1980s, called the Meese Commission "Sex Busters" and described its hearings as a "surrealist mystery tour of sexual perversity."[49]

Like the Presidential Commission in 1970, the Meese Commission disregarded advance negative publicity and released a final report in July 1986 that maintained its established perspective. The two-thousand-page report began with personal commissioner statements that left little suspense as to what would follow. First came the chair, Henry Hudson, declaring that he endorsed the final report with one exception: its suggestion that prosecutors decline to press obscenity charges against materials containing only printed text, which Hudson considered fair game for prosecution. Then came psychiatrist Park Dietz, declaring, "Pornography is both causal and symptomatic of immorality and corruption," which drew the concurrence of four other members. James Dobson delivered a lengthy sermon against adult bookstores, which "are often centers of disease and corruption." He went on to describe private-viewing booths like Dante describing hell: "The stench is often unbearable," Dobson wrote, and "the floor becomes sticky with semen, urine, and saliva." After Dobson's fire and brimstone, Bruce Ritter's statement sounded calm and composed, but its message was as fierce. Ritter's main argument was that "category III" material, described by the commission as sexually explicit but nonviolent and nondegrading, "does not exist," since such materials "profoundly indignify the very state of marriage and degrade the very notion of sexuality itself and are therefore seriously harmful to individuals and to society."[50]

Only commissioners Ellen Levine, Judith Becker, and child-abuse expert Deanne Tilton dissented. "We reject any judgmental and condescending efforts to speak on women's behalf as though they were helpless, mindless children," they wrote of the commission's construction of pornography's "victims." Levine and Becker went on to criticize the stacking of the hearings toward antiporn witnesses. Noting that the very nature of the public hearings made it difficult for ordinary citizens to testify about positive experiences with pornography, the two dissenters noted, "since such material is selling to millions of apparently satisfied consumers, it seems obvious that the data gathered is not well balanced." The duo also condemned the skewing of the materials examined "to the very violent and extremely degrading," the lack of support for sex education in the report, and the "simple solutions to complex problems" offered by antiporn leaders.[51]

These concerns remained absent from the body of the report, which began with a discussion of the First Amendment's place in porn debates. Both society and the amendment itself suffer "if the essential appeal of the First Amendment is dissipated on arguments so tenuously associated with any of [its] purposes or principles," the report asserted, explaining that the strength of the amendment lay not just in courts, but "must reside as well in widespread acceptance" of freedom of speech. "We fear this acceptance is jeopardized when the First Amendment too often becomes the rhetorical device by which pornography is defended," the commission elaborated.[52]

After reducing the First Amendment to a rhetorical device applicable only to material that draws no social opposition, the commission went on to render moot its own discussion by removing pornography from speech. Because the "predominant use of such material is as a masturbatory aid," the report claimed without citing evidence, "what this material involves is not so much portrayal of sex, or discussion of sex, but simply sex itself." With this reification in place, the commission considered pornography to be "properly removed from the First Amendment questions." With a similarly cavalier attitude toward free speech the report then offered a non sequitur regarding boycott tactics that foreclosed citizen access to protected speech: "We regret that legitimate bookstores have been pressured to remove from their shelves legitimate and serious discussions of sexuality, but none of us would presume to tell a Catholic bookseller that in choosing books he should not discriminate against books favoring abortion."[53] The unfounded analogy served no purpose but to legitimize coercion by equating it with the personal choice of booksellers.

The commission next discussed the "harm" of pornography. In a telling aside it wrote, "We do not wish in referring repeatedly to 'harm' to burden ourselves with an unduly narrow conception of harm." This vague and expansive notion of harm allowed the concept to encompass everything from rape to moral harms such as promiscuity. "Pornography," too, received a semantic modification, this time to "avoid the usual definitional morass"; in the commission's eyes it now included any sexually explicit media whatsoever, including sex-educational materials. Within this framework the commission reached predictable conclusions. Citing Malamuth and Donnerstein at length, it found great harm in violent pornography, though it admitted R-rated "slasher" horror films were "likely to produce the consequences discussed here to a greater extent than most materials available in 'adults only' pornographic outlets." Though the commission admitted it was "less confident" about nonviolent pornography, it still found much moral harm in it, even as the report tried to diminish the significance of such material by calling the category of nonviolent pornography "quite small in terms of currently available materials," again without any semblance of evidence.[54]

Four hundred pages into the first of its two lengthy volumes, the perversely structured Meese Commission report suddenly delivered its ninety-two policy recommendations. These began with a proposal to Congress to enact a forfeiture statute covering all proceeds and instruments used in any violation of federal obscenity law, added a suggestion that the Justice Department escalate its obscenity efforts, and included a recommendation of a one-year minimum prison sentence for any repeat violation of federal obscenity laws. More than forty-five of the ninety-two recommendations dealt with child pornography, including a proposal for legislation prohibiting the use of models under the age of twenty-one. Though the report had earlier called child pornography "largely distinct from any aspect" of the adult porn industry, it saw no problem with integrating child porn recommendations with those involving such topics as telephone-based "dial-a-porn" services, thus preserving the illusion of a monolithic porn industry that preyed on children.[55]

Having delivered its recommendations, the Meese Commission next turned to "victimization." Editorial choices reflected the commission's sympathies, as the section began with a solid three-page quote from antiporn feminist Andrea Dworkin. "In this country where I live as a citizen," Dworkin said, "women are penetrated by animals and objects for public entertainment, women are urinated on and defecated on." With the mood thus set, the report compiled an extensive list of anecdotes from commission hearings in which pornography was involved in various abuses. A molested daughter testified that her father left a *Playboy* centerfold on her bed with her name written on it; in the report's awkward wording, "He joined her in bed that night and taught her about sex." Other examples included gang rapists who left smut magazines behind in their camping grounds; a racial murder allegedly suggested by a pornographic picture; a teenage boy who died during autoerotic asphyxiation he had allegedly learned about in *Hustler*; and numerous stories involving guilt, shame, fear, embarrassment, "situations in which pornography has been used to instill feelings of racial inferiority," drug use, alcoholism, venereal diseases, and even financial loss. The only commonality linking the anecdotes was that the various harms were related, at least tangentially, to porn. Some tales seemed geared to horrify the devout: "I experienced everything from date rape to physical abuse, to group sex and finally to fantasizing homosexuality," said one former *Playboy* bunny in a tragic narrative that conflated sexual coercion with "deviation" (the articulation inexplicably suggesting the greatest horror was the lesbian fantasies). Perhaps the most bizarre story came from a woman whose husband was "extremely excited by the story of a man who had fish in an aquarium, stuck his organ in the aquarium and they nibbled on it until he orgasmed." The husband then decided to purchase his own fish tank, the woman explained, before adding, "At that time John was physically abusing me by pulling my hair, slapping me, kicking me, stomping on my feet." What connection this had to his porn consumption remained unclear.[56]

Among pornography's victims the commission counted its performers, who "seem to share troubled or at least ambivalent personal backgrounds," the report claimed. Yet it also admitted the lack of actual representative evidence. Despite possessing "severely limited" information, the report proceeded to more specifically describe porn performers as "normally young, previously abused, and financially strapped." Nowhere did the report endorse social welfare measures that might relieve the suffering of such young abuse victims. Instead, despite the unsubstantiated victim model, the report's number-one policy recommendation was to legally classify porn work as "a subset of prostitution"—thus criminalizing the very group it had just presented as victims one single page earlier.[57]

By foregrounding Andrea Dworkin's "eloquent testimony," as the report called her undeniably powerful words, the Meese Commission seemed to align itself with feminist efforts against porn. Indeed, throughout, the report cloaked itself in a veneer of feminism, using feminist rhetoric to call porn "a practice of discrimination on the basis of sex." Yet most of the commissioners diverged radically from feminist notions of harm against women, which stemmed from gendered inequalities rather than moral damage; Chairman Hudson, for instance, referred in his personal statement to porn's tendency to "distort the moral sensitivity of women and undermine the values underlying the family unit," a profoundly antifeminist perspective rooted in the upholding of traditional gender roles. Invoking feminism even as it called for the arrest of those "victims" allegedly driven to sex work, the commission report sought to avoid categorization as a direct offspring of the Christian Right. While this effort failed among the general public, it did exacerbate some of the feminist fault lines I will discuss in chapter 7.[58]

In its second volume the Meese Commission report spent several hundred pages linking the porn industry to organized crime. It then offered several suggestions for antiporn protestors; though the section was titled "Methods by Which Citizens Can Express Concern About Pornography," the suggestions were full of "should" statements rather than "could" or "can" statements, making abundantly clear the already evident direction in which the commission's sympathies lay. Most inexplicably, the report concluded with three hundred pages of graphic sexual descriptions. First came a list of 2,325 magazines, 725 books, and 2,370 film titles, apparently included simply to shock. Then, after a parade of titles beginning with *A Cock Between Friends*, marching through highlights such as *Anal Fuck* and *Vicky's Cock Fucking Throat* to conclude benignly with *800 Fantasy Lane*, came extended descriptions of magazines such as *Asian Slut*. Next came book summaries, with a summary of *Tying Up Rebecca* delivered in a porn-degree-zero writing style as graphic as the real book: "The boy ejaculated in the tub. Vern stood on the tub and urinated on them. The urine landed in Svetlana's mouth. The boy performed cunnilingus on Svetlana. Vern then got dressed and left." And finally, to conclude on a fever pitch of filth worthy of a Citizens for Decent Literature erotic monologue, the report printed re-constructed screenplays of some porn films, with protagonists yelling, "You want a good stiff dick in your mouth. . . . Oh suck on it, suck."[59]

Thus the Meese Commission's *Final Report* provided a complement to other New Right attempts to repeal the permissive society and return to an imagined past that lacked the array of sexually deviant attacks on the family unleashed by the sexual revolution, fitting snugly into the Christian Right's culture war. Pornography had provided a malleable trope for de-monization, and conservatives deployed it widely. The Parents' Music Re-source Center (PMRC), a group interested in preventing youthful access to music with explicit lyrics, pitted itself against what it called "porn rock." As historian Gillian Frank observes, both the PMRC and the private-action-endorsing Meese Commission resonated with the New Right's de-regulatory corporate sympathies, as "the regulation of sexuality occurred in increasingly privatized and less democratic forms of governance," which he also links to the Christian Right's influential efforts to scale back public-school sex education to cater to the movement's abstinence-only bent.[60]

Meanwhile, the profitable phone-sex industry was decried as "Dial-a-Porn" by New Right politicians, eager to display their Christian credibility. The Senate Committee on the Judiciary was staffed with several luminaries of the New Right, such as Paul Laxalt, Strom Thurmond, Alan Simpson, John East, and Jeremiah Denton, and when it held hearings on "Dial-a-Porn" in 1985, it stacked the witness list with conservative sympathizers, in-cluding Jesse Helms. When the ACLU's Barry Lynn arrived, the acting chair, Denton, treated him curtly. Denton compared phone sex to shouting "fire" in a crowded theater, and when Lynn attempted to "respond to that analogy," Denton cut him off to deliver a four-paragraph soliloquy about the "harms" of phone sex.[61]

Pornography was not the only trope of the culture wars; sometimes "war" itself took on a literal meaning. Bombings and other violence against abortion clinics escalated rapidly in the 1980s. The crusade against homo-sexuality also continued unabated, fueled by exploitation of the AIDS crisis. As a Christian Family Renewal mailing explained, "Homosexuality is not going to go away until you take an *official* stand on the issue." The group in-cluded an "Immunity from AIDS" mandate demanding a quarantine of all AIDS patients, a category it casually conflated with all gay men. This vitri-olic homophobia was given official credence by the Supreme Court, which upheld a Georgia sodomy law in 1986. In his lead opinion Byron White adopted a Christian Right slippery-slope argument in claiming the decriminalization of "homosexual conduct" in the privacy of the home would lead to similar treatment for adultery, incest, and "other sexual crimes." Leaving behind the vast difference between consensual gay sex and abusive molestation, White simply wrote, "We are unwilling to start down that road." In his concurrence Chief Justice Burger cited "millennia of moral teaching," with oddly chosen examples such as Blackstone's description of "the infamous crime against nature" as an offense of "deeper malignity" than rape. Into this regressive social atmosphere the Meese Commission report was launched. Despite the report's intellectual incoherence and manipulative presentation, it indeed marked a resuscitation of governmental attacks on pornography in the late 1980s.[62]

Rollback

Predictably, the Meese Commission report drew accolades from the evangelical Christian press. *Christianity Today* endorsed the report enthusiastically, emphasizing violent and child pornography without reference to the commission's own government-sponsored textual smut. Phyllis Schlafly also applauded the report in her newsletter, calling the commission "a very diverse group, professionally and ideologically." Schlafly soon published a compilation of excerpts from the hearings, titling the book *Pornography's Victims.*[63]

More common, however, were scathing condemnations of the report. Numerous works attacked the commission, from *The Meese Commission Exposed*, a book featuring numerous intellectuals and artists from Kurt Vonnegut to Betty Friedan, to *United States of America vs. Sex*, a journalistic expose published by Penthouse. The ACLU issued the most detailed critique, addressing commission points by juxtaposing report text and commentary. Also rejecting the "victims of pornography" model, the ACLU instead pinpointed abusive relationships, substance abuse, and various family crises as the actual issues at stake, with pornography "a tangential afterthought." Rejecting the commission's divorcing of pornography and speech, and reflecting the distance it had come since the 1950s, the ACLU argued that the sexual themes of pornography, even when abhorrently sexist, were "quintessentially political," since they concerned "the distribution and use of power in social relations," and were thus protected speech. The ACLU sued to gain access to commission working papers, and it found that early drafts of the report had mentioned that dial-a-porn revenue had in some cases been used to subsidize lifeline services for the poor and elderly. These references were removed from the final report, an indication of ideological editing at play. The ACLU critique opposed most of the commission policy recommendations, finding reactionary intent even behind seemingly neutral suggestions. For instance, whereas the fourth recommendation of the commission involved modifying the 1910 Mann Act, which prohibited the interstate transportation of "any woman or girl" for immoral purposes, ostensibly merely to make it gender-neutral, the ACLU observed, this "would simply give prosecutors a new weapon against gay lifestyles."[64]

More damaging than ideological criticism, however, was criticism by social scientists. Edward Donnerstein and Daniel Linz published an essay in *Psychology Today* carefully explaining how the Meese Commission had misappropriated their research. "It is not sex, but violence, that is an obscenity in our society," the authors claimed, accusing the commission of "ignor[ing] the data" and "miss[ing] the boat" by focusing on the former instead of the latter. The social scientists went on to publish a book in 1987 elaborating on their assertion that the Meese Commission drew "unwarranted extrapolations from the available data." Instead of stricter laws, the social scientists called for "a more well-informed public."[65]

Negative publicity led to the report's immediate disappearance from public view. Attorney General Meese said he had not yet read the report when presented with it on July 9, 1986, but that he would offer his response in "two to four weeks." He failed to comment for three months, and after a brief and unpublicized endorsement the report was not mentioned again. The public showed no interest in reading it. While the official report on the *Challenger* spacecraft disaster sold thirty thousand copies, the Government Printing Office sold only five thousand of the commission's report. Still more telling was the fact that the 1970 Presidential Commission report had been sold in a mass-market edition by Bantam, whereas the only publishing company to take advantage of the noncopyrighted Meese Commission report was Nashville's Rutledge Hill Press, whose biggest seller to date had been *The Original Tennessee Homecoming Cookbook.*[66]

The disappearance of the Meese Commission report did not indicate widespread rejection of it among the Christian Right or its political representatives, however. Indeed, the Right simply disregarded Donnerstein's repeated rejections of pornography's causal ties to violence. Though conservative critics of the 1970 Presidential Commission report had faulted its reliance on data obtained from prison interviews, which were seen as overtly self-serving, they embraced the method when it supported their conclusions. In 1988 *Conservative Digest* told of Arthur Gary Bishop, executed in Utah for raping and killing five young boys. Uncritically calling Bishop a "victim," the digest explained that he "readily acknowledged that pornography had played an important role in distorting his values, destroying his character, and instigating his crimes." In this rhetorical framework anecdotal evidence overshadowed social science data when it came to proving pornography's harms. Meanwhile, the ACLU's thorough critique went entirely unheeded by politicians, who were learning to avoid affiliation with the group. In the 1988 presidential debates George Bush would famously use Michael Dukakis's status as a "card-carrying member" of the ACLU to discredit him, asking, "Do we want this country to go that far left?" With the term *liberal* itself reconfigured as an epithet, the ACLU's critique found no vocal proponents in the halls of power.[67]

Neither, however, did the Meese Commission report's poor reception suggest a lack of follow-through on behalf of the government. If the Meese Commission entered historical memory mostly as a joke, its ideology regarding obscenity law nonetheless shaped federal policy in the late 1980s. Though a June 1986 state obscenity referendum in Maine—the first such measure in the nation in more than a decade—was resoundingly defeated, officials elsewhere cracked down on pornography that year. Federal obscenity prosecutions had lagged for much of the 1980s, with fewer than ten per year on average during the Reagan administration. This changed abruptly following the report's release; from ten indictments in 1986, the statistics flew to eighty in 1987. Local prosecutors read this as an invitation to commence their own efforts. In Denver a deputy district attorney helped draft a new state law "aimed at hard-core pornography involving children, violence, rape, and torture" but immediately prosecuted commonplace magazines "showing close-ups of men and women engaged in sex acts." Two video-store owners in Beaufort, South Carolina, were arrested late in 1986 for renting out nonviolent adult pornography.[68]

At times the Justice Department blatantly abused its powers, threatening companies in liberal states with prosecution in the most conservative districts it could find. For instance, the Connecticut company Consumer's Marketing Group, which sold adult materials through the mail, was simultaneously indicted in 1986 in Utah, Mississippi, Indiana, and Delaware. In North Carolina PHE, better known as Adam & Eve, faced obscenity charges in 1986. Federal officials first pressured the local district attorney to prosecute the firm, but he refused, calling the project "a total waste of time and law enforcement resources." The Justice Department next succeeded in persuading the neighboring county to press charges, which resulted in a jury acquittal delivered in under five minutes of deliberation. Finally the Justice Department itself took over and charged Adam & Eve's owner, Phil Harvey, with distributing obscenity in Utah, threatening him with further charges unless he agreed to cease distribution of all materials more explicit than R-rated Hollywood films, including magazines like *Playboy* and best-selling books like *The Joy of Sex*. When Harvey refused, he suddenly faced another indictment, this time in Kentucky.[69]

In court, records emerged detailing a "coordinated, nationwide prosecution strategy" against adult companies; a letter from Utah's U.S. attorney Brent Ward to Attorney General Edwin Meese had proposed simultaneous multiple prosecutions against individual firms in numerous locations. This, Ward wrote, would "strike a serious blow" against the pornography industry by "test[ing] the limits of the pornographers' endurance" and "undermine profitability to the point that the survival of obscenity enterprises will be threatened." The sheer flagrance of this abuse of power ultimately assisted the persecuted firms. Consumer's Marketing Group won injunctive relief against the Justice Department, as did Adam & Eve in a federal court decision that accused the Justice Department of using "harassment and threats of multiple prosecutions, to suppress [Adam & Eve's] constitutionally protected activities."[70]

As these cases suggested, the Reagan Justice Department took a hard-line stance against pornography. Another particularly vindictive approach to obscenity law involved deployment of the Racketeer Influenced and Corrupt Organizations Act (RICO) to porn merchants. This law allowed for the prosecution of any crime involving two or more parties as a syndicated racket, and included provisions for the seizure of property. In one 1987 case Dennis and Barbara Pryba, a Virginia couple who ran several video stores described as 75 percent to 80 percent nonerotic, but with backroom "adults only" sections included, forfeited approximately $1 million in personal assets after being convicted of selling $105 worth of obscene merchandise. The case traveled all the way to the Supreme Court, which denied certiorari in 1990, thus letting stand the RICO seizures. RICO quickly became a common prosecutorial approach to obscenity cases.[71]

Meanwhile, though its attrition tactic of multiple prosecutions had been reined in, the Justice Department continued to indict adult merchants in the most conservative and provincial districts available. Thus Vivid Video's founder, Steven Hirsch, pleaded guilty to obscenity charges and paid a $500,000 fine in Mississippi in 1991, and VCA's founder, Russell Hampshire, accepted a plea bargain of $2 million and one year in jail as a result of an Alabama indictment that same year. Adult entrepreneur Mark Carriere paid even more, $3.5 million, in fines in Florida the next year. As a result of these prosecutions the major firms in the adult entertainment industry began a careful monitoring of their product to avoid offending government tastes. Discussing the cases, even an FBI obscenity investigator testified that fellow agents had become "zealots" whose "religious belief overstepped good judgment."[72]

By 1988 the Justice Department possessed ninety-three trained "Obscenity/Child Exploitation Specialists," whose very title indicated the department's eagerness to conflate child pornography and abuse with the mainstream adult porn industry. The Justice Department also went well beyond the conclusions of the Meese Commission in its discussion of pornography and children. Claiming its goal was to "eliminate trafficking in child pornography, thereby reducing child molestation," the department went beyond even the furthest-reaching Meese Commission conclusion. In fact, the "only remaining commercial producer of kiddie porn in the United States" was, as the *Progressive* wrote, "Uncle Sam." Instead of combating the largely nonexistent child pornography industry, the Justice Department's project involved entrapping pedophiles susceptible to solicitations sent by covert government operations. This effectively resulted in an exploitation and criminalization of pedophilia but did nothing to address actual child abuse or the production of child pornography.[73]

A department report issued that year listed "obscenity and child sexual exploitation" alongside drugs, terrorism, and organized crime as the "top criminal justice priorities." Following the Meese Commission, the Justice Department minimized perception of ordinary sex acts in pornography, haphazardly characterizing the market as consisting of "child sexual abuse, bondage, torture, rape, incest, orgies, sex with animals, excretory functions, lesbian, homosexual and transsexual activity" in a typical scare-tactic manner that gave equal legitimacy to protecting children and preserving hetero-normative Christian values. Going even beyond the commission, the Justice Department claimed—in a conspicuous use of the passive voice that suggested the utter lack of supporting evidence—that pornography consumers "have been reported to have a frightening but not surprising degree of overlap with the police blotters' list of sex criminals and violent assailants." When it came to protecting children from exposure to adult pornography, the Justice Department again revealed an overtly Christian perspective. Instead of continuing to advance obsolete theories of "antisocial" behavior or sex crimes, it simply claimed youthful exposure could "have a substantial impact upon the way they view sex, marriage, women, and the conduct of men in our society toward these important social relationships," thus effectively criminalizing one side of the so-called culture war.[74]

Predictably, the Christian conflation of pornography and homosexuality persisted in the context of this constant legitimization of repression. In the Senate Jesse Helms took offense to some artworks funded by the National Endowment for the Arts and pushed for a ban on future NEA funding for "obscene or indecent" material, a definition that included "homoeroticism" as one of its criteria. Helms's ban passed a voice vote in the Senate but was ultimately scaled back to merely bar funding for "obscene" material, dropping the term *indecency* after the House took exception. The attention Helms brought to photographers Andres Serrano (whose "Piss Christ" depicted a crucifix in a urinal) and Robert Mapplethorpe (who often focused on interracial gay sadomasochism) resulted in obscenity charges against the director of a Cincinnati art gallery after he held a Mapplethorpe exhibit. Though the director was ultimately acquitted in 1990, the overt homoeroticism of Mapplethorpe's critically acclaimed photographs clearly precipitated the prosecution. Most significant, when groups like Gay Men's Health Crisis responded to the Reagan administration's absence of leadership on the AIDS crisis with sexually graphic educational materials, Helms once again targeted them as obscene, introducing a legislative amendment barring the use of CDC resources for projects that "promote or encourage, directly, homosexual sexual activities" in 1987. Even after gay rights groups defeated the Helms Amendment in court, it left a residual chilling effect on prevention programs, as political moralism continued obstructing lifesaving public health efforts.[75]

In Fort Lauderdale, Florida, obscenity law was stretched to unprecedented new lengths in 1990 when the rap group 2 Live Crew's album *As Dirty As They Wanna Be* was declared obscene by a federal judge, resulting in the prosecution and conviction of a local record store owner for selling the album. The case took on racial overtones; the jury was described as "all-white, mostly female," and black defendant Charles Freeman angrily told local media, "They don't know nothing about the [goddamn] ghetto."[76] Though the conviction was predictably overturned on appeal, the episode showed the newfound extent to which obscenity laws could be pushed in a political climate favorable to prosecution.

As the 1990s began, the Christian Right had failed to repeal the permissive society but had strongly impacted public policy regarding pornography and obscenity. Politicized evangelicals voted Republican, in return for moralistic policies intended to preserve the sanctity of the heterosexual nuclear family. Attacks on pornography fit into a larger framework of attacks on gay rights, abortion, and feminism, and although the Christian Right failed to impose its normative standards to the extent it would have preferred, the political landscape in 1990 looked vastly different than it had in 1976. Outward displays of piety grew more common, while obscenity prosecutions reached a fervor unseen since the brief explosion of repression after the 1973 *Miller* decision. In a reflection of how thoroughly postwar liberalism had failed, even some radical feminists began to side with the Right rather than liberals on the issue of pornography. We turn now to the development of that anomalous alliance.

7. PORNOGRAPHY IS THE PRACTICE, WHERE IS THE THEORY?
Second-Wave Feminist Encounters with Porn

EXPLAINING LATE IN 1978 WHY organized feminist antiporn activism had taken a decade to appear after the women's liberation movement began in 1968, Robin Morgan wrote, "Many of us have been coerced into silence" on the issue.[1] This silence has been transposed onto the historiography of the modern feminist movement, but it might better be described as a strategic deafness on Morgan's part. In fact, feminists were active, engaged, and above all, vocal in considering pornography from the early years of the women's liberation movement, though they failed to conform to the interpretive model later dictated by antiporn feminists. The architects of the antiporn wing of the movement, however, effectively rewrote the narrative of modern feminism to obscure several years of diverse thought on the topic and instill their own position as the singular and inevitable outcome of feminism.

Historians have yet to penetrate the fog of this myth with much clarity, but this chapter recovers the shifting analytical terrain of second-wave feminism's confrontations with pornography, which were much more varied than antiporn advocates acknowledged. "Most feminists have chosen to ignore the degrading nature of pornography," claimed Diana Russell in 1977, but a more accurate assessment reveals that they instead chose not to assign it a position of centrality in their analysis of women's oppression. Though in 1979 the antiporn leader Andrea Dworkin would categorically describe pornography as "inextricably tied to victimizing, hurting, exploiting," a half-decade earlier even she had found sufficient redeeming social value in the pornographic magazine *Suck* to credit it with taking a "relevant, respectable stand" in its advocacy of oral sex.[2]

Despite this, most scholars of feminism and women's history continue to date feminist analysis of pornography as beginning in the late 1970s.[3] The originators of the antiporn movement endorse this perspective, as seen in Susan Brownmiller's memoirs, which paint antiporn feminism as the dominant feminist framework dating back to the movement's beginning.

Though exciting scholarship continues to approach second-wave feminism, too often this work uncritically accepts antiporn claims, as seen in a 2003 article that mistakenly calls the sexually inexplicit 1976 horror film *Snuff* "the most egregious example" of the pornographic genre. Scholars seem uneager to reassess the topic—a recent collection of papers on women and popular culture in the 1970s discusses everything from cookbooks to disco but makes no mention of pornography—and the result is to allow a retroactive determinism to shape the course of feminist history. Here I seek to restore the full narrative of feminist thought on pornography, tracing the issue as it evolved from epiphenomenal annoyance to the root cause of women's oppression. This trajectory was not inevitable, nor did it move by force of intellectual dialectics stemming from any fundamental tenets of women's liberation.[4]

From the start second-wave feminists took a hostile stance toward sexism in pornography, decrying such masculinist fantasies as the 1972 film *Deep Throat*, which heralded in the "porno chic" phenomenon. But even as they vigilantly monitored this oppressive pabulum, early feminists envisioned and sometimes created an alternative pornography in which women held erotic agency. The antiporn introduction of a distinction between pornography and "erotica" in the late 1970s helped suppress this vision, both by rendering a "feminist pornography" inherently oxymoronic and by outlining the qualities of erotica in such a way as to deprive female sexuality of any pleasurable prurience, reintroducing femininity to a movement initially predicated on the annihilation of gender roles.

Antiporn feminism also parted ways with the initial direction of the women's liberation movement through its willingness to call on the powers of the state in the name of suppression. At the start of the 1970s, proponents of women's liberation, upset at the pornography they encountered, made it abundantly clear that the risks of state censorship far outweighed any potential benefits, but by the mid-1980s leading figures of the antiporn movement endorsed precisely this expansion of state power. Lesbian feminists—especially wary of censorship, given the lengthy history of their sexuality being seen as "obscene"—in particular, resisted these efforts; indeed, lesbian resistance to censorship provides a far more continuous thread within modern feminism than does antiporn activism.

Feminist analyses of women's labor provided another site of transition facilitated by antiporn feminists. The feminist occupations of several sexually explicit publishers in the early 1970s took shape over labor issues, namely women's relegation to what they called "shit work." These actions recognized the importance of controlling the means of production and of structural changes in the nature of women's labor. When women's labor resurfaced in the antiporn movement, these organizing principles had been effaced to make way for an image of women in pornography as victimized pawns on a male chessboard—brutalized, infantilized, and deprived of all agency.

This scaling back of feminist demands—this cessation of the radical, structural interrogations that marked the women's liberation movement—was perhaps the greatest break with the aspirations of feminism wrought by the antiporn movement. In taking a movement wracked by internecine conflict, particularly over sexuality, and attempting to eliminate that conflict by introducing a topic around which all women could seemingly rally, antiporn feminists promoted a pared-down version of the women's liberation project. Their cause effectively diverted attention from other institutional sites of oppression such as marriage and the nuclear family—a diversion the New Right was all too eager to assist in as it aligned itself with antiporn feminists in the 1980s. While radical feminism unquestionably persisted at the local level, the mainstream media continued to ignore such efforts, preferring to highlight antiporn activism in ways that failed to link it to other feminist issues, an obfuscation in which antiporn feminists would prove complicit.

Early feminist activism against porn clearly emanated out of women's participation in the anticapitalist Left, but as a formal antiporn movement developed, it came unmoored from that framework. This development stemmed partly from calculated antiporn decisions to detach themselves from the class analysis, multiracial organizing, and other radical elements that kept feminism invisible or demonized in the status-quo-embracing mass media. Of equal importance, though, was the ongoing failure of American liberalism to meaningfully endorse a platform of sexual rights; from sexist "progressive" men heckling female speakers at New Left events to liberal politicians articulating abortion rights in terms of privacy rather than women's bodily autonomy, both leftist and liberal men seemed incapable of integrating a substantive gender analysis into their frameworks. For many feminists "liberal" and "conservative" proved empty signifiers for two ostensibly opposed political forces, both premised on heteronormative defenses of patriarchal social structures.

Activists who had once broken with the New Left for its insufficient progressivism found themselves willing to work on the opposite end of the political spectrum, in a marriage of convenience with the profoundly anti-feminist New Right. Andrea Dworkin reflected the strange new political formations this generated; in 1979 she accused "so-called radical men" of "us[ing] images of rape and torture to terrorize women into silence," and in a 1983 book she credited right-wing women with a more thorough understanding of gender oppression than liberal feminists.[5] Though Dworkin and other antiporn feminists clearly fell under classification as leftist, the issue of pornography took on such a newfound prominence that it overshadowed their commitment to a broad radical agenda and acquired singular importance by the 1980s. Although antiporn feminism ultimately failed to achieve most of its goals, the outcome was as much a failure of American liberalism to provide the space for a dialogue on sexual politics that might have incorporated feminists of various positions into a unified front against the New Right agenda.

Controlling the Means of Production

Although historians have refuted the long-held myth that the years between the suffrage movement and the 1960s passed devoid of feminist activity, a visible surge in women's gender-oriented activism marked the mid-1960s. The formation of the National Organization for Women (NOW) in 1966 embodied one thread of this activism, appealing most noticeably to middle-class white women inspired by Betty Friedan's 1963 salvo *The Feminine Mystique*. Meanwhile, young women inspired by the civil rights movement but alienated by the sexism of the male-dominated New Left would also join the women's liberation movement, often rejecting what they saw as NOW's reformist bent in favor of a radical analysis.[6]

For these feminists the fundamental institutions of contemporary society were aggressively targeted for destruction. Not just patriarchy as a loose, overarching concept but rather specific instantiations of it were often singled out. While Redstockings claimed, "Women are an oppressed class. Our oppression is total, affecting every facet of our lives," the New York Radical Feminists supplied the details, listing marriage, motherhood, love, sexual intercourse, and the nuclear family as the primary institutions "constructed and maintained to keep women in their place." The Feminists added sex roles, whose destruction was necessary to foreclose perpetuation of the sex caste system. These women, generally white and college educated, often overlooked the differences in women's oppression as mediated by the intersecting social hierarchies of race, class, and sexuality; indeed, the very trope of the "second wave" used to describe their movement reinscribes their privilege by creating an implicit chronology of "hegemonic feminism" less attentive to the activism of women of color, as Becky Thompson and other scholars note.[7]

Certainly these "second wavers" were the most visible feminists of the period, and crucial to their developing analysis was an emphasis on controlling the means of production. On one level this meant devising a theoretical apparatus independent of the New Left's restrictive class analysis, which like male socialism before it downplayed the significance of gendered social subjugation. On a more literal level it meant women actually controlling the machinery of industry, particularly the press. While New Left Marxism informed such efforts, a less-theoretical pragmatism also figured in. As Patricia Bradley shows, the mass media carried damaging impact for feminists of the late 1960s and early 1970s, depicting the movement in images and terms detrimental to its public reception. As a movement coalesced, feminists recognized the importance of accessing the institutions of the media, and they confronted its sexist barriers accordingly. Pornography surfaced in some of these efforts, but feminists never saw fit to place it in a position of centrality in women's oppression.[8]

For instance, Kate Millett reached the pivotal insight that "sex has a frequently neglected political aspect" in her groundbreaking *Sexual Politics*. Her book finally gave the lie to the postwar liberal fantasy of a depoliticized sexual sphere as something simply emanating out of the natural order of things, and Millett developed her analysis of sexual politics through a systematic survey of modern literature, showing how the "counterrevolutionary sexual politicians" D. H. Lawrence, Henry Miller, and Norman Mailer used sex as a mode of asserting male dominance in their writings. But Millett refrained from reducing these writers to pornographers, nor did she isolate pornography for criticism; to do so, in fact, would have weakened the force of her argument, which showed the ubiquity of sexual politics in places less predictable than mere porn. Indeed, Roxanne Dunbar of the Boston group Cell 16 complemented Millett's arguments in a 1969 essay that claimed pornography "expresses a masculine ideology of male power over females." Dunbar examined porn as simply one facet of the ongoing "sexual liberation" project she condemned for coercing women into nominal consent, and though she felt "utterly disgusted" with porn, Dunbar noted that critics such as herself were "reacting against what is *behind* pornography," namely the power imbalances of contemporary sexuality.[9]

Embedding porn criticism within a larger framework, such analyses found pornographic sexism to represent simply one virulent strain of the pervasive media sexism found everywhere. Media critiques continued as women's liberation developed; for instance, a 1969 article titled "The Art of Maiming Women" in *Women: A Journal of Liberation* focused on television images of housewives rather than violent or sexual imagery. Robin Morgan's massive 1970 anthology *Sisterhood Is Powerful* devoted its two essays on media oppression to advertisements and body odor products, without any mention of pornography. When New York feminists demanded $100 million in reparations for "sexploitation," they targeted Madison Avenue advertisers, not pornographers. The underlying problem was reification itself.[10]

This theme of pornography as one more form of commodification in a society already saturated with the process appeared when *Playboy* representatives visited Iowa's Grinnell College in 1969. Again, the "stereotyping and commercializing of the female body in order to sell the magazine" drew protest from Grinnell Women's Liberation, who with the support of a cadre of male affiliates held a "nude-in" in the form of arriving to the magazine's speech unclothed. This time, the protesters tied their objections to a more expansive critique of the capitalist commodification of the body. With women commercialized to sell copies, men too fell prey to "dehumanizing manipulation . . . for the benefit of the magazine and its advertisers." To further emphasize pornography's association with capitalism, the Grinnell protest used pointed biblical language to call *Playboy* "the money changer in the temple of the body."[11]

Similar tropes recurred when the Twin Cities Female Liberation group chided the Minneapolis poster shop Electric Fetus for the "traditional straight, capitalistic manner which you are displaying in your store" by selling sexist posters, comics, and magazines. Meanwhile, in Boston feminists demonstrating outside a Playboy Club explained, "Sex should not be treated like a consumer item," again highlighting the capitalist reification of women. Grounded in Marxist theory, these feminist protests nonetheless stayed true to the tenets of women's liberation by foregrounding gender, but in neglecting to even use the word *pornography* where it was clearly applicable, they also made clear that they saw the issue of porn as inseparable from the broader issue of sexism and as a sign of deeper, structural mechanisms of oppression rather than a central mechanism in and of itself.[12]

Pornography thus remained peripheral to feminist analyses of oppression in the late 1960s and early 1970s; echoing Kate Millett's and Roxanne Dunbar's perspective, Barbara Burris wrote in *It Ain't Me Babe* in 1970 that "the sexual exploitation and dehumanization of women into male toys and objects in *Playboy* and other magazines, in movies, and in other entertainment and communications media is just one example of this male counterrevolution." More important to Burris and women's liberation was the demise of institutionalized inequality in the home, the workforce, and the social world. In this framework the root causes of oppression remained distinct from their surface effects, and pornography clearly fell among the latter. As the Feminists had written of sex roles, "If any part of these role definitions is left, the disease of oppression remains and will reassert itself again in new, or the same old, variations throughout society." For early women's liberationists, anything less than a complete cure was no cure at all, and porn was less disease than symptom, less a structural component of patriarchal institutions than the ugly wallpaper covering them.[13]

Dissatisfaction with pornographic images of women did not go unremarked. In a 1969 gesture Bay Area Women's Liberation (BAWL) literally stormed the towers when an underground, male-run San Francisco group decided to publish a porn magazine to raise revenue for its radical political paper. "A liberation movement which furthers the prostitution and degradation of women and permits men to act like pimps is closer to fascism than the 'socialism' they profess to work toward," BAWL explained after confronting one of the editors and persuading him to cancel the porn magazine. Born of an "honest response to rage," the BAWL episode reflected the anger women felt at the distortion of their sexualities in male-dominated media. It even earned mention in *Time*, as an article on feminism began, "Pornographers, take note." But as BAWL admitted, "We have not developed any program for attacking this shit," and no discernible further effort went into doing so. The project of restructuring society, and attempting to wrench the levers of representational power from the grip of patriarchy, took precedence.[14]

Feminist actions against a series of publishers in 1970 revealed the limited role of opposition to pornography as an organizing principle of women's liberation. In three separate protests porn appeared in a rhetorically prominent but substantively peripheral manner, bringing an attention-grabbing surface sheen to struggles centered on the gendering of labor and control over the means of media production.

When women took over the New York underground newspaper *Rat* in February 1970, they felt definite antagonism to the paper's frequent pictures of naked women. But after a brief reference to the "porny photos, the sexist comic strips, the 'nudie-chickie' covers," Robin Morgan's mission statement for the takeover, "Goodbye to All That," left porn behind for a far more encompassing rebuttal to the sexual revolution in its entirety, comparing its effect on women to that of Reconstruction on former slaves: "reinstituting oppression by another name." No other articles in the first women-printed issue of *Rat* addressed pornography, though one article criticized the obscenity charges pending against the radical and sexually graphic play *Che*. Indeed, the women occupying *Rat* were forced into a defense of the magazine the very next week, when police showed up with an arrest warrant on obscenity charges over a cartoon rendition of a castration. When "a woman staffer of *Rat*" recalled the takeover one year later, she made clear her displeasure over the pornographic content but emphasized equally that women had done "most of the shitwork" while men had monopolized the lofty editorial positions. She recalled that "it was obvious we had to control the means of production ourselves," and the obviousness stemmed as much from structural labor issues as from control over content.[15]

Shortly thereafter, a similar occupation at Grove Press also stemmed from labor conflicts. Known for its subversive willingness to push First Amendment boundaries by publishing and distributing such controversial works as Henry Miller's novel *Tropic of Cancer* and the film *I Am Curious (Yellow)*, Grove displayed a far more traditional nature when its owner, Barney Rosset, fired several employees for attempting to unionize the press in April 1970. Among those fired was the feminist leader Robin Morgan, who led eight women in an occupation of the Grove offices in protest. The occupiers released a protest flier that began by charging Grove with earning millions of dollars "off the base theme of humiliating, degrading, and dehumanizing women through sado-masochistic literature, pornographic films, and oppressive and exploitative practices against its own female employees." Their list of demands began with the immediate cessation of all books, films, and magazines that "degrade women," but then the list quickly went on to call for child-care centers for employees, training programs for disadvantaged groups, funds for abortion and birth control, the redistribution of profits from *The Autobiography of Malcolm X* into the black community, funds for the treatment of rape victims, and, finally, the placement of women in control of 51 percent "of all decisions, editorial and otherwise." On the back the flier proclaimed, "No more use of women as shit-workers to produce material that degrades them . . . No more union-busting by rich-man Rosset!"[16]

When the occupiers were arrested, the story became newsworthy, and reporters recognized the occupation as a result of labor organizing thwarted. The *New York Times* quoted the occupiers' lawyer as explaining that the demonstration "had been triggered by the dismissal of eight Grove Press employees . . . for union activities." She went on to note, "Grove Press won't let women be anything but secretaries, scrub women and sex symbols." The *Village Voice* reported the story similarly, and the feminist paper *It Ain't Me Babe* concluded, "Grove better watch out"—not, notably, because of its pornographic publications but because "by the end of the day over half of its 110 workers had signed up to form a union." Again, pornography entered a debate that was fundamentally predicated on issues of labor and power. The same dynamic shaped a feminist boycott of the *Los Angeles Free Press* later that year, as the radical but sexist paper was labeled the "PORNO FREEP" while its female staff focused four of their five demands on labor issues.[17]

The broader issues of gendered labor and sexist images of women tie the occupations of the sexually explicit publications to other feminist media undertakings of 1970. Women's liberationists occupied the offices of CBS and *Ladies' Home Journal*, and forty-six women employed by *Newsweek* filed suit with the Equal Employment Opportunities Commission on the grounds that the magazine systematically discriminated against women in hiring and promotion; the very physical arrangement of the *Newsweek* office, where men had private offices and women sat next to one another at desks, was "designed to reinforce women's sense of being kept in their place."[18]

The entire series of 1970 occupations illustrated the difficulty of negotiating the boundary between theory and action faced by women's liberationists. A clear understanding of the underlying institutions of oppression did not lead to a shared vision of which surface manifestations offered the best access into those structures, though the media clearly drew the most attention from feminists for the social power contained in its imagery. That language used against *Ladies' Home Journal* could be equally applicable to porn indicated again that porn had not yet been isolated as something separate from the general glut of media outlets for patriarchy nor as something more insidious and pressing than issues of labor. As women interrogated the means of theoretical and industrial production by formulating their own analytical frameworks and challenging the structure of the media, porn was evidently a product of the existing arrangements, not a causal factor in their construction.

"Censorship Sucks Shit"

If consensus was rare among early women's liberationists, it did exist in opposition to governmental suppression. When the Presidential Commission on Obscenity and Pornography released its libertarian report in late September 1970, conservatives united in outrage, while liberal politicians dodged the topic. Feminists, however, offered a more supportive reception, indicating an awareness of the dangers of censorship. Lesbians displayed particular concern regarding suppression. Improving porn rather than banishing it emerged as a frequent feminist goal in the years before 1976.

Bobbie Goldstone, writing for *off our backs* in 1970, rejected commissioner Charles Keating's conservative dissenting opinion even though she questioned the social science methodologies used to validate the commission's conclusions. Admitting that Keating's stark descriptions of pornographic content made his challenge to the commission "appealing," since the content was "pretty horrible," Goldstone added, "its [*sic*] no secret that pornography degrades women. But so, in all fairness to pornographers, do Doris Day movies." Goldstone even hypothesized that feminists "may have to climb in next to the pornographers" to combat repressive campaigns enacted under the guise of public decency, since "the pornography issue can and will be used for the suppression of almost everything," especially radical feminist literature—she pointed out that *off our backs* itself had lost a printer who found its content "obscene."[19]

Pseudonymous Brenda Starr expressed similar sentiments in the pages of *Everywoman*. "I don't trust the motives of those who endorse censorship," she wrote, like Goldstone observing the likelihood that political publications would be felled with the same censorial axe as porn. Starr also raised "the question of definition," on the grounds that "anything that degrades anyone is pornographic, and that includes practically our whole culture." In contemplating noncensorial solutions to the porn problem, Starr ultimately arrived at the issue of labor, connecting the eradication of pornography to the ineluctable "drudge" work available to women in a gender-segregated economy. Seeing the choice between "dehumanizing yourself" in porn work or "robotizing yourself" on an assembly line as "no real choice," Starr made clear once more that pornography was a surface manifestation of the masterfully concealed dynamics of gender oppression.[20]

When a group of feminists in Eugene, Oregon, entered two "sex stores" to survey the goods in 1971, they recoiled at the "impersonal attitude toward women," concluding that the store might as well "put up a fence with a hole with some hair around it and get the same effect." Despite their disgust, when the state of Oregon passed a "porno bill" two years later to reduce the prosecution's burden of proof in obscenity cases, the women's liberationists of Eugene strongly opposed the bill, opting for porn and civil liberties over censorship. As the Iowa feminist paper *Ain't I a Woman?* phrased it, "Censorship sucks shit. Not only does it result in the suppression of controversial political views; . . . it makes for Amerikan pig society!" The *Lesbian Tide* in California similarly opposed a restrictive law taking the definition of *obscenity* out of the Supreme Court's hands and allowing local law enforcers to take their own initiatives in regulating pornography in 1972. "This proposition would abridge one of our basic freedoms, freedom of the press," the paper argued, going on to note that "we as homosexuals have an even greater stake, we would be most severely oppressed if this proposition passes."[21]

Indeed, along with gay men lesbians had long borne the brunt of obscenity prosecutions used to stifle their public visibility. From the obscenity charges against Radclyffe Hall's "invert" novel *The Well of Loneliness* in 1920s New York to a 1969 Boston conviction of a theater owner for screening the tepid Hollywood film *The Killing of Sister George*, the targeting of lesbian texts as obscene was systematic and pervasive in the heteronormative

United States. This trend continued even into the 1970s, keeping lesbians all too aware of the dangers inherent in antiobscenity crusades—an awareness that would help shape lesbian responses to antiporn feminism when it coalesced later in the decade.[22]

During these same years in the early 1970s, feminists began to speculate about the possibilities of pornography, examining the problem of porn as one of content rather than form. The existing material generally repulsed them; "Is this sex or is it conquest," wondered the author of an *Everywoman* article upon her visit to a Los Angeles adult bookstore. Representational imbalances disturbed her, such as the depiction of oral sex, in which "the only pictures were of fellatio by women to men but not of cunnilingus." In Michigan *her-self* offered the same response to the film *The Devil in Miss Jones.* "Oral sex is an act of great intimacy," it declared, before noting, "any such act can easily turn unsavory and exploitative if it isn't reciprocated." Though both articles excoriated the works they examined, implicit in their arguments was an acknowledgment that porn could be done correctly, with an egalitarian aspect sorely lacking in the existing dreck.[23]

In the Boston paper *Hysteria* Peggy Hopper more bluntly articulated this tacit corollary. Agreeing that "most pornography is degrading to women," she warned that censorship and suppression encouraged conservative moralism, no matter how feminist the intentions. Instead, she proposed, "Maybe what we need is more female pornographers." Striking a blow against sexual normativity from Left or Right, Hopper called for "greater acknowledgment that the way people's minds work is not always nice, wholesome and pure." Precisely this feigned purity rendered the program on Eroticism at the First International Festival of Women's Films in 1972 too "clinical and dull" for the *off our backs* reporter Maryse Holder. She objected not to graphic sex but to the "mechanical and begrudging" nature of films too hesitant to break free from traditional standards of femininity and express the unwholesome facets of desire. Holder concluded her report with a call for "freer films on sex," listing piety and timidity as "our most damaging legacy."[24]

Holder's wish was granted. In late 1973 she was able to revel in "the fecuncy, the fecuntitty, of cuntassy," when she surveyed a spate of "pornography written by women." From Judy Chicago's vaginal art to Niki de Saint Phalle's *Daddy*, a film full of graphic shots of masturbating women, Holder found herself in "another cuntree." She argued that "this aggressive presentation of the cunt is a first step at self-definition," noting that the term itself became "de-obscenified" when reclaimed by women. Women's depictions of male nudes also drew Holder's praise, as *all* bodies became eroticized, rather than the traditional pornographic emphasis on women alone. Holder recognized the precariousness of these developments; "Let us record an amazing phenomenon before some old gent in Boise puts on the clamps," she wrote, assuming the inevitable clamps would come from such "gents" and not her fellow feminists.[25]

By the time Holder wrote her piece in 1973, pornography had begun its brief cultural ascent. Porn films were prevalent enough to merit an annual Erotic Film Festival beginning in 1972, and *Women & Film* reporter Lucille Iverson attended to deliver a feminist critique. No fan of films in which "women are degraded, submissive, adoring of the large, erect penis," Iverson preferred portrayals of sexuality as "a gratifying, pleasurable human experience not associated with shame, guilt, [or] fear" and based on "equal participation and gratification." She found both visions at the festival, sometimes within the same film. *Room Service 75*, for instance, showed lesbians captivated by "the myth of supposedly greater satisfaction achieved via the big male cock," but the film had redeeming qualities in other scenes, where "the women are treated equally with the men" and "the clitoris is important and so is fondling and kissing." Iverson took particular glee in a film adaptation of Chaucer's *The Miller's Tale*, in which "a lot of fun is made of the acts of pissing, farting, and fucking." Again, a feminist vision of porn demanded the reclaiming of sexuality from both male supremacy and the bonds of femininity or any other normative imposition except autonomous desire.[26]

When *Deep Throat* crystallized the "porno chic" moment in 1973, the feminist response to the film recapitulated the theme of antagonism to contemporary porn based on content rather than form. Redstockings cofounder Ellen Willis, also a music and film critic, reviewed the film for the *New York Review of Books*. Willis castigated it as "witless, exploitative, and about as erotic as a tonsillectomy," in contrast to earlier stag films, which were "amusingly, whimsically naughty" and less "mechanical," though equally explicit. Going one step further, she specified exactly why "movies like *Throat* don't turn me on": "partly because they objectify women's bodies and pay little attention to men's," but mostly because such films stifled the creation of more authentic sexual fantasies. Lamenting the fact that "women have no pornographic tradition," Willis admitted, "I've had fantasies about making my own porn epic for a female audience." Her formula for success in the genre included moving beyond the merely genital to include psychological complexity as well as a more body-encompassing eroticism. It did not include forsaking the explicit or even the prurient.[27]

In another response to *Deep Throat*, Christine Stansell covered the film for *off our backs*, describing an almost quintessentially Cartesian reaction to the film, which starkly polarized her body and mind. Physically, Stansell "freaked out" at the film, rushing to the restroom ten minutes in after "building up a physical pressure of rage in my stomach." But after her body offered its repulsed review, her mind took a more dispassionate approach in writing; Stansell admitted her "purposeful, rational plan to determinedly collect images of Degraded Women was thwarted from the start." The cunnilingus-to-fellatio ratio was about even; images of sadism were absent, much to her surprise; and the "real titillation of the film" was not male, but female, orgasm. She hated it, but Stansell intellectually granted the possibility of better-made porn in a semantically elusive conclusion that "stag films . . . have the potential to embrace the correct genital party line," but "pornography will always be a woman hater." The sudden introduction of an unexplicated distinction between "stag films" and "pornography" portended the shape of theory to come. At the time, however, it was evident that "pornography" in this context referred to what critics like Willis might call "bad pornography." The possibility of good in the genre remained open even to a critic who had shed "explosive tears" over the travesty of *Deep Throat*.[28]

When the Nixon-stacked Supreme Court issued its conservative 1973 *Miller v. California* ruling, returning the definition of obscenity to states and localities after fifteen years of increasingly permissive rulings, feminists recognized the decision as an open invitation to state repression. Calling the ruling "blatant paternalism" and "invasion of my dignity and privacy" in the *San Francisco Chronicle*, Eleanor Jackson Piel reiterated the already-established feminist resistance to governmental checks on free speech. Complementing this in the *Chicago Journalism Review*, Terri Schultz elaborated on the notion of feminist porn, claiming that "pornography, far from being evil, has a valid and constructive place in our lives," that of allowing for the vicarious exploration of fantasies. Again like earlier feminists, Schultz duly noted that "most pornography degrades women," though she was quick to add that women were also "exploited and degraded in most other areas of life." Rejecting the Court's stance, Schultz argued, "We should maintain access to pornography as a legitimate means of personal expression that sometimes reveals the best of us, often reveals the worst of us."[29]

Although not unanimous, these attitudes were pervasive among mid-1970s feminist circles. When Ti-Grace Atkinson, who did not subscribe to them, listed pornography as one of the five institutions—along with marriage, motherhood, prostitution, and rape—that oppressed women, a respondent in *off our backs* pointed out that porn could also be seen as "a result rather than a cause of female oppression." The *Lesbian News* ran articles such as "*Ecstasy*: Pornography for Women?" which claimed, "Erotic material that reflects the *real* fantasies of women will appeal to women." And, as I noted earlier, future antiporn leader Andrea Dworkin, too, found reasons to preclude categorical dismissals of the value of porn.[30]

Negotiations over the nature of pornography and the representation of women came to a head in Dworkin's debut book, *Woman Hating*, published in 1974. Returning to the style of the early manifestos, Dworkin proclaimed that "the destruction of middle-class lifestyle is crucial," as it embodied the nuclear family. *Woman Hating* rooted out male supremacy in its sundry shapes and forms. The manifestations Dworkin identified ranged from Chinese foot-binding to European witch-burning. The ideology of traditional narratives, too, drew fire, as fairy-tale heroines from Cinderella to Snow White were exposed as illustrating through their passivity "the cardinal principle of sexist ontology—the only good woman is a dead woman." Unsurprisingly, pornography received some attention, as well, and Dworkin fit the tenor of then-contemporary radical feminist discourse, contending that pornography, in general, earned a description as "simple-minded, brutal, and very ugly." But just as the door there remained open to something better, Dworkin's text did the same, even going beyond that to find merit in the otherwise sexist journal *Suck*.[31]

Filled with pornographic pictures, *Suck* emphasized oral sex. Dworkin applauded this, noting, "Sucking is approached in a new way. . . . Sperm tastes good, so does cunt. In particular, the emphasis on sucking cunt serves to demystify cunt in a spectacular way—cunt is not dirty, not terrifying, not smelly and foul." Because oral sex was still taboo, even illegal in many states, *Suck*'s publishing of such pictures took on the status of an "act of political significance"; by contributing to the breakdown of repressive bourgeois laws, it assisted in the destruction of the family. While Dworkin ultimately placed this admission of value in a larger rejection of *Suck* for perpetuating the ideas of the phallocentric sexual revolution, her limited celebration of the journal is notable, given the stark contrast in which it stands to her later work.[32]

At middecade, then, feminists had staked out a measured critique of pornography, while often articulating and manifesting a coherent vision of nonsexist porn. Feminist masturbation advocate Betty Dodson called herself a pornographer because she thought "the word ought to be legitimized" by women taking its helms. Graphic photographs of sexuality and nudity recurred throughout various feminist publications, putting theory into practice.[33]

After early criticisms had largely declined to situate porn centrally in the institutional structure of women's oppression, feminists had turned away from attacking pornography as an institution and rather condemned existing porn for its failures to live up to its nonsexist potential. A critic for *Ms.* even ushered in "a totally new kind of 'human' porn" while reviewing the documentary *Exhibition* in early 1976. That analysis, and the optimism concomitant with it, would soon surrender to a simpler equation that stripped pornography of its multifaceted ramifications, exchanging nuance and complexity for a simplified formal elegance as feminist theory moved the genre to the institutional center of women's oppression.[34]

Rape, Snuff, and the New Pornocentrism

Key to the emergence of antiporn arguments were developments in the understanding of rape. The two discourses of pornography and rape stayed very separate for the first half of the 1970s. When Aljean Harmetz published "Rape—An Ugly Movie Trend" in 1973, her disparaging examples covered a wide range of mainstream Hollywood product, including *The Exorcist*, *Straw Dogs*, and *Frenzy*, but no porn. Other feminist writers followed suit, and when Molly Haskell published *From Reverence to Rape: The Treatment of Women in the Movies* in 1974, her sarcastic declension model ended not in the realm of porn but, again, in mainstream Hollywood films. Even Michigan feminists discussing rape in protesting the 1972 porn film *Behind the Green Door* reflected not a theoretical linking of porn and rape but rather the literal content of the film, which featured a woman kidnapped and brought to a sex club. To clarify that they did not want the film banned, they insisted, "All we asked was that women NOT SPEND MONEY" on it. For these women nothing inherently linked pornography to rape.[35]

The understanding of rape developed in the early years of women's liberation conceived it as an act of violence. The literature on rape swelled in the early 1970s, and most works followed the model set by Susan Griffin, emphasizing the violence and aggression of rape as an act of domination, as well as the implicit permission society allowed men to rape. As Griffin phrased it in her influential 1971 essay "Rape: The All-American Crime," "Many men appear to take sexual pleasure from nearly all forms of violence." The right to coerce women into sex, Griffin recognized, was given to men by nearly every imaginable institution, from the law to marriage. The mass media, too, impacted men's perceptions of women's willingness to submit. "James Bond alternately whips out his revolver and his cock," she wrote, tacitly asking whether any difference existed between them. While Griffin briefly mentioned a stag film in passing, her thesis made clear that rape-culture propaganda was not the province of the marginal world of porn but rather the predominant aesthetic of mainstream patriarchal society.[36]

Griffin's analysis proved influential. Mass media were often targeted as a key site of rape-friendly ideology, with pornography rarely singled out. Andra Medea and Kathleen Thompson blamed "the John Wayne brand of masculinity," calling attention to a standard male icon. Likewise, when the New York Radical Feminists published a rape sourcebook for women, its discussion of cinema made no mention of porn, isolating Stanley Kubrick's A Clockwork Orange as the most venomous cinematic advocate of rape. The book mentioned pornography only in an appendix, listed after "advertising" and "major novels," as examples of the culture based on masculine objectification of women. One section, "Suggestions on the Elimination of Rape," suggested that pornography would disappear effortlessly along with many other institutions when sex roles were finally annihilated. Even Diana Russell, soon to become a leader of the antiporn movement, saw nothing noteworthy about porn in her 1975 book The Politics of Rape. A collection of case-study interviews with analysis, it included a tale of a woman raped by her husband as part of a porn film shoot, but Russell's analysis merely observed that marital rape was not always socially perceived as such. Later Russell argued, "The virility mystique, expounded by magazines like Playboy ... predisposes men to rape." Pornography occupied no place of importance in this analysis, and Russell's other examples of this mystique were Norman Mailer and Ogden Nash.[37]

Not every women's liberationist agreed, and in a 1974 essay Robin Morgan coined the slogan "pornography is the theory, and rape the practice." But Morgan grew evasive when it came to moving her sound bite from metaphor to causal assertion, admitting that "we know less about the effects of pornography" than those of rape and that porn, rather than direct causal agent, "is sexist propaganda, no more and no less." Morgan's essay would later become known as a classic, but its impact was delayed; in Andrea Dworkin's most frequently delivered speech of 1975, "The Rape Atrocity and the Boy Next Door," no mention was made of pornography, even as the lengthy speech covered various other social institutions supporting rape, such as marriage and the nuclear family.[38]

It was Susan Brownmiller who most powerfully advocated a rape-porn connection in her 1975 surprise best seller *Against Our Will: Men, Women, and Rape*. Brownmiller had already argued against pornography in a 1973 editorial celebrating the *Miller* ruling as "wholly consistent" with feminist ideals. "One has to be hopelessly masochistic or strongly male-identified to get an electric charge from porn if one is a woman," Brownmiller argued, calling the development of a "pro-female pornographic idiom" "wildly quixotic." In attempting to reframe the Nixon-appointed Chief Justice Burger's opinion as profeminist, Brownmiller made several concessions, admitting that Burger's phrasing of "sexually explicit" material would be better articulated in terms of the degradation of women. She also acknowledged as a "genuine concern" that a community that banned *Deep Throat* might also censor *Our Bodies, Ourselves*, though her vague solution to this consisted of a suggestion that juries include more than businessmen and prudes.[39]

This analysis held limited feminist appeal, and in *Against Our Will* the author found a more effective antiporn trope. Brownmiller offered an expansive survey covering the history of rape, the legal constructs surrounding it, its portrayal in various media, its racial and class features, and its nature as an act of male aggression, among other topics. Pornography entered the text only briefly, but memorably, first in comparison to rape as "a male invention, designed to dehumanize women, to reduce the female to an object of sexual access," and then as actively promoting "a climate in which acts of sexual hostility directed against women are not only tolerated but ideologically encouraged."[40] Brownmiller offered little specific evidence, but after hundreds of pages of rigorously footnoted references, the book carried the implicit authority of the expert. Its position as a best seller ensured its ideas a far wider dissemination than that of the typical women's liberation journal article. *Against Our Will* fused pornography and rape in the feminist consciousness, laying the groundwork for further expansion of the theme.

Before the theoretical dust had time to settle, Brownmiller's analysis was seemingly validated when a *New York Post* article in October 1975 alerted the nation to snuff films, with the attention-grabbing headline, "'Snuff' Porn—The Actress Is Actually Murdered." Citing no factual support for these films' existence, the article merely insinuated the underground circulation among a "select clientele" of wealthy perverts of films featuring the unsimulated deaths of porn actresses. When evidence of snuff failed to surface, the B-movie distributor Allen Shackleton saw an opportunity to capitalize on the topic. After purchasing *The Slaughter*, an unreleased horror film set in Argentina, he added an unrelated scene at the conclusion, purporting to show the real director actually murdering a script girl.[41]

Retitled *Snuff*, the film entered theaters in early 1976 to little initial notice. In New York City a crowd of fifty apparent protestors gathered in Times Square, but they revealed no feminist agenda and were quite likely hired by Shackleton himself to draw attention to *Snuff*. At first underplaying the negative reaction, the *New York Times* reported the demonstration in a minute notice buried on page 22. Whatever the origin, in subsequent weeks the protests continued and began to draw notice, and by March the film had become newsworthy. While patrons of the grindhouse theaters that usually played similar exploitation films would have recognized *Snuff* as akin to the typical filler, Shackleton released the film in generally mainstream theaters to increase its publicity appeal as an affront to social values. Critics unused to such lowbrow fare were suddenly writing about it in the pages of the *New York Times, Washington Post*, and *San Francisco Chronicle*. In the definitive academic article on the film Eithne Johnson and Eric Schaefer attribute the uproar over *Snuff* to "genre confusion." At the heart of the controversy, though, was uncertainty not about genre but rather the veracity of the film's final murder scene.[42]

Film critics uniformly dismissed the murder as not only a hoax but a poorly faked hoax with cheap special effects. Some feminists, though, alerted to the affinities Brownmiller had argued for between pornography and rape, quickly linked *Snuff* to that equation. Despite the fact that only one woman was murdered in the climactic faux-vérité scene and Manhattan district attorney Robert Morgenthau had already reported her alive, *off our backs* claimed "the bodies of the two women were found sometime after the film was made." A subsequent wave of feminist protest ensued. *Snuff* drew feminist protesters in New York, successful boycotts to close it in Los Angeles and later Denver, and vandalism toward a theater showing it in Rochester, New York.[43]

With the film discredited as a concrete link between cinema and violence, but with energy running high, *Snuff* was discursively reconfigured as evidence of pornography's harm to women. *Los Angeles Times* film critic Kevin Thomas had noted the film's "minimal sex and nudity," but a Denver group persisted in distributing leaflets that claimed, "*Snuff* is a pornographic film which shows on screen the actual murder and dismemberment of a woman." The group used that assertion to substantiate the more categorical claim that "all pornography relates directly to the countless crimes of violence against women." Further tying *Snuff* to the porn genre, Molly Haskell titled her response "The Night Porno Films Turned Me Off." And crystallizing the feminist sentiments in a sound bite, Susan Brownmiller herself offered neither trope nor metaphor but instead presented porn as an action. "Pornography is violence against women," she said, meaning it quite literally.[44]

Concurrent with the *Snuff* controversy, attention toward media violence against women resulted in the formation of the group Women Against Violence Against Women (WAVAW). Begun in Los Angeles in June 1976 to protest a billboard advertising the Rolling Stones album *Black and Blue*, which featured a bruised woman tied up and seemingly happy, WAVAW directed its critique toward all sexist mass media. The group initiated several record-label boycotts in response to sexist album covers and made clear in December 1976, "We aren't out here to object to pornography. We're objecting to the violence." Many WAVAW branches took part in *Snuff* protests, based on the film's depiction of violence against women. But even as WAVAW presented its all-encompassing critique of sexist media, very much in keeping with established traditions in the women's liberation movement, the reconstitution of *Snuff* as pornography heralded a new emphasis in feminist analyses that left the group superseded by more narrowly focused organizations.[45]

After a late 1976 conference on violence against women in the San Francisco Bay Area, a group of local women gathered to organize around the theme. At an early meeting in January 1977 they called themselves Women Against Media Violence and Degradation. But the group found the name insufficiently memorable, and in February it debated other titles. Women Against Media Sexist Propaganda, Women Against Media Violence, and Women Against Sexist Pornography were all suggested, but the discussion at the meeting repeatedly drifted back to porn. Finally, a vote was held, and Women Against Pornography and Violence in Media tied Women Against Misogynist Propaganda, leaving the one male present to break the tie by voting for the former; helping the cause was a member who pointed out the importance of "paying attention to our name in concrete situations, i.e., demonstrations, press releases, etc." Pornography clearly carried the greatest visceral impact. At the next meeting, though, a "long discussion" ensued over whether the group's emphasis should fall on violence or porn; "we evolved from the VIOLENCE conference," one member reminded the group. As a result, the group modified its name to Women Against Violence in Pornography and Media (WAVPM) and became the first feminist group dedicated to fighting porn. When the New York branch splintered off to become simply Women Against Pornography (WAP) approximately a year later, a movement was born.[46]

Rejecting the idea that pornography merely constituted a "reflection of men's sexual fantasies, unrelated to larger structures," antiporn feminists like political scientist Irene Diamond instead considered it "one of the mechanisms that has sustained the systematic domination of women by men throughout history."[47] This theoretical stance marked a break from the general consensus established in the first decade of second-wave feminism. For the first time feminists placed pornography at the center of women's oppression. Key to this argument was a newfound distinction between pornography and erotica, a distinction that in effect desexed pornography and semantically reconstructed it as violence against women.

The separation of pornography from erotica was in itself no innovation. Similar distinctions had previously been undertaken outside a feminist context. In 1929 D. H. Lawrence distinguished obscenity—"mild little words that rhyme with spit or farce"—from pornography, "the attempt to insult sex." Eberhard Kronhausen and Phyllis Kronhausen described "erotic realism" as "the reaction against hypocrisy in art and literature," porn as mere "erotic psychological stimulant" in 1959. And Steven Marcus marked "literature," with its "multitude of intentions," as mutually exclusive from "pornography," which had "only one" intention, in his 1966 study of Victorian smut. Each of these distinctions relied on heavily subjective and arbitrary criteria but also offered an appealingly simple means of categorizing culture that left the dualism ripe for revival. "Erotica and Pornography," a 1978 *Ms.* cover asked: "Do You Know the Difference?"[48]

Antiporn feminists strove to inject rigor into their definitions. It was an important distinction because the approval of erotica refuted stereotypes of feminists as prudes or puritans and thus distanced them from their socially conservative forebears in the temperance and suffrage movements. With the erotica-pornography distinction secured, porn could be demonized not just in its individually flawed manifestations but as an entire category. Gloria Steinem used etymological differences to distinguish the words ontologically: *porne* and *graphos* in ancient Greece meant describing whores, while *eros* entailed passion or love. Insisting "it's clear there is a substantive difference" beyond the merely semantic, she brought in the example of snuff films to associate porn with rape and death. Erotica, by contrast, encompassed the life-affirming sexuality of love and mutual pleasure. Women Against Violence in Pornography and Media further clarified the distinction, listing attributes of each category in its *Newspage*. Erotica received descriptions including "personal," "emotional," "natural," and "fulfilling," while pornography earned such tags as "defined by penis," "for titillation of men," "power imbalance," and "produces violence." Porn was "something you buy and sell"; erotica was "just there." This distinction proved influential; by 1979 the Denver paper *Big Mama Rag* could state, "Erotica concerns sex, pornography power," as an axiom that need not be elaborated.[49]

Separating pornography from sex added weight to the connection between porn and violence against women. Rather than a medium predicated on sexually explicit representations, the new line held, pornography "is only secondarily concerned with sex; its main function is to be a vehicle for male power"; "The Obscene Use of Power," another article called it. The logic proceeded inexorably, as Wendy Kaminer of WAP claimed pornography consisted of "pictures or graphic descriptions of women being bound, beaten, or mutilated." Ultimately, the division allowed Diana Russell to divorce porn from sex completely, writing, "Some pornography I saw recently doesn't even include sex: women are kidnapped, beaten, tied up, then hung upside down like pieces of meat." Because "pornography" was now encapsulated by violence against women, feminist pornography became inherently untenable, foreclosed by its own internal contradiction.[50]

Despite this separation of pornography from sex and the highly specific meaning of the term *pornography* in their theories, the antiporn groups often persisted in using vernacular understandings of the term, in which it generally referred simply to explicit portrayals of sex. This allowed the charged connotations of their idiosyncratic definitions to carry over into the everyday meanings of pornography by blurring semantic lines. Thus, when WAVPM addressed the "Questions We Get Asked Most Often," one question asked to what the group's name referred. The answer listed films such as *Cry Rape, Love Gestapo Style*, and *Angels in Pain*, which "depict women being bound, beaten and abused." But when the next question read, "Do you object to pornography in which there is no violence," the group answered in the affirmative, maintaining that while violent content was integral to pornography, violent effects could earn the label as well. Because "even the most banal pornography objectifies women's bodies" and objectification is "an essential ingredient of much rape," the violence was attached to the sex by virtue of male viewer actions.[51] The statement by WAP's founding member, Susan Brownmiller, that "pornography is violence against women," then, came to take on at least three meanings within the antiporn movement: first, that—as per *Snuff*—porn consisted of actual violence against unwilling women; second, that porn committed violence against women because its manifest content of sex concealed a latent content of objectification-as-violence; and third, that porn *caused* men to commit violence against women or at least created a hostile climate actively conducive to such behavior.

The last of these meanings contrasted with most contemporary social science literature. The 1973 issue of the *Journal of Social Issues* devoted to the topic of pornography, for example, concluded that "pornography is an innocuous stimulus . . . [and] public concern over it is misplaced." Some male social scientists, such as Victor Cline, challenged the benign view of pornography, however, calling porn a "causal instigator" of "sexual deviations, crime, [and] delinquency." As we saw in chapter 6, other men began to question the existing consensus in the 1970s, but only with WAVPM and WAP did feminists join the social science debate in large numbers. WAP sometimes operated at a reductionist level, asserting on a poster that "there is a strong connection between the spread of pornography and the increase in rape, battering of women, and molesting of children," without offering more than analogy in the way of evidence. When the situation demanded it, though, the group offered more solid arguments. In the peer-reviewed academic journal *Signs*, for instance, Irene Diamond supported the claim that "pornography contributes to actual violence against women" with evidence from recent psychology experiments and official city statistics. Much of her argument depended on undermining the objectivity of the Presidential Commission, whose social scientists made many flagrant errors in their calculations.[52]

Indeed, antiporn feminists revealed significant research shortcomings of the commission, such as the fact that the much-heralded sex-crime drop in Denmark stemmed from the legalization of homosexuality and concomitant drops in arrests; rape itself may have actually increased. But their critical acumen often failed them in their own assertions. When Gloria Steinem, Robin Morgan, and Diana Russell cited and recommended Victor Cline for his claim of empirical support for porn as a causal factor in rape, they disregarded the Citizens for Decent Literature supporter's ideologically reactionary research framework. Cline's actual case was that porn caused "sexual deviation," which he defined broadly enough to encompass rape, homosexuality, and even divorce. At one point Cline's example of "the power of deviant modeling in films or books to suggest sexual activities destructive to the self-interest of the viewer" even included wives led into swinging; 65 percent reported they "would rather 'turn on' to the female than to the males," warned the homophobic Cline, leaving one to wonder whose "self interest" he was guarding, that of women and their morality or that of men and their wifely possessions. In either case his antifeminist agenda clearly shaped his conclusions, though antiporn feminists blithely overlooked the former in promoting the latter.[53]

By the late 1970s feminism was in disarray. Conflicts over race, class, and sexuality all revealed the internal fault lines of the movement, as working-class women and women of color found the predominantly white, middle-class public figures in charge of the movement unresponsive to their needs. Black and Chicana feminists often showed their disaffection with white-dominated organizations through nonparticipation and separatist groups.[54] Meanwhile, landmark feminist victories had given way to conservative retrenchment, as the Hyde Amendment sought to roll back the 1973 *Roe v. Wade* abortion decision, and antifeminist grassroots resistance prevented the required state ratifications to add the Equal Rights Amendment, which had passed Congress in 1972, to the Constitution. Awareness that the institutions of women's oppression remained far from being dismantled suffused feminist literature as the decade wore on. "What if the revolution isn't tomorrow?" asked Carol Anne Douglas, already aware it would not be. One magazine, perhaps a bit overeager, even published a "Requiem for the Women's Movement" in 1976. The weariness was real, though; calling the movement a "dispersed silent majority," Patricia Beyea offered a similarly mournful assessment of the defeatism that had set in for many feminists.[55]

One response to this impasse was a renewed emphasis on local efforts, and rape-prevention workshops, domestic-abuse shelters, college Women's Studies programs, communal living, and other grassroots feminist activity proliferated in the second half of the 1970s, almost always outside the scope of mass-media coverage. Another solution to the fragmentation and indirection of feminism was to shift emphasis from radical politics to "an insistence on women's essential sameness to each other," which the historian Alice Echols has labeled "cultural feminism." Through this notion of universal sisterhood, cultural feminism attempted to restore an artificial unity to the movement by effacing the differences that had flared up among various groups of women. Antiporn feminism participated wholly in this shift. "Pornography affects the life of every woman," a WAP flier claimed, attempting to recreate a universal sisterhood by promoting a theoretical commonality among the Harvard undergraduate, the Arizona housewife, the inner-city single mother, and the women of the Kentucky coal mines.[56]

The shift to a pornocentric feminist platform hardly went uncontested. Even after *Snuff*, antirape activists Deb Friedman and Lois Yankowski reiterated the call for a "feminist pornography," and Friedman went on to challenge antiporn doctrine in 1977, directly rejecting a causal connection between porn and actual violence against women. Ellen Willis called the appeals for government intervention after *Snuff* "mistaken and dangerous," noting that the Memphis prosecution of *Deep Throat* star Harry Reems on conspiracy charges could set a precedent "that will inevitably be used against us" (indeed, no feminists—nor anyone in the national press, for that matter—appeared to notice that Reems's *The Devil in Miss Jones* costar Georgina Spelvin also faced charges in Memphis for her participation in that film, a seemingly shocking assault on female sexual freedom). And while two authors for *off our backs* began an essay with, "We hate pornography," they went on to reject censorship, banning, or firebombing porn shops, instead reminding women of the original goal of feminism: "What we are after is a re-making of society from the ground up."[57]

WAVAW, too, continued to push for a broader analysis of oppressive imagery, often agreeing with condemnations of porn but insisting that *pornography* "is not a useful word for naming what it is we are fighting." The group's newsletter focused instead on "the essence of the problem itself—the gratuitous use of images of violence against women," in its most prevalent form: mainstream, legitimate media. The group also explained its "political considerations," which centered on the "current right wing attack on porn"; "we cannot be identified with them," WAVAW insisted.[58]

Among feminists countering the developing antiporn party line, lesbians led the charge. In the early 1970s lesbians had been marginalized within the feminist movement and even, notoriously, purged from the New York National Organization for Women. But by middecade lesbians had effectively politicized love for women as a core component of feminism and dominated the radical wing of the movement. This did not, however, insulate lesbians from repeated suppression. Police in Provincetown, Massachusetts, pressured the owner of a lesbian bar not to show the film *A Comedy in Six Unnatural Acts* in 1976, warning her that if she did, police would send in the alcoholic beverage commission to "find something wrong" and shut the bar down. In 1978 *The Joy of Lesbian Sex* was confiscated from bookstores in Lexington, Kentucky, and B. Dalton Book Company ordered the book removed from shelves in its three hundred stores. Such was lesbian concern over suppression that Cincinnati lesbians defended even *Hustler* publisher Larry Flynt when he faced obscenity charges in 1977, on the grounds that "there's a great deal of concern about where this is all going to lead."[59]

If many lesbians were not predisposed to suppress pornography, though, neither did the new antiporn groups welcome them in. Lesbians remained vigilantly aware of veiled homophobia within the movement, such as Elinor Langer's 1974 *Ms.* review of Kate Millett's *Flying*, in which the critic called the bisexual memoir "heavily pornographic." As Julia Stanley noted in the lesbian journal *Sinister Wisdom*, "At no point does [Langer] attempt to define her use of the word" *pornographic*, suggesting it was based less on the graphic nature of the sex scenes than their lesbianism. So when WAVPM founding member Diana Russell claimed, "It is upsetting—particularly for heterosexual women—to face the depth and extent of men's antipathy" in porn, most lesbians could not have read the comment as an invitation.[60]

Likewise, at a 1979 WAP conference antagonism erupted when a lesbian in the audience yelled at WAP speaker Susan Brownmiller that she was tired of the movement "being run by cocksucking straight women," since "the cock was fucking ultimately responsible for all violence against women." Brownmiller, who had allegedly rejected an offer to speak before the prominent lesbian group Daughters of Bilitis in 1970 because she considered lesbians "hypersexual and aggressively male," grew angry. Sinking to the woman's personal attack, Brownmiller responded to the crowd by pointing at the tie-wearing protestor and exclaiming, "See, she even *dresses* like a man." The incident did little to endear WAP to lesbians, and a reporter covering the conference for the *Lesbian Tide* also noted its less-sensational problems, such as the lack of attention to lesbian concerns and the conspicuous omission of the word *lesbian* from conference publicity. That same year WAP declined to endorse the National March on Washington for Lesbian and Gay Rights on the grounds that the group was a single-issue organization. As one "suspicious" observer wrote WAP, another motive might have been fear that such an endorsement "would offend your more conservative antiporn allies."[61]

Antiporn feminists recognized these fissures in the movement and sought to rectify them. Susan Brownmiller claimed, "We have never had a gay/straight split in [WAP] and we never will," though an earlier apology for her dress comment was tempered by her assertion that "fashion is very political" and that "I was trying to make a serious political comment." The title of Brownmiller's 1980 essay "Let's Put Pornography Back in the Closet" surely failed to help. Even before the contentious conference, WAP issued a statement on "Lesbian Feminist Concerns" in the antiporn movement. It recognized the "special threat" that suppression posed to lesbians but countered that, because "rapists and murderers do not distinguish" between gay and straight women, "it is very much in the self-interest of lesbian women to participate in the feminist antipornography movement."[62]

At times these conciliatory gestures worked. WAP attracted a sizeable lesbian membership. Charlotte Bunch and Audre Lorde, leading lesbian theorist/activists, contributed essays to a WAP-dominated antiporn anthology in 1980. Other times antiporn feminists burned bridges to lesbian communities. For instance, WAVPM listed sadomasochism alongside pornography and media violence as things it opposed. When the San Francisco–area lesbian s/m group Samois called for "dialogue" with WAVPM to discuss the feminist value of sadomasochism, WAVPM rebuffed the group, dismissively explaining that its refusal to meet was "due to the urgency we felt about our own work." This antiporn-s/m rift would turn explosive in the 1980s.[63]

More important than social niceties, though, was the fact that many lesbians felt not only marginalized but overtly threatened by the antiporn movement. "What many of these women fail to realize," a 1978 *Lesbian Tide* article argued, "is that their support of censorship only lends fuel to the enemies of feminism and gayness," such as the right-wing, antigay Florida crusader Anita Bryant. Considering it a profoundly naive mistake to assume that only woman-hating material would be suppressed if antiporn forces had their way, the article noted that "once allowed and supported, there is *no* end to censorship." This theme permeated the lesbian press; after seeing how precarious their own publications already were, lesbians remained all too painfully aware that if antiporn laws passed, "all of the gay and half of the feminist press would have to cease publishing," as an article titled "Feminists and the Right—Merging over Porn?" noted. Wondering "where did the word 'violence' go" in 1980, s/m advocate and feminist Pat Califia denounced WAVPM as "a group with a right-wing philosophy masquerading as a radical feminist organization." Expressing resentment toward the antiporn worldview of victimized women in need of protection, Califia compared the movement's rhetoric to the "Victorian imagery" of "pure women controlling the vile, lustful impulses of men"—precisely the feminine stereotype feminists should combat, Califia added. The threat of a normative sexuality and a rearticulated femininity frightened lesbians who had spent years escaping those impediments.[64]

Indeed, WAP grew steadily more dogmatic and normative in its rhetoric. Several antiporn feminists contributed to the 1982 anthology *Against Sadomasochism*, which described lesbian s/m as "firmly rooted in patriarchal sexual ideology." In response to s/m lesbian claims that their practices subverted patriarchy instead of internalizing it, Catharine MacKinnon offered a dismissive analogy: "If Blacks owned Black slaves, would that express the white supremacist structure or subvert it?" But WAP moved beyond attacking already-marginalized fringe groups; a late 1982 press release condemned a sex-positive feminist group by claiming that when sex "is shared with a stranger . . . the beauty is diminished altogether." The statement's author continued, "I don't think the gift of a shared sexuality should be taken so casually." In contrast to early feminist critiques of the sexual revolution, WAP called not for women's freedom from male "sexual liberation" but rather for a new, conservative sexual normativity, comparable in part to the "passionlessness" imposed on women in the last century. The group allowed for no diverging feminist perspectives; "We believe we represent all women," it said in a 1984 press release.[65]

Deradicalizing Feminism

In the face of so much vocal, informed dissent, antiporn activists clearly lacked a solitary claim to the mantle of feminism. But by maintaining a highly visible public presence, antiporn feminists obtained access to academia and the mass media, which in turn conferred respectability, financial resources, and national prominence on the movement. Scholars have debated the nature of feminism's evolution in the mid-to-late 1970s. Alice Echols presents a declension narrative of cultural feminism supplanting radical women's liberation, while subsequent scholars challenge this assessment, showing how feminist resistance persisted in politically hostile times.[66] This scholarly dialogue hinges on the *actual* social history of feminism. The antiporn movement has, in effect, superseded the debate itself, both at the time and in historical memory; by assuming the national public face of feminism, it dramatically overshadowed the sustained grassroots efforts focused on a greater range of issues. Feminism did not deradicalize in the 1970s or 1980s, but the antiporn movement ultimately invited that perception by positioning itself as the center of feminist activity and offering a vision of feminism stripped of many of its radical aspects.

Many feminist efforts did take a turn toward pragmatism in the mid-1970s. Exigency dictated some of this, as tangible endeavors like creating battered women's shelters replaced the more abstract project of annihilating gender as a social construct. New knowledge brought other changes; for instance, as authors like Louise Armstrong and Judith Herman brought the pervasiveness of incest into public discussion, earlier radical feminist notions of smashing the incest taboo gave way to more pressing concerns of preventing abusive incest. Plans to destroy the nuclear family also faded; Betty Friedan, who had never been comfortable with the radical direction women's liberation had taken after the formation of NOW, called the family (in which household and other labor would be reallocated more equitably) the "new feminist frontier" in her 1981 book *The Second Stage*. Antiporn feminists, too, reflected these trends, effacing the earlier critique of capitalism and dropping the emphasis on women's control over the means of production. They also went beyond the new moderate consensus, showing a willingness to work with members of the reactionary New Right. This only added to the tensions among feminist camps, vindicating fears that antiporn activism would ultimately contribute to an exacerbation of conservative repression.[67]

WAVPM began its efforts with marches and pickets against San Francisco porn shops. When it planned the first National Feminist Conference on Pornography in 1978, it anticipated 350 attendees, with 500 more for a postconference march. More than one thousand joined the march, and San Francisco mayor George Moscone assisted by proclaiming it "Take Back the Night" night for women. Even smarmy reporting, such as *San Francisco Chronicle* columnist Warren Hinckle's sexist joke that the women would protest porn and topless clubs by marching "on the sidewalk three abreast, if you will pardon the expression," helped publicize the cause. New York University lent credence to the antiporn cause by hosting a colloquium at its law school on pornography in early 1979. Though token civil libertarians and conservatives were invited, the colloquium served primarily as a forum for antiporn feminism. When the *NYU Review of Law and Social Change* published several of the proceedings, it bestowed to the antiporn activists a seeming monopoly on feminism by failing to include dissenting feminist perspectives.[68]

As the antiporn movement coalesced in 1978–79, WAP eclipsed its mother group WAVPM. Holding its own conferences and marches—drawing five thousand at one in 1979—and offering tours of Times Square, porn capital of America, WAP proved shrewd in its media front. Appearing on *The Phil Donahue Show* in September 1979, for instance, Brownmiller and other WAP members studiously avoided framing their critique as radical or even particularly feminist. This elusiveness helped generate a flurry of support from uncomprehending conservatives, who wrote letters of support with frequent financial contributions. "Thank you for your stand on bible morality," wrote one woman, while another noted approvingly that "the only permanent solution it seems to me goes back to the home and religion. . . . The laws of nature are not permissive." A male *Donahue* viewer applauded "you fine American mothers" as "the best indications yet of a new revitalization of our traditional American standards and character." Letters from conservative Christians worried about "moral decay" far outnumbered letters from feminists, and a typical $25 donation came from a man who warned WAP not to let itself be "overrun by queer (homo) subgroups." Just as a marcher in a 1977 WAVPM protest had told a reporter, "I can see myself with pro-lifers or Catholics on this," the converse also clearly held true.[69]

When feminists did write to WAP, they often expressed alarm and dismay. One woman called the downplaying of feminist ideology on the *Donahue* show "an opportunistic approach and a dangerous one" for inviting the support of those who opposed sexual and reproductive freedom. The letter writer also accused WAP of failing to discuss the wider context of capitalism that generated objectification and porn. One reason for this was WAP's immersion in capitalism. Its Times Square office was donated in June 1979 by the Midtown Enforcement Agency and the 42nd Street Redevelopment Corporation, two organizations dedicated to driving porn out of the area and fostering business growth. In its script for Times Square tours WAP called redevelopment "an interesting, fluid situation." The *Village Voice* described it differently, as "the inexorable march west by big real estate." The nearby neighborhood of Clinton, a rare remaining specimen of class and ethnic heterogeneity in Manhattan by the late 1970s, vigorously protested redevelopment. Neighborhood coalitions objected to higher rents and taxes that would drive out low-income residents, "outrageous tax breaks" for private developers, and the transformation of Times Square into a "glass, chrome, and concrete canyon . . . devoid of light during the day and devoid of people at night." The Midtown Enforcement Agency never disguised its motive of "restoring consumer and investor confidence in the Times Square area," and the free office for WAP was a successful attempt to enlist feminism in its corporate rehabilitation of 42nd Street. Foreshadowing future antiporn alliances, WAP said nothing on the topic.[70]

With such powerful resource mobilization behind it, WAP had a clear effect on feminist discourse. References to feminist porn largely vanished,

244 • PORNOGRAPHY IS THE PRACTICE, WHERE IS THE THEORY?

and antiporn influence extended beyond the feminist community. Mainstream women's magazines showed the impact; whereas a 1976 *Redbook* article had discussed "What I Like About Porn Flicks," a late 1979 *Glamour* poll revealed that 78 percent of its readers believed porn "affects real-life behavior." Asked "What's most offensive to you?" 50 percent of the readers said pornography, while 37 percent said media portraying "women as being bound, degraded or killed for sexual stimulation or pleasure." The very fact that women saw these categories as separate showed the failure of antiporn feminists to effectively convey their actual analyses rather than simply their conclusions, since the categories were coextensive in the eyes of WAVPM and WAP.[71]

At one of its first meetings WAVPM had concluded that legal definitions of pornography and obscenity were "confusing because of their subjectivity." This did not compel the group to hold its own analysis of porn to objective standards. "We shouldn't be concerned with being subjective—only that we're right," one member explained. From the start antiporn feminists had used the term *pornography* in many ways, leading critic Ellen Willis to accuse them of "playing games with the English language." But as porn came to occupy its new position of centrality, writers grew even more cavalier. Essays in one antiporn anthology offered at least five definitions of porn, ranging from specific to wildly subjective. Robin Yeaman straightforwardly defined the term as "any use of the media which equates sex and violence." But Charlotte Bunche hearkened back to Supreme Court Justice Potter Stewart's infamous "I know it when I see it" quip in simply claiming, "Every woman that I know . . . can draw the line. We can tell the difference between eroticism and anti-female pornography." The presentation of an effective demonology took precedence over analytical rigor.[72]

The true installation of antiporn ideology as the dominant public voice of feminism came with a spate of books from 1979 to 1981 by WAVPM or WAP members, all of which firmly entrenched porn at the center of women's oppression. Andrea Dworkin's *Pornography: Men Possessing Women* construed porn as an all-encompassing metaphysical system in which "the only choice for the woman has been to embrace herself as whore." "We will know we are free," Dworkin intoned, "when the pornography no longer exists." Susan Griffin recast porn as gender-holocaust in *Pornography and Silence*, offering an extended quasi-allegory in which Hitler was a "master" among pornographers, the concentration camp "resembled an enacted pornographic fantasy," and the final effect of porn on women, as of the Holocaust on Jews, was to silence them. Kathleen Barry included a lengthy discussion of porn in *Female Sexual Slavery*, terming it "the ideology of cultural sadism" and arguing that porn "cannot be separated from behavior." And Laura Lederer's anthology *Take Back the Night: Women on Pornography* collected thirty-eight essays that unanimously condemned porn from various angles.[73]

Dworkin's *Pornography* provided the centerpiece of antiporn feminism. A true powerhouse of a book, it contended that the "major theme of pornography as a genre is male power" and that "the degradation of the female is the means of achieving this power." Dworkin offered brilliant textual analyses of the power dynamics in several pornographic works. For instance, a photograph from *Hustler* titled "Beaver Hunters" used the purported humor of two armed men "hunting" a naked woman to obscure the dehumanization and terrorism it contained, and Dworkin argued that the picture gave men "the power of naming" while the woman—"beaver"—was "diminished to the point of annihilation; her humanity is canceled out." Dworkin's vivid language solicited emotional response. "In the male system," she wrote, women were "the lowest whore, the whore who belongs to *all* male citizens: the slut, the cunt." Her persuasiveness, though, went beyond mere visceral impact, and certainly Dworkin's analysis resonated with many women horrified by the normalization of rape and sexual violence that cropped up with systematic regularity in 1970s porn films.[74]

For Dworkin pornography constituted an ethos, the central ethos of the entire male-dominated world. Her broad radical agenda of demolishing that world rarely surfaced in antiporn activism, however. Unwilling to challenge capitalism because of its single-issue focus—or, as critics alleged, fear of alienating its conservative allies and corporate benefactors—the antiporn movement offered none of the Marxist rhetoric that had marked the occupations of *Rat* and Grove Press. Instead of emphasizing power structures or control over the means of production in looking at women's labor in sex-related media, antiporn writers devised a simpler interpretive model based on victimization. Because women were abused in pornography, the new line of reasoning held, women working in porn were victims. Thus Laura Lederer, interviewing a former porn model for WAVPM's *Newspage* in 1978, asked why women get involved in porn. "J. J." replied, "Alot [*sic*] of women are hurt or crazy. . . . It's all a form of rape because women who are involved in it don't know how to get out." J. J. went on to describe her own molestation by her father, rape and abuse on the job, and the effect of her porn career in ruining her own perception of sex. These details established an image of porn models as psychologically damaged, coerced, and abused. But when J. J. suddenly took a defensive stance, noting that working-class women never asked her "the 'How could you have done anything like that?' question" that middle-class feminists—who "have no consciousness about what it is like out there"—often did, Lederer abruptly shifted the conversation away by asking a non sequitur about snuff films.[75]

This unwillingness to acknowledge matters beyond their preconceptions also plagued antiporn feminists in their reception of Linda Lovelace. The famous *Deep Throat* star had been an icon of the porno chic movement, a living testament to the splendors of sexual liberation. But her 1980 autobiography *Ordeal* revealed an unseen side of her existence: for years she had been sexually and physically abused by her husband, Chuck Traynor, who had forced her to perform degrading sex acts in and out of pornography. Antiporn feminists rallied to Lovelace's cause, using her revelations as a platform to denounce porn for brutality toward its female performers. Law professor Catharine MacKinnon cited Lovelace to write, "The first victims of pornography are the ones in it"; Susan Griffin and Gloria Steinem also used her to make sweeping, categorical claims about porn actresses. This frequent referencing of pornography obscured the actual theme of the book, however, which was the danger of spousal domination and abuse. The villain of *Ordeal* was Chuck Traynor, not pornography. Of the *Deep Throat* shoot, Lovelace wrote, "I hated to see it end" because the cast and crew treated her kindly, despite failing to intervene when Traynor beat her. Andrea Dworkin even put words in Lovelace's mouth, calling her a "strong feminist" when in fact Lovelace herself wrote, "I don't call myself a feminist."[76]

In constructing the porn actress and model as victim, Dworkin quantified: "perhaps three-quarters of the women in pornography are incest victims," she wrote in 1984, though two years later she adjusted this number to claim, "sixty-five to seventy percent of them we believe are victims of incest or child abuse." When pressed for a source for this information, Dworkin cited a study of two hundred prostitutes that asked no questions about porn and was not, in her own words, "scientifically valid." Like the Meese Commission, she refrained from approaching actual porn actresses and sex workers for their input. Nonetheless, she persisted in asserting that women in porn were coerced; admitting the "hypothetical" possibility that some were not, she added, "we can't find that group." This victim model extended to womankind in general, including the antiporn leaders. Dworkin claimed "the most powerless women" were those fighting porn, while MacKinnon described women as "silenced" by "a publishing industry that virtually guarantees that if they ever find a voice it leaves no trace in the world," despite the fact that MacKinnon's and Dworkin's publishing profile, on mass-market imprints and prestigious academic publishers like Harvard University Press, towered over the small-press distribution of their feminist challengers.[77]

Working together, Dworkin and MacKinnon used this victim model to pioneer the most regressive feature of antiporn feminism, its call for state intervention and suppression. The First Amendment had entered antiporn discourse early on, approached in different ways. In the late 1970s Diana Russell framed porn as "an *abuse* of freedom of speech" and agreed with Susan Brownmiller that it should be banned, while Kathy Barry called the First Amendment question a "side issue." Robin Morgan suggested investigating the "clear and present danger" test used to bar shouts of "fire" in a crowded theater. Wendy Kaminer of WAP, while arguing that only the government could violate the First Amendment and that protesting women could not, added, "We simply cannot look to the government to rid us of pornography." The general tenor of these stances was a rejection of the civil libertarian position but also a hesitancy to call on state power in any specific manner. That hesitancy disappeared as Dworkin and MacKinnon rose to prominence.[78]

As MacKinnon framed it, sex inequality was so endemic to patriarchal American culture that at the dawn of the nation, gender "was simply assumed out of legal existence, suppressed into a presumptively preconstitutional social order through a constitutional structure designed not to reach it." Thus, constitutionally guaranteed negative freedoms such as the freedom from abridgement of speech were never meant to ensure a voice to all; "no one who does not have [speech] socially is granted [it] legally," she wrote. Dworkin, the more direct writer, further articulated the idea: the First Amendment "was written by white men who were literate and who owned land. Many of them owned slaves and many of them owned women." From the start, Dworkin explained, literacy was a sign of social power, kept from slaves, and the First Amendment "was written to preserve that power." Two centuries later "it protects a different kind of power, a more vulgar power": that of money. Because "it was never intended" to empower women, Dworkin argued, women owed no allegiance to it.[79]

MacKinnon, in particular, directed her critique toward liberalism, whose abstract ideals of "equality, liberty, privacy, and speech" worked to ratify the existing social order by atomizing rights as strictly individual matters and thus deflecting investigations into institutionalized inequalities. She carefully distinguished antiporn feminism from obscenity law, which has "literally nothing in common with this feminist critique." Obscenity law "is more concerned with whether men blush, pornography with whether women bleed," she explained, rejecting the moralistic framework that traditionally guided policy as another male invention.[80]

Having thus distanced themselves from the free-speech debate, Dworkin and MacKinnon transferred their activism from the theoretical to the legislative. In 1984 the duo introduced an antiporn ordinance in Minneapolis, adopting not an obscenity-law approach—which would, of necessity, carry attendant free-speech implications—but what they called a "civil rights" approach to suppressing porn, which was classified as "discrimination on the basis of sex." Using an expansive definition of porn that encompassed images of rape and torture, as well as material in which "women are presented dehumanized as sexual objects, things or commodities," the ordinance served several functions. It allowed women who were damaged by porn to sue producers and distributors for injuries ranging from coercion into performance to imposed exposure to porn. The ordinance also regulated media and behavior that did not directly impact women. Because porn equaled sex discrimination, for instance, private porn clubs were declared "a conspiracy to violate the civil rights of women." Based in civil rather than criminal law, the ordinance nonetheless shared with obscenity law the goal of suppressing pornography.[81]

The ordinance passed the Minneapolis City Council twice but was vetoed both times by Mayor Donald Fraser. Undaunted, MacKinnon took the civil rights approach to Indianapolis. In the more conservative city Dworkin's fiery presence was more liability than asset, so MacKinnon worked instead with conservative councilwoman Beulah Coughenour, who had led the fight against the ERA in Indiana and opposed abortion rights, as well as marital rape laws. The ordinance, too, lost some of its feminist edge, as its definition of porn was scaled back to emphasize rape and violence without the "dehumanization" clause. This time the measure succeeded, though it was quickly overturned at the judicial level on free-speech grounds.[82]

By the time the Meese Commission began its investigation in 1986, these political activities of antiporn feminists made them valuable allies. Dworkin, MacKinnon, and several others testified before the commission eagerly and to warm response. The final report quoted Dworkin at great length, and Commissioner Park Dietz even wrote a tribute to her in the report's personal statement section, describing the tears she brought to his eyes. The report also singled out the Dworkin/MacKinnon civil rights ordinances for praise and adopted their language, calling porn "a practice of discrimination on the basis of sex." That this represented a blatant co-optation of feminist rhetoric rather than any meaningfully feminist bent on behalf of the commission was apparent. The commission did absolutely nothing to embrace feminist goals and saturated its report with homophobic, "profamily" themes. Chairman Henry Hudson's paternalistic explanation that porn "distort[ed] the moral sensitivity of women" stood in direct opposition to Dworkin's and MacKinnon's positions. Though the commission's only two feminists, Judith Becker and Ellen Levine, dissented from its report and criticized the commission for seeking only victims and considering a "paucity" of perspectives, Women Against Pornography issued a statement commending the commission for its work.[83]

As lesbians had feared in the 1970s, the Christian Right quickly co-opted the antiporn feminist platform, adopting the MacKinnon/Dworkin civil rights framework in a proposed Suffolk, New York, ordinance later in 1984. With the substance of the ordinance overhauled to reflect a fundamentalist agenda, the Republican county legislator proposing it explained, "I don't want to tell anyone what to do as long they live by the Ten Commandments." Though MacKinnon, Dworkin, and WAP denounced the Suffolk ordinance (which failed, as did similar but feminist-run efforts in Los Angeles and Cambridge, Massachusetts), they did little to distance themselves from the Right. "When women get raped they're not asked first whether they're Democrats or Republicans," Dworkin explained in defense of her conservative allegiances. Elsewhere she added, "when Jerry Falwell starts saying there's real harm in pornography, then that is valuable to me." That the converse—antiporn feminism was also of value to right-wing efforts—might as well be true went unaddressed, as did acknowledgment that Falwell's notion of harm, based on challenges to the heterosexual nuclear family, was precisely Dworkin's idea of progress.[84]

Ambivalent Liberals Redux

Again, none of this went uncontested. Visions of a feminist pornography refused to die, and a group of lesbians distraught by the direction of the antiporn movement began publishing *On Our Backs* in 1984. The title parodied the longtime feminist paper *off our backs*, and the first issue proclaimed, "Yes, finally a sex magazine for lesbians!" With a "Bulldagger of the Season" pictorial, prurient erotic stories, and informed political essays, *On Our Backs* presented a sex-positive feminism intended to dispel notions of a monolithic patriarchy without losing sight of such feminist goals as autonomy and equality. That same year, former porn star Candida Royalle formed Femme, a film company dedicated to reshaping porn; its films featured egalitarian sex devoid of violence against women, embedded in narratives portraying women as premedical students and executives. In Ohio a group called Women for Pornography offered its own salvo in 1986, arguing that antiporn feminism "reinforces the notion that sex is for men only."[85]

These groups, however, remained small and easily marginalized. When Gloria Steinem dismissed lesbian porn as involving "a woman assuming the 'masculine' role of victimizing another woman," she reached an audience vastly wider than that of *On Our Backs*, which, in fact, routinely proved Steinem wrong with its varied pictorials. Likewise, Women for Pornography never established a national following; in contrast, when Andrea Dworkin explained why some women claim to enjoy porn by writing, "Women have two choices: lie or die," it was in a best-selling book. And though Royalle made a tidy profit, when the *New York Times* covered her work, the article prefaced its discussion with a lengthy quote from Robin Morgan dismissing Femme because "women are interested in relationships, in intellect and emotion as part of eroticism, not fetishized individual body parts, whether male or female." The antiporn movement, with its access to mainstream mass media, thus rendered dissenting prosex feminists seemingly suspect and irrelevant.[86]

Feminists opposed to the antiporn movement more successfully organized around traditional liberal principles of free speech and expression.

While groups like the ACLU and NOW afforded resources and prestige to anti-antiporn efforts, their mainstream liberalism muted the message of sex-positive feminism. Instead of opposing the antiporn movement with a radical politics of pleasure, anti-antiporn feminists recognized the necessity of a more palatable anticensorship framework, more easily conveyed to a mass audience than nuanced discussions of sexuality. As radical lesbian Lisa Duggan later explained, "We appropriated the rhetoric of 'anticensorship'... because 'censorship' was a negative we hoped would be powerful enough to set against 'pornography.'" The Faustian bargain gave anti-antiporn feminists social capital but at the cost of their radicalism.[87]

The Feminist Anti-Censorship Taskforce (FACT) emerged as the standard-bearer of this approach. Active in combating the Dworkin-MacKinnon ordinances, FACT explained that, instead of truly addressing violence against women, "the movement against pornography is a diversion" built on the fact that "sex has always been an easy, vulnerable target and has always been something from which the culture has 'protected' women." Responding to the Meese Commission, FACT pointed out that the Reagan administration was using the nominal feminist rhetoric of the commission to draw attention from the various ways its policies were "harming women" in its quest to destroy the welfare state. FACT press releases followed the pattern of drawing attention to the antiporn movement's "dangerous alliance with the Right Wing," then following it up by refuting the antiporn position in negative terms: censorship adversely impacted women, social science did not establish causal ties between porn and rape, and so on.[88]

FACT proved successful in mobilizing support. Its amicus curiae brief in the legal battle against the Indianapolis antiporn ordinance drew signatures from Betty Friedan, Kate Millett, Ellen Willis, and numerous other feminists. While the brief, written by Nan Hunter and Sylvia Law, immediately pointed out the ordinance's fallacy in assuming that "women are incapable of choosing for themselves what they consider to be enjoyable, sexually arousing material," FACT nonetheless presented itself as strictly opposed to censorship rather than as focused on the sexual dynamics of porn. When several FACT members published essays in a 1985 anthology, they occasionally examined the potential feminist pleasures of porn, but the anthology's title similarly framed it more broadly: *Women Against Censorship*. To challenge the antiporn movement on grounds other than censorship was clearly to risk marginalization and obscurity.[89]

The ambivalence of the National Organization for Women reflected the difficulties of challenging the antiporn movement from within liberal feminism. The California NOW branch passed a resolution in 1982 rejecting state intervention in the control of porn. Such laws, it declared in a show of wariness toward New Right co-optation, "run the grave risk of backfiring into serious attacks on First Amendment rights, sex education, and access to birth control information." Instead of legal mechanisms, California NOW proposed to eradicate porn "through change in social awareness such that it no longer will be tolerated." While the national organization shared this free-speech orientation, it, too, expressed hostility toward porn. In a 1984 general resolution NOW found porn to be "a factor in creating and maintaining sex as a basis for discrimination." Showing how thoroughly the antiporn movement had set the terms of debate, NOW declared pornography "distinct from erotica," defining it as "a systematic practice of exploitation and subordination based on sex which differentially harms women and children." Within this framework advocacy of feminist porn was clearly unwelcome.[90]

NOW's response to the Meese Commission likewise indicated ambivalence, as unease with porn preceded insistence on free speech. In a press release NOW began with its support for aspects of the commission's report, such as the forum offered to women and "civil remedies for harm directly attributable to pornography." Only after some time spent on these virtuous qualities of the Meese Commission did NOW reach its criticisms, rejecting obscenity laws and warning that the Christian Right "will use the revulsion that many Americans feel" toward porn "as an excuse to spread bigotry and hatred against lesbians and gay men." The press release also noted the "disturbing undertone" in several commissioners' comments, which suggested porn could be defined as "any sexually explicit material that does not reflect 'traditional family values.'"[91]

Despite these caveats, NOW's position was sufficiently Meese-friendly to draw "deep concern" from some members. The cochairs of the San Francisco NOW Prostitution, Pornography, and AIDS Task Force noted that NOW's uncritical reference to the "harms" of porn might be construed as support for the Meese Commission's own take on those harms, which included promiscuity and homosexual behavior. The NOW members pointed out that three of the four women on the commission issued dissents from its report and wondered why NOW would side with right-wingers over fellow women.[92]

Still other liberal feminists took similar stances against the antiporn movement in related debates. When Cambridge debated an antiporn ordinance in 1985, the Boston chapter of Women Against Violence Against Women opposed it, arguing that porn had "monopolized feminists' attention," diverting attention from more pressing issues such as abortion rights and actual male violence. Several NOW leaders involved themselves in the issue. Karen DeCrow, NOW president from 1974 to 1977, contributed a 1985 essay to *Penthouse* calling antiporn feminists and the New Right "Strange Bedfellows." Even Betty Friedan entered the fray with a scathing denunciation of the Meese Commission. Calling censorship "extremely dangerous to women," she distinguished porn from "actual violence" and pointedly observed, "The forces that want to suppress pornography are not in favor of suppressing guns." Murder and poverty constituted "the ultimate obscenity" to Friedan, who also suggested conservatives hoped to use porn "to take our attention away" while they enacted policies detrimental to the well-being of women, the working class, racial minorities, and other groups.[93]

Liberal feminists thus displayed open antagonism to repression, but the broad anticensorship framework they adopted spoke little to sex radicals beyond the pale of the mainstream. "I think the most radical and visionary voices on women's sexuality, especially lesbian sexuality, have chosen silence in the face of the vicious attacks they suffered at the hands of the antiporn movement," wrote one woman to *off our backs* in 1987. She added, "There is a paltry amount of visual material that supports my lesbian sexuality," all of which would be banned under the Dworkin/MacKinnon laws. Indeed, even without such laws lesbians and gay men remained targets. An Atlanta lesbian newsletter, for example, documented repeated harassment and obscenity charges against a local queer bookstore in 1984. Though by the 1980s mainstream liberal feminists had moved beyond the homophobia of the early 1970s, by transforming the debate into one of abstract free-speech principles rather than sexuality, they reactively ceded the analysis of pornography to the antiporn movement.[94]

Narrativizing the Sex Wars

Antiporn feminists had a ready response to FACT and other liberal, free-speech feminists: to brand them as "collaborators." Catharine MacKinnon, who used that term in a 1985 speech, also invoked false consciousness in accounting for FACT, saying that "oppressed people often respond by identifying with the oppressor." Andrea Dworkin simply wrote FACT out of feminism: "They are collaborators, not feminists." And a WAP book reviewer equated FACT with Christian fundamentalist Marabel Morgan and reactionary activist Phyllis Schlafly in 1987—the same year, ironically, that Schlafly's book *Pornography's Victims* quoted extensively and approvingly from WAP supporters while itself equating pornographers with an even more demonized group for Christian fundamentalists, abortionists.[95]

The narrativization of the porn debates by antiporn feminists was disingenuous at times. In 1990 WAP founding member Dorchen Leidholdt called it a "rumor" devoid of evidence that antiporn feminists had "formed an alliance with conservatives to fight pornography." She went on to accuse free-speech feminists of "collaboration with antifeminists," both on the grounds of their occasional financial ties to groups like the Playboy Foundation and because some of them had made arguments for the legalization of prostitution. Dworkin partook of this construct as well, calling the *Hudnut* decision that overturned the Indianapolis ordinance "the right-wing position" and even describing the presiding judge in the case as "a Reagan-appointed judge, a woman, a right-wing woman."[96]

Of her own collaboration with the reactionary Indianapolis councilwoman Beulah Coughenour, MacKinnon said little. Years later she would skirt the topic by pointing to a factual error in the *New York Times* regarding her other allies in the Minneapolis effort and briefly mentioning Coughenour in the same context, as if to suggest her image had been distorted by "taint through innuendo." It had not, though MacKinnon went further, citing conservative Attorney General Edwin Meese's lack of involvement with the press-named Meese Commission in an attempt to distance the body from its origins on the political right. Employing her own taint through innuendo, she also inaccurately described the earlier liberal Presidential Commission on Obscenity and Pornography as "appointed by President Nixon." As late as a 2005 book MacKinnon continued to defend the Meese Commission's "cautious and measured" approach.[97]

MacKinnon's misleading evasions showed how reluctant antiporn feminists were to be affiliated with the New Right and its antifeminist policies. As important, however, was the title of the last significant WAP effort, the 1990 book *The Sexual Liberals and the Attack on Feminism.* Though the liberalism of the title came from the British concept of classical liberalism, a laissez-faire philosophy somewhat (though not entirely) removed from contemporary American liberalism, WAP eagerly exploited the homonym. The historian Sheila Jeffries defined sexual liberalism as an ideology predicated on "the assumption that sexual expression is inherently liberating and must be permitted to flourish unchecked, even when it entails the exploitation or brutalization of others."[98] This straw-woman concept described no members of the anti-antiporn feminist brigade, who opposed government intervention only in the realm of consensual activity but remained united on the necessity of laws and intervention to prevent sexual coercion and abuse. The fact that WAP tarnished their opponents with the brush of "liberalism" did, however, reflect the abject failure of mainstream American liberalism to aggressively embrace a progressive sexual politics. Just as liberal arguments for abortion rights privileged abstract "privacy" over women's rights, the liberal defense of free speech paid little heed to the important gender analysis offered by MacKinnon and others. Conservatives, supporting similar antiporn goals, even for different reasons and toward different ends, could thus at times claim greater single-issue affinities with feminists.

This benefited conservatism immensely more than it did feminism. As the decade drew to a close, antiporn feminists had achieved few tangible results besides a divisive intrafeminist battle that weakened feminism when it most needed a united front, in the face of Reagan administration policies that waged what one formerly Republican author called "the Republican war on women."[99] The power of pornography to effect political realignments nowhere showed so clearly as it did within the internecine feminist conflicts, as some women preferred to work with profoundly antifeminist politicians rather than defend the free speech of pornographers. To these women liberalism had little to offer but apologetics. Meanwhile, to free-speech feminists the foulness of porn was a small price to pay for the hard-won freedoms over their bodies and beliefs women had won in the twentieth century. Lost in this debate were the politics of pleasure. This aspect would move to the forefront of academic work on sexuality in the 1990s, but outside the Ivory Tower the New Right would continue to dominate the political landscape, even as Democrats recaptured the White House. In chapter 8 we will see how conservatives have continued to exploit antiporn moral panics well into the new century, while a weakened liberalism struggled merely to temper the Right's blows against free expression.

8. VANILLA HEGEMONY
Policing Sexual Boundaries in the
Permanent Culture-War Economy

AN INDICATION OF THE EXTENT to which social perceptions of pornography had changed since the 1980s came during the February 2005 premiere of the documentary film *Inside Deep Throat*. After the screening a panel discussion featured film critics, First Amendment lawyers, and the antiporn feminist leader Catharine MacKinnon. Two decades earlier MacKinnon had stunned her audiences into horrified silence with her descriptions of the brutal "throat rapes" inspired by *Deep Throat*. But when she repeated this in 2005, claiming the "deep throat" fellatio technique was inherently unsafe and could be performed only under hypnosis, the response came in the form of audience giggles. "What's so funny?" MacKinnon reportedly demanded, to which one man in the crowd eagerly shouted, "I can do it!" As the Internet blogosphere reported, "The room echoed with a chorus of gay men going, 'me too!'"[1]

The anecdote illustrates several significant themes: the increasing irrelevance of antiporn feminists, the legacy of their insensitivity to the queer experience, and a shifting cultural disposition toward porn. Indeed, *Inside Deep Throat* went on to garner positive reviews and receive widespread distribution despite carrying the scarlet letter of the NC-17 rating. Rejection of antiporn ideologues went beyond MacKinnon. Father Bruce Ritter, a Meese commissioner and the founder of Covenant House, was transferred to India after Franciscan investigators found evidence of his long-term sexual exploitation of numerous young men at the runaway shelter. St. Louis state prosecutor George Peach, who had spent fifteen years focused on obscenity cases, was arrested in 1992 for soliciting sex from an undercover police officer.[2] It seemed many of the criticisms leveled at Citizens for Decent Literature in the 1960s regarding the misplaced sexual obsessions of antiporn activists had some basis in fact.

Indeed, the most public antiporn fall from grace centered on CDL leader Charles Keating, though for financial rather than sexual improprieties. Keating was named executive vice president of American Financial

Corporation in 1972, and the subsequent plummeting of CDL's public profile was no coincidence. From the start Keating had been CDL's public face and spokesman, and with his attention focused elsewhere, the group floundered. Using the same organizational genius that had built CDL, Keating created a massive financial empire. He left AFC in 1978 after an SEC investigation into his murky accounting and investment behaviors, but after relocating to Phoenix and taking over an AFC subsidary, he promptly began again. Keating acquired a savings and loans bank in 1984, and taking full advantage of Reagan-era deregulation he joined Michael Milken in pioneering "junk bond" marketing. By selling these unsecured bonds to thousands of retirees and funneling the money back into an elaborate network of phony corporate fronts, Keating essentially embezzled upwards of $1 billion. Ironically, he was tried under RICO, the federal racketeering statute that CDL had once called an "important new tool" in fighting porn. Convicted on seventy-three counts of racketeering, fraud, and conspiracy in early 1993, he served fewer than five years of a twelve-year sentence before engineering a new deal that saw him plead guilty to four counts of fraud and receive a reduced sentence to time served.[3]

The undeniable corruption of Charles Keating gave great pleasure to his longtime opponents (*Playboy*, for instance, enjoyed the savings-and-loan fiasco greatly, ridiculing Keating's "inordinate lust for money" and calling his story "Profit Without Honor"), but to dismiss CDL—or Ritter's Meese Commission, or MacKinnon's work alongside Women Against Pornography—on the basis of ad hominem attacks does a great disservice to the historical significance of these bodies and their work.[4] To be sure, as this chapter will show, the years since 1989 have looked to some like a radical sex bacchanalia in the halls of academia, the currents of mainstream culture, and the postspatial world of the Internet. But even as antiporn public leaders were displaced by a more relaxed culture, beneath this veneer of sophistication, urbanity, and the public mockery of hypocrites and bluenoses lay a further consolidation of the Christian Right's political influence.

Though the first Bush administration took shape as a "kinder, gentler" extension of the Reagan years, the Clinton administrations of the 1990s provided even more fertile ground for the Christian Right. As president, Bill Clinton exhibited a personal tolerance that effectively disguised his conservative leanings to many observers, but in fact his policy of "triangulation" represented a series of concessions to conservative forces. In the realm of pornography this facilitated a distinct moral panic regarding child porn. That this was a real social problem cannot be denied; even the scholar Philip Jenkins, after dismissing it as myth in a 1998 book, returned to admit Internet child porn's prevalence and significance in a later work.[5] But in the hands of the Christian Right the juridical underpinnings of child pornography laws would be entirely forgotten, as the logic of preventing sexual abuse was abandoned for a more widespread crusade against diverse forms of counternormative sexuality. If law operates as the "border patrol of sexual citizenship," as the legal scholar Brenda Cossman writes, it is clear that the Christian Right established and fiercely guarded this border, as obscenity charges continued to shore up traditional notions of normalcy.[6]

These efforts reached their apex under the George W. Bush regime, as antiporn efforts extended beyond child porn in an effort to regulate adult sexual behavior and representation. The Bush II administration took a normative and openly regressive approach to sexuality, privileging abstinence over birth control and abortion rights. Its gay-baiting anti-same-sex-marriage efforts, meanwhile, presented state recognition of same-sex unions as a "threat" to the already wildly unstable nuclear family. Pornography fit into this framework well, and the Bush Justice Department expanded its adult obscenity suppression in an effort to scale back sexual freedom and appease the Christian Right. These developments reflect the logical conclusion of this book's overarching narrative: a topic once controlled and defined by cautious liberals whose discourse of civil liberties concealed fundamentally conservative sexual politics gave way to a sexualized consumer culture that existed within parameters set by reactionary religious activists.

This chapter begins with an examination of developments in academia, where sex radicalism found something of a niche. The intellectual efforts of queer theorists and feminist scholars, as well as gay men inside and outside the Ivory Tower, definitively refuted the analytical foundations of antiporn feminism, calling into question its facile equation of porn with power. Popular culture embraced much of this sex-positive attitude but without any of its radical sexual politics, and an increasing normalization of porn occurred within contested boundaries, which the Bush administration fought hard to tighten. The twenty-first century began with sexual normativity alive and well in the United States, if somewhat concealed behind a sex-driven media swirl.

Queering the Debate

While antiporn feminists and the New Right claimed greater social profiles than their opponents in the 1980s, opposition to both coalesced within academia. Feminist scholars alienated by the essentialist qualities of the antiporn movement, criticized for constructing an image of women more feminine than feminist, joined gay activists in undermining the antiporn theoretical framework. As queer theory coalesced in the early 1990s, the insights of these two groups fused in a renaissance of sex-positive radical feminism, which returned to the initial emphasis of the women's liberation movement, interrogating the power structures that shape gender and sexual identity. The resulting critique of mainstream porn found much to celebrate in some forms of porn, as well as much to condemn, though outside the Ivory Tower these theoretical developments were paralleled by a facile "postfeminism" that omitted the radical politics and substituted an implied endorsement of the status quo. The fruits of queer theory would be consumed by the public only after a dilution process that left their insights closer to sickly sugared water.

Feminist academics had taken a frequently critical stance toward the antiporn movement from its inception, a perspective solidified by the controversy surrounding a 1982 Barnard College conference called "Towards a Politics of Sexuality." Women Against Pornography protested the conference, distributing a leaflet accusing its planners of "silencing" the views of "a major portion of the feminist movement" by neglecting to invite any representatives of the antiporn movement. The leaflet went on to single out several members of the conference by name, associating them with sado-masochistic and antifeminist activity.[7]

Nearly three hundred feminists and academics signed a letter of protest against the WAP leaflet, claiming it had directly caused the Barnard administration to take measures against the conference. Turning WAP rhetoric back on itself, the protest added that no feminist dialogue on sexuality could occur when "one segment of the feminist movement uses McCarthyite tactics to silence other voices." The matter might have ended with mutual bad feelings and little public awareness, but the academic journal *Feminist Studies* published both the leaflet and the protest, leading to an outpouring of outrage, both at the journal for bringing greater publicity to those named by WAP and at WAP for printing the leaflet in the first place. *Feminist Studies* issued an apology condemning the leaflet and opened its pages to responses by those singled out. The result was an explosive burst of resistance to the antiporn movement. Gayle Rubin argued that "all dissent has been labeled anti-feminist" by WAP, Carole Vance called the leaflet a "slimy and vicious attack on individual women," and Pat Califia (who would later transition his gender but then still self-identified as a lesbian) compared WAP to the Catholic Church in its acceptance of "deviants" such as s/m lesbians "as long as they are searching for a cure." "I spit on that invitation," he continued, rejecting any movement "which wants to make me feel shitty about how I get off." Although these responses had little impact on the public face of the antiporn movement, they helped establish an infrastructure of resistance that quickly blossomed in academia. A subsequent WAP response noting that all of the women named in the leaflet had already discussed their sexualities in public did little to redeem the group's tarnished image among academics, to whom charges of McCarthyism were very serious.[8]

When papers from the Barnard conference were published in book form as *Pleasure and Danger* in 1984, Carole Vance's introduction disavowed the antiporn movement, describing sexuality as a realm of "restriction, repression, and danger," as well as "exploration, pleasure, and agency" in women's lives. Pointing out that antiporn ideology attended to only one aspect of this duality, Vance also accused it of making "new forms of shaming possible" for women by attacking them for their interest in sexual material deemed antifeminist. In another essay, leading women's historians Ellen DuBois and Linda Gordon drew parallels between groups like WAP and the nineteenth-century Women's Christian Temperance Union. *Powers of Desire*, a similar anthology from 1983, also positioned its essays on sexuality in opposition to the antiporn movement. Both books carried essays by Alice Echols, the most cogent critic of WAP at the time, who found in the group a retreat from the goals of women's liberation into an acceptance of the gender status quo. Most of the essays in these books had little direct bearing on the porn debate, but nearly all of them implicitly refuted WAP by insisting on an analysis of sexuality more complicated than the victimized-woman model.[9]

While antiporn feminism carried on its prominent activities in the 1980s, feminist scholars continued to undermine its basic premises. Kathy

Peiss, a contributor to *Powers of Desire*, enshrined the "pleasure and danger" model of female sexuality in her 1986 book *Cheap Amusements*. The book, an important social-history monograph, looked at working-class women's culture in early-twentieth-century New York, adopting a theoretical framework that style, fashion, and romance "could be a source of autonomy and pleasure as well as a cause of [women's] continuing oppression." This became the most common framework for women's historians and historians of sexuality in the 1980s. For instance, Christine Stansell, onetime *Deep Throat* critic and *Powers of Desire* editor, referenced the "pleasures and the dangers" of nineteenth-century working women's lives in her *City of Women*. Using history to refute the victimized-woman model of sex work, Stansell showed that prostitution "was not a surrender to male sexual exploitation but a way of turning a unilateral relationship into a reciprocal one." By discussing this without ever losing sight of the fundamental patriarchy shaping women's lives, Stansell deftly depicted a dialectic of oppression and agency that, by implication, stripped the WAP monolithic-oppression analysis of historical accuracy. Women's sexuality was simply more complicated than the antiporn movement would admit, these feminist scholars showed.[10]

Gay men had never displayed much sympathy for the antiporn movement, and as feminist scholars discredited it, so, too, did gay men inside and outside academia. Gay liberation had paralleled women's liberation following the 1969 Stonewall rebellion, with similar analyses of gender identity and other social institutions as oppressive, but pornography played a dramatically different role in the gay male experience. In a homophobic, repressive culture homoerotic works were often deemed obscene, as we saw in earlier chapters. But for isolated, closeted gay men, such works historically provided comfort and even markers of identity. The case of Smith College professor Newton Arvin, whose life was torn apart by 1960 obscenity charges related to his erotic beefcake collection, is only one documented incident in a legion of unrecorded lives that sought solace in physique magazines and other gay material and were adversely impacted by obscenity laws. As the gay liberation movement took shape in the late 1960s, gay porn films such as Wakefield Poole's *Boys in the Sand* (1971) and Fred Halsted's *L.A. Plays Itself* (1972) adopted a liberationist ethos and served as purposeful efforts to smash the closet and affirm the varieties of queer experience. Even the physical space of porn theaters often served to facilitate makeshift sexual communities, as participant Samuel Delany would later recall, describing them as "humane and functional, fulfilling needs that most of our society does not yet know how to acknowledge."[11]

When *Deep Throat* star Harry Reems was arrested in 1976, the *Gay Community News* warned that gays and lesbians, as fellow "lifestyle dissenters," risked comparable persecution. As the antiporn movement took shape, the straight women in command proved as insensitive to specific gay male concerns as they did to lesbian issues. When Gloria Steinem dismissed gay male porn as involving a "feminized" partner and thus paralleling hetero porn in reflecting patriarchal hierarchies and power abuses, journalist Michael Bronski took vigorous exception: "This is not applicable to any homosexual male pornography (unless one equates 'passive' with 'feminine'—which I hope is not the case here)." He also noted that Robin Morgan advocated newspapers restricting space for pornographic advertising; when the *New York Times* implemented such a policy, they quickly banned ads for *GULP—A Gay Musical*. Morgan did little to calm gay nerves in a 1979 *Gay Community News* interview. Addressing gay male concerns, she wondered, "*Which* gay publications do they fear will be censored for being obscene?" Answering her own rhetorical question, Morgan mused, "What I mean to say is: if the shoe fits . . ."[12]

Returning the fire, gay historian John D'Emilio wrote about WAP for *Christopher Street* in 1980. Recounting his participation in a WAP Times Square tour, D'Emilio accused the group of willfully distorting the contents of porn and denouncing rather than debating the women participating in the tour who failed to see violence in depictions of consensual sex. Calling WAP "at best misguided and at worst downright dangerous," D'Emilio compared the group to the social purity campaigns of the late nineteenth century and warned of its ideological affinities to the New Right. He concluded his essay with an autobiographical anecdote about a random sexual encounter in an adult bookstore. Because public sex figured so importantly in the liberated gay identity, D'Emilio observed, "My sex life, according to the definitions of many, is pornographic."[13]

This defense of pornography by gay activists would be overshadowed in the 1980s, as the burgeoning AIDS crisis assumed center stage in queer communities. As the Reagan administration's silence regarding AIDS went from deafening to deadly, anonymous public sex became a contested topic among gay communities, thus diminishing the significance of porn theaters to gay identity. In the midst of crisis and the absence of substantive governmental assistance, though, gay porn staged its own political intervention, as filmmakers like Al Parker attempted to integrate condoms and safe-sex practices into the gay erotic imagination. Meanwhile, gay scholars persisted in approaching porn on friendly terms. Michael Bronski discussed it at length in his 1984 book *Culture Clash: The Making of Gay Sensibility*, explaining that "for many gay men, pornography was one of the few ways to assess and affirm their sexual feelings and desires." The next year, an issue of the film journal *Jump Cut* provided a forum for gay male film scholars to discuss pornography, as Richard Dyer and Tom Waugh found both pleasure and political importance in hardcore gay cinema. All of these authors voiced support for feminism but found oversimplification and misrepresentation in the antiporn wing of the movement.[14]

Waugh published the magnum opus of gay male porn scholarship with his expansive *Hard to Imagine* in 1996, which argued for the importance of porn to gay history, uncovering the circulation of gay smut from the dawn of photography to Stonewall. Listing desire, lust, and prurience as some of "the real motivations for this study," Waugh decried the "right-wing feminist backlash" against porn. According to him, gay porn had been systematically suppressed and underdocumented but was crucial to understanding the development of gay consciousness in a relentlessly homophobic society. "Fuck photos have always had to serve not only as our stroke materials but also, to a large extent, as our family snapshots and wedding albums, as our cultural history and political validation," he wrote. Waugh's powerful case inspired an entire body of scholarship on gay porn that continued into the twenty-first century.[15]

Meanwhile, queer theory took shape in the academy. Michel Foucault's 1976 book *The History of Sexuality, Vol. 1* portrayed society as a nexus of interlocking, multilateral power relations in which identities—sexual and otherwise—emerged always already entangled in the discursive webs of social regulation. The book carried enormous influence in the humanities, and queer theory emerged as a formidable scholarly project dedicated to dismantling heteronormativity by exposing the numerous ways "normalcy" had been historically constructed as a natural rather than political condition.[16]

In this post-Foucauldian academic world that saw the workings of power everywhere, the antiporn equation of porn with power and erotica with "natural" sex was exposed as vastly simplistic, hardly worthy of debate. The time was ripe for a sustained examination of pornography that bypassed liberal feminism's squeamishness regarding prurience, and in 1989 film scholar Linda Williams's *Hard Core* provided it. Williams found the genre to be both a medium of phallic power and a site of feminist pleasure and agency, often simultaneously. Emphasizing the need to accept disparities between politics and sexual fantasies, she concluded, "Hard core is not the enemy. Neither are fantasies, which by definition are based on unruly desires rather than politically correct needs." Informed by various theoretical frameworks from psychoanalysis to deconstruction, Williams saw porn as neither more nor less than an effort to "make sex speak," something it shared with many other projects of modernity.[17]

Hard Core helped usher in a massive body of feminist film criticism that found pornography too complex to reduce to simple oppression. Instead, it became seen as a site of contestations over gender, class resentments, racialization, and sexual subjectivity. The developing feminist porn-studies movement rejected antiporn feminism as reductionist and distorting. Indirectly referencing Susan Griffin's porn/holocaust analogies without finding them relevant enough to directly address, Constance Penley considered "white trash" porn films "closer to *Hee Haw* than Nazi death camp fantasies." Eithne Johnson, meanwhile, examined how self-identified "dyke porn" carried radical perspectives that depicted sex as "a culturally informed activity" rather than something simply "natural."[18]

Beyond academia, pornography made by and for women proliferated. Pat Califia, who had argued that "more of us have to start saying that we use porn, like it, and want it to be accessible" in response to the Meese Commission in 1986, suddenly jumped from the marginalized fringe of gay and lesbian magazines to the best-seller charts with the 1994 compilation *Public Sex*.[19] Susie Bright, who like Califia spent the 1980s in the sexual margins, also achieved a measure of national prominence in the 1990s with her humorous, sex-positive books. Covering everything from her own masturbation to the Meese Commission's detailed descriptions of porn to the entertaining power dynamics of "men getting fucked, completely in a heterosexual context," by women with strap-ons in straight-oriented amateur porn, Bright reclaimed porn and sexual experimentation as a feminist enterprise. Both Califia and Bright also copiously published written porn that gleefully proclaimed its own prurience. Former porn star Annie Sprinkle likewise reclaimed the means of production in her onstage performances of the "Herstory of Porn," in which she screened her sex scenes while delivering commentary, claiming a sex-worker voice that Andrea Dworkin had denied existed. A veritable stream of feminist porn practically saturated the market, such as the 2000 literary anthology *Gynomite: Fearless, Feminist Porn*, which announced, "Many of these stories will be jack-off fodder. That's a good thing." By 2002, the "100% dyke-produced" San Francisco porn company SIR had even won the best all-girl feature award from *Adult Video News*, a leading publication of the mainstream porn industry.[20]

As if trapped in a zero-sum game, antiporn feminists lost stature as sex-positive feminists and queer theorists achieved greater visibility in the 1990s. While these challengers replaced the monolithic antiporn analysis with a more nuanced perspective, more damaging to the antiporn case than any theoretical debates were actual events in society. In 1991 customs officials in Boston seized a shipment of photographer Della Grace's book *Love Bites*, published in the United States by the gay firm Alyson; the book depicted gay pride marches and lesbians holding hands but no explicit sexuality. Though the U.S. attorney's office quickly released the books without charges, the publisher denounced the homophobia of the seizure. Gay men and lesbians sensitive to their historical susceptibility to spurious obscenity charges found the episode chilling, but it was quickly surpassed by developments across the border in Canada. When the Canadian Supreme Court gave a MacKinnon-inspired reading of an obscenity statute in 1992, authorities moved quickly to suppress numerous queer-themed works, such as the American lesbian s/m magazine *Bad Attitude*. The resulting outcry by queer communities and progressive allies served in many ways as the headstone on the grave of antiporn's credibility.[21]

When Catharine MacKinnon published *Only Words* in 1993, reviews greeted the book not as a threat to speech, or even as a serious analysis, but as an overwrought exercise in futility. In the book MacKinnon again portrayed women in porn as "poor, desperate, homeless, pimped women who were sexually abused as children," arguing that porn was properly conceived of not as speech but action. Consequently, in her view, banning it was most accurately seen not as a violation of the First Amendment but rather as the enforcement of the Fourteenth Amendment's promise of equal protection of law to the women victimized in porn. MacKinnon's often loose reasoning did her argument no favors. She employed dubious logic in her syllogism that "Pornography is masturbation material. It is used as sex. It therefore is sex," while her assertion that "There is no evidence that pornography does no harm" relied on an insinuating and misleading double negative. Feminist reviewers of the book often approached it with sarcasm and disdain, and the *Boston Globe* found MacKinnon's construct of the "victims" of pornography "remarkably condescending toward women."[22]

Antiporn feminists continued publishing in the 1990s, remaining sturdy in their beliefs. In 1995 WAP member Kathleen Barry continued to bracket the "Feminist" in quotation marks when referring to the Feminist Anti-Censorship Taskforce, maintaining that defenders of pornography could not be feminists. In a display of antiporn feminism's intellectual inconsistencies, Diana Russell also self-published a book full of graphic hardcore material accompanied by textual analysis. She justified this by claiming "the effects of seeing pornography are different when such material is presented within an anti-pornography framework," but she provided no discussion of how other contextual factors involved in everyday consumption might exacerbate or mitigate the supposed ill effects of porn. Russell unintentionally revealed the uselessness of the porn/erotica distinction in her 1998 book *Dangerous Relationships: Pornography, Misogyny, and Rape*; attempting to offer concrete examples of erotica, she listed Georgia O'Keefe's flower paintings and a short film "depicting the peeling of an orange." A "highly sensual and erotic" scene of two snails "making love" in the insect documentary *Microcosmos* constituted her only other example. The growing irrelevance of the antiporn movement was apparent in Russell's own observation that her causal theory of porn and rape "has not yet received the critical attention that I think it deserves."[23]

No such attention was forthcoming as the new century began. Feminist scholars largely ignored the antiporn movement and its side of the 1980s sex wars, writing its legacy out of existence. When Lisa Sigel published a monograph on nineteenth-century British smut in 2002, she dispensed with the antiporn movement in two paragraphs, giving Dworkin and MacKinnon credit for good intentions but explaining, "They lack a historical perspective, which deeply flaws the theoretical underpinnings of their work." In Linda Williams's 2004 edited collection *Porn Studies*, only her own introduction engaged antiporn theory, and it did so in a frankly dismissive manner. MacKinnon received only two mentions in the sixteen essays, both negative.[24]

The reclaiming of feminism by women who recognized the polysemous nature of pornographic texts did not, however, signify a mass-movement return to the initial women's liberation project. As the media highlighted (and thus created) an emergent "postfeminist" movement spearheaded by straight, white, privileged leaders like Naomi Wolf and Katie Roiphe, radicalism and queerness fell out of the picture. While the more sophisticated participants of the sex wars never lost sight of class and racial realities, the dangers of the state, or the plight of the marginalized, postfeminist authors in the 1990s presented a celebration of pleasure that implicitly ratified the status quo. Sallie Tisdale's popular *Talk Dirty to Me*, for instance, erased the political history of censorship in her rejection of antiporn feminism; her "main reason" for rejecting censorship "is a selfish one," based on the fact that "sooner or later something I write or something I want to read or see or talk about is going to be forbidden." In presenting censorship as something that affected her privately, Tisdale removed from sight the gay men, lesbians, and birth-control advocates whose systematic suppression via obscenity laws carried more historical import than her own personal reading proclivities. In a similar vein Wendy McElroy distorted and oversimplified early second-wave feminism by praising porn as "part of a larger trend toward sexual liberation—a liberation that [late 1960s] feminists applauded." By obscuring the much more critical attitude of early feminists toward the male-dominated sexual revolution, McElroy helped assure that their complaints would not be revisited.[25]

These authors wrote for popular audiences, attracting a readership much larger than the most renowned queer theorists. The mainstream media latched onto this apolitical postfeminism; *Esquire* labeled it "do me" feminism and quoted Naomi Wolf as saying, "Well, we need sluts for the revolution," sounding like Germaine Greer's uncritical endorsement of the sexual revolution reiterated for a new generation.[26] Obscured in all of this was the critical issue of social power understood by both antiporn feminists and porn-friendly scholars, albeit in different ways. In this sense postfeminism made for the perfect complement to the political tenor of the 1990s, perhaps best described as postliberal. Bill Clinton carried two presidential elections, but he did so by erasing from his own Democratic Party much of what it once stood for. Concealed behind such terms as *centrism* and *triangulation* was the ceding of the Democratic platform to the long-held desires of many conservative Republicans. Though Clinton was nominally a social liberal, his domestic policies often catered to the power of the Christian Right. Pornography played a minor role in the controversies of the decade, but it reflected the institutionalization of New Right moralism in national politics even when the New Right was ostensibly out of power.

Triangulation, Indeed: Father, Son, and Holy Ghost

When Steve Bruce published his study of the Christian Right in 1988, he titled it *The Rise and Fall of the New Christian Right*. The title seemed appropriate at the time: Jerry Falwell had recently disbanded the Moral Majority; the leading Republican presidential hopeful, George Bush, had tenuous ties to the evangelical movement at best; and a series of sexual and financial scandals had tarnished the reputations of leading televangelists. Bush went on to win the 1988 election, and he met expectations by failing to satisfy the Christian Right. Bruce's prognosis nonetheless came too early; by 1993 another scholar, Michael Lienesch, noted that "reports of the demise of the movement have been very much exaggerated," while Clyde Wilcox extended his acquiescence in metaphor, predicting "the Christian Right could rise like Lazarus from the grave in the 1990s."[27]

As it happened, the Christian Right did not rise quite like Lazarus; instead of returning in a blinding flash, it amassed power as what Bush might call "a thousand points of light." Rebuilding itself quietly, outside the attention of the national media, the Christian Right consolidated power at the state and local levels over the course of the 1990s. While it appeared less visible nationally than it had in the 1980s, the movement's imprint was evident in several aspects of federal policy, including approaches to porn. Bush's failure to arouse the Christian constituency opened the door to Democrat Bill Clinton's two terms in office. As president, Clinton pacified the left with a veneer of social liberalism, even as he co-opted much of the New Right's platform, including moralistic appeals to Christian voters.

An early indication of evangelical disaffection toward Bush came in the 1988 campaign for the Republican nomination, in which the Pentecostal televangelist Pat Robertson beat the then–Vice President Bush repeatedly in several early caucus skirmishes before Bush finally took the lead in the first significant primary, New Hampshire. Once in office, Bush tended to downplay moral issues, focusing instead on his neoconservative ideal of a "New World Order." For instance, while Jesse Helms continued to combat the National Endowment for the Arts, Bush took a surprisingly firm stance against Helms's efforts. Declaring himself "against government censorship of the arts," the president angered conservative Republicans by suggesting he would oppose legislation aimed at restricting NEA grants and projects.[28]

Bush also dismayed the Religious Alliance Against Pornography in 1990. When the group visited the White House, it received a presidential snub due to what a White House spokesperson called a "scheduling thing." But when the alliance learned Bush had found time to meet with magazine editors, including *Playboy*'s Christie Hefner, the group voiced its dissatisfaction with the president. A return invitation to the White House the next year served as slender compensation. In an address to the Religious Alliance Bush's comments were measured, telling the group to "keep up the good fight" but offering no policy plans; indeed, in place of obscenity prosecutions the president asked the alliance to support his new crime bill that contained "provisions to protect women and children from violence and abuse," apparently deciding it was close enough to porn.[29]

Faring as badly on other evangelical fronts, Bush repeatedly declared himself prolife but appointed the moderate David Souter to the Supreme Court, robbing the Christian Right of its dream of overturning *Roe v. Wade*. He also proved insufficiently homophobic for the Christian Right, signing both the Hate Crimes Statistics Act and the Americans with Disabilities Act, which respectively addressed gay-bashing victims and people with HIV/AIDS. In response, when the party congregated for its 1992 convention, the resulting platform was a fiercely moralistic diatribe, emphasizing family values before Bush's own prized globalism. Railing against abortion and gay rights, the platform also declared that "the time has come for a national crusade against pornography."[30]

One measure endorsed by the GOP in 1992 was the Pornography Victims Compensation Act. Inspired by the Meese Commission's co-optation of antiporn feminism, the act proposed to leave porn producers and distributors open to civil suits by victims of attackers influenced by porn. The bill's sponsor, Kentucky senator Mitch McConnell, defended it before Judiciary Committee hearings in 1991. When committee chair Joseph Biden (D-Delaware) asked McConnell whether the act distinguished between violent porn and the merely sexual, McConnell responded with a series of obfuscations. "Well, I, like the chairman, am not an expert on pornography," he began. When pressed, the sponsor said, "A lot of the child pornography, I suppose you [could] argue was not violent," but an unsatisfied Biden pressed the point, grilling McConnell on whether explicit sex or rather violence ought to be legislated as a causal factor. Again McConnell dodged, explaining that "violent pornography has been implicated in numerous cases." An exasperated Biden conceded child porn and violent porn but continued to press McConnell on whether he could cite examples of sex crimes inspired by nonviolent porn. Finally the Kentucky senator admitted, "Not that I am aware of."[31]

McConnell failed to persuade his peers, and the Compensation Act died without a vote in 1992. Bush, too, fell short of convincing the Christian Right of his moral credentials, losing to Arkansas governor Bill Clinton in a tightly contested three-way race that saw the incumbent's support among white Protestants drop significantly. Though a Baptist, Clinton also held little appeal to fundamentalists, promising in his campaign to overturn the obsolete ban on gays and lesbians in the military. Winning with only 43 percent of the popular vote (a victory because of Texas billionaire H. Ross Perot's strong third-party challenge, which accounted for much of Bush's lost Christian support), the new president reflected awareness of his lack of a mandate when he failed to follow through on this promise. Indeed, much of Clinton's appeal came from his ability to position himself as a centrist by adopting traditional Republican economic policies. Under his administration several longtime Republican agenda items would finally pass, most notably the North American Free Trade Agreement (NAFTA) and the further evisceration of the welfare state under the guise of "welfare reform." Nonetheless, because of his symbolic association with the sexual revolution (married to a self-avowed feminist, at least rhetorically supportive of gay and lesbian rights, and notorious for his extramarital sexual appetite), Clinton incurred the wrath of Christian Right supporters less interested in his neoliberal economics than appalled by his cultural position.[32]

This "New Democrat" had little to say about pornography, but he quickly learned the importance of appeasing those who did. When he took office, a pending federal appellate case involved child porn charges against Stephen Knox, a Pennsylvania graduate student. Knox had been convicted of possessing illegal material on the basis of several videos depicting young girls and adolescents wearing bikinis and thong underwear. Though the videos were devoid of sexual acts or even nudity, the filmmaker had zoomed in on the girls' crotches and allowed his camera to linger there. As Knox's appeal reached the Supreme Court, the Bush Justice Department had urged affirmation of the conviction, but as the Clinton staff took their positions, the new solicitor general, Drew Days, filed a brief asking the Court to set Knox's conviction aside on the grounds that the lower courts had given an overly broad interpretation to the 1984 child porn statute.[33]

The case occurred well outside the scope of the national eye, until congressional Republicans seized on it as an example of Clinton administration depravity. Representative Christopher Smith of New Jersey commenced the fusillade of condemnations on October 20, 1993, holding the president personally responsible for the "outrageous" brief: "If Mr. Clinton prevails," Smith warned, "efforts to curb this hideous form of child abuse will be seriously undermined." Senator William Roth of Delaware followed, crediting the administration with "responsibility for having opened the floodgates to a new wave of child pornography and sexual exploitation that is likely to ensue," while back in the House Thomas Lewis of Florida expressed his "bitterness" that the administration "care[d] more about the perverts" than children.[34]

With such polarizing rhetoric capturing media attention, Democrats had little opportunity to articulate a nuanced defense of the Justice Department's position. Joe Biden, for instance, explained on the Senate floor that the Knox case had little connection to child sexual abuse, since it lacked any actual victims, but when the Senate voted on a resolution expressing opposition to the solicitor general's brief, Biden and all the other Democrats joined in a unanimous vote for fear of receiving the child-porn-supporter label.[35]

As he did with regard to gays in the military, Clinton triangulated, repudiating his own Justice Department in order to defuse the chorus of Republican condemnation. Taking the unusual step of composing an open letter to Attorney General Janet Reno, the president informed her, "I fully agree with the Senate about what the proper scope of the child pornography law should be." As with the "don't ask, don't tell" policy, Clinton framed this categorical concession as a victory, something the complacent media accepted at face value; the *New York Times* reported that the administration sought stronger legislation to "prevent gains by conservative groups," failing to recognize the gains those groups had just made by forcing the president to conform to their view of victimless child porn. Reno went on to personally direct the change of policy; on remand from the Supreme Court, Knox's conviction was affirmed, and in 1995 he began a five-year prison sentence. *The Nation* rued "how apathetic and frightened the civil liberties lobbies have become in the face of gathering fundamentalist fury," but Clinton dispensed with the topic, eager to be rid of it.[36]

Clinton's capitulation indicated the extent to which the New Right controlled the terms of the porn debate in the 1990s. As we saw in chapter 6, the Supreme Court's 1982 *Ferber* decision had allowed for special restrictions on child pornography because of the direct connection between child porn and child sexual abuse, in that the latter was a necessary precondition of the former. In the *Knox* case no such connection held, and the defendant was convicted on the basis of his distasteful proclivities rather than any actual harm along the production-distribution-consumption continuum.

Children had, of course, always figured in the foreground of the national obscenity debates. In the decades after the 1957 *Butler* case, however, that role was restricted by the Supreme Court's insistence that materials could not be regulated for adults simply because they were inappropriate for children. The 1968 *Ginsberg* decision even allowed for a variable obscenity standard to "protect" minors from porn. When child porn entered the national consciousness in the late 1970s the nature of the debate shifted to emphasize it, but in the 1990s children surged toward becoming the sole governing trope of conservative obscenity discourse. Bill Clinton had little to say in the 1990s, but the Christian Right eagerly filled that discursive void, showing its confidence by blithely disregarding the four-decades-old standing *Butler* ruling to attempt categorical new regulations on the basis of children's standards. When that failed, the antiporn arguments shifted to exploiting fears about the technological advances of the Internet, constructing children as passive victims of aggressive online filth merchants.

From the early days of the Internet the dissemination of porn had figured prominently among its uses. By the mid-1990s Internet porn had grown into a multibillion-dollar industry, and the Christian Right eagerly capitalized on new social fears about children's access to online smut. Not all Republicans partook of this; Newt Gingrich, Speaker of the House after the Republican congressional conquest of the 1994 midterm elections, was a devoted technophile who embraced the net. In the "Contract with America," spearheaded by Gingrich, moralism played a minor role; it advocated increased sentences for porn delivered to minors via computers but otherwise focused on tax cuts, shrinking government, welfare reform, and balanced budgets. As Gingrich provided a technocratic national face to nominally libertarian conservatism, though, the Christian Right expanded its influence over the course of the decade, especially at the state level—not just in such predictable Bible-belt states as South Carolina and Oklahoma but also in Minnesota and Michigan.[37]

This groundswell of influence was also visible in the emergence of the Communications Decency Act (CDA), which entered law in 1996 as part of that year's Telecommunications Act. Exemplifying New Right policy, the Telecommunications Act deregulated several branches of media and communication, thus fostering further concentration of power in already oligopolistic markets in the name of small government, even as it expanded governmental moral surveillance in the provisions of the Decency Act.

Nebraska Democrat James Exon, a longtime antiporn conservative who had won the praise of Citizens for Decent Literature in the early 1970s, was the prime mover behind the CDA. Taking his cue from Charles Keating, Exon showed fellow senators a "blue book" full of hardcore pornography taken from the Internet. Accompanying this shock tactic was an emphasis on children's access to the material. Exon's goal was to regulate the Internet like the FCC regulated radio and television broadcasts, making it equally suitable for children. As the CDA took form in 1995, this seemed a plausible goal; many politicians had limited understandings of how the Internet functioned, and Internet law was far from established. In one notable 1993 precedent, downloaded material had been treated the same as physical obscenity when a Tennessee court imprisoned a married California couple for distributing GIF files over their electronic bulletin board system.[38]

In congressional debate Exon made no effort to disguise the Christian Right's open influence on the CDA. He began his presentation with a prayer: "Oh God, help us care for our children. Give us wisdom to create regulations that will protect the innocent" from "virtual but virtueless reality." Ally Dan Coats (R-IN) added that the home provided a safe place of refuge from the sinful world, but "the Internet has invaded that protected place and destroys that innocence. It takes the worst excesses of sexual depravity and places it directly in the child's bedroom." Exon also inserted several letters of support from Christian Right groups into the *Congressional Record*. With another Keating-like touch he fabricated the statistic that 75 percent of computer owners refused to go online for fear of encountering porn. "I do not know the authenticity of the statement," Exon admitted, before employing the familiar passive voice to explain that "it has been estimated."[39]

The substance of the CDA centered on prohibiting the online "knowing transmission" of "obscene or indecent" material to minors. The former category was already covered by obscenity laws, but the addition of the more loosely defined "indecency" vastly expanded the scope of government suppression. As the leading CDA opponent, Patrick Leahy (D-VT), argued on the Senate floor, the CDA could be used to prosecute everything from online versions of *Lady Chatterley's Lover* to rap music or discussion groups for rape victims. Even Newt Gingrich's science-fiction novel *1945*, which "contains some steamy scenes," could fall under its provisions. Leahy argued that legislation more consistent with conservative belief in small government would allow for parental responsibility over children's Internet behavior, assisted by filtering software to block adult sites. He proposed an alternative bill to fund a study of methods for protecting children, but to no avail. The Knox episode had heightened politicians' attention to avoiding linkage with pornographers, and the CDA passed the Senate in a bipartisan sweep, 84–16. Significantly, the Senate held hearings on cyberporn and children in July, *after* passing the CDA, a sequence that drew acerbic comments from Leahy at the hearings.[40]

While the CDA encountered unexpected resistance in the House from Gingrich, ultimately deregulation superseded losing the Telecommunications Act over the CDA, and the bill passed. Though President Clinton had threatened to veto the bill if it contained the CDA, he, too, could not resist the allure of communications deregulation and signed the bill in early 1996. A vast array of websites mourned the act by joining a "Thousand Points of Darkness" protest. Breast cancer support groups, gay and lesbian organizations, and music sites all replaced their usual graphics with stark black backdrops and statements such as, "This is what the World Wide Web is going to look like" under the CDA.[41]

Predictably, the ACLU and an associated consortium of free-speech groups and websites immediately filed for an injunction pending legal testing of the act. In a Philadelphia federal court a government witness admitted that the then-famous *Vanity Fair* cover featuring the pregnant actress Demi Moore posing nude might be susceptible to CDA prosecution in some provincial towns. As free-speech lawyer and scholar Marjorie Heins writes, "If there was one moment during the hearings that prefigured the likely outcome of [the case], this was it. The government's expert had just testified that posting the photograph of a naked pregnant celebrity that had appeared on the cover of a mass circulation magazine might be a felony under the CDA." The case rose quickly to the Supreme Court, which affirmed the lower court's ruling finding the CDA unconstitutional. John Paul Stevens's opinion emphasized that indecency prohibitions applied to other broadcast media because the government's compelling interest in regulating their scarce bandwidth allowed for exaggerated scrutiny; because the Internet was limitless, no such qualifications applied. Stevens extended Leahy's warnings, noting that the CDA would permit prosecutions of safe-sex discussions and "arguably the card catalogue of the Carnegie Library."[42]

A recalcitrant Clinton issued a statement declaring his administration "firmly committed to the provisions—both in the CDA and elsewhere in the criminal code—that prohibit the transmission of obscenity over the Internet and via other media."[43] Though he backed this up with very little substance in the form of actual Justice Department effort, Clinton's avowal fit snugly into his general policy of conceding to moralists. After surrendering on gays in the military, Clinton had gone on to fire Surgeon General Jocelyn Elders after she made the medically sensible but morally unacceptable suggestion that children be taught masturbation as a form of safe sex. In 1996 the president signed the homophobic Defense of Marriage Act, designed for the express purpose of excluding same-sex marriage from federal recognition, despite the fact that no such marriages were legally recognized anywhere in the nation. Within the framework of Clinton's triangulation, such political cowardice was publicly reconfigured as success, in terms of nipping in the bud further conservative mobilization around the issues and even more dire outcomes.

As history would prove, such tactics failed. With the CDA still in limbo Congress rapidly attached a new amendment to a 1996 omnibus spending bill. The Child Pornography Prevention Act of 1996 (CPPA) outlawed not just actual child porn but depictions of what "appear[ed] to be" minors engaging in sexual conduct. As with the Knox case, the CPPA abandoned the initial source of opposition to child porn—the victimization of children—to directly criminalize the indulgence of socially unacceptable fantasies. As Utah Republican Orrin Hatch explained, "Computer generated child pornography has many of the same harmful effects" as actual child porn. Bruce Taylor of the National Law Center for Children and Families agreed, explaining that the CPPA was necessary because pedophiles were incited to act out fantasies by such imagery, and they also used the images to seduce children. Neither figure supported his contention with any actual evidence. Democrats showed some resistance to the measure, as Joseph Biden reminded CPPA supporters that the rationale behind the *Ferber* decision had been the harm caused to the children involved in child porn. By 1996, though, the Christian Right had perfected the machinery of polarization, and when Democrats briefly held up the bill in September, Iowa Republican Charles Grassley framed the action as opposition to "stiff new mandatory penalties for child pornographers," also included in the CPPA. Though the bill was vague enough to potentially include everything from animated porn to the recent critically acclaimed independent film *Kids*, it quickly passed. Clinton signed the spending bill without mentioning the CPPA.[44]

Once again an immediate injunction prevented the CPPA from taking effect, and once again the Christian Right extended what had become a war of attrition against civil libertarians by simply passing another openly unconstitutional measure, the Child Online Protection Act (COPA). This 1998 law, sponsored by CDA cosponsor Dan Coats, dropped the CDA's "indecency" and replaced it with "material harmful to minors" but otherwise carried the same thrust. The definition of "harmful to minors" reached broadly, encompassing both the legally obscene and also "patently offensive" material, including "lewd exhibition of the genitals or post-pubescent female breast," an anatomical feature that had not been considered obscene even before the 1957 *Roth* decision. As with the CDA and CPPA, COPA was included in a much larger bill, this time a budget bill, which helped it pass Congress. Clinton again signed it into law in October 1998, to little media attention. And, completing the cycle one more time, an ACLU-filed injunction blocked COPA from implementation awaiting court review. After much legal wrangling, the CPPA was struck down in 2002, and COPA finally fell before the Supreme Court in 2009.[45]

On the surface none of this legislation carried any impact, since all three major laws regarding children and Internet porn went straight into drawn-out court contests before implementation. Indeed, the most famous piece of sexually graphic media in the 1990s was the conservative-sponsored Starr Report, born of the prurient Republican-led investigation into the president's sex life after efforts to investigate other aspects of his career failed to provide anything incriminating. Through its relentless legislation, though, the Christian Right effectively fostered a legal atmosphere hostile to expressions of youthful sexuality, even when such expressions clearly fell short of qualifying as child pornography. In the movement's hands, "harm" was entirely divorced from the actual harm of child sexual abuse and reconceptualized as either youthful exposure to any sexuality whatsoever or any admittance of youthful sexuality into the public sphere.

The Clinton administration catered to this transformation as best it could without actual substantive commitment; thus, in 1995 the Justice Department announced a "preliminary investigation" into Calvin Klein's erotic jeans advertisements. The models were, in fact, of legal age, the ads went no further than salacious suggestions, and a full investigation never materialized; but the gesture resulted in Klein's aborting the ad campaign and displayed the administration's nominal concern for the issue. While this approach helped maintain some protection for mainstream porn merchants by making child porn an official Justice Department priority at the expense of adult obscenity cases, it also fueled the Christian Right's adventures in extremism.[46]

That concern over child porn had reached moral-panic proportions could be seen in a 1997 Oklahoma City episode. When a local Christian activist heard a conservative talk-show host mention that the 1979 Oscar-winning German film *The Tin Drum* could be considered pornographic, the man immediately called the police. A rapid investigation resulted in police raids on local video stores and private homes, as the R-rated film (tame enough to rent at the notoriously puritanical Blockbuster chain) was seized because it featured a suggested sex act between two minors. The case quickly evaporated into fodder for late-night comic humor, but it served as a telling barometer of the political climate.[47]

The Christian Right next turned its attention to the bookstore chain Barnes and Noble, which carried several art books by Sally Mann, Jock Sturges, and David Hamilton featuring adolescents in unclad or sexualized photographs. The Colorado group Focus on the Family and the antiabortion activist Randall Terry led the charge, and in August 1997 several protestors tore up copies of the books in a Denver Barnes and Noble. This tactic spread across the nation, with book-tearings in New York, Dallas, Kansas City, and Lincoln. Pressure to prosecute the bookstore soon followed, and though district attorneys in Atlanta and New Orleans resisted the pressure, misdemeanor charges were brought in Tennessee and felony charges in Alabama in 1998.[48]

As the Barnes and Noble uproar subsided, other consequences of the panic manifested themselves in several obscenity charges against mothers who took pictures of their own children naked. Though the Christian Right had earlier opposed domestic violence laws because they interfered with internal family business, the movement said nothing when an Oberlin, Ohio, bus driver, Cynthia Stewart, was arrested and put on trial in 1999 after a photo technician called police when developing Stewart's pictures. Facing sixteen years in prison, Stewart plea-bargained to avoid jail. Similar charges occurred elsewhere, based not on allegations of abuse but the simple presence of child nudity. A twenty-nine-year-old mother was acquitted in 2000, also in Ohio, and a sixty-six-year-old grandmother won her case in New Jersey the next year, though neither case reached completion without massive family trauma.[49]

By that time Bill Clinton was out of office, but his complacency in the face of Christian Right moral aggression had long since facilitated that movement's success in institutionalizing its framework in national politics. Signs of resurgent repression were pervasive. Alabama banned the sale of sexual devices such as vibrators under its obscenity law in 1998, and the state's attorney general explained that there was no fundamental right "to purchase a product to use in pursuit of having an orgasm." As the Clinton years drew to a close a county attorney in Newport, Kentucky, leveled obscenity charges at several stores for selling such common magazines as *Hustler*, *Swank*, and *Club*, which some had carried for a quarter-century; "less is tolerated in a predominantly Christian community," wrote the prosecutor in a local editorial.[50]

Public memory would quickly frame the 1990s as a secular decade, marked by the technology boom and its sophisticated coffeehouse patrons. Despite Clinton's Baptist ties he stood far apart from evangelicals in public image, more closely associated with the student movements of the 1960s. But if the slackers of Generation X had succeeded the hippies of the New Left, the 1990s ultimately bore a more significant comparison to the 1960s: while the cultural radicalism of that decade had obscured the grassroots coalescence of the New Right, so too did the hip urbanity of icons like Bill Gates, Kurt Cobain, and Jerry Seinfeld provide a secular cultural surface under which Christian Right activism grew ever more influential. Those efforts acquired a political face in 2000, and Clinton's successor in office showed no concern for the subtleties of triangulation, ruling instead with a regressive dualism that saw issues in sharp black or white. "You're either with us or against us," he told the world, in rhetoric the Christian Right understood. The early years of the new millennium would unfold as a counterfactual version of the 1920s in which William Jennings Bryan had gone from the Scopes Monkey Trial to setting national policy.

Bringing the War Home

After losing the national election of 2000 by more than five hundred thousand votes and being installed in office through an unprecedented judicial coup by the Supreme Court, George W. Bush held no Clintonesque qualms over lacking a mandate. Following the devastating attacks of September 11, 2001, Bush simply declared himself a "war president" and assumed powers far beyond his constitutional reach, as his administration condoned the torture of war prisoners and the warrantless wiretapping of American citizens, among numerous other violations of domestic and international law. Bush also brought his war mentality to culture, installing the Christian Right agenda in the White House. Reagan had offered rhetorical gestures, Clinton concessions, but the Bush II administration offered substance.[51]

Bush openly catered to the Christian Right. Though he himself had a checkered past containing shadowy allegations of cocaine abuse and a girlfriend's abortion, Bush benefited even from this, as his redemption through Christ fit the born-again model. As a young man in the late 1970s, still known as George Bush Jr., he had made a failed Texas bid for Congress in which the organizations of the New Right actually supported his Democratic opponent, seeing Bush as too liberal. Later, he observed his father's failure to connect with the Christian Right and the implications of that disjuncture in the 1992 election. Determined to avoid repeating the mistake, Bush reached out to conservative evangelicals, repeatedly professing his faith and taking a firm verbal antichoice stance on abortion. He would also gradually learn the value of obscenity in shoring up evangelical support. "There ought to be limits to freedom," Bush declared while gearing up for his presidential run in 1999, a statement that neatly anticipated the overarching policy framework of his eight years in office.[52]

Bush took office midway through a cultural shift regarding porn. In the years after the brief porno chic moment of the mid-1970s, pornography had fallen back into disrepute in its mainstream cultural depictions. Hollywood films like *Hardcore* (1979) and *52 Pick-Up* (1986) sensationalized the porn industry as a snuff-affiliated death factory, and the iconic porn stars of the 1980s included Linda Lovelace, now reconfigured into a "victim" of pornography; the famously well-endowed John Holmes, involved in sordid drug-related murders before dying from AIDS-related illness; and Traci Lords, revealed as an underage performer with fake identification in 1986.

This began to change in the 1990s, as the porn star Ron Jeremy reinvented himself as a lovable pop-culture icon, while Jenna Jameson emerged as a one-woman industry, with diversified product lines ranging from a best-selling autobiography to designer handbags in her name. The cultural climate of the United States in the new millennium regarded porn more casually, especially after politics itself took on a pornographic hue with the Republican-sponsored smut of the Starr Report, which described Bill Clinton's sex life in graphic, clinical detail. Homemade celebrity sex tapes proliferated, and two members of the industry even placed among the top ten vote-winners of the wild California gubernatorial recall election of 2003. Films featuring explicit, graphic sex regularly played arthouse theaters and became widely available through the popular mail-order rental company Netflix, which carried such titles as *The Brown Bunny* (2003), *9 Songs* (2004), and *Shortbus* (2006), while a seemingly endless series of documentaries investigated various porn stars.[53]

Such developments left Bush's religious voting base apoplectic. The administration appeased his fundamentalists in a plethora of manners, supporting the Christian Right's efforts to transform the government into a quasi-biblical apparatus as it endorsed abstinence-only education, removed condom references from the Centers for Disease Control's website, manipulated information on the National Cancer Institute website to spuriously suggest a connection between breast cancer and abortion, politicized the FDA to prevent final approval of the already medically approved "morning-after pill" RU-486, and took pronounced stances against reproductive rights and gay rights.[54] Under Bush-appointed chairman Michael Powell, the Federal Communications Commission closely scrutinized television (even as the ostensibly libertarian Powell supported the accelerating oligopolization of the media); while casual nudity and swearing had entered 1990s-era network evening-programming with shows like *NYPD Blue*, the Bush-era FCC cracked down on "indecency" with a vengeance, levying an unprecedented $500,000 fine on CBS for the split-second exposure of Janet Jackson's nipple during her performance at the 2004 Super Bowl.

On the porn front Bush initially moved slowly but eventually found remarkable success in chipping away at freedom of sexual expression at the margins, helping institute a vanilla hegemony whose flavor grew ever blander. This paralleled the Christian Right's antichoice tactics with regard to abortion, which increasingly emphasized parental notification laws, waiting periods, and other obstacles to convenient access. Even as porn infiltrated the mainstream, it did so within normative parameters established and policed by the Christian Right.

After the September 11 attacks the administration focused on national security issues, and the *New York Times* reported in October 2001 that even FBI child pornography investigations would be curtailed as resources flowed toward counterterrorism. Attorney General John Ashcroft's appointment of Andrew Oosterbaan as chief of the Criminal Division's Child Exploitation and Obscenity Section in November 2001 further disappointed the Christian Right. As a holdover from the Clinton administration, Oosterbaan initially persisted in following the Clinton-era pattern of prosecuting child porn cases but allowing free rein to material made by and for consenting adults.[55]

By 2003 the Department of Justice (DOJ) had commenced some token prosecutions of material on the sexual fringes to prove adult obscenity would still be pursued. Michael and Sharon Corbett, a West Virginia couple who ran the website Girlspooping.com, provided one easy target; charged with distribution of obscenity in March 2003 and facing up to twenty years in prison, the Corbetts pleaded guilty and received eighteen and thirteen months in federal prison, respectively. The Christian Right welcomed the charges, and the Concerned Women for America (CWA) declared, "The only 'community standards' where this stuff might be acceptable is Hell." But the CWA saw the Corbetts as a mere warm-up act rather than an end in themselves. "Come on DOJ," the group egged, "go after the big guys."[56]

Bush offered rhetoric to sate the Christian thirst for prosecutions, declaring Protection from Pornography Week in October 2003 and bemoaning porn's "debilitating effects on communities, marriages, families, and children." He promised further prosecutions and quickly delivered:

a western Pennsylvania indictment soon followed for the Los Angeles–based company Extreme Associates, specializing in adult rape-porn, while in Texas former police officer Garry Ragsdale and his wife, Tamara, were convicted for distributing the *Brutally Raped* series. Still, the Christian Right found the efforts lacking. A lengthy article in Focus on the Family's December issue of its *Citizen* magazine criticized Ashcroft for failing to pursue adult obscenity cases with sufficient gusto and singled out Andrew Oosterbaan as "the source of that timidity." The article cited a former DOJ employee's claim that Ashcroft was "reluctant to prosecute material that only portrayed close-ups of sexual penetration and nothing more extreme," and it also quoted with anger a Colorado postal inspector who said his focus was on child porn; "If two consenting adults have sex on film," he explained, "that's not obscenity."[57]

The administration recognized its constraints. Attempting to prosecute mainstream hardcore porn would result in likely failure and public mockery. A deputy assistant attorney general testifying before Congress in 2003 called pornography "constitutionally protected," as distinguished from "adult obscene material and child pornography."[58] The dividing line between porn and adult obscenity, in the administration's eyes, was one of normative sexuality, hence the emphasis on bestiality and rape porn. But with the Christian Right unsatisfied, more effort was required; as Bush lost public support in the face of an unpopular war in Iraq predicated on flagrantly false claims, maintaining the support of his evangelical base took on a paramount importance.

To this end the administration moved to politicize the obscenity wing of the DOJ. This followed Bush's precedent of politicizing various government agencies, including other DOJ branches like the civil rights division, which abruptly swerved away from defending minority rights after ideologically motivated staffing shifts. Filling the DOJ with established anti-porn warriors, the administration appointed Bruce Taylor "senior counsel" in February 2004. Taylor had a lengthy history of involvement with right-wing "profamily" groups, including work as CDL legal counsel, and he had been prominently quoted in the 2003 Focus on the Family critique. Significantly, the Justice Department declined to publicize Taylor's appointment, knowing the Christian Right would recognize it but hesitating to announce its porn-fighting imperative to mainstream America. This followed a familiar Bush tactic of sending concealed messages to his Christian base without alerting other citizens, a trick most gracelessly utilized later that year in the presidential debates, when Bush declared he would not appoint a Supreme Court justice who supported the *Dred Scott* decision. While millions of Americans wondered just who *would* support an 1857 decision stripping African Americans of their personhood, the antichoice movement recognized the phrase as coded language for *Roe v. Wade*, seen as the modern equivalent. In the case of Taylor's appointment it succeeded, as little mainstream media coverage ensued and the CWA declared itself "especially pleased."[59]

Along with Taylor, incoming attorney general Alberto Gonzales pledged himself to the antiporn cause. At the time of his February 2005 appointment Gonzales was viewed with some suspicion by the Christian Right. He lacked the personal prudery of his predecessor, even removing the drapes Ashcroft had notoriously placed over the bare-breasted "Spirit of Justice" statue in the DOJ's Great Hall. But he moved quickly to win evangelical support, and porn provided one convenient avenue for this. In a press release Gonzales declared his department "strongly committed to the investigation and prosecution of adult obscenity cases." The ploy worked, especially after Gonzales allowed Taylor's creation of a new Obscenity Task Force, as the conservative Family Research Council announced its "growing sense of confidence in our new Attorney General." Later in 2005 a memo circulated in the FBI, seeking members for a new obscenity squad to assist the DOJ and describing porn prosecutions as "one of the top priorities" for Gonzales, specifically framing the squad in terms of adult rather than child porn. As one sarcastic FBI agent told the *Washington Post*, "I guess this means we've won the war on terror."[60]

By 2007 even Brent Ward, the Utah-based Reagan-era U.S. attorney chided by a federal judge for his reckless prosecutorial attrition tactics of charging adult firms in multiple conservative districts, had been reappointed to the Bush DOJ, to cheers from the Christian Right. Even his old tactics recurred, as porn dealers from Cleveland were charged in clearly hostile Salt Lake City, Ward's home turf. As well, the administration encouraged obscenity prosecutions through both rewards and punishment. When prosecutors pursued obscenity cases, they won plum positions, as seen in Pennsylvania porn-chaser Mary Beth Buchanan, appointed to head the DOJ's Office on Violence Against Women in late 2006, or Montana porn-buster Bill Mercer, appointed to the third-ranking position in the DOJ around the same time. Meanwhile, as Gonzales stumbled into controversy for the politically motivated firings of U.S. attorneys seen as not adhering to the Bush agenda, it became clear in early 2007 that reluctance to pursue adult obscenity cases had contributed to the firings of two prosecutors in Nevada and Arizona, both of whom Brent Ward had complained about in messages to the attorney general.[61]

This reoriented Justice Department, and Bush's budget proposals calling for widespread austerity in regard to education and social services but listing obscenity prosecutions alongside antiterrorist efforts as one of the few areas receiving spending increases, matched the tenor of the Christian Right, which prioritized moral threats over material ones. In 2003 Nebraska's Republican representative (and former football coach) Tom Osborne asked, "What is America's greatest threat today?" Instead of al Qaeda, nuclear weapons, or the floundering economy, he declared it "the unraveling of the culture from within," which included porn. Like the examples discussed in chapter 4, this showed the New Right's continuing discursive displacement of tangible issues by moralistic ones, and it reflected the pervasive Spengler-by-way-of-Charles-Keating evangelical theory of history. A U.S. attorney in West Virginia even attempted to justify focusing on obscenity by comparing porn to other threats of the day, calling it "a lot like cancer, a highly contagious disease, a rabid dog, terrorism, or a weapon of mass destruction," on the tenuous ground that it "destroys people, relationships and normal societal functioning."[62]

With the framework in place and the personnel staffed, the Bush DOJ began to expand the scope of its obscenity prosecutions. By 2004 it was clear the United States was engulfed in a massive, systemic wave of corporate corruption, with the Enron and WorldCom scandals as mere tips of the iceberg. But while the administration downplayed this reflection on free-market capitalism by merely indicting symbolic CEOs rather than addressing the economic structures that facilitated the debacle, Bruce Taylor's obscenity wing of the DOJ subjected certain branches of capitalism to close scrutiny.

John Kenneth Coil, for instance, owner of twenty-seven adult-oriented businesses in New Mexico, Texas, and Arizona, pleaded guilty to a multimillion-dollar tax fraud charge in June 2004. Tacked on to the charges, and also receiving a guilty plea, was a single obscenity count, related to the film *Nympho Bride*. The DOJ described the film as "hardcore pornography with penetration clearly visible, depicting adults engaged in ultimate sex acts." This put the film well within the accepted mainstream of pornography and thus made it very unlikely to earn a sustainable conviction at trial; by coercing Coil—who faced much larger issues and was in no position to bargain—to plead guilty to the obscenity count, Taylor was able to frame his victory to the Christian Right as one against porn. He promptly did just that, initiating the *DOJ Obscenity Prosecution News* in early 2005 and declaring that the Coil case "underscores how successful law enforcement and the use of the federal laws can bring traffickers in hardcore obscenity to justice in the courts," as though *Nympho Bride* and not ordinary corporate fraud had been at the center of the case. Taylor repeated his technique in other cases, exploiting tight tax fraud cases to graft on obscenity charges. One Colorado merchant, Edward Wedelstedt, and a Texas storeowner, Leroy Moore, both fell prey to this approach in 2005, pleading guilty to obscenity charges in the face of irrefutable tax charges.[63]

Tax-related porn cases proved few, so the DOJ turned its attention to the margins of the porn industry, targeting a string of counternormative pornographers occupying the nation's sexual fringes. Bestiality, simulated rape, and the erotic deployment of vomit and bodily waste proved popular themes for obscenity charges, as a pattern developed: the DOJ worked with local prosecutors to devise "shotgun" charges, in which each defendant faced very lengthy jail terms, all in conservative regions likely to draw unsympathetic juries; the result was a series of pleas rather than trials that thus proved the success of the DOJ's approach.[64]

Outside Christian Right websites the national response to these prosecutions was extremely muted. The national media largely avoided them, unwilling to sully its pages with descriptions of such works as *In Need of Dog*, while even the ACLU showed little sign of interest. Thus, little national attention fell on the reinscription of normative sexuality being enacted through the DOJ's prosecutions. Alongside the sensational items mentioned above, federal obscenity charges also routinely cited sadomasochism, fisting, and bukkake (a group-ejaculation usually centered on one woman surrounded by several men), among other sexual practices. At least one prominent Christian Right figure, the former Reagan DOJ official Patrick Trueman, admitted the goal of imposing more conservative standards on the porn industry. Testifying before Congress in 2005, Trueman touted the Meese-era success in "changing the nature of hardcore material produced." According to him, "Themes of rape, incest, bestiality, pseudo-child pornography (in which adults dress and act like children while engaging in sex) . . . disappeared from store shelves." Given the Meese Commission's unsubtle appropriation of feminist discourse, it was clear that this disciplining of sexuality had nothing to do with feminist analyses of problematic gender politics and everything to do with protecting the sanctity of the (nonkinky) nuclear family. Likewise, proscribing fisting—a consensual, nonviolent practice popular in straight and lesbian circles—under the Bush DOJ represented another effort to shore up this vanilla hegemony, drawing lines of sexual citizenship that excluded practitioners of such "deviant" behaviors.[65]

This emphasis on adult porn reflected the increasing assertiveness of the Christian Right. As I described above, cultural conservatives had relied on a rhetoric of imperiled children during the 1990s. But with conservative control solidified over all three branches of government in the new century, a more openly normative discourse emerged. In its 2003 critique of Ashcroft, Focus on the Family counted among its complaints that "child porn is a higher priority" than adult obscenity cases; as the group explained, child porn "is unspeakably evil. Yet more children are harmed each day by adult pornography than by child porn." This assertion relied on an extremely elastic definition of *harm*, which rendered the actual harm of children sexually abused in the making of child pornography secondary to the supposed moral harm of children being exposed to pornographic material online. Concerned Women for America also preferred adult obscenity cases, this time using the logic that "pedophiles commonly use adult obscenity to seduce children." This argument disregarded the fact that laws already existed against adults seducing children, a task also often aided by alcohol, video games, or in the case of the rampant sexual abuse at the hands of clergymen, religious conventions.[66]

Because Christian Right discourse steadfastly remained in a vacuum, the obvious internal flaws of the monologue delivering these arguments went largely unchallenged. The thinly veiled corollary behind them, that the Christian Right eagerly sought to impose its normative sexual standards on American culture, went only indirectly articulated but pervaded the rhetoric. The CWA commended a DOJ official for his assertion that porn "can lead some to commit other degrading, and sometimes violent, sexual offenses against others" in 2003.[67] No social science supported this, but that mattered little to the Christian Right; as with *harm*, these terms were quite malleable. "Degrading" acts, like "antisocial behavior" in the hands of such earlier zealots as Victor Cline, could mean anything from homosexual activity to oral sex, while "violent offenses" might run the gamut from rape to consensual light s/m.

Even in the realm of case law this project won some success. Robert Zicari and Janet Romano, California-based owners of the violent-porn company Extreme Associates, were indicted on obscenity charges in western Pennsylvania. A temporary setback was dealt the Bush administration in January 2005 when federal district judge Gary Lancaster of Pennsylvania dismissed the charges. Citing the 1969 *Stanley* case that permitted private possession of obscenity, Lancaster also used the recent 2003 Supreme Court *Lawrence v. Texas* decision in his logic. That case had overturned the 1986 *Bowers* decision, finally recognizing the right of consenting adults to privately engage in sodomy. After *Lawrence*, Lancaster wrote, "the government can no longer rely on the advancement of a moral code, i.e., preventing consenting adults from entertaining lewd or lascivious thoughts, as a legitimate, let alone a compelling, state interest." The Christian Right reacted with outrage, applying its ubiquitous label of "activist judge" to Lancaster. Attorney General Gonzales, meanwhile, vowed to appeal, and the DOJ explained that the ruling, if upheld, would undermine not only obscenity prohibitions "but also laws against prostitution, bigamy, bestiality," and other behaviors proscribed "based on shared views of public morality." Ironically, this also echoed the *Lawrence* decision—in this instance, dissenting Justice Antonin Scalia's worry that granting a right to sodomy "called into question" the validity of state laws against bigamy, same-sex marriage, masturbation, fornication, and adultery.[68]

Lancaster's ruling for adult sexual freedom met swift reversal by the court of appeals, which in December 2005 reversed and remanded the *Extreme Associates* case, calling Lancaster's analysis of *Lawrence's* implications "impermissible . . . speculation." This followed a Texas case that had already refused to use *Extreme Associates* as a precedent. With the Supreme Court racing rightward under Bush appointees John Roberts and Samuel Alito, further appeals seemed hopeless, and the defendants ultimately pleaded guilty in early 2009, closing the possibility that Lancaster's initial opinion would ever become viable precedent.[69]

As the Bush DOJ grew increasingly aggressive, it made headway toward the porn-industry mainstream. Paul Little, whose "Max Hardcore" character was notorious for his misogyny but recognized as a significant porn-world figure, was convicted on obscenity charges in Florida in late 2008 and sentenced to forty-six months in federal prison. John Stagliano, owner of the influential Evil Angel Productions, also faced charges that year, for such films as *Milk Nymphos* and *Storm Squirters 2*. As his wife and business partner Karen Stagliano observed, the films showed "girls having fun doing things that maybe you don't always do in your normal bedroom, but that's kind of the point of porn." With lactation and female ejaculation now added to its list of obscene practices, the Bush DOJ further tightened the reins on acceptable normalcy.[70]

Perhaps the most evident display of sexual disciplining through obscenity law during the Bush era occurred in contests over vibrators and sexual representations of children made without the involvement of actual children. Such cases displayed obscenity law as an instrument of sexual normativity in its most naked form, used to stigmatize "prurient interests in autonomous sex and the pursuit of sexual gratification unrelated to procreation," as the state of Texas bluntly phrased it in 2008. They also completed the divorcing of simulated child porn from any connection to actual child protection, targeting counternormative fantasy representations instead.[71]

In Alabama, where criminalization of sex toys had begun in 1998, the state engaged in a protracted legal battle with Sherri Williams, owner of the adult store Pleasures. Williams won a federal district court victory against the ban in 2002, but the Eleventh Circuit Court of Appeals reversed this in 2004, denying the existence of a fundamental "right to sexual privacy." The appellate court invoked *Lawrence v. Texas*, noting that the Supreme Court itself invited this reading by avoiding the strict-scrutiny approach to sodomy laws that a fundamental-rights framework would entail and instead applying the rational-basis review used for lesser rights. While Williams defiantly proclaimed that Alabama would "have to pry this vibrator from my cold, dead hand," the court was unimpressed. It reaffirmed the constitutionality of the ban in early 2007, and the Supreme Court declined to hear Williams's challenge, just as it had refused to hear a 2006 challenge to a similar Texas law.[72]

The Mississippi State Supreme Court also supported sex-toy bans under the aegis of obscenity law, explaining in 2004 that the devices "have no medical purpose." While such a purpose might render them acceptable, their apparent use for sheer prurient pleasure put them beyond the pale. Indeed, the notion that only therapeutic sex-toy usage was legitimate marked numerous sex-toy hunts of the early twenty-first century. In Abilene, Kansas, a county attorney filed ten obscenity charges against a local adult store for selling sex toys such as vibrators and dildos in 2005. "A lot of the evidence we seized out there I don't think have a therapeutic or psychological use," the prosecutor explained, calling them "totally gross. And that has nothing to do with morality or sexuality." The case was dismissed, leading a local activist to declare, "We need to get past all these technicalities that are tripping us up," apparently referring to the First Amendment, but other efforts continued. Joanne Webb, a Texas woman who held private "Tupperware-type parties for suburban housewives," was arrested for selling vibrators in late 2003, and although her obscenity charge was ultimately dropped, another 2006 Texas police raid yielded several sex toys in the city of Kennedale. In that case a city official explained that "as an item becomes realistic, it becomes obscene," adding, "Things that are obviously only for sexual pleasure are against the penal code."[73]

In practice, "sex toy" is most often a euphemism for vibrators and dildos. Danielle Lindemann observes that emphasizing medical or therapeutic validations of such devices serves to reinforce the stigmatization of women's masturbation. This, of course, is precisely what enforcers of sex-toy bans intended, the redirection of female sexuality toward heterosexual, procreative purposes. Even defense attorneys proved complicit in upholding this social framework, privileging pragmatic tactics for their clients over abstract principle. Thus a Kansas defense lawyer in 2007 sought to fight obscenity charges by using expert testimony to show confiscated sex toys "have value linked to sexual treatment" as a means of justifying their sales. When a federal appeals court struck down Texas's sex-toy ban in early 2008, in a remarkably progressive decision that used *Lawrence v. Texas* to reject state control over "consensual private intimate conduct," within which the court included access to sex toys, an attorney for the firm challenging the law nonetheless reasserted the sexual status quo by telling the press that "the rights of ordinary people [were] being violated by this law," making sure to divest the products of any untoward connotations. While the boundaries of normalcy had arguably expanded to incorporate sex-toy use in "ordinary" ways, obscenity law continued to mediate the parameters of that normalcy.[74]

If sex-toy bans reflected a patriarchal sexual politics that extended back as far as the original 1873 Comstock law that also included contraceptives and other "obscene" devices, the regulation of sexual imagery of children in the absence of actual children was a novel production of the Christian Right. When the Supreme Court found the Child Pornography Prevention Act of 1996 unconstitutional in 2002, Reagan appointee Anthony Kennedy's lead opinion stressed that virtual child porn differed from actual child porn in that it lacked any tangible connection to abuse, which had been the basis of the 1982 *Ferber* opinion that allowed for the criminalization of child pornography. This did not stop Florida Republican congressman Mark Foley—himself four years away from a career-ending scandal involving sexually graphic Internet instant messages to teenage congressional pages—from articulating the Christian Right's predictable response, claiming the Court had "sided with pedophiles over children." Social conservatives immediately set out to reinstate control over simulated representations.[75]

The result was the PROTECT Act, passed by Congress and signed into law by President Bush in April 2003. The act, as Bush explained, deemed that "images of children, even those created with computer technology, will now be illegal, giving prosecutors a new tool" against child porn. It accomplished this by specifically prohibiting obscene virtual child pornography—in other words, through a redundant criminalization of already legally unprotected material. The PROTECT Act clearly served as a sheer expression of sexual normativity intended to encourage prosecutors, since the material it targeted was already, by definition, actionable under existing obscenity laws. While Bush drew applause from his audience at the bill's signing by claiming that "obscene images of children, no matter how they are made, incite abuse," he cited no actual evidence of this unproven claim.[76]

A "pandering" clause of the PROTECT Act also criminalized the offering or solicitation of child porn as a felony even in the absence of any actual obscene material, including the virtual. In other words, simply convincing someone that an Internet file contained child porn took on penalties comparable in severity to actually transmitting child porn. The Eleventh Circuit Court of Appeals struck the pandering provision in 2006, since its vague language allowed the government to establish a violation "with proof of a communication that it deems, with virtually unbounded discretion, to be reflective of perverse thought." This open-ended arbitrariness, the court claimed, "reflect[ed] a persistent disregard of time-honored and constitutionally-mandated principles relating to the Government's regulation of free speech and its obligation to provide criminal defendants due process."[77]

What the appellate court saw as a dangerous regulation of deviant fantasies and desires, though, the Supreme Court saw as justified in the name of child protection. In reversing the lower court, Justice Antonin Scalia brushed aside the possibility that citizens might be convicted of pandering under the PROTECT Act for advertising virtual child porn as the real thing, arguing that communication targeted by the act merely constituted "collateral speech introducing such material into the child-pornography distribution network." As David Souter complained in a fairly irate dissent, Scalia's lead opinion served as a stealth overturning of the 1982 *Ferber* decision and the 2002 *Free Speech Coalition*, which had killed the Child Pornography Prevention Act. While both of those decisions tethered child porn regulation to material documenting the sexual exploitation of minors, the new *U.S. v. Williams* decision unmoored this regulation from its originally intended design, allowing for prosecutions predicated on socially unacceptable desires rather than meaningful child protection.[78]

The *Williams* decision emanated out of a case in which Michael Williams had possessed and offered actual child pornography, and his challenge to the PROTECT Act's pandering clause thus operated as something of a tangent in his own legal efforts. Another equally unsympathetic defendant, Dwight Whorley of Richmond, Virginia, mounted another failed challenge to the PROTECT Act. Whorley had served time in the late 1990s on child porn charges and was arrested again in 2004, this time under the provisions of the PROTECT Act. In both cases he used public computers to download and transmit sexually explicit images of children. The seventy-four charges of which he was convicted in 2005 fell into three categories: first, actual images of child pornography, then a set of Japanese anime cartoons described as showing "prepubescent children engaging in graphic sexual acts with adults," with "actual intercourse, masturbation, and oral sex, some of it coerced." Finally, a set of emails describing "sexually explicit conduct involving children, including incest and molestation by doctors" rounded out the charges.[79]

When Whorley appealed his conviction, he challenged the constitutionality of all three categories, but only the latter two challenges merited serious court review. A federal appellate court rejected his challenge, citing the PROTECT Act to note that it was "not a required element of any offense under this section that the minor depicted actually exist." As the court explained, the PROTECT Act served as a "valid restriction on *obscene speech* under *Miller*, not a restriction on non-obscene pornography of the type permitted by *Ferber*," thus rendering the question of the anime characters' actual existence moot. Meanwhile, the court relied on the 1973 *Kaplan* decision to hold that text-only emails could also be obscene, despite the fact that no known convictions for purely verbal smut of any sort had been upheld in the intervening years.[80]

Working to blur distinctions between actual and virtual child porn, an FBI press release celebrated Whorley's conviction for sending "Japanese 'anime' cartoons showing graphic acts of child pornography," without clarifying that the cartoons involved no actual children. This lack of distinction, specifically invited by the phrasing of the PROTECT Act, extended to the prosecution of an Iowa manga collector, Christopher Handley, in 2007. Unlike Williams or Whorley, Handley possessed no actual child pornography whatsoever but faced obscenity charges for his imported manga comics, an often violent and sexually graphic Japanese comic genre consumed by a large American fan base. When he filed for a dismissal on the grounds that the fictional characters depicted in the manga—young boys and girls who had sex with animals at times—lacked ages, as they did not in fact exist, the federal district court displaced the convolutions of the PROTECT Act onto Handley, explaining that he "imprecisely blends the law of child pornography with the law of obscenity" by focusing on the ages of the characters. For the court the critical issue was that of obscenity, not child porn per se; in fact, it even read portions of the PROTECT Act as unconstitutionally overbroad for invoking only parts of the three-pronged 1973 *Miller* obscenity test in its definition of obscene "visual depictions not involving the use of actual minors."[81]

Though the court denied Handley's motion for a dismissal, its critique of the PROTECT Act did portend some hope for his case, as the court even alluded rather dismissively to the government's acknowledgment that its notion of "per se obscenity," which it used to defend the PROTECT Act, "has its genesis in Justice Department briefs and, as yet, awaits judicial support." Nonetheless, facing a potentially hostile Iowa jury and a lengthy prison sentence, Handley ultimately pleaded guilty to "possessing obscene visual representations of the sexual abuse of children," thus allowing the Department of Justice to maintain the illusion that actual children were involved in the case.[82]

While the PROTECT Act thus completed the utter divorcing of "child pornography" as a legal and social construct from the tangible exploitation of children that had first allowed its criminalization under the 1982 *Ferber* decision, the Bush Justice Department also relied on traditional obscenity law to target depictions of child sexuality that lacked actual children. Karen Fletcher, a fifty-six-year-old woman in western Pennsylvania who ran the website Red Rose Stories, featuring explicit stories of violent child sexual abuse, was charged with distributing obscenity online in 2006. Though the site featured no images, only text, U.S. attorney Mary Beth Buchanan claimed that it emboldened predators. Fletcher, an agoraphobic with a mere twenty-nine subscribers who paid $10 fees for access to her work, called the site "an effort to help her deal with her own pain from child sexual abuse." She pleaded guilty to avoid a trial and was sentenced to six months of house arrest and a $1,000 fine. Meanwhile, at the local level, a Florida elementary school principal was sentenced to five years in 2009 for "child pornography" consisting of children's faces cut out and glued to pornographic pictures of adult women. Prosecutors urged the harsh sentence to "drive home" to the defendant and "others like him that children are never ever objects of sexual desire."[83]

These developments revealed the extent to which the discourses of obscenity and child pornography served as regulatory devices employed to monitor and control sexual expression, in the absence of any actual victimization. Indeed, as the Bush era drew to a close, the new phenomenon of "sexting," in which teenagers texted or posted erotic self-images online or over electronic communications devices, also reflected a perverse cultural logic by which the ostensible victims of child pornography were prosecuted for its dissemination. In one 2009 case a Pennsylvania district attorney threatened a high school freshman with criminal charges for transmitting nude pictures of herself if she refused to take a "10-hour class dealing with pornography and sexual violence." When the young woman fought back, filing an injunction against the prosecutor on the grounds that the only pictures she had sent featured herself in a brassiere, from the waist up, it became apparent that sexting was being used as a ruse to discipline teen sexuality. With one-fifth of teenagers and a full third of twentysomethings admitting to sending nude or seminude images of themselves at some point, it was evident that sexting was widespread, and the attempt to regulate it rested on the same conservative myths of childhood innocence that had framed the 1950s comics scare.[84]

The chilling effect of these collective efforts to police the boundaries of acceptable sexuality by stigmatizing counternormative sexual expression as obscene went underreported but not unnoticed during the Bush years. As early as January 2001 adult industry lawyer Paul Cambria issued a list of imagery to avoid under the Bush DOJ. It included prohibitions on "food used as sex object," "peeing unless in a natural setting," wax dripping, fisting, squirting, transsexuals, and "black men–white women themes." As obscenity prosecutions accelerated, the gay newspaper *Houston Voice* expressed concern over the vulnerability of queer porn in such a hostile political climate, and further trepidation was on display as several long-running s/m sites began shutting down. Even the popular softcore Suicidegirls.com began removing any images featuring blood "to ensure that we are not targeted by the U.S. government's new war on porn."[85]

In another telling sign of the times, the popular blog-hosting site LiveJournal in 2007 suspended five hundred journals and communities in the name of "protecting children" when it fell under the scrutiny of an activist group called Warriors for Innocence. Ignored by the mainstream media, the LiveJournal purge ignited a firestorm of online controversy, since its deletions went beyond overt pedophile communities to include a wide swath of slash fiction, a popular form that places well-known cultural icons such as Harry Potter in often sexualized scenarios. When a staff member explained the logic of the purge to angry LJ members, he cited the repressive legal climate that held virtual child pornography criminal.[86]

While this transpired, conservative media continued to substitute the demonology of porn for actual analysis in attributing the causality of social ills. In one particularly egregious case the *Chattanooga Times Free Press* in early 2006 listed several "red flags that may indicate your spouse is involved" in porn consumption: "Does your spouse exhibit inappropriate anger," it asked, also wondering, "Do you constantly seem to have money problems?" Two symptoms of the massive upward redistribution of wealth transpiring under the Bush administration were thus ascribed not to the administration's class warfare on working Americans but rather to pernicious pornographic forces still associated with liberalism, a diversion that helped reconcile the socially conservative faction of the New Right with its corporate sponsors, a trade-off of economic security for moral sanctity that the historian Dagmar Herzog pointedly calls "the wages of straightness."[87]

As this book has shown, all of this frenzied attention to pornography represented yet another spin of the moral-panic wheel. In the 1950s, when cold war politics provided a normative model of healthy American sexuality, porn threatened to divert sexual energy from its proper channeling into procreative nuclear families, and outrage ensued. At the end of the next decade the obsolescence of racism and anticommunism—the tropes on which conservative politicians had traditionally staked their appeal—led the nascent New Right to discover the political capital of moralism. This was followed by a permissive lull in the 1970s, reflecting widespread ambivalence on the topic of porn as the sexual revolution hit the cultural mainstream. Indeed, the history of the postwar United States shows that the American public is often content to take a hands-off approach to pornography in the absence of moral entrepreneurs generating concern on the topic. Ending the lull, antiporn efforts resurfaced in the late 1970s as certain feminists attempted to efface the splintering of the women's liberation movement by constructing pornography as an ideological oppressor of all women. With the political awakening of evangelical Christians in the same period, the New Right attempted to capture and retain their votes by appealing to moral issues such as abortion, gay rights, and pornography. This trend was perhaps most evident in the 1986 Meese Commission report, and was revived by the Bush II administration. American culture remained deeply divided over pornography, as porn infiltrated the mainstream even amidst a wave of governmental moral retrenchment at the dawn of the twenty-first century.

In each turn of this cyclical wave of pornocentric moral panics, pornography has also served as a discursive displacement of more complicated issues: the origins of juvenile delinquency, the racial turbulence of the late 1960s, the fragmentation of the feminist movement, and the fact that New Right policies often work against the economic interests of its own Christian voting base. The Bush II administration relied heavily on such displacement tactics to maintain evangelical support. These tactics began to show their seams in the face of the administration's flagrant incompetence and corruption on almost every imaginable front, but this study nonetheless reveals the consistent profitability of "perversion" in the hands of public and political figures.

Liberals have shown little propensity for resisting this process in the past half-century. They ceded control over the pornography debate to the New Right in the late 1960s and have effectively disengaged themselves from the debate since then, challenging only the most egregious cases of suppression and only then through the sterilized abstraction of "free speech." While legal scholars in the Ivory Tower argue for a reading of the "historically neglected" Ninth Amendment's protection of otherwise-unenumerated rights that would ground sexual rights as fundamental, the courts continue to downplay this analysis, and liberal politicians do nothing to encourage it. The Declaration of Independence's promise of the pursuit of happiness notwithstanding, the politics of pleasure remain absent from the liberal framework.[88]

President Barack Obama showed little inclination toward modifying this trajectory in the early months of 2009, advancing no meaningfully progressive sexual politics in his first months in office. While his appointment of former Clinton-DOJ member Eric Holder as attorney general and onetime *Playboy* lawyer David Ogden as deputy attorney general angered some conservatives and suggested the Bush obscenity crusade had drawn to a close, the Obama administration showed no interest in reclaiming control over the political discourse on sexual expression from the Christian Right that had shaped its articulation, just as the administration shied away from challenging conservative control over the discourse on same-sex marriage, the failed Clintonian "don't ask, don't tell" military policy, and numerous other matters of sexual politics.[89]

In the absence of a strong and compelling challenge to sexual normativity, the nature of public discussion regarding sexuality in America remains such that concepts like pornography are all too easily constructed as one-sided demonologies that facilitate the stripping away of nuance from any dissenting perspectives. Such challenges are discredited by mischaracterization of their proponents as affiliated with the worst possible excesses of the moral issue in question. Precisely these tactics have allowed the New Right to shape and dominate public discourse not just on pornography but also on abortion, gay rights, sex education, and other complex issues that operate at the intersection of public policy and private belief. Modern liberalism remains complicit in this conservative domination by virtue of its passive acquiescence to the engines of normativity.

The cycle of recurring moral panics is unlikely to stop without a key ingredient: a better understanding of human sexuality by American citizens. One of the key arguments of the 1970 report of the Presidential Commission on Obscenity and Pornography held that only comprehensive sex education could facilitate open conversation about sexuality, and only open conversation—free from embarrassment, condemnation, or misinformation—could accommodate the subtleties necessary to devise effective and fair public policy in a pluralistic society. Few conservative sources have so much as acknowledged this argument, much less effectively refuted it. It holds true today, as it did in 1955 and 1968 and 1993, that demagogues can profit from perversion only in the absence of an informed public voice questioning their construction of the very notion of normalcy. Communists, welfare queens, terrorists, and immigrants have provided effective bogeymen for conservatives over the past several decades. Until America can hold a calm, reasonable discussion of sexuality and its sundry manifestations, pornography and other "perversions" will outlive all those demonized constructs, helping to divert attention from the many more pressing issues facing the nation and the world.

Notes

Introduction

1. Andrea Friedman, *Prurient Interests: Gender, Democracy, and Obscenity in New York City, 1909–1945* (New York: Columbia University Press, 2000); Donald Alexander Downs, *The New Politics of Pornography* (Chicago: University of Chicago Press, 1989).

2. See, as examples of the massive popular literature, Kenneth Turan and Stephen Zito, *Sinema: American Pornographic Films and the People Who Make Them* (New York: Praeger, 1974); Al Di Lauro and Gerald Rabkin, *Dirty Movies: An Illustrated History of Stag Films, 1915–1973* (New York: Chelsea House, 1976); Luke Ford, *A History of X: 100 Years of Sex in Film* (Amherst, NY: Prometheus, 1999); David Flint, *Hollywood Blue: An Illustrated History of Adult Cinema* (London: Creation, 1999); Legs McNeil and Jennifer Osborne, *The Other Hollywood: The Uncensored Oral History of the Porn Film Industry* (New York: Regan, 2005).

3. See Robert Haney, *Comstockery in America: Patterns of Censorship and Control* (Boston: Beacon, 1960); Montgomery Hyde, *A History of Pornography* (London: Heinemann, 1963); Max Ernst and Alan Schwartz, *Censorship: The Search for the Obscene* (New York: Macmillan, 1964); Ira Carmen, *Movies, Censorship, and the Law* (Ann Arbor: University of Michigan Press, 1966); Richard Kuh, *Foolish Figleaves? Pornography in and out of Court* (New York: Macmillan, 1967); Richard Randall, *Censorship of the Movies: The Social and Political Control of a Mass Medium* (Madison: University of Wisconsin Press, 1968); Felice Flannery Lewis, *Literature, Obscenity, and the Law* (Carbondale: Southern Illinois University Press, 1976); Edward de Grazia and Roger Newman, *Banned Films: Movies, Censors, and the First Amendment* (New York: Bowker, 1982); Donna Demac, *Liberty Denied: The Current Rise of Censorship in America* (New Brunswick, NJ: Rutgers University Press, 1990); Edward de Grazia, *Girls Lean Back Everywhere: The Law of Obscenity and the Assault on Genius* (New York: Random House, 1992); and Richard Hixson, *Pornography and the Justices: The Supreme Court and the Intractable Obscenity Problem* (Carbondale: Southern Illinois University Press, 1996). Crucial to note here, as well, is Joseph Slade's amazing three-volume *Pornography and Sexual Representation: A Reference Guide* (Westport, CT:

Greenwood Press, 2001), which, although not a straightforward historical study per se, nonetheless contains an endless wealth of information and analysis.

4. See Francis Couvares, ed., *Movie Censorship and American Culture* (Washington: Smithsonian Institution Press, 1996); Lee Grieveson, *Policing Cinema: Movies and Censorship in Early-Twentieth-Century America* (Berkeley: University of California Press, 2004); Lea Jacobs, *The Wages of Sin: Censorship and the Fallen Woman Film, 1928–1942* (Madison: University of Wisconsin Press, 1991); and Janet Staiger, *Bad Women: Regulating Sexuality in Early American Cinema* (Minneapolis: University of Minnesota Press, 1995).

5. Paul Boyer, *Purity in Print: The Vice-Society Movement and Book Censorship in America* (New York: Charles Scribner's Sons, 1968); Nicola Beisel, *Imperiled Innocents: Anthony Comstock and Family Reproduction in Victorian America* (Princeton, NJ: Princeton University Press, 1997); Leigh Ann Wheeler, *Against Obscenity: Reform and the Politics of Womanhood in America, 1873–1935* (Baltimore: Johns Hopkins University Press, 2004); Friedman, *Prurient Interests*. See also, for instance, David Pivar, *Purity Crusade: Sexual Morality and Social Control, 1868–1900* (Westport, CT: Greenwood Press, 1973); and Molly McGarry, "Spectral Sexualities: Nineteenth-Century Spiritualism, Moral Panics, and the Making of U.S. Obscenity Law," *Journal of Women's History* 12, no. 2 (2000): 8–29.

6. See Matthew Lasar, "The Triumph of the Visual: Stages and Cycles in the Pornography Controversy from the McCarthy Era to the Present," *Journal of Policy History* 7, no. 2 (1995): 181–207.

7. Joan DeJean, *The Reinvention of Obscenity: Sex, Lies, and Tabloids in Early Modern France* (Chicago: University of Chicago Press, 2002), 5.

8. Walter Kendrick, *The Secret Museum: Pornography in Modern Culture* (Berkeley: University of California Press, 1987), 1, xiii; Matthew Frye Jacobson, *Whiteness of a Different Color: European Immigrants and the Alchemy of Race* (Cambridge, MA: Harvard University Press, 1998), ix–x; Rickie Solinger, *Wake Up Little Susie: Single Pregnancy and Race Before* Roe v. Wade (New York: Routledge, 1992), 13–14.

9. Richard Randall, *Freedom and Taboo: Pornography and the Politics of a Self Divided* (Berkeley: University of California Press, 1989), 5; Margaret Jacob, "The Materialist World of Pornography," in *The Invention of Pornography: Obscenity and the Origins of Modernity, 1500–1800*, ed. Lynn Hunt (New York: Zone Books, 1996), 157–202 (quote at 158); Lynn Hunt, "Pornography and the French Revolution," in ibid., 301–40; Iain McCalman, *Radical Underworld: Prophets, Revolutionaries, and Pornographers in London, 1795–1840* (Cambridge, UK: Cambridge University Press, 1988); Peter Wagner,

Eros Revived: Erotica of the Enlightenment in England and America (London: Secker and Warburg, 1988).

10. Carolyn Dean, *The Frail Social Body: Pornography, Homosexuality, and Other Fantasies in Interwar France* (Berkeley: University of California Press, 2000), 5.

11. This trajectory can be followed in Julie Peakman, *Mighty Lewd Books: The Development of Pornography in Eighteenth-Century England* (Houndmills, UK: Palgrave Macmillan, 2003); Lisa Sigel, *Governing Pleasures: Pornography and Social Change in England, 1815–1914* (New Brunswick, NJ: Rutgers University Press, 2002); Di Lauro and Rabkin, *Dirty Movies*; Eric Schaefer, "Gauging a Revolution: 16mm Film and the Rise of the Pornographic Feature," *Cinema Journal* 41 (2002): 3–26; Frederick Lane III, *Obscene Profits: The Entrepreneurs of Pornography in the Cyber Age* (New York: Routledge, 2000).

12. Jay Gertzman, *Bookleggers and Smuthounds: The Trade in Erotica, 1920–1940* (Philadelphia: University of Pennsylvania Press, 1999); Alan Hunt, "The Great Masturbation Panic and the Discourses of Moral Regulation in Nineteenth- and Early-Twentieth-Century Britain," *Journal of the History of Sexuality* 8, no. 4 (1998): 575–615. .

13. See Richard Trexler, *Sex and Conquest: Gendered Violence, Political Order, and the European Conquest of the Americas* (Oxford: Polity, 1992); Stephanie Wood, "Sexual Violation in the Conquest of the Americas," in *Sex and Sexuality in Early America*, ed. Merril Smith (New York: New York University Press, 1998), 9–34; Stephen Nissenbaum, *Sex, Diet, and Debility in Jacksonian America: Sylvester Graham and Health Reform* (Chicago: Dorsey Press, 1980), 164; Sharon Ullman, *Sex Seen: The Emergence of Modern Sexuality in America* (Berkeley: University of California Press, 1997). See also the cornerstone book on the history of American sexuality: John D'Emilio and Estelle Freedman, *Intimate Matters: A History of Sexuality in America* (New York: Harper and Row, 1988).

1. The Rediscovery of Pornography

1. *Motion Picture Daily*, 16 May 1946; John S. Sumner to Motion Picture Division, 2 Aug. 1939, with attached "Report on Miami Theater" by Mr. Jacobson, n.d., New York Motion Picture Division Records, Subject Files, box 10, folder: Flick, Hugh, New York State Archives, Albany, NY; Director Esmond to Sumner, 3 Aug. 1939, ibid.

2. *New York Times*, 9 Jan. 1947 (hereafter *NYT*); NYSSV, *73rd Year Book—1946 Report*, John Saxton Sumner Papers, box 3, folder 6, Wisconsin Historical Society, Madison, WI; Society to Maintain Public Decency, "Report of the Secretary for the Month of June, 1948," Sumner Papers, box 3, folder 5. On Comstock see Helen

Lefkowitz Horowitz, *Rereading Sex: Battles over Sexual Knowledge and Suppression in Nineteenth-Century America* (New York: Knopf, 2002), 297–444.

3. Knowlton Durham (SMPD President) to Members of Society, 5 Feb. 1951, Ralph Ginzburg Papers, box 15, folder 4, Wisconsin Historical Society; Ginzburg note to self, 2 Feb. 1955, ibid.; Harry Maule to Sumner, 23 Feb. 1956, Sumner Papers, box 1, folder 2.

4. Samuel Walker, *In Defense of American Liberties: A History of the ACLU* (New York: Oxford University Press, 1990), 86; Andrea Friedman, *Prurient Interests: Gender, Democracy, and Obscenity in New York City, 1909–1945* (New York: Columbia University Press, 2000), 155–82; William Matchett, "Boston Is Afraid of Books," *Saturday Review of Literature*, 15 July 1944, 6–7; *NYT*, 15 June 1953. See also Paul Boyer, *Purity in Print: The Vice-Society Movement and Book Censorship in America* (New York: Charles Scribner's Sons, 1968), 207–74.

5. Nicola Beisel, *Imperiled Innocents: Anthony Comstock and Family Reproduction in Victorian America* (Princeton, NJ: Princeton University Press, 1997), esp. 104–27.

6. The literature on the cold war is massive, but see, for instance, Stephen Whitfield, *The Culture of the Cold War* (Baltimore: Johns Hopkins University Press, 1991); Ellen Schrecker, *Many Are the Crimes: McCarthyism in America* (Princeton, NJ: Princeton University Press, 1998); Reinhold Wagnleitner, *Coca-Colonization and the Cold War: The Cultural Mission of the United States in Austria After the Second World War*, trans. Diana Wolf (Chapel Hill: University of North Carolina Press, 1994); Lizabeth Cohen, *A Consumer's Republic: The Politics of Mass Consumption in Postwar America* (New York: Knopf, 2003).

7. Frank Costigliola, "'Unceasing Pressure for Penetration': Gender, Pathology, and Emotion in George Kennan's Formation of the Cold War," *Journal of American History* 83, no. 2 (1997): 1309–39; Elaine Tyler May, *Homeward Bound: American Families in the Cold War Era* (New York: Basic Books, 1988). On the sexualization of the cold war see also Robert Dean, *Imperial Brotherhood: Gender and the Making of Cold War* (Amherst: University of Massachusetts, 2001); K. A. Courdelione, *Manhood and American Political Cuture in the Cold War* (New York: Routledge, 2005).

8. Jessamyn Neuhas, "The Importance of Being Orgasmic: Sexuality, Gender, and Marital Sex Manuals in the United States, 1920–1963," *Journal of the History of Sexuality* 9, no. 4 (2000): 447–73, quoted at 470. See also Margot Canady, "Building a Straight State: Sexuality and Social Citizenship Under the 1944 G.I. Bill," *Journal of American History* 90, no. 3 (2003): 935–57; Estelle Freedman, "'Uncontrolled Desires': The Response to the Sexual Psychopath, 1920–1960," *Journal of American History* 74, no. 1 (1987): 83–106; Fred Fejes, "Murder, Perversion, and Moral Panic: The 1954 Media

Campaign Against Miami's Homosexuals and the Discourse of Civic Betterment," *Journal of the History of Sexuality* 9, no. 3 (2000): 305–47; David K. Johnson, *The Lavender Scare: The Cold War Persecution of Gays and Lesbians in the Federal Government* (Chicago: University of Chicago Press, 2004).

9. William Savage, *Comic Books and America, 1945–1954* (Norman: University of Oklahoma Press, 1990); Amy Kiste Nyberg, *Seal of Approval: The History of the Comics Code* (Jackson: University Press of Mississippi, 1998); Bradford Wright, *Comic Book Nation: The Transformation of Youth Culture in America* (Baltimore: Johns Hopkins University Press, 2001), 86–108.

10. See John Springhall, *Youth, Popular Culture and Moral Panics: Penny Gaffs to Gangsta-Rap, 1830–1996* (New York: St. Martin's, 1998).

11. Judith Crist, "Horror in the Nursery," *Collier's*, 27 March 1948, 22–23, 95–97. See also Andrea Friedman, "Sadists and Sissies: Anti-pornography Campaigns in Cold War America," *Gender & History* 15, no. 2 (2003): 201–27.

12. Fredric Wertham, "The Comics . . . Very Funny!" *Saturday Review of Literature*, 29 May 1948, 6–7, 27–29.

13. James Gilbert, *A Cycle of Outrage: America's Reaction to Juvenile Delinquency in the 1950s* (New York: Oxford University Press, 1986), esp. 21–41, 125–42. On "pachuco" youth culture, see Eduardo Obregon Pagan, *Murder at the Sleepy Lagoon: Zoot Suits, Race, and Riot in Wartime L.A.* (Chapel Hill: University of North Carolina Press, 2003).

14. Frankie Lymon and the Teenagers, "I'm Not a Juvenile Delinquent" (1956), from *The Very Best of Frankie Lymon and the Teenagers* (Rhino, 1998).

15. Allen Berube, *Coming Out Under Fire: The History of Gay Men and Women in World War II* (New York: Free Press, 1990), 128–74; Beth Bailey, *From Front Porch to Back Seat: Courtship in Twentieth-Century America* (Baltimore: Johns Hopkins University Press, 1988), 119–40; Rickie Solinger, *Wake Up Little Susie: Single Pregnancy and Race Before Roe v. Wade* (New York: Routledge, 1992), esp. 86–102.

16. Wertham, "The Comics . . . Very Funny!" 28.

17. Louise Pearson and Martin Wolfson, letters to the editor, *Saturday Review of Literature*, 19 June 1948, 24; "The Comics: Attack on Juvenile Delinquency," *NEA Journal*, Dec. 1948, 632–36; *Los Angeles Herald-Express*, 18 Aug. 1948; *NYT*, 25 June 1949; St. Cloud Ordinance No. 345, 23 March 1950, American Civil Liberties Union Papers, box 765, folder 8, Seeley G. Mudd Library, Princeton University (hereafter ACLU Papers).

18. Editorial, *Journal of Educational Sociology* 23, no. 4 (1949): 193–94; Frederic Thrasher, "The Comics and Delinquency: Cause or Scapegoat," ibid., 195–205.

19. *Juvenile Delinquency: A Compilation of Information and Suggestions Submitted to the Special Senate Committee to Investigate Organized Crime* (Washington: GPO, 1950), Hoover quote at 7.

20. Fredric Wertham, *Seduction of the Innocent* (New York: Rinehart and Co., 1954), 26, 174, 326, 178, 189–90.

21. Ibid., 177, 101, 336.

22. Ibid., 397.

23. "Cause of Delinquency," *Science News Letter*, 1 May 1954, 275; Wolcott Gibbs, "Books," *New Yorker*, 8 May 1954, 134–41.

24. Gregory Lisby, "Early Television on Public Watch: Kefauver and His Crime Investigation," *Journalism Quarterly* 62, no. 2 (1985): 236–42; Joseph Bruce Gorman, *Kefauver: A Political Biography* (New York: Oxford University Press, 1971), 197; "Horror Comics," *Time*, 3 May 1954, 78.

25. Senate Subcommittee to Investigate Juvenile Delinquency, *Comic Books and Juvenile Delinquency: Interim Report* (Washington: GPO, 1955), 2, 12–13.

26. St. Petersburg Ordinance No. 84-C, 18 Jan. 1955, ACLU Papers, box 770, folder 25; *NYT*, 2 Feb. 1956.

27. Special Commission to Investigate and Study the Relation Between Juvenile Delinquency and the Distribution and Sale of Publications Portraying Crime, Obscenity and Horror, *Report* (Boston: Wright and Potter, 1956), 5–6. See also the similar Rhode Island Commission to Study "Comic" Books, *Report* (Providence: House of Representatives, 1956).

28. Scott White Reed to Jeffrey Fuller, 19 March 1957, ACLU Papers, box 777, folder 9.

29. "Code of the CMAA," adopted 26 Oct. 1954, in Comics Magazine Association of America Fact Kit (1954), Edward Roybal Papers, box 9, folder: Crime and Horror Books, Charles E. Young Research Library, Special Collections, University of California, Los Angeles (hereafter UCLA Special Collections).

30. Wertham, "It's Still Murder," *Saturday Review*, 9 April 1955, 11–12, 46–48.

31. One measure of the declining fortunes of anticomics campaigns can be seen in the *Reader's Guide to Periodical Literature*'s indexing of the term *comics*. Covering an entire two-column page in the 1953–55 *Guide*, comics fell to only one column in the 1955–57 edition. By 1957–59 it mustered just twelve entries, only one of them alarmist.

32. "A Year of Community Activity for Youth Welfare to January 1945," n.d. (1945), Los Angeles Coordinating Council Records, box 1, folder: Minutes, 1944–48, Special Collections, University of Southern California, Los Angeles.

33. Albert Maisel, "The Smut Peddler Is After Your Child," *Woman's Home Companion*, Nov. 1951, 24–25, 49, 52, 54, 57; Minutes, Los Angeles Federation of Coordinating

Councils, 20 Nov. 1951, Los Angeles Coordinating Council Records, box 2, folder: 1947–52.

34. *NYT*, 18 Feb. 1953; *NYT*, 16 April 1954.

35. Herbert Monte Levy, memo to "LJ," 23 April 1954, ACLU Papers, box 769, folder 4; Receipt for Property Seized, n.d., ibid.

36. St. Petersburg Ordinance No. 84-C, 18 Jan. 1955, ACLU Papers, box 770, folder 25; "City Censors Ban Classics," *Nation*, 24 Jan. 1953, 9; Clifford Davidson, "St. Cloud— How the Flames Spread," *New Republic*, 29 June 1953, 13–14.

37. Jay Gertzman, *Bookleggers and Smuthounds: The Trade in Erotica, 1920–1940* (Philadelphia: University of Pennsylvania Press, 1999), 9.

38. Geoffrey O'Brien, *Hardboiled America: The Lurid Years of Paperbacks* (New York: Van Nostrand Reinhold, 1981), 33–45.

39. Finding and Recommendation of the Examiner, In the Matter of the May–June 1947 Issue of *Naturel Herald*, U.S. Post Office, 1 March 1948, ACLU Papers, box 758, folder 19.

40. Gay Talese, *Thy Neighbor's Wife* (New York: Dell, 1980), 83–84.

41. Al Di Lauro and Gerald Rabkin, *Dirty Movies: An Illustrated History of the Stag Film, 1915–1970* (New York: Chelsea House, 1976).

42. Benefit Corporation, "Latest Listings of 8 and 16mm Graphic Arts Films," n.d. (1949), ACLU Papers, box 756, folder 23; R. J. Ross, "Ross Presents Hollywood Beauties," n.d. (1950), ibid., box 758, folder 6; William H. Door, "Glamour Catalogue," n.d. (1950), ibid., box 756, folder 23.

43. Untitled editorial, *Playboy*, vol.1, no.1, n.d. (1953), 3; "Playkids," *Time*, 29 April 1957, 69–71; *Modern Man*, Aug. 1955.

44. "The Spread of Smut," *Newsweek*, 27 April 1957, 41–42; Howard Whitman, "Smut: The Poison That Preys on Our Children," *Good Housekeeping*, Nov. 1961, 64–65, 101–4, 173–75.

45. *NYT*, 1 June 1955.

46. *Long Island Press*, 7 Feb. 1962. To chart *America*'s shift from comics to pornography, see "Comic Books and Delinquency," 24 April 1954, 86; Harold Gardiner, "Comic Books: Cultural Threat?" 19 June 1954, 319–21; Gardiner, "Comic Books: Moral Threat?" 26 June 1954, 340–42; "Comic-Books Cease-Fire?" 5 March 1955, 580; "Comics, Obscenity and the Press," 2 April 1955, 7; then Auleen Bordeaux Eberhardt, "Teen-Agers Turn the Tide," 7 May 1955, 154–55; "Smut on the Defensive," 18 June 1955, 302; "Pornography Racket," 2 June 1956, 235–36; "Pornography in the PX," 7 July 1956, 336.

47. Senate Committee on the Judiciary, *Juvenile Delinquency (Obscene and Pornographic Magazines): Hearings Before the Subcommittee to Investigate Juvenile Delinquency* (Washington: GPO, 1955), 231, 194.

48. Ibid., 304. Langer may have felt the need to reassert some authority after earlier in the hearings having needed the concept of "bondage photos" explained to him (70).

49. Senate Committee on the Judiciary, *Obscene and Pornographic Literature and Juvenile Delinquency: Interim Report of the Subcommittee to Investigate Juvenile Delinquency* (Washington: GPO, 1956), 3, 61.

50. Ibid., 62.

51. Ibid., 68, 70; "Psychiatrists Say Sexy Books Don't Cause Crimes," *Science News Letter*, 3 Jan. 1953, 9.

52. J. Edgar Hoover, "Let's Wipe Out the Schoolyard Sex Racket!" reprint from *This Week Magazine*, 25 Aug. 1957, in City Council File 95330, Los Angeles City Archives; Courtney Cooper, "This Trash Must Go!" *Reader's Digest*, Feb. 1940, 20–24; Hoover, untitled statement, *FBI Law Enforcement Bulletin*, Jan. 1960, 1–2. On Hoover's obscenity file see Athan Theoharis and John Stuart Cox, *The Boss: J. Edgar Hoover and the Great American Inquisition* (Philadelphia: Temple University Press, 1988), 94–96.

53. Jack Harrison Pollack, "Newsstand Filth: A National Disgrace!" *Better Homes and Gardens*, Sept. 1957, 10–11, 197, 205.

54. California Assembly Subcommittee on Pornographic Literature, *Preliminary Report* (n.p., 1958), 18; ibid., *Report* (Sacramento: California Assembly, 1959), 11; New Jersey Commission to Study Obscenity in Certain Publications, *Final Report* (n.p., 1962); ibid., *Public Hearing, Trenton, October 17, 1961* (n.p., 1961).

55. Gregory Lisby, "'Trying to Define What May Be Indefinable': The Georgia Literature Commission, 1953–1973," *Georgia Historical Quarterly* 84, no. 1 (2000): 72–97; Oklahoma Statutes Annotated, Title 21, Sec. 1040 (1957), and Harry Culver, "Literature," UP print, 19 April 1957, both in Harry Culver Papers, box 8, folder 21, Carl Albert Congressional Research and Studies Center, University of Oklahoma, Norman; *Spokane Spokesman-Review*, 22 Feb. 1961; "Youth Protection Committee Information," 14 April 1961, Youth Protection Committee Records, box 1, folder: By-laws, Utah State Historical Society, Salt Lake City.

56. House Committee on Post Office and Civil Service, Subcommittee on Postal Operations, *Obscene Matter Sent Through the Mail* (Washington: GPO, 1959), 1; ibid., *Circulation of Obscene and Pornographic Material: Hearing Before the Subcommittee on Postal Operations* (Washington: GPO, 1960); *Obscene Matter Sent Through the Mail: Hearings Before the Subcommittee on Postal Operations* (Washington: GPO, 1962).

57. Arthur Summerfield, "Our Challenge: Decency and Dignity for Our Children," 27 Feb. 1960, Freedom of Information Center files, box 7, folder: CDL, University of Missouri, Columbia; Samples of postal stamp sent into ACLU office, all dated 1960–61, ACLU Papers, box 786, folder 6.

58. *Memphis Press-Scimitar*, 21 Sept. 1956; ibid., 30 Aug. 1956.

59. Subcommittee on Postal Operations, House of Representatives, *Obscene Matter Sent Through the Mail: Report to the Committee on Post Office and Civil Service* (Washington: GPO, 1959), 14.

60. See Gertzman, *Bookleggers and Smuthounds*, 113–17.

61. Committee on the Judiciary, Senate, *Scope of Soviet Activity in the United States*, Part 23 (Washington: GPO, 1956), 1195–1206.

62. *NYT*, 15 June 1953; *Christian Science Monitor*, 29 June 1953; ACLU News Release, 25 Feb. 1955, ACLU Papers, box 770, folder 17; *NYT*, 27 Feb. 1955 (the Legion ultimately traded "good" comics for "bad" ones rather than burning them).

63. Mary Dudziak, *Cold War Civil Rights: Race and the Image of American Democracy* (Princeton, NJ: Princeton University Press, 2002).

64. While many early civil rights activists were, in fact, affiliated with the Communist Party, as Robin D. G. Kelley shows in *Hammer and Hoe: Alabama Communists During the Great Depression* (Chapel Hill: University of North Carolina Press, 1990), many were very much local, and the "outsider" trope was never more than a rhetorical smokescreen.

65. See John Benedict, "Pornography: A Political Weapon," *American Mercury*, Feb. 1960, 3–21; *Brunswick* (Georgia) *News*, 26 Oct. 1960.

66. Jack Mabley, "Is Flood of Pornographic Material a Communist Plot?" in Citizens for Decent Literature, "Report No. 3," n.d. (1960), Freedom of Information Center files, box 7, folder: CDL.

67. House Committee on Post Office and Civil Service, *Obscene Matter Sent Through the Mail: Hearings Before the Subcommittee on Postal Operations* (Washington: GPO, 1962), 179; *Santa Ana Register*, 28 April 1961; *Los Angeles Mirror*, 6 Sept. 1961; *Los Angeles Times*, 13 Feb. 1961.

68. Undated, unidentified newspaper clipping (Oklahoma City, 1961), ACLU Papers, box 785, folder 23; W. Cleon Skousen, *The Naked Communist*, 9th ed. (Salt Lake City: Ensign Publishing, 1961), 261. On the book's right-wing popularity see Lisa McGirr, *Suburban Warriors: The Origins of the New American Right* (Princeton, NJ: Princeton University Press, 2001), 95, 101.

69. *Protecting Postal Patrons from Obscene and Obnoxious Mail and Communist Propaganda*, House of Rep. (Washington: GPO, 1963).

70. *South Omaha Sun*, 21 April 1966; *Indianapolis Star*, 23 Feb. 1966.

71. Sgt. P. A. Wellpott, Memo, 8 Aug. 1943, box 96, file: Massage, Griffith Family Papers, UCLA Special Collections; LAPD, *Annual Reports*, 1940–1947.

72. Berube, *Coming Out Under Fire*.

73. Daniel Hurewitz, *Bohemian Los Angeles and the Making of Modern Politics* (Berkeley: University of California Press, 2007); John D'Emilio, *Sexual Politics, Sexual Communities: The Making of a Homosexual Minority in the United States, 1940–1970* (Chicago: University of Chicago Press, 1983), esp. 57–74; Stuart Timmons, *The Trouble with Harry Hay: Founder of the Modern Gay Movement* (Boston: Alyson, 1990), 95–171.

74. Resolution by Lloyd Davies, adopted 11 Nov. 1947, City Council File 30874, Los Angeles City Archives; W. H. Parker to Board of Police Commissioners, 22 May 1951, City Council File 48346, ibid.; *Daily News*, 13 Dec. 1948; ibid., 10 Sept. 1949; Johnson, *The Lavender Scare*, 2. On the shifts in police mentality at the LAPD under Parker see Edward Escobar, "Bloody Christmas and the Irony of Police Professionalism: The Los Angeles Police Department, Mexican Americans, and Police Reform in the 1950s," *Pacific Historical Review* 72, no. 2 (2003): 171–99.

75. Ed Davenport, Resolution, 13 August 1952, City Council File 54627, Los Angeles City Archives; Don Parsons, "'The Darling of the Town's Neo-Fascists': The Bombastic Political Career of Councilman Ed J. Davenport," *Southern California Quarterly* 81 (1999): 467–505; *Los Angeles Times* (hereafter *LAT*), 23 Jan. 1961; *Hollywood Citizen-News*, 23 Jan. 1962; *Citizen-News*, 30 Jan. 1962.

76. Winston Leyland, ed., with photography by Bob Mizer, *Physique: A Pictorial History of the Athletic Model Guild* (San Francisco: Gay Sunshine Press, 1982); F. Valentine Hooven III, *Beefcake: The Muscle Magazines of America, 1950–1970* (Koln: Benedikt Taschen, 1995), 29–30, 46. See also Thomas Waugh, *Hard to Imagine: Gay Male Eroticism in Photography and Film from Their Beginnings to Stonewall* (New York: Columbia University Press, 1996), 215–83; and Cecile Whiting, *Pop L.A.: Art and the City in the 1960s* (Berkeley: University of California Press, 2006), 109–33.

77. *Los Angeles Mirror*, 4 May 1954; ibid., *Mirror*, 18 May 1954. John D'Emilio notes Coates's 1953 attack in *Sexual Politics, Sexual Communities*, 76.

78. *Los Angeles Mirror*, 18 May 1954; ibid., 19 May 1954.

79. *People vs. Mizer* (1954), Municipal Court Case File CR A 3216, Los Angeles County Record Center; Bob Mizer oral history interview by Pat Allen and Valentine Hooven, 24 Feb. 1992, cassette 1, ONE Institute and Archives, Los Angeles.

80. ONE's Legal Counsel, "The Law of Mailable Material," *ONE*, Oct. 1954, 4–6; *ONE, Inc. v. Oleson*, 241 F.2d 772 (1957); Jane Dahr, "Sappho Remembered," *ONE*, Oct. 1954, 12–15; Brother Gundy, "Lord Samuel and Lord Montagu," ibid., 18–19. On *ONE* and the early homophile press, see Rodger Streitmatter, *Unspeakable: The Rise of the Gay and Lesbian Press in America* (Boston: Faber and Faber, 1995), 17–50.

81. Ann Carll Reid, "Editorial," *ONE*, March 1957, 1; "*ONE* and the U.S. Postoffice," ibid., 7; "ONE, Inc. vs. Otto K. Oleson" (text of petition for writ of certiorari to Supreme Court), *Homophile Studies* (summer 1958): 62.

82. Rowland Watts to William Lambert, 17 July 1957, Southern California ACLU Papers, box 17, folder 4, UCLA Special Collections; Watts to Spencer Coxe, 1 Aug. 1957, ibid.; "ACLU Position on Homosexuality," 7 Jan. 1957, ACLU Papers, box 1127, folder 7, Seeley G. Mudd Library, Princeton University.

83. *ONE, Inc. v. Oleson*, 355 U.S. 371 (1958).

84. *NYT*, 14 Jan. 1958.

85. For *ONE* criticisms of prevailing conceptions of obscenity and pornography see "Homosexuality: A Way of Life," March 1958, 5–6; William Lambert, "Editorial," April 1958, 4–5; "Oleson and Other Censors," May 1958, 24–25; Lambert, "Editorial," Aug. 1958, 4–5; Dale Mallory, "Pornography They Say . . . " May 1961, 6–9; Robert Gregory, "Postal Censorship," Aug. 1961, 5–17.

86. Jim Kepner, interviewed in Paul Alcuin Siebenand, "The Beginnings of Gay Cinema in Los Angeles: The Industry and Its Audience" (PhD diss., University of Southern California, 1975), 14.

87. "Tangents," *ONE*, Feb. 1958, 18. On Anger and his L.A. avant-garde peers ("Wizards of the Id") see David James, *The Most Typical Avant-Garde: History and Geography of Minor Cinemas in Los Angeles* (Berkeley: University of California Press, 2005), 165–202.

88. *People vs. Rohauer*, Reporter's Transcript, Los Angeles Municipal Court No. 73460, 13 Jan. 1958, 22–25, 86, 96, 103, Stanley Fleishman Papers, box 12, file: Rohauer, UCLA Special Collections.

89. *Rohauer* transcript, 165, 205, 115, 38.

90. Memorandum Opinion, *People v. Rohauer*, Superior Court No. CR A 3911, printed in *Los Angeles Daily Journal Report Section*, 13 July 1959, 15–17; *LAT*, 28 Feb. 1959.

91. *Los Angeles Herald and Express*, 21 Nov. 1956; Edsel Newton, "Report on Pornography," booklet reprint of articles from the *Los Angeles Daily Journal*, n.d. (1958), Southern California ACLU Papers, box 1, folder 8.

92. *Manual Enterprises v. Day* 370 U.S. 478 (1962).

93. *People vs. Getz*, Los Angeles Municipal Court, No. 207224, Reporter's Transcript, vol. 1, 29 April–2 May 1964, 72, Fleishman Papers, box 250, no folder; Transcript, vol. III, 6 May 1964, 634, ibid.

94. *People vs. Getz*, Transcript, vol. 1, 83; vol. II, 5 May 1964, 396; vol. III, 496–98.

95. *People vs. Getz*, Transcript, vol. II, 354; vol. III, 626; *LAT*, 9 Dec. 1964.

96. Office of Estes Kefauver, "Proposed Amendment with Respect to Smut Peddling," undated press release (1959), Estes Kefauver Papers, series 1, box 72, folder: Comics, Obscene Lit., etc., University of Tennessee, Knoxville; draft, "Curbing the Smut Peddlers," 30 July 1960, Kefauver Papers, series 10, box 15, folder: Speeches.

97. *Congressional Record* 100 (14 May 1954): 6574.

2. Ambivalent Liberals

1. *Dennis v. U.S.*, 341 U.S. 494 (1951).

2. *New York Times* (hereafter *NYT*), 15 June 1953.

3. Collie Small, "What Censorship Keeps You from Knowing," *Redbook*, July 1951, 81.

4. Lionel Trilling, *The Liberal Imagination: Essays on Literature and Society* (New York: Doubleday, 1950), 5.

5. Alonzo Hamby, *Beyond the New Deal: Harry S. Truman and American Liberalism* (New York: Columbia University Press, 1973), vii; Alan Brinkley, *Liberalism and Its Discontents* (Cambridge, MA: Harvard University Press, 1998), ix. On progressivism see Daniel Rodgers, "In Search of Progressivism," *Reviews in American History* 10 (1982): 113–32.

6. Alan Brinkley, *The End of Reform: New Deal Liberalism in Recession and War* (New York: Knopf, 1995), esp. 259–64; Jonathan Bell, *The Liberal State on Trial: The Cold War and American Politics in the Truman Years* (New York: Columbia University Press, 2004), 161–73. Also see Richard Freeland, *The Truman Doctrine and the Origins of McCarthyism: Foreign Policy, Domestic Politics, and Internal Security, 1946–1948* (New York: Schocken, 1970).

7. Judy Kutulas, *The American Civil Liberties Union and the Making of Modern Liberalism, 1930–1960* (Chapel Hill: University of North Carolina Press, 2006), 4; Samuel Walker, *In Defense of American Liberties: A History of the ACLU* (New York: Oxford University Press, 1990), 130–49, 185–94.

8. Michal Belknap, *The Supreme Court Under Earl Warren, 1953–1969* (Columbia: University of South Carolina Press, 2005), xvii. Mark Tushnet agrees in "The Warren Court as History: An Interpretation," in *The Warren Court in Historical and Political Perspective*, ed. Mark Tushnet (Charlottesville: University Press of Virginia, 1993), 4. On the Court see also Bernard Schwartz, ed., *The Warren Court: A Retrospective* (New York: Oxford University Press, 1996); Morton Horwitz, *The Warren Court and the Pursuit of Justice: A Critical Issue* (New York: Hill and Wang, 1998); Lucas Powe Jr., *The Warren Court and American Politics* (Cambridge, MA: Belknap Press, 2000).

9. Belknap, *The Supreme Court Under Earl Warren*, 67.

10. Powe, *The Warren Court and American Politics*, 406.

11. John D'Emilio and Estelle Freedman, *Intimate Matters: A History of Sexuality in America* (New York: Harper and Row, 1988), 241; "ACLU Position on Homosexuality" (7 Jan. 1957). American Civil Liberties Union Papers, box 1127, folder 7, Seeley G. Mudd Library, Princeton University (hereafter ACLU Papers). See also David Johnson, *The Lavender Scare: The Cold War Persecution of Gays and Lesbians in the Federal Government* (Chicago: University of Chicago Press, 2004).

12. *Hoyt v. Florida*, 368 U.S. 57 (1961); Marc Stein, "*Boutilier* and the U.S. Supreme Court's Sexual Revolution," *Law and History Review* 23, no. 3 (2005): 491–536.

13. David Rabban, *Free Speech in Its Forgotten Years* (Cambridge, UK: Cambridge University Press, 1997), 44–76, 303; Zechariah Chafee Jr., *Freedom of Speech* (New York: Harcourt, Brace, 1920), 170–71.

14. Rabban, *Free Speech in Its Forgotten Years*, 311–13; Samuel Walker, *In Defense of American Liberties*, 83–86 (quote from Forest Bailey at 83). On Mary Ware Dennett's case see Constance Chen, "*The Sex Side of Life*": *Mary Ware Dennett's Pioneering Battle for Birth Control and Sex Education* (New York: Free Press, 1996), 269–304; ACLU report quoted in Paul Murphy, *The Constitution in Crisis Times, 1918–1969* (New York: Harper and Row, 1972), 172.

15. Roger Cottrell, *Roger Nash Baldwin and the American Civil Liberties Union* (New York: Columbia University Press, 2000), 166.

16. Morris Ernst and William Seagle, *To the Pure . . . A Study of Obscenity and the Censor* (New York: Viking, 1929), 275; Morris Ernst and Alexander Lindey, *The Censor Marches On: Recent Milestones in the Administration of the Obscenity Law in the United States* (New York: Doubleday, Doran, 1940), 188, 260.

17. Roger Baldwin to Post Office Solicitor, letter draft, 23 Sept. 1947, ACLU Papers, box 756, folder 12; Arthur Garfield Hays, redraft of Baldwin letter, 16 Oct. 1947, ibid.

18. Alan Reitman to George Biddinger, 18 Nov. 1949, ACLU Papers, box 757, folder 9; Herbert Monte Levy to E. L. Wilson, 28 Feb. 1951, ibid., box 763, folder 18; undated postcard by Ross Products, ibid., box 761, folder 7; Levy to Frederick Block, 15 Nov. 1951, ibid., box 761, folder 6.

19. Levy to Ernest Besig, 16 Oct. 1953, ACLU Papers, box 766, folder 31; Levy to Clifford Forster, 13 Nov. 1953, ibid.

20. *America's Need: A New Birth of Freedom; 34th Annual Report* (New York: ACLU, 1954), 12–13.

21. William Lockhart and Robert McClure, "Literature, the Law of Obscenity and the Constitution," *Minnesota Law Review* 38, no. 4 (1954): 295–395, 356, 390.

22. Bernard DeVoto, "The Easy Chair," *Harper's*, July 1944, 150; Rice to Baldwin, 4 June 1948, ACLU Papers, box 756, folder 13; National Council on Freedom from Censorship, council pamphlet, June 1946, ibid., box 755, folder 24.

23. Rice to Baldwin, 4 June 1948, ACLU Papers, box 756, folder 13.

24. Brief on Behalf of Defendant, *Capitol Enterprises v. Dept. of Education*, Ohio Supreme Court, n.d. (1954), Division of Film Censorship Records, box 50,732, folder: Capitol Enterprises Brief, Ohio State Historical Society, Columbus.

25. See Richard Hixson, *Pornography and the Justices: The Supreme Court and the Intractable Obscenity Problem* (Carbondale: Southern Illinois University Press, 1996), 9–10. The cases were *Rosen v. U.S.*, 161 U.S. 29 (1896), and *Swearingen v. U.S.*, 161 U.S. 446 (1896).

26. *United States v. One Book Entitled "Ulysses,"* 5 F. Supp. 182 (1933).

27. Ibid., affirmed, 72 F.2d 705 (1934); *Parmelee v. U.S.*, 113 F.2d 729 (1940).

28. *Hadley v. State*, 172 S.W.2d 237 (1943); *State v. Lerner*, 81 N.E.2d 282 (1948); *Commonwealth v. Isenstadt*, 62 N.E.2d 840 (1945).

29. *Schenck v. U.S.*, 249 U.S. 47 (1919); Zechariah Chafee Jr., *Government and Mass Communications* (Chicago: University of Chicago Press, 1947), 59.

30. *Roth v. Goldman*, 172 F.2d 788 (1949). On Frank's reputation—based largely on his 1930 book *Law and the Modern Mind*, a classic of legal realism that many considered a psychoanalysis of the legal system—see Morton Horwitz, *The Transformation of American Law, 1870–1960: The Crisis of Legal Orthodoxy* (New York: Oxford University Press, 1992), 175–87.

31. *Commonwealth v. Gordon*, 66 Pa. D. & C. 101 (1949).

32. Technically, the court upheld Bok's ruling by refusing to hear an appeal, but in a rare legal maneuver it specifically vacated his conclusions. American Book Publishers Council, Memo to All Members, 7 April 1950, ACLU Papers, box 758, folder 18.

33. *Roth v. Goldman*, 172 F.2d 788 (1949); Augustus Hand to Jerome Frank, 21 Jan. 1949, Jerome Frank Papers, box 101, folder 916, Manuscripts and Archives, Yale University Library, New Haven, CT; *Commonwealth v. Isenstadt*, 62 N.E.2d 840 (1945); *Dennis v. U.S.*, 341 U.S. 494 (1951).

34. *Besig v. U.S.*, 208 F.2d 142 (1953); Georgia House Bill No. 247, 19 Feb. 1953, ACLU Papers, box 769, folder 17.

35. Herbert Levy to Leon Despres, 13 March 1950, ACLU Papers, box 761, folder 24.

36. *Sunshine Book Co. v. Summerfield*, 128 F. Supp. 564 (1955).

37. Ibid.; "Editorial Comment," *Sunshine and Health*, July 1955, 13.

38. *U.S. v. Roth*, 237 F.2d 796 (1956).

39. *Chaplinsky v. New Hampshire*, 315 U.S. 568 (1942).

40. Minutes, Censorship Panel Meeting, 28 Nov. 1956, So. Cal. ACLU Papers, box 1, folder 4, UCLA Special Collections.

41. ACLU news release, 21 April 1957, ACLU Papers, box 1478, folder: *Kingsley Books v. Brown*; Minutes, Censorship Panel Meeting, 18 Dec. 1956, So. Cal. ACLU Papers, box 1, folder 4.

42. *Hannegan v. Esquire*, 327 U.S. 146 (1946); *Burstyn v. Wilson*, 343 U.S. 495 (1952). On film censorship see Laura Wittern-Keller, *Freedom of the Screen: Legal Challenges to State Film Censorship, 1915–1981* (Lexington: University Press of Kentucky, 2008).

43. *Butler v. Michigan*, 352 U.S. 380 (1957).

44. *Roth v. U.S.*, 354 U.S. 476 (1957).

45. Ibid.

46. Ibid.

47. *Yates v. U.S.*, 354 U.S. 298 (1957).

48. "The Supreme Court: The Temple Builder," *Time*, 1 July 1957, 11–17; "The Supreme Court: On Sex & Obscenity," ibid., 8 July 1957, 10–11; Harold Gardiner, "The Supreme Court on Obscenity," *America*, 13 July 1957, 403–4; Paul Kurtz, "What Is Obscenity?" *Nation*, 7 Sept. 1957, 112; Alan Reitman to Censorship Panel, ACLU Papers, 13 Dec. 1957, So. Cal. ACLU Papers, box 1, folder 4.

49. *Excelsior Pictures v. Regents*, 3 N.Y.2d 237 (1957); for examples of "indecent" and "immoral" as criteria for banning see censor elimination records for *Fire Under Her Skin* (31 Jan. 1957) and *The Scarlet Week* (6 Feb. 1957), among numerous others, in New York Motion Picture Division Records, box A1422-77, reel 9, New York State Archives, Albany; "obscene" became the sole criterion with *Children of the Sun*'s rejection, 15 July 1957, and remained such through the demise of the censor board in 1965.

50. *Times Film Corp. v. Chicago*, 244 F.2d 432 (1957), *reversed*, 355 U.S. 35 (1957); *One, Inc. v. Oleson*, 355 U.S. 371 (1958); *Sunshine Book Co. v. Summerfield*, 355 U.S. 372 (1958). See also *Mounce v. U.S.*, 355 U.S. 180 (1958).

51. *Kingsley International Pictures v. Regents*, 4 N.Y.2d 349 (1958), *reversed*, 360 U.S. 684 (1959); *Smith v. California*, 361 U.S. 147 (1959).

52. *Smith v. California*, 361 U.S. 147 (1959); *Times Film Corp. v. Chicago*, 365 U.S. 43 (1961); *State v. Chobot*, 106 N.W.2d 286 (1960), *cert. denied*, 368 U.S. 15 (1961).

53. Minutes, Censorship Panel Subcommittee on Local Obscenity Prosecutions, 16 Jan. 1958, ACLU Papers, box 80, folder 33; Reitman to Murphy, 6 Nov. 1959, ibid., box 207, folder 8.

54. Minutes, Censorship Committee, 14 April 1960, ACLU Papers, box 81, folder 31; House Post Office and Civil Service Committee, *Self-Policing of the Movie and Publishing Industry: Hearing Before the Subcommittee on Postal Operations* (Washing-

ton: GPO, 1960), 159; Minutes, Censorship Committee, 25 Oct. 1960, ACLU Papers, box 81, folder 31.

55. Minutes, Censorship Committee, 7 March 1961, So. Cal. ACLU Papers, box 1, folder 4.

56. *State v. Settle*, 90 R.I. 195 (1959); ACLU, *Justice for All: "Nor Speak with Double Tongue"; 37th Annual Report* (New York: ACLU, 1957), 39; California Assembly Interim Committee on Judiciary, Subcommittee on Pornographic Literature, *Report* (Sacramento: California Assembly, 1959), 27.

57. Robert Kirsch, "Obscenity—U.S. Style," *ALA Bulletin*, April 1964, 269–72; *U.S. v. West Coast News*, 30 F.D.R. 13 (1962).

58. Thomas Michael Gaume, "Suppression of Motion Pictures in Kansas, 1952 to 1972" (master's thesis, University of Kansas, 1975), 73–74; Abilene Ordinance, 20 April 1961, attached to Edward Kirk to Hubert Dyer, 26 April 1961, Georgia State Literature Commission Records, box 1, folder: Abilene Christian College, Georgia State Archives, Morrow; Anthony Lewis, "The Most Recent Troubles of 'Tropic,'" *New York Times Book Review*, 21 Jan. 1962; *San Francisco News-Call Bulletin*, 8 Dec. 1961.

59. Herman Womack to Hank, 1 Oct. 1959, H. Lynn Womack Papers, box 1, folder 6, Division of Rare and Manuscript Collections, Cornell University; *Manual Enterprises v. Day*, 289 F.2d 455 (1961). On Womack see Rodger Streitmatter and John Watson, "Herman Lynn Womack: Pornographer as First Amendment Pioneer," *Journalism History* 28, no. 2 (2002): 56–65.

60. *Manual Enterprises v. Day*, 370 U.S. 478 (1962); *Chicago New World*, 29 June 1962; "Obscenity and the Courts," *America*, 21 July 1962, 521. The school prayer decision was *Engle v. Vitale*, 370 U.S. 421 (1962).

61. *Bantam Books v. Sullivan*, 372 U.S. 58 (1963); *Richmond News Leader*, 2 March 1964.

62. *State v. Jacobellis*, 179 N.E.2d 777 (1962).

63. *Jacobellis v. Ohio*, 378 U.S. 184 (1964); *New York Times v. Sullivan*, 376 U.S. 254 (1964).

64. *Jacobellis v. Ohio*.

65. *Grove Press v. Gerstein*, 378 U.S. 577 (1964).

66. Wanda Albrecht to ACLU, 3 Dec. 1961, ACLU Papers, box 784, folder 4; *Motion Picture Daily*, 22 Oct. 1962; *Chicago New Crusader*, 24 Feb. 1962; *Detroit News*, 14 Nov. 1963; *New York Daily News*, 2 May 1963; *Dayton Daily News*, 4 Oct. 1963; *NYT*, 30 March 1965; *New York Herald Tribune*, 9 June 1965; *Milwaukee Sentinel*, 18 July 1965.

67. Henry Miller, *Tropic of Cancer* (New York: Grove, 1961), 5; *U.S. v. West Coast News*, 357 F.2d 855 (1966); Oscar Peck, *Sex Life of a Cop* (n.l.: Saber Books, 1959), 13; *U.S. v. Luros*, 260 F. Supp. 697 (1966); *People vs. Luros*, L.A. Superior Court, No. 295183 (14 June 1965), Stanley Fleishman Papers, box 667, folder: Luros, UCLA Special Collections.

68. John Paul Jones to Elmer Rice, 4 April 1962, So. Cal. ACLU Papers, box1, folder 4; ACLU News Release, 28 May 1962, ACLU Papers, box 83, folder 6.

69. *Memoirs v. Massachusetts*, 206 N.E.2d 403 (1965), *reversed*, 383 U.S. 413 (1966).

70. Ibid.

71. Bruce Allen Murphy, *Fortas: The Rise and Ruin of a Supreme Court Justice* (New York: William Morrow, 1988), 458.

72. *EROS* mailing, n.d. (1961), EROS Collection, box 2, folder 1, Kinsey Institute for Research in Sex, Gender, and Reproduction, Indiana University, Bloomington.

73. Bernard Harding to Saul Mindel, 19 March 1963, Ralph Ginzburg Papers, Accession, box 1, folder: Postal Inspector's Case File, Wisconsin Historical Society, Madison.

74. Several thousand response cards—most unsigned and undated—are preserved in the *EROS* Collection. The quoted examples come from box 1, folders 2 and 11. In box 1, folder 8 lies a biohazard bag reading, "Contents: response card with feces."

75. Herbert Miller to Attorney General, 5 April 1962; E. Lamar Sledge to Carl Belcher, 31 July 1962; Carl Belcher to Herbert Miller, 8 Nov. 1962; Sledge to Belcher, 5 Dec. 1962; Belcher to Miller, 7 Dec. 1962; Sledge to Belcher, 14 Dec. 1962; all in Ginzburg Papers, Accession, box 1, folder: Dept. of Justice Case File.

76. Rey Anthony, *The Housewife's Handbook on Selective Promiscuity* (New York: Documentary Books, 1962), 87, 7; Carl Belcher to Herbert Miller, 13 March 1963, Ginzburg Papers, Accession, box 1, folder: Dept. of Justice Case File.

77. James Symington, Memorandum to the Attorney General, 3 Dec. 1962, Ginzburg Papers, Accession, box 1, folder: Dept. of Justice Case File; *U.S. v. Ginzburg*, 224 F. Supp. 129 (1963).

78. Murphy, *Fortas*, 458. Fortas cited Ginzburg's "slimy" character in explaining his mistake.

79. *Ginzburg v. U.S.*, 383 U.S. 463 (1966).

80. Ibid.

81. C. Peter McGrath, "The Obscenity Cases: Grapes of Roth," in *Supreme Court Review 1966*, ed. Philip Kurland (Chicago: University of Chicago Press, 1966), 7–77, 59, 60; *NYT*, 3 April 1966; "An Analysis of the Ginzburg, Mishkin and Fanny Hill Decisions," *National Decency Reporter*, June-July 1966, 3.

82. *Mishkin v. New York*, 383 U.S. 502 (1966).

83. *Columbus Evening Dispatch*, 23 March 1966; *Denver Post*, 24 March 1966; Oklahoma Literature Commission, "Findings of the Commission and Notice of Proposed Order," 28 March 1966, Harry Culver Papers, box 8, folder 21, University of Oklahoma, Norman; *Minneapolis Star*, 27 April 1966.

84. *U.S. v. Hellenic Sun*, 253 F. Supp. 498 (1966); *Landau v. Fording*, 245 Cal. App. 2d 820 (1966).

85. *Redrup v. New York*, 386 U.S. 767 (1967).

86. Belknap, *The Supreme Court Under Earl Warren, 1953–1969*, 214–15.

87. *Aday v. U.S.*, 388 U.S. 447 (1967); *U.S. v. Potomac News*, 389 U.S. 47 (1967); *Landau v. Fording*, 388 U.S. 456 (1967); O. John Rogge, "[T]he High Court of Obscenity I," *University of Colorado Law Review* 41, no. 1 (1969): 59. For a complete list of the Court's redruppings see Joseph Kobylka, *The Politics of Obscenity: Group Litigation in a Time of Legal Change* (Westport, CT: Greenwood Press, 1991), 174–75.

88. *Ginsberg v. New York*, 390 U.S. 629 (1968).

89. *Stanley v. Georgia*, 394 U.S. 557 (1969).

90. *Brandenburg v. Ohio*, 395 U.S. 444 (1969); Leigh Ann Wheeler, *Making Liberties: The American Civil Liberties Union and the Transformation of Sexual Culture in the Twentieth-Century United States* (New York: Oxford University Press, forthcoming).

3. Arousing the Public

1. *St. Louis Globe-Democrat*, 17 May 1963; "CDL Films" mailing, n.d., Citizens for Decent Literature file, Wilcox Collection, University of Kansas, Lawrence.

2. *Perversion for Profit* (CDL, 1963). This film has fallen into the public domain and can be viewed at The Internet Archive, www.archive.org.

3. Harry Hollis, Memo, 17 April 1970, Christian Life Commission Papers, box 19, folder 4, Southern Baptist Convention Historical Society and Archives, Nashville, TN; Keating quoted in Edwin Roberts Jr., *The Smut Rakers* (Silver Spring, MD: National Observer, 1966), 116.

4. CDL, "Fight Newsstand Filth," pamphlet, 1960, Stanley Fleishman Papers, box 546, folder: Newsletters, UCLA Special Collections.

5. CDL mailing, March 1962, American Civil Liberties Union Papers, box 788, folder 19, Seeley G. Mudd Library, Princeton University (hereafter ACLU Papers).

6. Don Cortum to Los Angeles City Council, 28 April 1960, City Council File 95330, Los Angeles City Archives; Southern California CDL, "Statement of Policies," n.d., City Council File 93734, ibid.

7. CDL, "Urgent Memorandum," n.d. (1960), Freedom of Information Center, box 7, folder: CDL, University of Missouri, Columbia (hereafter FOIC).

8. Michel Foucault, *The History of Sexuality, Vol. 1*, trans. Robert Hurley (New York: Vintage, 1978), 45; Michel Foucault, *Power/Knowledge: Selected Interviews and Other Writings, 1972–1977*, ed. Colin Gordon (New York: Pantheon, 1980), 186, quoted in Janice Irvine, *Talk About Sex: The Battles over Sex Education in the United States*

(Berkeley: University of California Press, 2002), 152; Peter Wagner, "The Veil of Science and Morality: Some Pornographic Aspects of the *Onania*," *British Journal for Eighteenth-Century Studies* 4 (1983): 179–84; Christopher Looby, "'The Roots of the Orchis, the Iuli of Chesnuts': The Odor of Male Solitude," in *Solitary Pleasures: The Historical, Literary, and Artistic Discourses of Autoeroticism*, ed. Paula Bennett and Vernon Rosario II (New York: Routledge, 1995), 163–88.

9. One exception to this is Joseph Kobylka, *The Politics of Obscenity: Group Litigation in a Time of Legal Change* (Westport, CT: Greenwood Press, 1991), which discusses CDL at length but from a procedural framework regarding litigation rather than from a historical perspective.

10. See Gaines Foster, *Moral Reconstruction: Christian Lobbyists and the Federal Legislation of Morality, 1865–1920* (Chapel Hill: University of North Carolina Press, 2002); Paul Boyer, *Purity in Print: Book Censorship in America* (New York: Charles Scribner's Sons, 1968); Alison Parker, *Purifying America: Women, Cultural Reform, and Pro-Censorship Activism, 1873–1933* (Urbana: University of Illinois Press, 1997); Andrea Friedman, *Prurient Interests: Gender, Democracy, and Obscenity in New York City, 1909–1945* (New York: Columbia University Press, 2000); Leigh Ann Wheeler, *Against Obscenity: Reform and the Politics of Womanhood in America, 1873–1935* (Baltimore: Johns Hopkins University Press, 2004); Leonard Leff and Jerold Simmons, *The Dame in the Kimono: Hollywood, Censorship, and the Production Code from the 1920s to the 1960s* (New York: Grove Weidenfeld, 1990).

11. Gregory Black, *The Catholic Crusade Against the Movies, 1940–1975* (Cambridge, UK: Cambridge University Press, 1997); Thomas O'Connor, "The National Organization for Decent Literature: A Phase in American Catholic Censorship," *Library Quarterly* 65, no. 4 (1995): 386–414; Stephen Vaughn, "Morality and Entertainment: The Origins of the Motion Picture Production Code," *Journal of American History* 77, no. 2 (1990): 39–65; Frank Walsh, *Sin and Censorship: The Catholic Church and the Motion Picture Industry* (New Haven, CT: Yale University Press, 1996).

12. Una Cadegan, "Guardians of Democracy or Cultural Storm Troopers? American Catholics and the Control of Popular Media, 1934–1966," *Catholic Historical Review* 87, no. 2 (2001): 252–82; John Fischer, "The Harm Good People Do," *Harper's*, Oct. 1956, 14; ACLU, "Statement on Censorship by Private Organizations and the National Organization for Decent Literature," repr. in Harold Gardiner, *Catholic Viewpoint on Censorship*, rev. ed. (Garden City, NY: Image, 1961), 180–86. On anti-Catholicism between the 1830s and the 1950s see Barbara Welter, "From Maria Monk to Paul Blanshard: A Century of Protestant Anti-Catholicism," in *Uncivil Religion:*

Interreligious Hostility in America, ed. Robert Bellah and Frederick Greenspan (New York: Crossroad, 1987), 43–71.

13. *Albuquerque Journal*, 23 Feb. 1954; unidentified newspaper clipping, ACLU Papers, box 769, folder 16; Churchmen's Commission for Decent Publications, "Constitution and By-Laws," n.d., ACLU Papers, box 778, folder 20; Churchmen's Commission *Newsletter*, May 1958, ibid.; Unattributed ACLU report, 20 Sept. 1957, ibid.

14. *Cincinnati Times-Star* (hereafter *CTS*), 4 May 1957; *CTS*, 1 Feb. 1958.

15. House Committee on the Judiciary, Keating testimony, *Mailing of Obscene Matter: Hearings Before Subcommittee No. 1* (Washington: GPO, 1958), 72; "The War Against Smut," *Catholic Digest*, Jan. 1963, 14–22.

16. CDL, "Printed Poison" pamphlet, 1960, Underground, Alternative, and Extremist Literature Collection (hereafter UAE), box 60, folder: CDL, UCLA Special Collections; Kay Sullivan, "Cincinnati vs. Pornography," *Catholic Digest*, June 1959, 12–19; Raymond Gauer, "A Typical CDL Talk," 14 Sept. 1962, Youth Protection Committee Records, box 2, folder: Miscellaneous, Utah Historical Society, Salt Lake City.

17. "Pornography's Poison," *Advocate* (California CDL magazine), Oct. 1963, 1, UAE, box 60, folder: CDL.

18. Pitrim Sorokin, *The America Sex Revolution* (Boston: Porter Sargent, 1956).

19. *Roth v. U.S.*, 354 U.S. 476 (1957).

20. *Cincinnati Post and Times-Star* (hereafter *CPTS*), 18 June 1959; CDL, "Printed Poison" pamphlet, UAE.

21. *Cincinnati Enquirer* (hereafter *CE*), 2 Nov. 1958; *CE*, 3 Nov. 1958; *CPTS*, 16 June 1959; Sullivan, "Cincinnati vs. Pornography," 17–18; CDL mailing, 8 Sept. 1962, ACLU of Cincinnati Papers, box 2, folder: CDL, University of Cincinnati Special Collections (hereafter ACLU-C).

22. Eugene Freeman, "Obscenity: A Community Menace!" n.d. (1960), Raymond Tucker Papers, box 4, folder: Board of Review, Washington University Special Collections, St. Louis, MO; *Perversion for Profit*, *Burbank Herald Tribune and Valley Advertiser*, 2 Sept. 1962. On middle-class insecurities see Elaine Tyler May, *Homeward Bound: American Families in the Cold War Era* (New York: Basic Books, 1988); Kenneth Jackson, *Crabgrass Frontier: The Suburbanization of the United States* (New York: Oxford University Press), 231–82; Thomas Sugrue, *The Origins of the Urban Crisis: Race and Inequality in Postwar Detroit* (Princeton, NJ: Princeton University Press, 1996), 209–29; James Gilbert, *A Cycle of Outrage: America's Response to the Juvenile Delinquent in the 1950s* (New York: Oxford University Press, 1986).

23. "Partial Attendance Records" scrapbook, CDL/National Better Magazine Council Records, box 1, Historical Society of Western Pennsylvania, Pittsburgh; Sullivan, "Cincinnati vs. Pornography," 19.

24. CDL mailing, n.d. (ca. 1962), FOIC, box 7, folder: CDL; CDL, "Procedures for Establishing a Citizens for Decent Literature Group in *Your* Town," n.d. (ca. 1964–67), Kinsey Institute for Research in Sex, Gender, and Reproduction Vertical Files, Indiana University, Bloomington.

25. *CE*, 24 Oct. 1961; James J. Clancy, "A Guest Editorial," *National Decency Reporter* (hereafter *NDR*), 15 Sept. 1963, 2; Catherine Rymph, *Republican Women: Feminism and Conservatism from Suffrage Through the Rise of the New Right* (Chapel Hill: University of North Carolina Press, 2006), 131–59.

26. James Patterson, *Mr. Republican: A Biography of Robert A. Taft* (Boston: Houghton Mifflin, 1972); *CE*, 23 Jan. 1941; *State v. Lerner*, 81 N.E.2d 282 (1948); *Cincinnati Post* (hereafter *CP*), 11 Oct. 1949; *CTS*, 8 Nov. 1949; *CP*, 25 Nov. 1949; *CE*, 18 Jan. 1957.

27. *CP*, 3 Jan. 1957; *CP*, 10 Jan. 1957; *CP*, 26 June 1957.

28. *CP*, 5 March 1958; *CP*, 6 March 1958; *CE*, 9 July 1958; *CP*, 16 April 1958; *CPTS*, 16 Aug. 1958; *CPTS*, 18 Aug. 1958; *CE*, 17 Jan. 1959.

29. "Public Opinion Against Smut," *America*, 5 April 1958, 2; *CE*, 25 Oct. 1958; House Post Office and Civil Service Committee, *Obscene Matter Sent Through the Mail* (Washington: GPO, 1959), 33; Thomas Morgan, "When Is a Book Obscene?" *Cosmopolitan*, Aug. 1959, 58.

30. CDL Articles of Incorporation, 11 July 1958, Stanley Fleishman Papers, box 393, folder: AFAA-CDL; *CPTS*, 25 Oct. 1958; "Plan for a National Organization," n.d. (Oct. 1958), FOIC, box 7, folder: CDL; Program, 1960 CDL National Conference, ibid.

31. *CE*, 30 Oct. 1959; *CE*, 28 Feb. 1960.

32. *CE*, 27 Feb. 1960; Arthur Summerfield, "Our Challenge," Post Office press release, 27 Feb. 1960, FOIC, box 7, folder: CDL; Program, 1960 CDL National Convention, ibid.

33. CDL mailing, n.d. (1962), ACLU-C, box 2, folder: CDL; National ALARM, "Decency vs. the Obscenity Racket," undated pamphlet (ca. 1961–62), Harry Culver Papers, box 8, folder 21, Carl Albert Center, University of Oklahoma, Norman.

34. Terry Isaacs, "Politics, Religion, and the Blue Book: The John Birch Society in Eastern New Mexico and West Texas, 1960–1965," *New Mexico Historical Review* 71, no. 1 (1996): 51–73; Douglas Mackintosh et al., "Sex Education in New Orleans: The Birchers Win a Victory," *New South*, summer 1970, 46–56; Daniel Bell, ed., *The Radical Right* (Garden City, NY: Anchor Books, 1963).

35. Senate Committee on the Judiciary, *Control of Obscene Material: Hearings Before the United States Senate Committee on the Judiciary* (Washington: GPO, 1960), 54; "Keating Outlines Obscenity War," *Texas Catholic*, 15 April 1961; Jack Mabley, "Is Flood of Pornographic Material a Communist Plot?" in "Report No. 3," n.d. (1960), FOIC, box 7, folder: CDL.

36. Keating testimony, House Post Office and Civil Service Committee, *Protecting Postal Patrons from Obscene and Obnoxious Mail and Communist Propaganda: Hearings Before the Committee on Post Office and Civil Service* (Washington: GPO, 1963), 18–19.

37. William Riley testimony, House Post Office and Civil Service Committee, *Obscene Matter Sent Through the Mail: Hearings Before the Subcommittee on Postal Operations*, (Washington: GPO, 1962), 178–79; "Statement of Dr. Donald Cortum," n.d. (1961), City Council File 93734, Los Angeles City Archives.

38. *Hollywood Citizen-News*, 11 Nov. 1961; W. Cleon Skousen, *The Naked Communist*, 9th ed. (Salt Lake City: Ensign, 1961), 261; Skousen, "Obscene Literature—What Can the Police Do About It?" *Law & Order*, Aug. 1961, unpaginated clipping, Stanley Fleishman Collection About Obscenity and Its Legal Aspects, box 62, folder 23, UCLA Special Collections.

39. *CE*, 11 June 1961; Jonathan Schoenwald, *A Time for Choosing: The Rise of Modern American Conservatism* (New York: Oxford University Press, 2001), 101.

40. *New York Times*, 16 March 1964; Morris Lipton, "CDL National Convention, St. Louis, March 14–15, 1969," Presidential Commission on Obscenity and Pornography Records, Lyndon B. Johnson Library, Austin, Texas (hereafter PCOP), box 135A, folder: Meetings; "Nixon Appointment Helps Birches," *Group Research Report*, 4 Sept. 1969, 61.

41. Keating testimony, House Post Office and Civil Service Committee, *Protecting Postal Patrons from Obscene and Obnoxious Mail and Communist Propaganda: Hearings Before the Committee on Post Office and Civil Service* (Washington: GPO, 1963), 13; *Dayton Journal Herald*, 21 Nov. 1963; Frank Riley, "A Ballot Test for the Cleans and the Dirties," *Los Angeles*, Aug. 1966, unpaginated clipping in John Weaver Collection of Ephemera and Research Material on L.A., box 64, folder: Morals and Mores, UCLA Special Collections; W. Cody Wilson, "Memorandum for the Record, CDL National Convention," n.d., PCOP, box 42B, folder: Citizen Action Groups.

42. Evelyn Sturm to Hugh Hefner, 24 Jan. 1959, ACLU Papers, box 781, folder 4; *San Francisco Chronicle*, 6 Nov. 1959; ibid., 30 Nov. 1959.

43. *Indianapolis Times*, 18 June 1959; *Winona (MN) Daily News*, 2 Feb. 1960; Maricopa County Citizens for Decent Literature, "List of Objectionable Magazines," Jan. 1961,

Jean Provence Papers, unprocessed CDL folder (catalog no. 2003.445), Arizona Historical Society, Central Arizona Division, Tempe.

44. Roland Burk, Memorandum, 18 Oct. 1960, Fleishman Collection of Material, box 283, folder: Correspondence.

45. Rev. Wilfred Myll to Alan Reitman, 29 Oct. 1959, ACLU Papers, box 783, folder 28; Louis O'Connell to Richard Kinsella, 5 Aug. 1960, Georgia State Literature Commission Records, box 1, folder: Augusta, Georgia State Archives, Morrow; *Trenton (NJ) Monitor*, 21 April 1961; *Dayton Journal Herald*, undated clipping, Fleishman Collection of Material, box 282, folder: CDL; Roland Burke to Sidney Kramer, 16 June 1960, ACLU Papers, box 342, folder 2.

46. *CPTS*, 25 May 1961; Robert O'Brien to Gordon Rich et al., 20 Oct. 1961, ACLU-C, box 2, folder: Laws re: Obscenity.

47. *CE*, 24 Oct. 1961; Keating, CDL mailing, ACLU-C, 8 Sept. 1962, box 2, folder: CDL.

48. CDL mailing, 27 June 1960, Kinsey Institute Vertical Files; Alan Reitman to Marjorie Wright, 5 Nov 1962, ACLU-C, box 2, folder: CDL.

49. Wendell Pierce to Marjorie Wright, 5 Nov. 1962, ACLU-C, box 2, folder: CDL; Roger Blanchard to Keating, 15 Oct. 1962, ibid.; David Thornberry to Wright, 12 Dec. 1962, ibid.; Thornberry to Keating, 12 Dec. 1962, ibid.

50. *New Orleans Times-Picayune*, 18 July 1963; Southern California CDL information sheet, n.d., City Council File 93734, Los Angeles City Archives; *Providence (RI) Journal*, 11 Dec. 1964.

51. CDL mailing, n.d. (1963), ACLU-C, box 2, folder: CDL; *Milwaukee Journal*, 4 Feb. 1965; *Washington Post*, 14 Feb. 1966; ibid., 26 Feb. 1960.

52. Roberts, *The Smut Rakers*, 102, 103.

53. CDL, "Report No. 3," n.d. (1960), FOIC, box 7, folder: CDL; *St. Louis Globe-Democrat*, 14 Feb. 1960; "Report from Citizens for Decent Literature," n.d. (1960), UAE, box 60, folder: CDL.

54. "First Edition of CDL Newspaper," *NDR*, 15 Sept. 1963, 1.

55. Brooklyn Tablet, 13 Jan. 1962; CDL advertisement for *Pages of Death*, *CE*, 25 April 1962; "CDL Films" mailing, received 22 Sept. 1969, Wilcox Collection, CDL file; *Norwalk Hour*, 2 Feb. 1965; *Catholic Virginian*, 11 Oct. 1968.

56. CDL, Amicus curiae brief (and decision), *Jacobellis v. Ohio*, 378 U.S. 184 (1964); *CE*, 10 May 1965.

57. CDL, Amicus curiae brief; Charles Rembar, Supplemental brief in response to CDL; and decision, *Memoirs v. Massachusetts*, 383 U.S. 413 (1966).

58. *CE*, 24 March 1968; CDL, Amicus curiae brief, *Ginsberg v. New York*, 390 U.S. 629 (1968); Karen O'Connor and Lee Epstein, "Amicus Curiae Participation in U.S. Su-

preme Court Litigation: An Appraisal of Hakman's 'Folklore,'" *Law and Society Review* 16, no. 2 (1981–82): 311–21.

59. *Los Angeles Times*, 18 Dec. 1964; ibid., 30 Dec. 1964.

60. *Milwaukee Sentinel*, 13 Dec. 1965; *Washington Post*, 26 Feb. 1966; *Indianapolis Star*, 8 Feb. 1966.

61. ACLU, *By the People: Annual Report* (New York: ACLU, 1960), 13; Censorship Bulletin, June 1960; "Censorship Spreads Across U.S.," *Californian*, July 1961, 7–12; Hugh Hefner, "The Playboy Philosophy," *Playboy*, Nov. 1963, 57–58.

62. CDL flier, n.d., UAE, box 60, folder: CDL.

63. William Landau to Alan Reitman, 27 Feb. 1965, ACLU-C, box 1, folder: Laws re: Obscenity; St. Louis CDL mailing, 16 April 1964, Raymond Tucker Papers, box 14, folder: Decent Literature Commission.

64. William Landau, "Perversion for Profit," 10 March 1964, ACLU Papers, box 792, folder 11.

65. *St. Louis Post-Dispatch*, 11 March 1964; ibid., 15 April 1964; *St. Louis Globe-Democrat*, 19 Nov. 1964.

66. *Oklahoma Journal*, 9 March 1966; Untitled UPI print, dated 1967, Harry Culver Papers, box 8, folder 5; *New York Herald-Tribune*, 20 March 1968.

67. *St. Louis Review*, 21 March 1969; *St. Louis Post-Dispatch*, 15 March 1969; Jane Friedman, "Report on the National Convention of the Citizens for Decent Literature," 15 March 1969, PCOP, box 131, folder: Report; "Convention Huge Success," *NDR*, March-April 1969, 1.

68. Norman Mark, "Censorship: Fanatics and Fallacies," *Nation*, 5 July 1965, 5–7; CDL, *Printed Poison* (1965); Roberts, *The Smut Rakers*, 104.

69. *Perversion for Profit* brochure, n.d. (1963), Kinsey Institute Vertical Files; Eric Schaefer, *"Bold! Daring! Shocking! True!" A History of Exploitation Films, 1919–1959* (Durham, NC: Duke University Press, 1999), 103–19.

70. Schaefer, *"Bold! Daring! Shocking! True!"* 133; Charles Keating, "A Typical Talk," n.d. (1962), Youth Protection Committee Papers, box 2, folder: Published Material; Gauer, "A Typical CDL Talk," 14 Sept. 1962, ibid., box 2, folder: Miscellaneous.

71. *New York Herald-Tribune*, 23 Oct. 1965; *Washington Post*, 24 Oct. 1965; *Louisville Courier-Journal*, 24 Oct. 1965; "Nudist Magazines and Paperback Books Adjudged Obscene," *NDR*, March 1966, 14.

72. *Manual Enterprises v. Day*, 370 U.S. 478 (1962); CDL mailing, "Perversion for Profit," n.d. (1964), Kinsey Institute Vertical Files. Though the Manual Enterprises case had resulted in multiple opinions, Keating flatly misrepresented it; there was, in fact, a

very clear majority, as the case was decided 6–1, with two justices sitting out and only Tom Clark dissenting.

73. *Savannah News*, 13 Oct. 1965; "Hon. E. Richard Barnes' Address," *NDR*, Feb. 1966, 13; CDL mailing, 6 May 1972, UAE, box 60, folder: CDL.

74. Keating, "A Typical Talk"; CDL, "Procedures for Establishing a Citizens for Decent Literature Group in *Your* Town," n.d., Kinsey Institute Vertical Files.

4. Damning the Floodtide of Filth

1. John Stormer, *None Dare Call It Treason* (Florissant, MO: Liberty Bell Press, 1964), back cover, 226, 35, 47, 62, 220.

2. John Stormer, *The Death of a Nation* (Florissant, MO: Liberty Bell Press, 1968), 9.

3. James Pickett Wesberry, "Some Things I Have Learned in My Fight Against Obscenity," undated speech (1965), Wesberry Papers, box 10, folder 49, Mercer University Special Collections, Macon, GA.

4. Thomas Byrne Edsall, with Mary Edsall, *Chain Reaction: The Impact of Race, Rights, and Taxes in American Politics* (New York: Norton, 1991); Ronald Formisano, *Boston Against Busing: Race, Class, and Ethnicity in the 1960s and 1970s* (Chapel Hill: University of North Carolina Press, 1991); Michael Flamm, *Law and Order: Street Crime, Civil Unrest, and the Crisis of Liberalism in the 1960s* (New York: Columbia University Press, 2005); Kevin Kruse, *White Flight: Atlanta and the Making of Modern Conservatism* (Princeton, NJ: Princeton University Press, 2005); Matthew Lassiter, *The Silent Majority: Suburban Politics in the Sunbelt South* (Princeton, NJ: Princeton University Press, 2006); Donald Mathews and Jane Sherron De Hart, *Sex, Gender, and the Politics of ERA: A State and the Nation* (New York: Oxford University Press, 1990), 172; Lisa McGirr, *Suburban Warriors: The Origins of the New American Right* (Princeton, NJ: Princeton University Press, 2001); John Andrew III, *The Other Side of the Sixties: Young Americans for Freedom and the Rise of Conservative Politics* (New Brunswick, NJ: Rutgers University Press, 1997); Mary Brennan, *Turning Right in the Sixties: The Conservative Capture of the GOP* (Chapel Hill: University of North Carolina Press, 1995); Dan Carter, *The Politics of Rage: George Wallace, the Origins of the New Conservatism, and the Transformation of American Politics* (New York: Simon and Schuster, 1995); Jonathan Schoenwald, *A Time for Choosing: The Rise of Modern American Conservatism* (New York: Oxford University Press, 2001).

5. Rick Perlstein, *Nixonland: The Rise of a President and the Fracturing of America* (New York: Scribner, 2008), 113.

6. Jerome Himmelstein, *To the Right: The Transformation of American Conservatism* (Berkeley: University of California Press, 1990), 85.

7. Janice Irvine, *Talk About Sex: The Battles over Sex Education in the United States* (Berkeley: University of California Press, 2002).

8. *Arkansas Gazette*, 11 Feb. 1966.

9. Robert Mason, *Richard Nixon and the Quest for a New Majority* (Chapel Hill: University of North Carolina Press, 2004), 41, 182 (italics added).

10. M. Stanton Evans, *The Future of Conservatism: From Taft to Reagan and Beyond* (New York: Holt, Rinehart and Winston, 1968), 290; M. Stanton Evans and Margaret Moore, *The Lawbreakers: America's Number One Domestic Problem* (New Rochelle, NY: Arlington House, 1968), 15.

11. Evans and Moore, *The Lawbreakers*, 42. Earlier conservatives had dealt obliquely with the tension between their libertarianism and traditionalism, resulting in "fusionism," which attempted to remove theoretical imperfections by deigning capitalism the most moral economic system. See Himmelstein, *To the Right*, 53–59. On the key theorist of Old Right fusion see Kevin Smant, *Principles and Heresies: Frank S. Meyer and the Shaping of the American Conservative Movement* (Wilmington, DE: ISI Books, 2002).

12. Brennan, *Turning Right in the Sixties*, 119; Thomas Payne, "The 1966 Elections in the West," *Western Political Quarterly* 20, no. 2, Part 2 (1967): 517–23.

13. "Governor Says State Does Not Need New Pornography Laws," *Legislative Bulletin*, 4 Dec. 1959; Matthew Dallek, *The Right Moment: Ronald Reagan's First Victory and the Decisive Turning Point in American Politics* (New York: Free Press, 2000), 42–61.

14. Carter, *The Politics of Rage*, 205–12; Ethan Rarick, *California Rising: The Life and Times of Pat Brown* (Berkeley: University of California Press, 2005), 288–89.

15. *Los Angeles Times*, 22 April 1966 (hereafter *LAT*); ibid., 7 Oct. 1966. On the real estate industry's exploitation of racism see Kevin Fox Gotham, *Race, Real Estate, and Uneven Development: The Kansas City Experience, 1900–2000* (Albany: State University of New York Press, 2002); W. Edward Orser, *Blockbusting in Baltimore: The Edmondson Village Story* (Lexington: University Press of Kentucky, 1994).

16. Totton Anderson and Eugene Lee, "The 1966 Election in California," *Western Political Quarterly* 20, no. 2, Part 2 (1966): 535–54, quoted at 543.

17. Californians for Reagan, "A message to ALL voters," undated pamphlet (1966), California Republican Assembly Papers, box 3, folder 2, UCLA Special Collections.

18. Northern California ACLU, "Analysis of the Obscenity Initiative Sponsored by CLEAN," 7 Sept. 1966, Southern California ACLU Papers, box 135, folder: Obscenity Legislation, UCLA Special Collections.

19. *LAT*, 6 Sept. 1966; *LAT*, 2 Nov. 1966; *LAT*, 20 Sept. 1966; *LAT*, 13 Sept. 1966; William Wingfield, "California's Dirty Book Caper," *Nation*, 18 April 1966, 457; *LAT*, 12 Sept. 1966.

20. *LAT*, 27 Sept. 1966; Richard Bergholz, *LAT*, 22 Oct. 1966.

21. *LAT*, 9 Nov. 1966; Michael Paul Rogin and John Shover, *Political Change in California: Critical Elections and Social Movements, 1890–1966* (Westport, CT: Greenwood Press, 1970), 168.

22. League of Women Voters, "California Election Extra," 7 June 1966, Charles Gant California Democratic Council Papers, box 5, folder 10, UCLA Special Collections; "Spencer Williams for Attorney General," undated mailing (1966), Joseph Wyatt California Democratic Council Papers, box 12, folder 5, UCLA Special Collections; *LAT*, 22 May 1966.

23. *LAT*, 15 Jan. 1967; *LAT*, 11 Jan. 1967; *LAT*, 13 June 1968; *Los Angeles Herald Examiner*, 5 June 1969; ibid., 17 June 1969.

24. *LAT*, 17 March 1967; on Reagan's years in Sacramento see Lou Cannon, *Governor Reagan: His Rise to Power* (New York: Public Affairs, 2003).

25. News Release, 28 June 1968, Strom Thurmond Papers, box 100-11A-2689, Clemson University Special Collections, Clemson, SC; "One Minute Broadcast by Senator Strom Thurmond," 22 July 1968, ibid., box 100-11A-2782. On Thurmond see Nadine Cohodas, *Strom Thurmond and the Politics of Southern Change* (Macon, GA: Mercer University Press, 1993).

26. *Washington Sunday Star*, 9 June 1968; Liberty Lobby, "Emergency Liberty Letter Number 21," 6 July 1968, Special File Pertaining to Abe Fortas and Homer Thornberry (hereafter Fortas File), box 2, folder: Chronological File, 7/1–7/6, Lyndon B. Johnson Library. See also Liberty Lobby, "The Abe Fortas Record," Paul Porter Papers, box 1, folder: Personal Correspondence, LBJ.

27. *New York Times* (hereafter *NYT*), 28 June 1968; AFL-CIO Press release, 28 June 1968, Fortas File, box 1, folder: Chron. File, 6/13–6/25; telegram, Mike Manatos to LBJ, 29 June 1968, ibid. Johnson had befriended Fortas during their youthful New Deal days in Washington, and in many ways the president owed his political career to the justice, who several years earlier had formulated LBJ's strategy for avoiding a vote count in the notorious Texas election of 1948, which Johnson won by the likely phony "87 votes that changed history" (see Robert Caro, *The Years of Lyndon Johnson: Means of Ascent* [New York: Vintage, 1990], 368–73).

28. Fortas biographers acknowledge CDL but often treat its presence in the hearings as a deus ex machina. Bruce Allen Murphy covers the group's involvement best in *Fortas: The Rise and Ruin of a Supreme Court Justice* (New York: William Morrow,

1988), 441–62; see also Laura Kalman, *Abe Fortas: A Biography* (New Haven, CT: Yale University Press, 1990), 342–45.

29. Senate Committee on the Judiciary, *Nominations of Abe Fortas and Homer Thornberry: Hearings Before the Committee on the Judiciary* (Washington: GPO, 1968), 294, 303.

30. *Chicago's American*, 25 July 1968; "Fortas on Filth," *Strom Thurmond Reports to the People*, 5 Aug. 1968; William Buckley, "Obscenity Ruling Needs Explaining," *Washington Evening-Star*, 21 Aug. 1968; James J. Kilpatrick, "Suggestion: Let a Movie Decide Fortas' Fate," ibid., 13 Aug. 1968; I. A. Wozny to LBJ, 29 July 1968, Fortas File, box 6, folder: AF–NF 8/1–8/7; Mr. and Mrs. Armand Albertoli to LBJ, 6 Sept. 1968, ibid., box 6, folder: AF–NF 8/8–8/31.

31. *Mobile (AL) Press*, 5 Sept. 1968; *Nominations of Abe Fortas and Homer Thornberry, Part 2* (Washington: GPO, 1968); Mike Manatos to LBJ, 16 Sept. 1968, Fortas File, box 2, folder: CF 9/16–9/30.

32. "Memorandum Re the Views of Justice Fortas on Obscenity," attached to memo, Larry Temple to Barefoot Sanders, 29 July 1968, Fortas File, box 2, folder: CF 7/14–7/31; Marvin [no last name] to Larry Temple, 20 Sept. 1968, ibid., box 2, folder: CF 9/16–9/30.

33. Fortas to LBJ, 1 Oct. 1968, ibid., box 2, folder: CF 10/1–12/20; "Fortas Confirmation Defeated," *National Decency Reporter*, Sept.-Oct. 1968, 1–4.

34. *Congressional Record* 115 (28 Jan. 1969): 1996; Barry Goldwater, *The Conscience of a Conservative* (New York: Hillman, 1960), 16–17, 35; *Phoenix Gazette*, 29 March 1969; *NYT*, 2 Oct. 1969. On the election of 1960 (and for "ducks" quote) see Laura Jane Gifford, *The Center Cannot Hold: The 1960 Presidential Election and the Rise of Modern Conservatism* (DeKalb: Northern Illinois University Press, 2009); on Goldwater and the New Right see Rick Perlstein, *Before the Storm: Barry Goldwater and the Unmaking of the American Consensus* (New York: Hill and Wang, 2001).

35. *Cincinnati Enquirer*, 14 June 1969; William Lockhart to Keating, 24 June 1969, Records of the Presidential Commission on Obscenity and Pornography (hereafter PCOP), box 25, folder: Lockhart, LBJ Library.

36. Freeman Lewis to Lockhart, 18 Aug. 1969, PCOP, box 43, folder: Commission Correspondence; Keating to Lockhart, 17 Sept. 1969, PCOP, box 25, folder: Lockhart; Don Cortum to Jackson Betts, 25 Sept. 1969, attached to W. Cody Wilson to Betts, 8 Oct. 1969, PCOP, box 37, folder 1; Keating to Wilson, 17 Sept. 1969, PCOP, box 25, folder: Lockhart.

37. Otto Larsen to Keating, 15 Oct. 1969, PCOP, box 25, folder: Lockhart; Commission Minutes, 29 Oct. 1969, box 46, PCOP, folder: Full Commission Meeting.

38. Commission Progress Report, July 1969, PCOP, box 38, unlabeled folder; Lockhart to Keating, 14 Nov. 1969, PCOP, box 39, folder: Commission Correspondence.

39. Keating to Lockhart, 22 Nov. 1969, PCOP, box 39, folder: Commission Correspondence.

40. Lockhart, "Memo for File: Confidentiality," 4 Dec. 1969, PCOP, box 25, folder: Lockhart; Keating to Lockhart, 10 Jan. 1970; Lockhart to Keating, 19 Jan. 1970; and Keating to Wilson, 18 March 1970, all ibid.

41. Lockhart to Edward Elston, 17 Aug. 1970, PCOP, box 50, folder: July/Aug. 1970; *St. Louis Globe-Democrat*, 12 Aug. 1970; Commission Minutes, 11 and 12 Aug. 1970, PCOP, box 50.

42. *St. Louis Globe-Democrat*, 1 Aug. 1970; Commission Minutes, 26 and 27 Aug. 1970, PCOP, box 50; Lockhart to Keating, 27 Aug. 1970, PCOP, box 38, folder 2; *NYT*, 9 Sept. 1970.

43. *The Report of the Commission on Obscenity and Pornography* (New York: Bantam, 1970), 456, 53, 581, 610, 595.

44. *Cincinnati Enquirer*, 1 Oct. 1970; "Statement of William B. Lockhart," 1 Oct. 1970, PCOP, box 135C, folder: Press Releases; *Nashville Banner*, 17 Aug. 1970; *Fort Wayne News-Sentinel*, 16 Oct. 1970. For sympathetic coverage see *St. Louis Post-Dispatch*, 1 Oct. 1970.

45. *NYT*, 13 Sept. 1970; *Congressional Record* 116 (25 Sept. 1970): 33829–30 (hereafter *Cong. Rec.*); ibid. (28 Sept. 1970): 34012, 34016; ibid. (1 Oct. 1970): 34498.

46. *Cong. Rec.* 116 (1 Oct. 1970): 34497; ibid. (13 Oct. 1970): 36461.

47. *Cong. Rec.* 116 (13 Oct. 1970): 36459–78; ibid. (14 Oct. 1970): 37081, 37143; Richard Nixon, "Statement About the Report of the Commission on Obscenity and Pornography," 24 Oct. 1970, American Presidency Project, www.presidency.ucsb; Keating, "The Report That Shocked the Nation," *Reader's Digest*, Jan. 1971, 37–41; W. Cody Wilson, "Facts versus Fears: Why Should We Worry About Pornography?" *Annals of the American Academy of Political and Social Science* 397, no. 7 (1971): 105–17.

48. George Gallup, *The Gallup Poll: Public Opinion, 1935–1971, Vol. 3: 1959–1971* (New York: Random House, 1972), 1966, 2201; Weldon T. Johnson, "The Pornography Report: Epistemology, Methodology, and Ideology," *Duquesne Law Review* 10, no. 2 (1971): 190–219, esp. 207–10.

49. *NYT*, 8 Oct. 1970; *NYT*, 12 Oct. 1970; *NYT*, 19 Oct. 1970.

50. *Macon (GA) News*, 11 Aug. 1969; *Birmingham (AL) News*, 10 July 1969; Carter, *Politics of Rage*, 367, 386.

51. On Helms see William Link, *Righteous Warrior: Jesse Helms and the Rise of Modern Conservatism* (New York: St. Martin's, 2008).

52. Strom Thurmond to Sam Hair, 4 Dec. 1959, Strom Thurmond Papers, box 4, folder: Communications-Movies, Subject Correspondence; Thurmond, *The Faith We Have Not Kept* (San Diego: Viewpoint, 1968), 17.

53. *Strom Thurmond Reports to the People*, 7 July 1969; ibid., 19 Oct. 1970; *Cong. Rec.* 116 (13 Oct. 1970): 36474; Thurmond to Edward Kennedy, 13 Oct. 1970, Thurmond Papers, box 100-11A-3531; "Statement by Strom Thurmond," 14 Sept. 1971, ibid., box 100-11A-4063.

54. Cohodas, *Strom Thurmond and the Politics of Southern Change*, 412.

55. Whitney Strub, "Black and White and Banned All Over: Race, Censorship, and Obscenity in Postwar Memphis," *Journal of Social History* 40, no. 3 (2007): 685–715.

56. *Memphis Press-Scimitar*, 8 July 1959 (hereafter *PS*); *PS*, 2 Oct. 1963.

57. Loeb to Lynn Walker et al., 6 Nov. 1969, Henry Loeb Papers, box 67, folder: Negro Protest—Black Monday, Memphis/Shelby County Public Library; Loeb to William Simmons, 19 Jan. 1971, Loeb Papers, box 67, folder: Negro Militants; *PS*, 5 April 1968; *PS*, 8 April 1968.

58. Mr. and Mrs. Farrell Evans to Loeb, 23 Sept. 1969; Mrs. John Helton to Loeb, 1 Oct. 1969; and Loeb to Mrs. Leva Osbirn, 2 Sept. 1969, in Loeb Papers, box 76, folder: Pornography—Citizens' Letters, 1969–70.

59. *PS*, 18 Nov. 1969; *Memphis Commercial Appeal*, 16 Jan. 1968; *PS*, 16 Jan. 1968; *Commercial Appeal*, 16 July 1969.

60. Loeb to Spiro Agnew, 4 June 1970, Loeb Papers, box 3, folder: Agnew; Loeb to Stephen Bennett et al., 30 Oct. 1969, Loeb Papers, box 67, folder: Negro Protests; Robert James to Marjorie Weber, 31 July 1969, Robert James Papers, box 8, folder: Pornography/Obscenity Correspondence, Memphis/Shelby County Public Library; James to Mr. and Mrs. Russell Kirn, 4 Aug. 1969, ibid.

61. Memphis Board of Review, "Report to the Mayor and City Council," 17 Nov. 1969, Loeb Papers, box 10, file: BOR 1970; *PS*, 2 Oct. 1969.

62. Loeb to Lewie Polk, 29 June 1971, Loeb Papers, box 10, folder: Board of Review 1971.

63. Loeb to Polk and George Morrow, 19 March 1970, Loeb Papers, box 10, folder: Board of Review, 1970.

64. Jefferson Cowie, "Nixon's Class Struggle: Romancing the New Right Worker, 1969–1973," *Labor History* 43, no. 3 (2002): 257–83; Kimberly Morgan, "A Child of the Sixties: The Great Society, the New Right, and the Politics of Federal Child Care," *Journal of Policy History* 13, no. 2 (2001): 215–50; Dean Kotlowski, *Nixon's Civil Rights: Politics, Principles, and Policy* (Cambridge, MA: Harvard University Press, 2001).

65. H. R. Haldeman, *The Haldeman Diaries: Inside the Nixon White House* (New York: Putnam, 1994), 181 (entry for 13 July 1970).

66. Richard Nixon, handwritten note on Alexander Butterfield's Memorandum for the President, 12 March 1969, box 1, folder: Presidential Handwriting, March 1–15, White House Special Files-Staff Members and Office Files-Presidential Office Files, Richard Nixon Archives, National Archives and Records Administration, College Park, MD; Haldeman, *The Haldeman Diaries*, 43 (28 March 1969); Nixon, "Special Message to the Congress on Obscene and Pornographic Materials," 2 May 1969, American Presidency Project, www.presidency.ucsb. Thanks to Rick Perlstein for the Haldeman citation.

67. Nixon, "Annual Message to the Congress on the State of the Union," 22 Jan. 1970; Jeff Donfeld to Bud Krogh, 11 March 1970, box 16, folder: Obscenity and Pornography, Bill Krogh Papers, Nixon Archives; Nixon, "Remarks to Newsmen in Denver, Colorado," 3 Aug. 1970; Nixon, "Remarks in Kansas City, Missouri," 19 Oct. 1970; Nixon, "Special Message to Congress Resubmitting Legislative Proposals," 26 Jan. 1971, all at American Presidency Project, www.presidency.ucsb.

68. Nixon, "Statement About the Report of the Commission on Obscenity and Pornography," 24 Oct. 1970, ibid.; *NYT*, 23 Aug. 1970; Winton Blount, "Let's Put the Smut Merchants Out of Business," *Nation's Business*, Sept. 1971, 34–39.

69. Bud Krogh to John Ehrlichman, 10 June 1970, box 16, folder: Obscenity & Pornography, Krogh Papers, Nixon Archives.

70. H. R. Haldeman to Pat Buchanan, 7 Sept. 1970, box 1, folder: 1965–1970, FG 95, White House Central Files-Subject Files, Nixon Archives; John Dean to Larry Higby, 18 Sept. 1970, box 52, folder: Obscenity Com. 2, John Dean Papers, Nixon Archives; Geoff Shepard to Richard Nixon, 11 July 1973, box 28, file: PU 2–6, White House Special Files—PU, Nixon Archives.

71. *Cain v. Kentucky*, 397 U.S. 319 (1970); *Walker v. Ohio*, 398 U.S. 434 (1970).

72. O. K. Armstrong, "The Problems of Pornography," *American Legion Magazine*, Aug. 1969, 22–25, 53–57; *Washington Post*, 15 May 1969; "Communists Are Right About Some Things," *Christianity Today*, 6 June 1969, 26–27; "Obscenity Report and Personal Response," *America*, 7 Nov. 1970, 366; Gerard Reedy, "That Obscenity Report!" ibid., 371–73.

5. The Permissive Society

1. Boris Sokoloff, *The Permissive Society* (New Rochelle, NY: Arlington House, 1971), 5.

2. Leonard Leff and Jerold Simmons, *The Dame in the Kimono: Hollywood, Censorship, and the Production Code from the 1920s to the 1960s* (New York: Grove Weidenfeld, 1990), 250–66; Jon Lewis, *Hollywood v. Hard Core: How the Struggle over Censorship Saved the Modern Film Industry* (New York: New York University Press, 2000).

3. Richard Gilman, "There's a Wave of Pornography/Obscenity/Sexual Expression," *New York Times Magazine*, 8 Sept. 1966, 82; Maryland Board of Censors Minutes, 28 March and 11 Oct. 1967, Board of Censors Records, box 11, Maryland State Archives, Annapolis; *New York Times* (hereafter *NYT*), 19 Jan. 1968; ibid., 30 Sept. 1969.

4. Todd Gitlin, *The Sixties: Years of Hope, Days of Rage* (New York: Bantam, 1987), 209. On the sexual revolution see John Heidenry, *What Wild Ecstasy: The Rise and Fall of the Sexual Revolution* (New York: Simon and Schuster, 1997); Beth Bailey, *Sex in the Heartland* (Cambridge, MA: Harvard University Press, 1999); David Allyn, *Make Love, Not War: The Sexual Revolution, an Unfettered History* (Boston: Little, Brown, 2000). On the New Left see James Miller, *"Democracy Is in the Streets": From Port Huron to the Siege of Chicago* (New York: Simon and Schuster, 1987). On the counterculture see Peter Braunstein and Michael William Doyle, eds., *Imagine Nation: The American Counterculture of the 1960s and '70s* (New York: Routledge, 2002).

5. Tom Brom, "Deep Throat," *Dragonseed*, Sept. 1972, 9; Kenneth Turan and Stephen Zito, *Sinema: American Pornographic Films and the People Who Make Them* (New York: Praeger, 1974), 105; Joseph Duong, "Hardcore Politics," in *Sex Scene: Media and the Sexual Revolution*, ed. Eric Schaefer (Durham, NC: Duke University Press, forthcoming); Elena Gorfinkel, "Wet Dreams: Erotic Film Festivals of the Early 1970s and the Utopian Sexual Public Sphere," *Framework* 47, no. 2 (2006): 59–86.

6. "Sex and the Arts," *Newsweek*, 14 March 1969, 67–70; "Sex as a Spectator Sport," *Time*, 11 July 1969, 61–66; "Sex, Shock and Sensuality," *Life*, 4 April 1969, 22–35; Elana Levine, *Wallowing in Sex: The New Sexual Culture of 1970s American Television* (Durham, NC: Duke University Press, 2007). On the media mainstreaming of the sexual revolution see also Rick Perlstein, *Nixonland: The Rise of a President and the Fracturing of America* (New York: Scribner, 2008), 401–11.

7. *Dallas Morning-News*, 9 April 1969; *Variety*, 23 July 1969; *Catholic Film Newsletter*, 15 March 1969. The first three films were *Last Summer*, *If . . .*, and *Laughter in the Dark*. The Office of Motion Pictures was the weakened remnant of the Legion of Decency.

8. On the history of Mundt's bill see Board of Directors to Office, with attachments, 19 Feb. 1965, Southern California ACLU Papers, box 115, folder: Censorship Committee, UCLA Special Collections; S. 309, *Congressional Record* (hereafter *Cong. Rec.*) 112 (30 June 1966): 14769 (the bill was initially introduced in 1965 but left hanging when the session ended); H.R. 10347, *Cong. Rec.* 113 (7 Aug. 1967): 21522.

9. Committee on Education and Labor, *Creating a Commission on Obscenity and Pornography: Hearing Before the Select Subcommittee on Education*, (Washington: GPO, 1967), 15–16; *Cong. Rec.* 113 (7 Aug. 1967): 21524.

10. "ACLU Position," 19 Feb. 1965, in Board of Directors to Office, So. Cal. ACLU Papers; *Creating a Commission on Obscenity and Pornography*, 79, 86–88; *Variety*, 27 Sept. 1967.

11. Jim Gaither to Joe Califano, 24 April 1967, White House Central Files (hereafter WHCF), box 373, folder: FG619, Lyndon Johnson Library, Austin, TX; Handwritten addendum to Gaither memo, no author or date; Ernest Goldstein to LBJ, 1 March 1968, ibid.

12. E. Ernest Goldstein to LBJ, 21 Nov. 1967, WHCF, "Citizens, D" Name File.

13. Robert McClure to Clifford Forster, 31 March 1953, American Civil Liberties Union Papers, box 766, folder 18, Seeley G. Mudd Library, Princeton University; William Lockhart and Robert McClure, "Censorship of Obscenity: The Developing Constitutional Standards," *Minnesota Law Review* 45, no. 5 (1960): 5–121, quoted at 26.

14. Legal Panel to Commission, 6 Nov. 1968, Presidential Commission on Obscenity and Pornography Records (hereafter PCOP), box 131, folder: Legal Panel, LBJ; see also Elizabeth Alison Smith, "Charged with Sexuality: Feminism, Liberalism, and Pornography, 1970–1982" (PhD diss., University of Pennsylvania, 1990), 97–98.

15. Weldon Johnson to Commission Staff, 15 Sept. 1969, PCOP, box 68, folder: Memo: Loneliness.

16. Morton Hill, "Separate Remarks," in Commission Progress Report, July 1969, PCOP, 21, box 38, untitled folder; "Response to Separate Remarks by Commissioner Morton Hill," Progress Report, 25–26.

17. Lloyd Meeds to W. Cody Wilson, 12 Aug. 1969, and Thomas Downing to Wilson, 12 Aug. 1969, PCOP, box 38, untitled folder, LBJ Library; Robert Cairns, James Paul, and Julius Wishner, "Sex Censorship: The Assumptions of Anti-Obscenity Laws and the Empirical Evidence," *Minnesota Law Review* 46, no. 6 (1962): 1009–41, quoted at 1040; J. Edgar Hoover, "Sex Books and Rape: FBI Chief Sees Close Links," *U.S. News & World Report*, 11 March 1968, 14; Paul Gebhard et al., *Sex Offenders: An Analysis of Types* (New York: Harper and Row and Paul Hoeber, 1965), 678, 404.

18. Eugene Levitt and John Paul Brady, "Sexual Preferences in Young Adult Males and Some Correlates," *Journal of Clinical Psychology* 21, no. 4 (1965): 347–54; Leon Jakobovits, "Evaluational Reactions to Erotic Literature," *Psychological Reports* 16, no. 1 (1965): 985–94; N. McConaghy, "Penile Volume Change to Moving Pictures of Male and Female Nudes in Heterosexual and Homosexual Males," *Behaviour Research and Therapy* 5, no. 1 (1967): 43–48; Eugene Levitt and Roger Hinesley, "Some Factors in the Valences of Erotic Visual Stimuli," *Journal of Sex Research* 3, no. 1 (1969): 63–68; Rosalind Dymond Cartwright et al., "Effect of an Erotic Movie on the Sleep and Dreams of Young Men," *Archives of General Psychiatry* 20, no. 3 (1969): 262–71.

19. Eugene Levitt, "Pornography: Some New Perspectives on an Old Problem," *Journal of Sex Research* 5, no. 4 (1969): 247–59; "What Should Parents Do When They Find Their Children in Possession of Pornographic Material?" *Medical Aspects of Human Sexuality* 3, no. 3 (1969): 6–12; "Pornography and Antisocial Behavior," *School and Society*, Feb. 1970, 76–78.

20. "COOP Progress Report," *Intellectual Freedom Newsletter*, Sept. 1969, 81.

21. Lockhart to Wilson, n.d. (Feb. 1969), PCOP, box 24, folder: White House.

22. Jules Witcover, "Civil War over Smut," *Nation*, 11 May 1970, 552; *San Francisco Examiner*, 14 May 1970.

23. *Report of the Commission on Obscenity and Pornography* (New York: Bantam, 1970), 4.

24. Ibid., 24–25, 255, 53, 311, 54.

25. Ibid., 63–68, 446–48.

26. Ibid., 54. On consent see Pamela Haag, *Consent: Sexual Rights and the Transformation of American Liberalism* (Ithaca, NY: Cornell University Press, 1999).

27. *San Francisco Chronicle*, 14 June 1969; AMA Council on Mental Health, "Statement on Obscenity and Pornography," 5 June 1970, PCOP, box 24, folder: Solicited Info.

28. New Jersey Commission to Study Obscenity and Depravity in Public Media, *Report to the Governor and Legislature* (n.p., 1970), 42–43; San Francisco Committee on Crime, *A Report on Non-victim Crime in San Francisco, Part II: Sexual Conduct, Gambling, Pornography* (n.p., 1971), 57.

29. *Hayse v. Van Hoomissen*, 321 F. Supp. 642 (1970); Paul Meyer and Daniel Seifer, "Censorship in Oregon: New Developments in an Old Enterprise," *Oregon Law Review* 51 (1972): 537–52.

30. Michael Goldstein et al., "Exposure to Pornography and Sexual Behavior in Deviant and Normal Groups," *Technical Report of the Commission on Obscenity and Pornography*, vol. 7, *Erotica and Antisocial Behavior* (Washington: GPO, 1971–), 1–89; C. Eugene Walker, "Erotic Stimuli and the Aggressive Sexual Offender," ibid., 91–147; Robert Cook and Robert Fosen, "Pornography and the Sex Offender," ibid., 149–62; Weldon Johnson et al., "Sex Offenders' Experience with Erotica," ibid., 163–71; Richard Ben-Veniste, "Pornography and Sex Crime: The Danish Experience," ibid., 245–61; James Howard et al., "Effects of Exposure to Pornography," *Technical Report of the Commission on Obscenity and Pornography*, vol. 8, *Erotica and Social Behavior*, 97–132; Terrence Thornberry and Robert Silverman, "Exposure to Pornography and Juvenile Delinquency," *Technical Report of the Commission on Obscenity and Pornography*, vol. 1, *Preliminary Studies*, 175–79.

31. Louis Zurcher and R. George Kirkpatrick, *Citizens for Decency: Antipornography Crusades as Status Defense* (Austin: University of Texas Press, 1976); Jon Van Til, *Citi-*

zens for Decency review, *Contemporary Sociology* 7, no. 5 (1978): 634–35. See also Michael Goldstein and Harold Sanford Kant, *Pornography and Sexual Deviance* (Berkeley: University of California Press, 1973); and *Journal of Social Issues* 29, no. 3, edited by W. Cody Wilson (1973).

32. Howard Whitman, "Smut: The Poison That Preys on Our Children," *Good House-keeping*, Nov. 1961, 64–65, 101–4, 173–75; Dr. Joyce Brothers, "What Women Think of Pornography," *Good Housekeeping*, May 1970, 56, 58; "Our Son Was Reading Pornography," ibid., March 1972, 20–34.

33. *Karalexis v. Byrne*, 306 F. Supp. 1363 (1969).

34. *U.S. v. Various Articles*, 315 F. Supp. 191 (1970); *U.S. v. Dellapia*, 433 F.2d 1252 (1970).

35. *Art Films International v. Vavrek*, U.S. District Court, Dist. of Minnesota (1970), Stanley Fleishman Papers, box 599, folder: Aquedalo, UCLA Special Collections; *U.S. v. "Language of Love,"* 432 F.2d 705 (1970); *U.S. v. Stewart*, 336 F. Supp. 299 (1971).

36. *U.S. v. 37 Photographs*, 402 U.S. 363 (1971); *U.S. v. Reidel*, 402 U.S. 351 (1971); *Grove Press v. Maryland*, 401 U.S. 480 (1971); "The Douglas Case (Cont'd.)," *Time*, 11 May 1970, 78; *Bloss v. Michigan*, 402 U.S. 938 (1971); *Burgin v. South Carolina*, 404 U.S. 806 (1971); *Rabe v. Washington*, 405 U.S. 313 (1972); *Cohen v. California*, 403 U.S. 15 (1971); *Kois v. Wisconsin*, 408 U.S. 229 (1972); *State v. Hartstein*, 469 S.W.2d 329 (1970), reversed, *Hartstein v. Missouri*, 404 U.S. 988 (1971).

37. The history of the underground porn market remains a murky topic with relatively little scholarship to illuminate it. On porn films see Al Di Lauro and Gerald Rabkin, *Dirty Movies: An Illustrated History of the Stag Film, 1915–1970* (New York: Chelsea House, 1976); and Joseph Slade, "Eroticism and Technological Regression: The Stag Film," *History and Technology* 22, no. 1 (2006): 27–52; on print media in nineteenth-century England see Lisa Sigel, *Governing Pleasures: Pornography and Social Change in England, 1815–1914* (New Brunswick, NJ: Rutgers University Press, 2002). The best discussion of the midcentury American porn underground appears in Eric Schlosser, *Reefer Madness: Sex, Drugs, and Cheap Labor in the American Black Market* (Boston: Houghton Mifflin, 2003), 109–210.

38. *My Name Is Bonnie* (City of Industry: Collector's Publications, 1968), H. Lynn Womack Papers, box 1, folder 29, Division of Rare and Manuscript Collections, Cornell University; *Intercourse* (City of Industry: Collector's Publications, 1968), i, PCOP, box 10.

39. Donald Gilmore, *Sex, Censorship, and Pornography* (San Diego: Greenleaf, 1969); Dale Armstrong mailing, 7 Nov. 1970, Womack Papers, box 2, folder 70.

40. *NYT*, 9 June 1969; see also Eithne Johnson, "The 'Coloscopic' Film and the 'Beaver' Film: Scientific and Pornographic Scenes of Female Sexual Responsiveness," in

Swinging Single: Representing Sexuality in the 1960s, ed. Hilary Radner and Moya Luckett (Minneapolis: University of Minnesota Press, 1999), 301–26; *San Francisco Chronicle*, 9 June 1969; Eric Schaefer, "Gauging a Revolution: 16mm Film and the Rise of the Pornographic Feature," *Cinema Journal* 41, no. 3 (2002): 3–26.

41. Adult Film Association of America Newsletter, 15 May 1970, PCOP, box 62, folder: AFAA.

42. *Kansas City Star*, 25 May 1970; *San Francisco Chronicle*, 16 Nov. 1970; *Cincinnati Enquirer*, 1 July 1969; ibid., 23 Nov. 1970; *Cincinnati Post and Times-Star*, 30 April 1971; *Variety*, 12 Aug. 1970; *Des Moines Register*, 15 April 1973; *NYT*, 11 March 1973; "List of Films Submitted," 31 Jan. 1973, Maryland Board of Censors Records, box 1, folder: Peep Shows List.

43. *Variety*, 15 April 1970; ibid., 29 April 1970; ibid., 22 Dec. 1971; ibid., 22 April 1970; ibid., 22 April 1970.

44. *NYT*, 10 May 1970; Arthur Knight, "Dirty Movies," *Saturday Review*, 30 Sept. 1972, 84; *Wall Street Journal*, 15 Sept. 1972.

45. *Mona* (Howard Ziehm, 1970); *San Francisco Chronicle*, 16 Nov. 1970.

46. *Deep Throat* (Gerard Damiano, 1972).

47. *NYT*, 21 Jan. 1973; Clive Barnes, "Sex Shockers: Hard Porno-Cash," *Vogue*, April 1973, 20; Herbert Gans, "*Deep Throat*: The Pornographic Film Goes Public," *Social Policy*, July/Aug. 1973, 119–21.

48. Ralph Blumenthal, "Porno Chic," *NYT Magazine*, 2 March 1973, 28–34; Bruce Williamson, "Porno Chic," *Playboy*, Aug. 1973, 132–37, 153–61; *Film Comment* 9, no. 1 (1973); "School for Scandal," *Newsweek*, 15 Oct. 1973, 79–80; Paul Bryan, Affidavit, n.d. (1973), Fleishman Papers, box 24, folder: Sun Film Group; "Pornography: The Vice Goes on Ice," *Newsweek*, 23 July 1973, 47.

49. Carolyn See, *Blue Money: Pornography and the Pornographers* (New York: David McKay, 1974), 234, 126; Turan and Zito, *Sinema*, 115–16. For a more grimly realistic portrayal of Holmes see the documentary film *Wadd: The Life and Times of John C. Holmes* (Wesley Emerson, 1998).

50. Gerald Ford, "House Floor Speech: Impeach Justice Douglas," 15 April 1970, box D29, Gerald R. Ford Congressional Papers, Gerald R. Ford Library, available at www.ford.utexas.edu/library/speeches/700415a.htm.

51. The Burger Court's conservatism was, however, a far less radical philosophical overhauling of Warren Court liberalism than contemporary observers expected. See the essays—summarized by the subtitle—in Vincent Blasi, ed., *The Burger Court: The Counter-Revolution That Wasn't* (New Haven, CT: Yale University Press, 1983).

52. *U.S. v. Orito*, 413 U.S. 139 (1973); *U.S. v. 12 200-Ft. Reels of Film*, 413 U.S. 123 (1973); *Paris Adult Theatre I v. Slaton*, 413 U.S. 49 (1973).

53. *Kaplan v. California*, 413 U.S. 115 (1973).

54. Bob Woodward and Scott Armstrong, *The Brethren: Inside the Supreme Court* (New York: Simon and Schuster, 1979), 203, 199.

55. *Miller v. California*, 413 U.S. 15 (1973); Woodward and Armstrong, *The Brethren*, 252.

56. *New Orleans States-Item*, 22 June 1973; Charles Keating, "Green Light to Combat Smut," *Reader's Digest*, Jan. 1974, 147–50; *NYT*, 5 Aug. 1973.

57. *New Orleans Times-Picayune*, 28 June 1973; *Richmond Times-Dispatch*, 29 June 1973; Sol Goodman to Merchants of the City of Hopewell, 25 June 1973, ACLU Papers, box 1545, folder: Miller; W. B. Porter to All Distributors of Reading Materials, 1 Oct. 1973, ibid.

58. *Variety*, 19 March 1975; *Warner Bros. v. Nichols*, U.S. District Court, Southern Dist. of Mississippi (1974), Fleishman Papers, box 495, folder: AFAA; *Jenkins v. State*, 230 Ga. 726 (1973); "Pornography: The Vice Goes on Ice," *Newsweek*, 23 July 1973, 45.

59. *San Francisco Chronicle*, 18 July 1973.

60. *Jenkins v. Georgia*, 418 U.S. 153 (1974).

61. *NYT*, 26 Nov. 1974; Kenneth Samuelson to David Preller, 13 Jan. 1976, Maryland Board of Censors Records, box 27, folder: North Cinema Theatre.

62. *Los Angeles Times*, 30 May 1973; unidentified news clipping, John Downing Weaver Collection of Los Angeles Ephemera, box 16, folder: City Attorney, UCLA Special Collections.

63. Stephen Ziplow, *The Film Maker's Guide to Pornography* (New York: Drake, 1977), 123; *NYT*, 17 May 1977; Obscenity Law Project, "An Empirical Inquiry into the Effects of *Miller v. California* on the Control of Obscenity," *New York University Law Review* 52 (1977): 810–939, quoted at 810.

64. *Detroit Free Press*, 21 June 1972; William Toner, *Regulating Sex Businesses* (Chicago: American Society of Planning Officials, 1977), 3–4.

65. Boston City Council Minutes, 28 April 1969 and 19 May 1969, Boston City Archives; *NYT*, 9 June 1974.

66. *Los Angeles Times*, 31 May 1977; *U.S. v. American Mini Theatres*, 427 U.S. 50 (1976); *Kansas City Star*, 10 Dec. 1976; *Des Moines Register*, 29 June 1976; ibid., 16 Dec. 1976; Toner, *Regulating Sex Businesses*, 11; *NYT*, 24 Feb. 1978.

67. On CDL's decline see Whitney Strub, "Perversion for Profit: Citizens for Decent Literature and the Arousal of an Antiporn Public in the 1960s," *Journal of the History of Sexuality* 15, no. 2 (2006): 287–91.

68. *Cong. Rec.* 116 (13 Oct. 1970): 36474; Alan Reitman to Larry Speiser, 17 Nov. 1970, ACLU Papers, box 796, folder 23; National Book Committee, Press Release, 21 Jan. 1971, ACLU Papers, box 796, folder 28.

69. *NYT*, 12 Oct. 1972.

70. The Democratic and Republican platforms of 1972 are both available at the American Presidency Project, www.presidency.ucsb.edu. Geoff Shepard to Don Santarelli, 18 Jan. 1972, box 28, folder PU 2–6, WHSF-PU, Richard Nixon Archives, National Archives and Records Administration, College Park, MD.

71. Earl Kemp, ed., *Illustrated Presidential Report of the Commission on Obscenity and Pornography* (San Diego: Greenleaf, 1970), 4.

72. Frank Moore to Jimmy Carter, 25 Oct. 1973, Legal Division Subject Files, Records of the Governor's Office, box 23, folder: Literature Commission, Georgia State Archives, Morrow. Ultimately, the Carter administration killed the State Literature Commission through attrition; when two of the three members died, leaving James Wesberry the sole remaining member, Carter declined to appoint replacements, and the attorney general informed Wesberry that two members were required to constitute a quorum. Arthur Bolton to James Wesberry, 10 Dec. 1973, Records of the Attorney General's Office, box 9, folder: Correspondence Files, Georgia State Archives, Morrow.

73. Governor's Office Press Release, 15 Sept. 1972, Legal Division Subject Files, Records of the Governor's Office, box 23, folder: Literature Commission, Georgia State Archives, Morrow. On Carter's dubious 1970 campaign techniques see Randy Sanders, "'The Sad Duty of Politics': Jimmy Carter and the Issue of Race in His 1970 Gubernatorial Campaign," *Georgia Historical Quarterly* 76, no. 3 (1992): 612–38.

74. Robert Scheer, "Playboy Interview: Jimmy Carter," *Playboy*, Nov. 1976, 86, 70, 68.

75. *Washington Post*, 7 Feb. 1978; *Memphis Press-Scimitar*, 4 Feb. 1977; W. J. Michael Cody, Motion to Dismiss Indictment, *U.S. v. DeSalvo*, 22 Aug. 1979, U.S. District Court for the Western District of Tennessee Case Files, box 7, folder: CR 75-90, #2, National Archives and Records Administration, Southeast Branch, East Point, GA; Cody, Motion to Dismiss Indictment, *U.S. v. Carter*, 26 Feb. 1979, ibid., box 1, folder: CR 73-27.

76. *Washington Post*, 15 Feb. 1980.

6. Resurrecting Moralism

1. Americans for Moral Decency flyer, n.d. (1960s), Youth Protection Committee Records, box 2, folder: Misc., Utah Historical Society, Salt Lake City; Citizens for Happy Family Living, "Statement of Purpose," 30 June 1966, ibid.

2. Robert William Fogel, *The Fourth Great Awakening and the Future of Egalitarianism* (Chicago: University of Chicago Press, 2000); Donald Miller, *Reinventing American Protestantism: Christianity in the New Millennium* (Berkeley: University of California Press, 1997), 2. On the Christian Right see also Robert Liebman and Robert Wuthnow, eds., *The New Christian Right* (New York: Aldine, 1983); Steve Bruce, *The Rise and Fall of the New Christian Right* (Oxford: Clarendon Press, 1988); Matthew Moen, *The Transformation of the Christian Right* (Tuscaloosa: University of Alabama Press, 1992); Michael Lienesch, *Redeeming America: Piety and Politics in the New Christian Right* (Chapel Hill: University of North Carolina Press, 1993); William Martin, *With God on Our Side: The Rise of the Religious Right in America* (New York: Broadway, 1996).

3. "Southern States," *Newsletter for Intellectual Freedom*, Jan. 1971, 5; Utah County Council for Better Movies and Literature Newsletter, Jan. 1973, Youth Protection Committee Records, box 1, folder: Newsletter.

4. Legal Defense Fund for Religious Freedom mailing, 30 May 1973, Stanley Fleishman Papers, box 393, file: AFAA-CDL, UCLA Special Collections. On American familial fears of the 1970s see Philip Jenkins, *Decade of Nightmares: The End of the Sixties and the Making of Eighties America* (New York: Oxford University Press, 2006); Natasha Zaretsky, *No Direction Home: The American Family and the Fear of National Decline, 1968–1980* (Chapel Hill: University of North Carolina Press, 2007); Gillian Frank, "Save Our Children: The Sexual Politics of Child Protection in the United States, 1965–1990" (PhD diss., Brown University, 2009).

5. William Rusher, *The Making of a New Majority Party* (New York: Sheed and Ward, 1975), 216; Marabel Morgan, *The Total Woman* (Old Tappan, NJ: Revell, 1973); Tim and Beverly LaHaye, *The Act of Marriage: The Beauty of Sexual Love* (Grand Rapids: Zondervan, 1976), 11, 296.

6. C. Brant Short, *Ronald Reagan and the Public Lands: America's Conservation Debate, 1979–1984* (College Station: Texas A&M University Press, 1989), 71.

7. James Findlay, *Church People in the Struggle: The National Council of Churches and the Black Freedom Movement, 1950–1970* (New York: Oxford University Press, 1993); Mark Hulsether, *Building a Protestant Left: Christianity and Crisis Magazine, 1941–1993* (Knoxville: University of Tennessee Press, 1999); Francine du Plessix Gray, *Divine Disobedience: Profiles in Catholic Radicalism* (New York: Knopf, 1970).

8. "The Temptations of Pornography," *Christian Century*, 11 Nov. 1970, 1339; "Obscenity Report and Personal Response," *America*, 7 Nov. 1970, 366; Gerard Reedy, "That Obscenity Report!" *America*, 7 Nov. 1970, 373; "Platform for Permissiveness," *Christianity Today*, 23 Oct. 1970, 27. On the magazine's history see Mark Toulouse, "*Christianity*

Today and American Public Life: A Case Study," *Journal of Church and State* 35, no. 2 (1993): 241–84.

9. James Wall, "Two Payments for Freedom," *Christian Century*, 7–14 July 1976, 619; Trevor Beeson, "Outcry over Pornographic Film on Jesus," ibid., 27 Oct. 1976, 934–36; "Catharsis or Corruption?" *Christianity Today*, 22 Nov. 1974, 201; Robert Cleath, "Pornography: Purulent Infection," ibid., 10 Oct. 1975, 21–22.

10. "Mailing List for CDML," n.d. (1974), Wilcox Collection, Ephemeral Material, University of Kansas Special Collections, Lawrence; Neil Gallagher to local retailers, 10 Jan. 1974, ibid; "Victory in Victoria," *Christianity Today*, 1 Feb. 1974, 530; Gallagher, *How to Stop the Porno Plague* (Minneapolis: Bethany Fellowship, 1977), 155.

11. *La Crosse (WI) Tribune*, 3 April 1977; ibid., 5 Oct. 1977; Proposed Ordinance (n.d.), Dale Kendrick La Crosse Pornography Ordinance Compiled Papers, 1977–1980, box 1, folder 2, University of Wisconsin–La Crosse Special Collections.

12. *Good News for Neighbors*, n.d., Kendrick Papers, box 1, folder 2; *La Crosse (WI) Tribune*, 26 March 1978; ibid., 12 March 1978.

13. *UW-La Crosse Racquet*, undated clipping, Kendrick Papers, box 1, folder 1; *La Crosse (WI) Tribune*, 1 April 1978; John Jacobson to Hal Scheie, n.d. (1978), Kendrick Papers, box 1, folder 2; *La Crosse (WI) Tribune*, 5 April 1978; *Gastonia Gazette*, 5 April 1978.

14. *La Crosse (WI) Tribune*, 19 Jan. 1980.

15. "MM Man of the Month," *Morality in Media Newsletter*, Nov. 1977, 4.

16. *Variety*, 20 Oct. 1976; *Washington Post*, 10 Dec. 1976; *Memphis Commercial Appeal*, 5 March 1978; Transcript, *U.S. v. Peraino* (1978), CR 75–91, U.S. District Court of Western Tennessee, box 7, National Archives and Record Administration, Southeast Branch, East Point, GA; *Issues and Answers: Pornography*, undated pamphlet (1967), Christian Life Commission Publications and Promotional Material, box 5, folder 3, Southern Baptist Convention Historical Library and Archives, Nashville, TN; Southern Baptist Convention, "Resolution on Pornography," June 1978, www.sbc.net/resolutions.

17. Robert Scheer, "Playboy Interview: Jimmy Carter," *Playboy*, Nov. 1976, 86, 84; Andrew Flint and Joy Porter, "Jimmy Carter: The Re-emergence of Faith-Based Politics and the Abortion Issue," *Presidential Studies Quarterly* 35, no. 1 (2005): 28–51.

18. Southern Baptist Convention [hereafter SBC], "Resolution on Abortion," June 1971; SBC, "Resolution on Abortion and Sanctity of Human Life," June 1974; SBC, "Resolution on Abortion," June 1980, all at www.sbc.net/resolutions. Abortion has generated a massive bibliography. Some key texts that address it in the context of religion, politics, and the New Right include Rosalind Pollak Petchesky, *Abortion and Women's Right: The State, Sexuality, and Reproductive Freedom* (Boston: Northeastern Univer-

sity Press, 1984); Kristin Luker, *Abortion and the Politics of Motherhood* (Berkeley: University of California Press, 1984); William Saletan, *Bearing Right: How Conservatives Won the Abortion War* (Berkeley: University of California Press, 2004).

19. Jane Mansbridge, *Why We Lost the ERA* (Chicago: University of Chicago Press, 1986); Donald Mathews and Jane Sherron De Hart, *Sex, Gender, and the Politics of ERA: A State and the Nation* (New York, 1990); Donald Critchlow, *Phyllis Schlafly and Grassroots Conservatism: A Woman's Crusade* (Princeton, NJ: Princeton University Press, 2005), 212–42; Martin, *With God on Our Side*, 163–67.

20. Fred Fejes, *Gay Rights and Moral Panic: The Origins of America's Debate on Homosexuality* (New York: Palgrave Macmillan, 2008); Anita Bryant, *The Anita Bryant Story: The Survival of Our Nation's Families and the Threat of Militant Homosexuality* (Old Tappan, NJ: Revell, 1977); William Turner, "Mirror Images: Lesbian/Gay Civil Rights in the Carter and Reagan Administrations," in *Creating Change: Sexuality, Public Policy, and Civil Rights*, ed. John D'Emilio, William B. Turner, and Urvashi Vaid (New York: St. Martin's, 2000), 3–28.

21. Richard Viguerie, *The New Right: We're Ready to Lead* (Falls Church, VA: Viguerie, 1980), 156.

22. Martin, *With God on Our Side*, 57, 68–69; *La Crosse (WI) Tribune*, 23 July 1978.

23. Robert Liebman, "Mobilizing the Moral Majority," in Liebman and Wuthnow, *The New Christian Right*, 50–73.

24. Jerry Falwell, *Listen, America!* (New York: Doubleday, 1980), 200, 201; Charles Keating, "How to Clean Up America by Eliminating Pornography—Step 2," in *How to Clean Up America*, ed. Jerry Falwell (Washington: Moral Majority, 1981), 17, 19.

25. Tim LaHaye, *The Battle for the Public Schools* (Old Tappan, NJ: Revell, 1983), 136, 145; Tim LaHaye, *The Battle for the Family* (Old Tappan, NJ: Revell, 1982), 73, 18; Tim LaHaye, *The Battle for the Mind* (Old Tappan, NJ: Revell, 1980), 20, 21.

26. Murray Friedman, *The Neoconservative Revolution: Jewish Intellectuals and the Shaping of Public Policy* (Cambridge, UK: Cambridge University Press, 2005), 121. See also Peter Steinfels, *The Neoconservatives: The Men Who Are Changing America's Politics* (New York: Simon and Schuster, 1979).

27. Irving Kristol, *On the Democratic Idea in America* (New York: Harper and Row, 1972), 43, 42, vii–viii.

28. Irving Kristol, *Two Cheers for Capitalism* (New York: Basic Books, 1978); Viguerie, *The New Right*, 16.

29. Falwell, *Listen, America!* 13, 203. On anti-Semitism in the Christian wing of the New Right—something in which Falwell quite often took part—see Friedman, *The Neoconservative Revolution*, 205–22.

30. Patrick Allit, *Catholic Intellectuals and Conservative Politics in America, 1950–1985* (Ithaca, NY: Cornell University Press, 1993), 140; David Brudnoy, "Comstock's Nemesis," *National Review*, 24 Sept. 1971, 1064–65; "Support Your Local Police," ibid., 20 July 1973, 770–72; "Topsy-Turvy," ibid., 29 Aug. 1986, 54–55. See also D. Keith Mano, "The Gimlet Eye," ibid., 19 Dec. 1975, 1480; M. J. Sobran Jr., "I Say Lock 'em Up, Spank Them, and Send Them Home," ibid., 24 June 1977, 712–13, 738.

31. David Pietrusza, "Government Pays to Publish Porno Book," *Conservative Digest*, May 1978, 47.

32. Nicol Rae, *The Decline and Fall of Liberal Republicans: From 1952 to the Present* (New York: Oxford University Press, 1989), 78; Martin, *With God on Our Side*, 208; Viguerie, *The New Right*, 1.

33. "The New Right: A Special Report," *Conservative Digest*, June 1979, 10; Alan Crawford, *Thunder on the Right: The "New Right" and the Politics of Resentment* (New York: Pantheon, 1980), 215–16; Short, *Ronald Reagan and the Public Lands*, 55–80; Martin, *With God on Our Side*, 248–57. On Joseph Coors see Russ Bellant, *The Coors Connection: How Coors Family Philanthropy Undermines Democratic Pluralism* (Boston: South End Press, 1992).

34. Moen, *The Transformation of the Christian Right*, 95; *Congressional Record* (hereafter *Cong. Rec.*) 127 (22 Oct. 1981): 24975; *Cong. Rec.* 128 (10 May 1982): 9189; ibid. (13 Dec. 1982): 30379.

35. Randy Frame, "Citizens Battle a Booming Pornography Business," *Christianity Today*, 7 Sept. 1984, 72–73; "Boycott Closes Store," *Christian Century*, 30 Jan. 1985, 96–97; "Mobilizing Against Pornography," *America*, 16 June 1984, 450.

36. Reo Christenson, "It's Time to Excise the Pornographic Cancer," *Christianity Today*, 2 Jan. 1981, 22; Donald Wildmon with Randall Nulton, *The Man the Networks Love to Hate* (Wilmore, KY: Bristol Books, 1989), 7.

37. Jerry Kirk, *The Mind Polluters* (Nashville: Thomas Nelson, 1985), 24–25; *Memphis Commercial Appeal*, 25 Oct. 1982; John Harris, "Plan to Regulate Adult Arcade Passes Amid Concern over AIDS," *Citizens Against Pornography Newsletter*, June 1987; "Demonstration Features Mass Wedding of Gay, Lesbian Couples," ibid., Nov. 1987; Citizens Against Pornography flier (1987), all in Wilcox Collection, Ephemeral Material; Mark Weaver, "Pornography and AIDS in Parks of Austin," *Citizens Against Pornography Newsletter*, Aug. 1987, Wilcox Collection. Not only does the article lack pornography; it also lacks any evidence of AIDS in the activities observed by Weaver.

38. Ronald Reagan, "Remarks at the Annual Convention of the National Association of Evangelicals in Orlando, Florida," 8 March 1983, American Presidency Project, www

.presidency.ucsb.edu; Ronald Reagan, "Remarks at the Annual Convention of the National Association of Evangelicals in Columbus, Ohio," 6 March 1984, ibid.; Ronald Reagan, "Remarks on Signing the Child Protection Act of 1984," 21 May 1984, ibid.

39. California State Senate Select Committee on Children and Youth, *Children in Pornography*, Public Hearing, 1 April 1977 (n.p., 1977), 22, 32.

40. "Child Pornography Banned," *State Government News*, Aug. 1977, 8; ACLU Communications Media Committee Minutes, 17 March 1977, American Civil Liberties Union Papers, box 116, folder 8, Seeley G. Mudd Library, Princeton University; "Child's Garden of Perversity," *Time*, 4 April 1977, 55; Peter Bridges, "What Parents Should Know and Do About 'Kiddie Pornography,'" *Parents* magazine, 1978, 42–43, 69, 43.

41. Judianne Densen-Gerber, "What Pornographers Are Doing to Children: A Shocking Report," *Redbook*, Aug. 1977, 86–90; Reo Christensen, "It's Time to Excise the Pornographic Cancer," *Christianity Today*, 2 Jan. 1981, 20–23; *Milwaukee Journal*, 27 Feb. 1977.

42. California Select Committee on Children, *Children in Pornography*, 55; California Assembly Committee on Criminal Justice, *Obscenity and the Use of Minors in Pornographic Material*, Public Hearing, 31 Oct. 1977 (n.p., 1977), 61–62; Viguerie, *The New Right*, 195; Attorney General's Advisory Committee on Obscenity and Pornography, *Report to the Attorney General on Child Pornography in California* (n.p., 1977), n.p.; "The Case Against Pornography," *Homemakers* magazine, June 1982, 8.

43. "St. Martin's Wins Round Against N.Y. Obscenity Law," *Publishers Weekly* (hereafter *PW*), 12 Dec. 1977, 23; *Ferber v. U.S.*, 458 U.S. 747 (1982); "President Reagan Signs Severe 'Kidporn' Bill," *PW*, 1 June 1984, 16.

44. Harry Clor, "Science, Eros, and the Law: A Critique of the Obscenity Commission Report," *Duquesne Law Review* 10, no. 1 (1971): 63–76.

45. Neil Malamuth, "Aggression Against Women: Cultural and Individual Causes," in Neil Malamuth and Edward Donnerstein, *Pornography and Sexual Aggression* (Orlando: Academic Press, 1984), 19–52, 32; Donnerstein, "Pornography: Its Effect on Violence Against Women," ibid., 53–81, 78.

46. Donnerstein, "Pornography," 79; Dorf Zillman and Jennings Bryant, "Effects of Massive Exposure to Pornography," in Malamuth and Donnerstein, *Pornography and Sexual Aggression*, 115–38, 134; Paul Abramson and Haruo Hayashi, "Pornography in Japan: Cross-Cultural Considerations," ibid., 173–83.

47. On the commissioners see Carole Vance, "The Meese Commission on the Road," *Nation*, 2 Aug. 1986, 1, 76; Philip Nobile and Eric Nadler, *United States of America vs. Sex: How the Meese Commission Lied About Pornography* (New York: Minotaur, 1986), 16–22.

48. Attorney General's Commission on Pornography, *Final Report* (Washington: Department of Justice, 1986), 225; Vance, "The Meese Commission on the Road," 77; Carole Vance, "Negotiating Sex and Gender in the Attorney General's Commission on Pornography," in *Sex Exposed: Sexuality and the Pornography Debate*, ed. Lynne Segal and Mary McIntosh (New Brunswick, NJ: Rutgers University Press, 1993), 29–49, 29–30.

49. Vance, "Negotiating Sex and Gender in the Attorney General's Commission on Pornography," 47; Maxwell Lillienstein, "Meese Commission Vigilantes," *PW*, 11 July 1986, 43–44; John Baker, "An American Dilemma," ibid., 31; Richard Stengel, "Sex Busters," *Time*, 21 July 1986, 12–21.

50. Attorney General's Commission on Pornography, *Final Report*, 51, 81, 97.

51. Ibid., 194, 196, 199, 211.

52. Ibid., 265–66.

53. Ibid., 266, 273.

54. Ibid., 302, 902, 329, 1006, 335.

55. Ibid., 433–58, 406.

56. Ibid., 769, 775, 816, 779, 797.

57. Ibid., 856, 888, 889.

58. Ibid., 769, 756, 27.

59. Ibid., 1316–50, 1663, 1679.

60. Susanna McBee, "Now It's Labels on 'Pornography Rock' to Protect Kids," *U.S. News & World Report*, 26 Aug. 1985, 52; Gillian Frank, "Save Our Children," 243.

61. Senate Committee on the Judiciary, *Cable-Porn and Dial-a-Porn Control Act: Hearings Before the Subcommittee on Criminal Law* (Washington: GPO, 1986), 103–4.

62. *New York Times* (hereafter *NYT*), 5 Nov. 1984; Christian Family Renewal mailing, July 1984, Wilcox Collection, Ephemeral Materials; *Bowers v. Hardwick*, 478 U.S. 186 (1986).

63. Beth Spring, "How Harmful Is Pornography?" *Christianity Today*, 11 July 1986, 26–27; "The New Pornography Commission Report," *Phyllis Schlafly Report*, July 1986; Phyllis Schlafly, ed., *Pornography's Victims* (Alton, IL: Pere Marquette Press, 1987).

64. *The Meese Commission Exposed* (New York: National Coalition Against Censorship, 1987); American Civil Liberties Union, *Polluting the Censorship Debate: A Summary and Critique of the Final Report of the Attorney General's Commission on Pornography* (n.p., 1986), 3, 31, 123.

65. Edward Donnerstein and Daniel Linz, "The Question of Pornography," *Psychology Today*, Dec. 1986, 56–59; Edward Donnerstein, Daniel Linz, and Steven Penrod, *The Question of Pornography: Research Findings and Policy Implications* (New York: Free Press, 1987), 172, 179.

66. Terry Teachout, "The Pornography Report That Never Was," *Commentary*, Aug. 1987, 51–57.

67. Robert Lee, "Waging War on Smut," *Conservative Digest*, Nov. 1988, 45; "First Bush-Dukakis Presidential Debate," 25 Sept. 1988, American Presidency Project.

68. "Maine Soundly Defeats Obscenity Referendum," *PW*, 27 June 1986, 18; U.S. Department of Justice, *Beyond the Pornography Commission: The Federal Response* (Washington: GPO, 1988), 49; *Denver Post*, 24 June 1986; *Beaufort (SC) Gazette*, 24 Oct. 1986.

69. *Freedberg v. U.S. Department of Justice*, 703 F. Supp. 107 (1988); Bob Cohn, "The Trials of Adam & Eve," *Newsweek*, 7 Jan. 1991, 48; *PHE, Inc. v. U.S. Department of Justice*, F. Supp. 15 (1990).

70. Brent Ward to Edwin Meese, quoted in *U.S. v. PHE, Inc.*, 965 F.2d 848 (1992); *PHE, Inc. v. U.S. Department of Justice*, F. Supp. 15 (1990). Adam & Eve's founder, Philip Harvey, describes his legal ordeals in *The Government vs. Erotica: The Siege of Adam & Eve* (Amherst, NY: Prometheus Books, 2001).

71. Robert Corn-Revere, "Putting the First Amendment Out of Business," *Nation*, 26 Sept. 1988, 234–38; *Pryba v. U.S.*, 498 U.S. 924 (1990). On RICO and obscenity see Richard Hixson, *Pornography and the Justices: The Supreme Court and the Intractable Obscenity Problem* (Carbondale: Southern Illinois University Press, 1996), 182–99; *NYT*, 12 Jan. 1988.

72. Steven Hirsch discussed the Mississippi case in early 2006, explaining, "It made us much more conservative." M. J. McMahon, "Steven Hirsch, CEO, Vivid Entertainment," *AVN Online*, Jan. 2006, *Los Angeles Times*, 8 Aug. 2003; Stephen Rae, "X-Rated Raids," *Playboy*, June 1992, 44.

73. U.S. Department of Justice, *Beyond the Pornography Commission*, 43, iii; Bruce Johansen, "The Meese Police on Pornography Patrol," *Progressive*, June 1988, 20–22.

74. U.S. Department of Justice, *Beyond the Pornography Commission*, iii–iv, 6.

75. *NYT*, 27 July 1989; *NYT*, 8 Oct. 1989; *Philadelphia Inquirer*, 6 Oct. 1990; Jessica Tourk, "Controlling Expression: The Stagnant Policy of the Centers for Disease Control in the Second Decade of AIDS," *Cardozo Arts and Entertainment Law Journal* 13 (1993): 601.

76. *Miami Herald*, 7 June 1990; ibid., 4 Oct. 1990.

7. Pornography Is the Practice, Where Is the Theory?

1. Robin Morgan, "How to Run the Pornographers Out of Town," *Ms.*, Nov. 1978, 55.

2. Diana E. H. Russell, "On Pornography," *Chrysalis* 4 (1977): 11–15, 11; Andrea Dworkin, *Pornography: Men Possessing Women* (New York: Perigee, 1979), 69; Andrea Dworkin, *Woman Hating* (New York: Dutton, 1974), 80.

3. Barbara Ryan, *Feminism and the Women's Movement: Dynamics of Change in Social Movement, Ideology, and Activism* (New York: Routledge, 1992), 113–17; Cassandra Langer, *A Feminist Critique: How Feminism Has Changed American Society, Culture, and How We Live from the 1940s to the Present* (New York: HarperCollins, 1996), 34–37; Kathleen Berkeley, *The Women's Liberation Movement in America* (Westport, CT: Greenwood Press, 1999), 70–71; Myra Marx Ferree and Beth Hess, *Controversy and Coalition: The New Feminist Movement Across Three Decades of Change*, 3rd ed. (New York: Routledge, 2000), 120–22; Ruth Rosen, *The World Split Open: How the Modern Women's Movement Changed America* (New York: Viking, 2000), 191–94; Jane Gerhard, *Desiring Revolution: Second-Wave Feminism and the Rewriting of American Sexual Thought, 1920 to 1982* (New York: Columbia University Press, 2001), 173–82; Estelle Freedman, *No Turning Back: The History of Feminism and the Future of Women* (New York: Ballantine, 2002), 270–72. Alice Echols briefly discusses pre-antiporn feminist thought on porn in the epilogue (and its footnotes) to *Daring to Be Bad: Radical Feminism in America, 1967–1975* (Minneapolis: University of Minnesota Press, 1989), 288–89, 361–63. The best work on this topic is Carolyn Bronstein, "Porn Tours: The Rise and Fall of the American Feminist Anti-pornography Movement" (PhD diss., University of Wisconsin, 2001).

4. Susan Brownmiller, *In Our Time: Memoir of a Revolution* (New York: Dial, 1999), 295–325; Stephanie Gilmore, "The Dynamics of Second-Wave Feminist Activism in Memphis, 1971–1982: Rethinking the Liberal/Radical Divide," *NWSA Journal* 15, no. 1 (2003): 94–117, quoted at 109; Sherrie Innes, ed., *Disco Divas: Women and Popular Culture in the 1970s* (Philadelphia: University of Pennsylvania Press, 2003).

5. Andrea Dworkin, "Why So-Called Radical Men Love and Need Pornography," in *Take Back the Night: Women on Pornography*, ed. Laura Lederer (New York: William Morrow, 1980), 148–54, 148; Andrea Dworkin, *Right-Wing Women* (New York: Perigee, 1983).

6. On women's activism between "waves" see Cynthia Harrison, *On Account of Sex: The Politics of Women's Issues, 1945–1968* (Berkeley: University of California Press, 1988); and Joanne Meyerowitz, ed., *Not June Cleaver: Women and Gender in Postwar America, 1945–1960* (Philadelphia: Temple University Press, 1994).

7. "Redstockings Manifesto," in *Sisterhood Is Powerful: An Anthology of Writings from the Women's Liberation Movement*, ed. Robin Morgan (New York: Vintage, 1970), 533–36; "Politics of the Ego: A Manifesto for New York Radical Feminists," in *Radical Feminism*, ed. Anne Koedt, Ellen Levine, and Anita Rapone (New York: Quadrangle, 1973), 379–83; "The Feminists: A Political Organization to Annihilate Sex Roles," ibid.,

368–78; Becky Thompson, "Multiracial Feminism: Recasting the Chronology of the Second Wave," *Feminist Studies* 28, no. 2 (2002): 337–60.

8. Patricia Bradley, *Mass Media and the Shaping of American Feminism, 1963–1975* (Jackson: University Press of Mississippi, 2003). Kathryn Thoms Flannery offers a valuable discussion of the formation of a feminist press in *Feminist Literacies, 1968–1975* (Urbana: University of Illinois Press, 2005), 23–59; see also Amy Erdman Farrell, *Yours in Sisterhood: "Ms." Magazine and the Promise of Popular Feminism* (Chapel Hill: University of North Carolina Press, 1998). On the plight of socialist feminists of the early twentieth century see Mari Jo Buhle, *Women and American Socialism, 1780–1920* (Urbana: University of Illinois Press, 1981).

9. Kate Millett, *Sexual Politics* (New York: Doubleday, 1970), 233; Roxanne Dunbar, "'Sexual Liberation': More of the Same Thing," *No More Fun & Games*, Nov. 1969, 53, 52. At least one sexual counterrevolutionary offered a rebuttal to Millett, albeit one so overtly hostile (and ridiculous) it found little support anywhere: Norman Mailer, *The Prisoner of Sex* (Boston: Little, Brown, 1971).

10. Donna Keck, "The Art of Maiming Women," *Women: A Journal of Liberation*, fall 1969, 40–42; Alice Embree, "Media Images 1," and Florika, "Media Images 2," in *Sisterhood Is Powerful*, 170–75, 175–91, respectively; "Reparations for Sexploitation," *Everywoman*, 31 July 1970, 4.

11. "Censorship Sucks Shit," *Ain't I a Woman?* 26 June 1970, 7; "Playboy Fucked Up," *Women: A Journal of Liberation*, fall 1969, 53; "money changer" line from *Grinnell Herald Register*, quoted in Judith Hole and Ellen Levine, *Rebirth of Feminism* (New York: Quadrangle, 1971), 324.

12. "Minneapolis," *It Ain't Me Babe*, 1–23 July 1970, 3; *Variety*, 1 April 1970.

13. Barbara Burris, "What Is Women's Liberation?" *It Ain't Me Babe*, Feb. 1970, n.p.; "The Feminists," 370 (see note 7 above).

14. Bay Area Women's Liberation, "Stop the Pornies," *Tooth & Nail*, Oct. 1969, 12–13; "The New Feminism," *Time*, 21 Nov. 1969, 53. See also *Los Angeles Free Press*, 7 Nov. 1969, 11.

15. Robin Morgan, "Goodbye to All That," originally in *Rat*, 6 Feb. 1970 (repr. in Robin Morgan, *The Word of a Woman: Feminist Dispatches, 1968–1992* [New York: Norton, 1992], 57–69); "Che!" *Rat*, 6–23 Feb. 1970, 23; "*Rat* Busted!" *Rat*, 24 Feb. 1970, 2; "A Year Ago . . . A Sister Remembers," *Rat*, 12 Jan., 1971, 11, 14. Another anonymous participant in the takeover emphasized that "the hierarchical structure of the paper would change" with women at the helm, placing that imperative ahead of content control. "Keep on Truckin', Sisters," *It Ain't Me Babe*, 7 April 1970, 11.

16. "Women Have Seized the Executive Offices of Grove Press," undated flier (1970), Robin Morgan Papers, Box S18, File: Grove Press 1, Rare Book, Manuscript, and Special Collections Library, Duke University: Durham, NC.

17. *New York Times* (hereafter *NYT*), 14 April 1970; *Village Voice*, 16 April 1970; Karen Kearns, "Grove Press," *It Ain't Me Babe*, 28 April 1970, 2; Z. Bartha, "Starve a Pimp Today, Boycott the FREEP," *L.A. Women's Liberation Newsletter*, Sept. 1971, 2; Varda One, "Free Press Women Fight Sexism," *Everywoman*, 31 July 1970, 1.

18. "March 8 Women Invade CBS," *Rat*, 30 March 1970, 25; Karla Jay, "Ladies Home Journal 1," *Rat*, 4 April 1970, 4, 22; on the *LHJ* occupation see Echols, *Daring to Be Bad*, 195–97; "*Newsweek*: The Man's Media," *Rat*, 4 April 1970, 4, 22.

19. Bobbie Goldstone, "The Politics of Pornography," *off our backs*, 14 Dec. 1970, 10.

20. Brenda Starr, "Pornography and Women's Liberation," *Everywoman*, Jan. 1971, 4.

21. Pat, "Sexist Bookstores in Eugene," *Women's Press*, Aug. 1971, 3; Susan and Paula, "Oregon's Censorship Bill," *Women's Press*, Sept. 1973, 3; "Censorship Sucks Shit," *Ain't I a Woman?* 26 June 1970, 7; Tyler, "No, on Proposition 18," *Lesbian Tide*, Nov. 1972, 6.

22. Leslie Taylor, "'I Made Up My Mind to Get It': The American Trial of *The Well of Loneliness*, New York City, 1928–1929," *Journal of the History of Sexuality* 10, no. 2 (2001): 250–86; *New York Post*, 12 March 1969. See also Whitney Strub, "Lavender, Menaced: Lesbianism, Obscenity Law, and the Feminist Antipornography Movement," *Journal of Women's History* 22, no. 2 (2010): 83–107.

23. Varda One, "Woman as Masochist, Man as Sadist," *Everywoman*, 19 June 1970, 1; Joan Matthews, "The Power Trip of Porn," *her-self*, 19 May 1973, 7.

24. Peggy Hopper, "I Don't Want to Change My Lifestyle, I Want to Change My Life," *Hysteria*, July 1971, 3; Maryse Holder, "First International Festival of Women's Films," *off our backs*, 30 Sept. 1972, 15.

25. Holder, "Another Cuntree," *off our backs*, 30 Sept. 1973, 11.

26. Lucille Iverson, "Feminist Critique of the First Annual Erotic Film Festival," *Women & Film* 1, nos. 3/4 (1973): 23–29.

27. Ellen Willis, "Hard to Swallow: *Deep Throat*" (1973), in *Beginning to See the Light: Sex, Hope, and Rock-and-Roll* (Hanover, NH: Wesleyan University Press, 1992), 68–75.

28. Christine Stansell, "*Deep Throat*," *off our backs*, 30 April 1973, 11.

29. *San Francisco Chronicle*, 2 Sept. 1973; Terri Schultz, "A Feminist Defends Porn," *Chicago Journalism Review*, July-Aug. 1974, 25.

30. Brooke, "Amazon Expedition," *off our backs*, 28 Feb. 1974, 16; "*Ecstasy*: Pornography for Women?" *Lesbian News*, Sept. 1975, 6.

31. Dworkin, *Woman Hating*, 22, 41, 53.

32. Ibid., 79, 80.

33. Jamaica Kincaid, "Art: Erotica!" *Ms.*, Jan. 1975, 30.

34. Judith Thurman, "What Is the 'Real Thing' for a Porn Star?" *Ms.*, March 1976, 37–39.

35. Aljean Harmetz, "Rape—An Ugly Movie Trend," *Media Report to Women* (repr. from *NYT*), 1 Nov. 1973, 7; Molly Haskell, *From Reverence to Rape: The Treatment of Women in the Movies* (New York: Holt, Rinehart, and Winston, 1974); Beth Lindberg, "Women Protest!" *her-self*, 19 May 1973, 7. See also Jo Ann Fuchs, "Rape in the Movies," *Women: A Journal of Liberation*, fall 1972, 52; Joan Robbins, "Media Ups and Downs," *Sister*, Nov. 1974, 12.

36. Susan Griffin, "Rape: The All-American Crime," *Ramparts*, Sept. 1971, 26–35.

37. Elaine Schroeder, "The Mythology of Rape," *Pandora*, 27 Dec. 1972, 5; Andra Medea and Kathleen Thompson, *Against Rape* (New York: Farrar, Straus, and Giroux, 1974), 22; New York Radical Feminists, *Rape: The First Sourcebook for Women* (New York: Plume, 1974), 267; Diana E. H. Russell, *The Politics of Rape: The Victim's Perspective* (New York: Stein and Day, 1975), 72, 264.

38. Robin Morgan, "Theory and Practice: Pornography and Rape" (1974), in *The Word of a Woman*, 78–89; Andrea Dworkin, "The Rape Atrocity and the Boy Next Door," in *Our Blood: Prophecies and Discourses on Sexual Politics* (New York: Perigee, 1976), 22–49.

39. Susan Brownmiller, "Is Porn Liberating?" *Boston Globe*, 11 Sept. 1973.

40. Susan Brownmiller, *Against Our Will: Men, Women, and Rape* (New York: Simon and Schuster, 1975), 394, 395.

41. *New York Post*, 1 Oct. 1975.

42. *NYT*, 16 Feb. 1976; Eithne Johnson and Eric Schaefer, "Soft Core/Hard Gore: *Snuff* as a Crisis in Meaning," *Journal of Film and Video* 45, nos. 2–3 (summer-fall 1993): 40–59. On Shackleton and the film see David Kerekes and David Slater, *Killing for Culture: An Illustrated History of Death Film from Mondo to Snuff* (London: Creation Books, 1994), 11–23.

43. *NYT*, 27 Feb. 1976; *Washington Post*, 9 March 1976; *San Francisco Chronicle*, 19 March 1976; Madeleine Janover, "Deadly Snuff," *off our backs*, 31 March 1976, 23; *NYT*, 10 March 1976. Mary Lou Fox first reported the falsity of *Snuff*'s murder scene to the feminist press, satirizing the film's ad line, "Made in South America, Where Life Is Cheap," in "Made in the Media, Where Talk Is Cheap," *Majority Report*, 6–22 March 1976, 4. On *Snuff* see *Majority Report*, 20 March 1976, 10; *Sister*, April-May 1976, 1; *NOW! Los Angeles Chapter*, May 1976, 2; *Big Mama Rag*, Nov./Dec. 1977, 9; *Rochester Patriot*, 12–25 Oct. 1978, 6.

44. *Los Angeles Times*, 19 March 1976; "We Are Women Against Violence Against Women," *Big Mama Rag*, Nov./Dec. 1977, 1; Molly Haskell, "The Night Porno Films Turned Me Off," *New York*, 29 March 1976, 56–60; Brownmiller quoted in Barbara Mehrhof and Lucille Iverson, "When Does Free Speech Go Too Far?" *Majority Report*, Aug./Sept. 1977, 1.

45. "Questions That People Will Ask," Dec. 1976, Women Against Violence Against Women Records, box 1, folder 1, Northeastern University Special Collections, Boston, MA. See also Carolyn Bronstein, "No More *Black and Blue*: Women Against Violence Against Women and the Warner Communications Boycott, 1976–1979," *Violence Against Women* 14, no. 4 (2008): 418–36.

46. Women Against Media Violence and Degradation Minutes, 29 Jan. 1977, COYOTE Records, box 9, folder 494, Schlesinger Library, Radcliffe Institute, Harvard University, Cambridge, MA (hereafter COYOTE Records); Women Against Pornography and Violence in Media Minutes, 12 Feb. 1977, ibid.; Women Against Violence in Pornography and Media Minutes, 26 Feb. 1977, ibid.

47. Irene Diamond, "Pornography and Repression: A Reconsideration of 'Who' and 'What,'" in *Take Back the Night: Women on Pornography*, ed. Laura Lederer (New York: Bantam, 1980), 187–203, 188.

48. D. H. Lawrence, "Pornography and Obscenity," in *Selected Literary Criticism*, ed. Anthony Beal (London: William Heinemann, 1955), 32–51, 33, 37; Eberhard Kronhausen and Phyllis Kronhausen, *Pornography and the Law: The Psychology of Erotic Realism*, rev. ed. (New York: Ballantine, 1964; orig. 1959), 25, 220; Steven Marcus, *The Other Victorians: A Study of Sexuality and Pornography in Mid-Nineteenth-Century England* (New York: New American Library, 1964), 278; *Ms.*, front cover, Nov. 1978.

49. Gloria Steinem, "Erotica vs. Pornography" (1978), in *Outrageous Acts and Everyday Rebellions* (New York: Holt, Rinehart, and Winston, 1983), 219–30; Sue Scope, "Erotica Versus Pornography: An Exploration," *Newspage*, 1979, 1; "Women Take to Stage in Porn Protest," *Big Mama Rag*, May 1979, 6.

50. Laura Shapiro, "Violence: The Most Obscene Fantasy," *Mother Jones*, Dec. 1977, 12; Gloria Steinem, "Pornography—Not Sex but the Obscene Use of Power," *Ms.*, Aug. 1977, 43–44; Wendy Kaminer, "Where We Stand on the First Amendment," *Aegis: Magazine on Ending Violence Against Women*, Sept./Oct. 1979, 52; Diana E. H. Russell, "Pornography: A Feminist Perspective," *Newspage*, Aug. 1977, 1.

51. "Questions We Get Asked Most Often," *Newspage*, Nov. 1977, 1.

52. James Howard, Myron Liptzin, and Clifford Reifler, "Is Pornography a Problem?" *Journal of Social Issues* 29, no. 3 (1973): 133–45, 133; Victor Cline, "Another View: Pornography Effects, the State of the Art," in *Where Do You Draw the Line? An Ex-*

ploration into Media Violence, Pornography, and Censorship, ed. Victor Cline (Provo: Brigham Young University Press, 1974), 203–44, 231; Women Against Pornography, "Six Questions About Pornography," undated poster, Schlesinger Library Vertical Files for Women's Studies, microfiche 2593; Irene Diamond, "Pornography and Repression: A Reconsideration," *Signs* 5, no. 4 (1980): 686–701, quoted at 698.

53. Cline, "Another View," 214.

54. See Benita Roth, *Separate Roads to Feminism: Black, Chicana, and White Feminist Movements in America's Second Wave* (Cambridge, UK: Cambridge University Press, 2004); and Kimberly Springer, *Living for the Revolution: Black Feminist Organizations, 1968–1980* (Chapel Hill: University of North Carolina Press, 2005). Alice Echols discusses class conflict in *Daring to Be Bad*, 204–10; and Anne Enke examines the intersection of race and class issues in *Finding the Movement: Sexuality, Contested Space, and Feminist Activism* (Durham, NC: Duke University Press, 2007).

55. Carol Anne Douglas, "What if the revolution isn't tomorrow?" *off our backs*, 30 Sept. 1977, 10; Veronica Geng, "Requiem for the Women's Movement," *Harper's*, Nov. 1976, 49–68; Patricia Beyea, "ERA's Last Mile," *Civil Liberties Review*, July/Aug. 1977, 49. On abortion see Kristin Luker, *Abortion and the Politics of Motherhood* (Berkeley: University of California Press, 1984); and Rosalind Pollack Petchesky, *Abortion and Woman's Choice* (Boston: Northeastern University Press, 1984); on the ERA see Jane Mansbridge, *Why We Lost the ERA* (Chicago: University of Chicago Press, 1986).

56. WAP flier, "March on Times Square Against Pornography," 20 Oct. 1979, WAVAW Records, box 5, folder 155. Echols discusses the ascent of cultural feminism in *Daring to Be Bad*, 243–86, though she later revisited her distinction to observe that the transition was more fluid than the linguistic separation of radical and cultural feminism would suggest, and that "I now think that calling it all radical feminism would have raised fewer hackles." See Alice Echols, *Shaky Ground: The Sixties and Its Aftershocks* (New York: Columbia University Press, 2002), 7. On feminism in the 1970s see Stephanie Gilmore, ed., *Feminist Coalitions: Historical Perspectives on Second-Wave Feminism in the United States* (Urbana: University of Illinois Press, 2008).

57. Deb Friedman and Lois Yankowski, "Snuffing Sexual Violence," *Quest*, fall 1976, 29; Deb Friedman, "Pornography—Cause or Effect," *Aegis*, winter/spring 1981, 44–46 (orig. in July/Aug. 1977 *FAAR Newsletter*); Ellen Willis, "Sexual Counterrevolution I," *Rolling Stone*, 24 March 1977, 29; Janis Kelly and Fran Moira, "A Clear and Present Danger," *off our backs*, 31 Jan. 1979, 7.

58. Joan Howarth, "Response to 'On Porn,'" *WAVAW Newsletter*, n.d. (c. Jan. 1979), WAVAW Records, box 1, folder 7; Los Angeles WAVAW, "Money Silences," *Lesbian*

Tide, May/June 1978, 11; "WAVAW History," n.d. (c. 1978), WAVAW Records, box 1, folder 24.

59. Echols, *Daring to Be Bad*, 210–41; Tom McNulty, "Censorship Is an Unnatural Act," *Majority Report*, June 1976, 8; Bridget Overton, "Short Currents," *Lesbian Tide*, Sept./Oct. 1978, 20; *Dinah*, quoted in Susan Freeman, "From the Lesbian Nation to the Cincinnati Lesbian Community: Moving Toward a Politics of Location," *Journal of the History of Sexuality* 9, nos. 1–2 (2000): 137–74, 150.

60. Elinor Langer, "Confessing," *Ms.*, Dec. 1974, 70; Julia Stanley, "Fear of FLYING?" *Sinister Wisdom*, fall 1976, 59–60; Russell, "On Pornography," 11.

61. Susan Chute, "Backroom with the Feminist Heroes," *Sinister Wisdom*, fall 1980, 2–4; on Brownmiller and the DOB see Echols, *Daring to Be Bad*, 211; Lynne Shapiro, "Lesbian-Straight Split . . . Round II?" *Lesbian Tide*, Nov./Dec. 1979, 24; [ ] to WAP, 17 Oct. 1979, Women Against Pornography Records, box 6, folder: Correspondence, 29 Oct. 1979, Schlesinger Library, Harvard University (names have been redacted from this and all subsequent WAP archival material related to nonpublic figures, as specified by archival policy).

62. Susan Brownmiller, letter to Susan Chute, *Sinister Wisdom*, fall 1980, 111; Susan Brownmiller, "Let's Put Pornography Back in the Closet," in *Take Back the Night: Women on Pornography*, ed. Laura Lederer (New York: Bantam, 1979), 251–54; WAP, "Lesbian Feminist Concerns in the Feminist Antipornography Movement," press release, Oct. 1979, WAVAW Records, box 6, folder 155.

63. WAVPM information packet, 1 Sept. 1977, Robin Morgan Papers, Box S17, Folder: Antiporn 3; "S/M Challenges Antiporn," *Lesbian Tide*, Nov./Dec. 1979, 25.

64. Bloomington Gay Rights Coalition, "Censorship: Whose Side Are We On?" *Lesbian Tide*, May/June 1978, 10–11; Jeanne Cordova and Kerry Lobel, "Feminists and the Right—Merging over Porn?" *Lesbian Tide*, May/June 1980, 17; Pat Califia, "Among Us, Against Us—The New Puritans," *Advocate*, 17 April 1980, 14–18.

65. Robin Ruth Linden, introduction to *Against Sadomasochism: A Radical Feminist Analysis*, ed. Robin Ruth Linden et al. (East Palo Alto: Frog in the Well, 1982), 1–15, 4; Catharine A. MacKinnon, *Toward a Feminist Theory of the State* (Cambridge, MA: Harvard University Press, 1989), 119; WAP Press Release, 19 May 1982, WAP Papers, box 9, folder: Feminine Rights to Erotic Expression Demo; WAP Press Release, n.d., WAP Papers, box 2, folder: Office Correspondence, 1984.

66. Echols, *Daring to Be Bad*; for challenges to Echols see Verta Taylor and Leila Rupp, "Women's Culture and Lesbian Feminist Activism: A Reconsideration of Cultural Feminism," *Signs* 19, no. 1 (1993): 32–61; Nancy Whittier, *Feminist Generations: The Persistence of the Radical Women's Movement* (Philadelphia: Temple University

Press, 1995); Laurel Clark, "Beyond the Gay/Straight Split: Socialist Feminists in Baltimore," *NWSA Journal* 19, no. 2 (2007): 1–31.

67. Louise Armstrong, *Kiss Daddy Goodnight: A Speak-Out on Incest* (New York: Pocket Books, 1978); Judith Lewis Herman with Lisa Hirschman, *Father-Daughter Incest* (Cambridge, MA: Harvard University Press, 1981); Betty Friedan, *The Second Stage* (New York: Summit, 1981), 83–123.

68. "National Porn Conference," *Newspage*, Aug. 1978, 1; *San Francisco Chronicle*, 18 Nov. 1978, 4; *New York University Review of Law and Social Change* 8, no. 2 (1978–79).

69. *NYT*, 21 Oct. 1979; [ ] to WAP, 15 Aug. 1979, WAP Records, box 3, folder: Corr.—Tues. Aug. 21; [ ] to WAP, n.d., ibid., box 3, folder: Corr.—Aug.15–16; [ ] to WAP, 15 Aug. 1979, ibid., box 3, folder; Religious Fanatics; [ ] to WAP, 26 Sept. 1979, ibid., box 12, folder: Corr., April 1980; [ ] to WAP, 24 July 1980, ibid., box 12, folder: Corr., July '80; *San Francisco Examiner*, 2 May 1977.

70. [ ] to WAP, 14 Aug. 1979, WAP Records, box 3, folder: Corr., Sat. Aug. 18; WAP press release, "Women Open Times Square Office," 16 June 1979, ibid., box 1, folder: Literature; WAP Tour Script, June 1979, ibid., box 10, folder: Tour Script; Richard Goldstein, "The Fate of Theatre Row," *Village Voice*, 22 April 1981; Clinton Coalition of Concern, undated flier, WAP Records, box 14, folder: Times Square; Office of Midtown Enforcement, *Annual Report*, 1981, 1, ibid., box 10, folder: Midtown Enforcement Agency. Samuel R. Delany charts the devastating effects of redevelopment on local gay communities in *Times Square Red, Times Square Blue* (New York: New York University Press, 1999).

71. Charlotte Weaver-Gelzer, "What I Like About Porn Flicks," *Redbook*, Sept. 1976, 47–48, 51; "This Is What You Thought About . . . Women and Violence," *Glamour*, Dec. 1979, 27.

72. Women Against Pornography and Violence in Media Minutes, 12 Feb. 1977, COYOTE Records, box 9, folder 494; Ellen Willis, "Feminism, Moralism, and Pornography" (1979), in *Beginning to See the Light*, 220; Robin Yeamans, "A Political-Legal Analysis of Pornography," in *Take Back the Night: Women on Pornography*, ed. Laura Lederer (New York: Bantam, 1979), 248–51, 248; Charlotte Bunch, "Lesbianism and Erotica in Pornographic America," ibid., 82.

73. Dworkin, *Pornography*, 207, 224; Susan Griffin, *Pornography and Silence: Culture's Revenge Against Nature* (New York: Harper and Row, 1981), 182, 189; Kathleen Barry, *Female Sexual Slavery* (Englewood Cliffs, NJ: Prentice-Hall, 1979), 174, 214.

74. Dworkin, *Pornography*, 24, 25, 28, 202. Rape scenes abound in 1970s American porn; for some examples see *Forced Entry* (1971), *Winter Heat* (1974), *Fiona on Fire* (1977), *Expensive Tastes* (1978), and many, many more.

75. Laura Lederer, "Then and Now: Views of a Former Pornography Model," *Newspage*, Sept. 1978, 1–11.

76. Catharine MacKinnon, *Feminism Unmodified* (Cambridge, MA: Harvard University Press, 1987), 179; Griffin, *Pornography and Silence*, 112–19; Gloria Steinem, "The Real Linda Lovelace," in *Outrageous Acts and Everyday Rebellions*, 243–52; Linda Lovelace, with Mike McGrady, *Ordeal* (New York: Berkley, 1980), 138; Andrea Dworkin, "Letter from a War Zone," in *Letters from a War Zone* (New York: Lawrence Hill, 1993), 313; Linda Lovelace, with McGrady, *Out of Bondage* (New York: Berkley, 1986), 273.

77. Dworkin, *Letters from a War Zone*, 181, 278, 301, 302, 322; MacKinnon, *Toward a Feminist Theory of the State*, 239.

78. Russell, "On Pornography," 14; Morgan, "How to Run the Pornographers Out of Town," 79; Wendy Kaminer, "Pornography and the First Amendment," in *Take Back the Night: Women on Pornography*, ed. Laura Lederer (New York: Bantam, 1979), 241–47, 247.

79. MacKinnon, *Toward a Feminist Theory of the State*, 163; Dworkin, "Feminism: An Agenda," in *Letters from a War Zone*, 150.

80. MacKinnon, *Toward a Feminist Theory of the State*, 163, 199.

81. "An Ordinance of the City of Minneapolis," repr. in Dworkin and MacKinnon, *Pornography and Civil Liberties: A New Day for Women's Equality* (Minneapolis: Organizing Against Pornography, 1988), 99–105.

82. On the Minneapolis/Indianapolis ordinances see Donald Alexander Downs, *The New Politics of Pornography* (Chicago: University of Chicago Press, 1989); on Coughenour see ibid., 109–11; "Code of Indianapolis and Marion County, Indiana," *Pornography and Civil Rights*, 106–32; *American Booksellers Association v. Hudnut*, 598 F. Supp. 1316 (1984).

83. Attorney General's Commission on Pornography, *Final Report* (Washington: Department of Justice, 1986), 769–72, 52, 756, 27; Statement of Dr. Judith Becker and Ellen Levine, ibid., 201; "WAP Responds to Attorney General's Commission on Pornography," *Women Against Pornography Newsreport*, fall 1987, 6.

84. Mary Kay Blakely, "Is One Woman's Sexuality Another Woman's Pornography?" *Ms.*, April 1985, 45; Aric Press, "The War Against Pornography," *Newsweek*, 18 March 1985, 66; *NYT*, 26 Aug. 1985.

85. "Year of the Lustful Lesbian," *On Our Backs*, summer 1984, 4; *NYT*, 6 Oct. 1986; Women for Pornography mailing, n.d. (1986), Dorothy Teer Papers, box 5, folder: F.A.C.T., Rare Book, Manuscript, and Special Collections Library, Duke University.

86. Steinem, "Erotica vs. Pornography," 221; Dworkin, "Nervous Interview," in *Letters from a War Zone*, 60; Dullea, "X-Rated 'Couples Films.'"

87. Lisa Duggan and Nan D. Hunter, *Sex Wars: Sexual Dissent and Political Culture* (New York: Routledge, 1995), 8. Duggan and Hunter acknowledge the shortcomings of the censorship framework: "We wanted to separate ourselves from the civil liberties framework to make a specifically feminist argument in defense of sexually explicit expression," they write, but the immediate exigencies of fighting repression necessitated the simpler approach.

88. FACT, "Violence Against Women: No Simple Solution," undated flier, Dorothy Teer Papers, box 5, folder: F.A.C.T. 2; FACT, "Feminism and Censorship: Strange Bedfellows?" n.d. (1985), American Civil Liberties Union Papers, box 141, folder 7, Seeley G. Mudd Library, Princeton University.

89. Hunter and Law's FACT brief is reprinted in Duggan and Hunter, *Sex Wars*, 210–47; Varda Burstyn, ed., *Women Against Censorship* (Vancouver: Douglas and McIntyre, 1985).

90. California NOW, Resolution on Abusive Images of Women in the Media and Pornography, July 1982, COYOTE Records, box 1, folder 32; NOW, General Resolution, 1984, ibid.

91. NOW News Release, 9 July 1986, National Organization for Women Papers, box 200, folder 33, Schlesinger Library, Harvard University.

92. Priscilla Alexander and Paula Lichtenberg to NOW National Officers, 14 July 1986, COYOTE Records, box 1, folder 32.

93. Boston WAVAW, "A Letter Addressed to Boston-Area Feminists," 29 Oct. 1985, Schlesinger Library Vertical Files for Women's Studies, microfiche 1448; Karen DeCrow, "Strange Bedfellows," *Penthouse*, May 1985, 96–97; Betty Friedan, untitled essay, in *The Meese Commission Exposed* (New York: National Coalition Against Censorship, 1987), 24–25.

94. Nancy Polikoff, "Fighting Sexual Repression," *off our backs*, July 1987, 25; "Queers and Cops Meet Again," *Atalanta*, July 1984; "Arrests Made at Gay Bookstore," ibid., Aug. 1984.

95. MacKinnon, "On Collaboration," in *Feminism Unmodified*, 198–205; Karen Davis, "Antiporn Initiative in L.A. County," *Newsreport*, spring 1985, 17; Dworkin, "Letter from a War Zone," 321; Evelyn Radinson, "Book Review: *Intercourse*," *Newsreport*, fall 1987, 15; Phyllis Schlafly, ed., *Pornography's Victims* (Alton: Pere Marquette Press, 1987), viii.

96. Dorchen Leidholdt, introduction to *The Sexual Liberals and the Attack on Feminism*, ed. Dorchen Leidholdt and Janice Raymond (New York: Pergamon Press, 1990), ix–xvii, xv–xvi; Dworkin, "Woman-Hating Right and Left," in ibid., 28–40, 37.

97. Catharine MacKinnon, "The Roar on the Other Side of Silence," in *In Harm's Way: The Pornography Civil Rights Hearings*, ed. Catharine MacKinnon and Andrea

Dworkin (Cambridge, MA: Harvard University Press, 1997), 3–24, 10, 14; Catharine MacKinnon, *Women's Lives, Men's Laws* (Cambridge, MA: Harvard University Press, 2005), 342.

98. Quoted in Leidholdt, introduction, ix.

99. Tanya Melich, *The Republican War on Women: An Insider's Report from Behind the Lines* (New York: Bantam, 1996).

8. Vanilla Hegemony

1. World of Wonder blog, "The Talk of New York," 8 Feb. 2005, http://worldofwonder. net/insidedeepthroat/archives/2005/feb/08/talk.wow.

2. On Father Ritter's case see the *Washington Post*, 13 Aug. 1991. Ritter was never charged with a crime, in what appeared to be a questionable deal with prosecutors that he would refrain from further contact with minors. On George Peach's case see the *New York Times* (hereafter *NYT*), 13 March 1992.

3. *NYT*, 7 April 1999. The rise and fall of Keating's financial empire is covered in Michael Binstein and Charles Bowden, *Trust Me: Charles Keating and the Missing Millions* (New York: Random House, 1993). Binstein and Bowden also show Keating to be a racist and a sexist who leered at the attractive young women he hired— "all young, mainly blond, often buxom"—and frequently pressured them into having breast enlargement surgery (61). When the authors asked Keating to explain his passion for fighting porn, he grew quiet and inarticulate, "mumbl[ing] something about his Catholic education, his moral training" (61). On CDL's praise for RICO see "Obscenity Made Federal RICO," *National Decency Reporter*, Nov.-Dec. 1984, 1.

4. Robert Scheer, "Of Saviors and Loans," *Playboy*, Sept. 1990, 58; Joe Morgenstern, "Profit Without Honor," ibid., April 1992, 68–70, 86, 151–56.

5. Philip Jenkins, *Beyond Tolerance: Child Pornography on the Internet* (New York: New York University Press, 2001), 8.

6. Brenda Cossman, *Sexual Citizens: The Legal and Cultural Regulation of Sex and Belonging* (Stanford, CA: Stanford University Press, 2007), 27.

7. Leaflet reprinted in "Notes and Letters," *Feminist Studies* 9, no. 1 (1983): 177–82, 180–82.

8. Ibid., 177–80; letters from Gayle Rubin, Carole Vance, and Pat Califia in "Notes and Letters," *Feminist Studies* 9, no. 3 (1983): 598–602; letter from WAP Steering Committee, "Notes and Letters," *Feminist Studies* 10, no. 2 (1984): 363–67. On McCarthyism in academia and its lasting scars see Ellen Schrecker, *No Ivory Tower: McCarthyism and the Universities* (New York: Oxford University Press, 1986).

9. Carole Vance, "Pleasure and Danger: Toward a Politics of Sexuality," in *Pleasure and Danger: Exploring Female Sexuality*, ed. Carole Vance (Boston: Routledge and Kegan Paul, 1984), 1–27, 1, 6; Ellen Carol DuBois and Linda Gordon, "Seeking Ecstasy on the Battlefield: Danger and Pleasure in Nineteenth-Century Feminist Thought," ibid., 31–49, 31, 43; Alice Echols, "The Taming of the Id: Feminist Sexual Politics, 1968–83," in *Pleasure and Danger*, 50–72; Alice Echols, "The New Feminism of Yin and Yang," in *Powers of Desire: The Politics of Sexuality*, ed. Ann Snitow, Christine Stansell, and Sharon Thompson (New York: Monthly Review, 1983), 439–59.

10. Kathy Peiss, *Cheap Amusements: Working Women and Leisure in Turn-of-the-Century New York* (Philadelphia: Temple University Press, 1986), 6; Christine Stansell, *City of Women: Sex and Class in New York, 1789–1860* (Urbana: University of Illinois Press, 1987), 87, 185. See also Judith Walkowitz, *Prostitution and Victorian Society: Women, Class, and the State* (Cambridge, UK: Cambridge University Press, 1980).

11. On Newton see Barry Werth, *The Scarlet Professor: Newton Arvin, a Literary Life Shattered by Scandal* (New York: Anchor, 2001); Samuel Delany, *Times Square Red, Times Square Blue* (New York: New York University Press, 1999), 90.

12. Bill Callahan, "Harry Reems—Unlikely Civil Liberties Cause," *Gay Community News*, 20 Nov. 1976; Michael Bronski, "Notes and Thoughts by One Gay Man on Pornography and Censorship," ibid., 23 Dec. 1978; Jill Clark, "Interview: Robin Morgan," ibid., 20 Jan. 1979 (ellipses in original).

13. John D'Emilio, "Women Against Pornography: Feminist Frontier or Social Purity Crusade?" (orig. 1980), in *Making Trouble: Essays on Gay History, Politics, and the University* (New York: Routledge, 1992), 202–15, 211, 214.

14. On Parker see Cindy Patton, *Fatal Advice: How Safe-Sex Education Went Wrong* (Durham, NC: Duke University Press, 1996), 122–24; Michael Bronski, *Culture Clash: The Making of Gay Sensibility* (Boston: South End Press, 1984), 161; Richard Dyer, "Male Gay Porn: Coming to Terms," *Jump Cut* 30 (1985): 27–29; Tom Waugh, "Men's Pornography: Gay vs. Straight," ibid., 30–35. On the contestations over public sex in the wake of the AIDS crisis see Dangerous Bedfellows, eds., *Policing Public Sex: Queer Politics and the Future of AIDS Activism* (Boston: South End Press, 1996).

15. Thomas Waugh, *Hard to Imagine: Gay Male Eroticism in Photography and Film from Their Beginnings to Stonewall* (New York: Columbia University Press, 1996), xv, 5; see also Jake Gerli, "The Gay Sex Clerk: Chuck Vincent's Straight Pornography," and Nguyen Tan Hoang, "The Resurrection of Brandon Lee: The Making of a Gay Porn Star," in *Porn Studies*, ed. Linda Williams (Durham, NC: Duke University Press, 2004), 198–220, 223–70.

16. Michel Foucault, *The History of Sexuality, Vol. 1: An Introduction*, trans. Robert Hurley (New York: Vintage, 1978); William Turner, *A Genealogy of Queer Theory* (Philadelphia: Temple University Press, 2000).

17. Linda Williams, *Hard Core: Power, Pleasure, and the "Frenzy of the Visible"* (Berkeley: University of California Press, 1989), 277, 2.

18. Constance Penley, "Crackers and Whackers: The White Trashing of Porn," in *White Trash: Race and Class in America*, ed. Matt Wray and Annalee Newitz (New York: Routledge, 1997), 89–112, 95; Eithne Johnson, "Excess and Ecstasy: Constructing Female Pleasure in Porn Movies," *Velvet Light Trap* 32 (1993): 30–49.

19. Pat Califia, *Public Sex: The Culture of Radical Sex*, 2nd ed. (San Francisco: Cleis, 2000; orig. 1994), 52.

20. Susie Bright, *The Sexual State of the Union* (New York: Touchstone, 1997), 77, 161; Annie Sprinkle, *Hardcore from the Heart: The Pleasures, Profits, and Politics of Sex in Performance* (London: Continuum, 2001), 45–64; Liz Belile, ed., *Gynomite: Fearless, Feminist Porn* (New Orleans: New Mouth from the Dirty South, 2000), 8; Ragan Rhyne, "Hard-core Shopping: Educating Consumption in SIR Video Production's Lesbian Porn," *Velvet Light Trap* 59 (2007): 42–50.

21. "Not Banned in Boston," *Publishers Weekly*, 28 June 1991, 9. On the Canadian suppression see Brenda Cossman et al., *Bad Attitude/s on Trial: Pornography, Feminism, and the Butler Decision* (Toronto: University of Toronto Press, 1997).

22. Catharine MacKinnon, *Only Words* (Cambridge, MA: Harvard University Press, 1993), 20, 17, 37; *Boston Globe*, 6 Oct. 1993. See also Alice Echols, *Shaky Ground: The Sixties and Its Aftershocks* (New York: Columbia University Press, 2002), 97–102; Susie Bright, *Sexwise* (San Francisco: Cleis, 1995), 122.

23. Kathleen Barry, *The Prostitution of Sexuality* (New York: New York University Press, 1995), 3; Diana E. H. Russell, *Against Pornography: The Evidence of Harm* (Berkeley: Russell, 1993), 17; Diana E. H. Russell, *Dangerous Relationships: Pornography, Misogyny, and Rape* (Thousand Oaks, CA: SAGE, 1998), 3, xiv.

24. Lisa Sigel, *Governing Pleasures: Pornography and Social Change in England, 1815–1914* (New Brunswick, NJ: Rutgers University Press, 2002), 5–6; Williams, *Porn Studies*, 70, 80.

25. Sallie Tisdale, *Talk Dirty to Me: An Intimate Philosophy of Sex* (New York: Doubleday, 1994), 334; Wendy McElroy, *Sexual Correctness: The Gender-Feminist Attack on Women* (Jefferson, NC: McFarland, 1996), 39.

26. Tad Friend, "Yes," *Esquire*, Feb. 1994, 49.

27. Steve Bruce, *The Rise and Fall of the New Christian Right* (Oxford: Clarendon Press, 1988); Michael Lienesch, *Redeeming America: Piety and Politics in the New Christian*

Right (Chapel Hill: University of North Carolina Press, 1993), 3; Clyde Wilcox, *God's Warriors: The Christian Right in Twentieth-Century America* (Baltimore: Johns Hopkins University Press, 1992), 211.

28. William Martin, *With God on Our Side: The Rise of the Religious Right in America* (New York: Broadway Books, 1996), 285–90; *Washington Post*, 24 March 1990.

29. "Pornographic Priorities," *Maclean's*, 27 Aug. 1990, 7; George Bush, "Remarks to the Religious Alliance Against Pornography," 10 Oct. 1991, American Presidency Project, www.presidency.ucsb.edu.

30. Joe Rollins, "Beating Around Bush: Gay Rights and America's 41st President," in *Creating Change: Sexuality, Public Policy, and Civil Rights*, ed. John D'Emilio, William B. Turner, and Urvashi Vaid (New York: St. Martin's, 2000), 29–42; Republican Party Platform of 1992, American Presidency Project, www.presidency.ucsb.edu.

31. Senate Committee on the Judiciary, *Legislative Proposals for Compensation of Victims of Sexual Crimes: Hearing Before the Committee on the Judiciary* (Washington: GPO, 1992), 10, 11, 14.

32. "Porn Victims' Compensation Bill Dead for Now," *Publishers Weekly*, 26 Oct. 1992, 7; Gerald Pomper, "The Presidential Election," in Gerald Pomper et al., *The Election of 1992: Reports and Interpretations* (Chatham, NJ: Chatham House, 1993), 139–40; Michael Meeropol, *Surrender: How the Clinton Administration Completed the Reagan Revolution* (Ann Arbor: University of Michigan Press, 1998).

33. *NYT*, 12 Nov. 1993.

34. *Congressional Record* (hereafter *Cong. Rec.*) 139 (20 Oct. 1993): 2494; ibid. (28 Oct. 1993): 14169; ibid. (3 Nov. 1993): 8709.

35. *Cong. Rec.* 139, daily ed. (4 Nov. 1993): 1247.

36. Bill Clinton, "Letter to Attorney General Janet Reno on Child Pornography," 10 Nov. 1993, American Presidency Project, www.presidency.ucsb.edu; *NYT*, 16 Nov. 1993; *U.S. v. Knox*, 32 F.3d 733 (1994); *NYT*, 19 Feb. 1995; "Porn Again," *Nation*, 6 Dec. 1993, 679–80.

37. Ed Gillespie and Bob Schellas, eds., *Contract with America: The Bold Plan by Rep. Newt Gingrich, Rep. Dick Armey, and the House Republicans to Change the Nation* (New York: Random House, 1994), 82. On Internet porn see Frederick Lane III, *Obscene Profits: The Entrepreneurs of Pornography in the Cyber Age* (New York: Routledge, 2000), esp. 183–294; Mark Rozell and Clyde Wilcox, eds., *God at the Grass Roots: The Christian Right in the 1994 Elections* (Lanham, MD: Rowman and Littlefield, 1995). Rozell and Wilcox helped edit several other books tracking the power of the Christian Right in subsequent elections; see, e.g., John Green, Mark Rozell, and Clyde Wilcox, eds., *Prayers in the Precincts: The Christian Right in the 1998 Elections* (Washington: Georgetown University Press, 2000).

38. The couple was Robert and Carleen Thomas of Milpitas, convicted in Memphis; on their case see Jonathan Wallace and Mark Mangan, *Sex, Laws, and Cyberspace* (New York: Henry Holt, 1996), 1–40. Robert appealed his conviction all the way to the Supreme Court, which denied certiorari and thus let it stand.

39. *Cong. Rec.* 141 (14 June 1995): 8310, 8336.

40. Ibid., 8340–41, 8347. The Vermont senator called the CDA's passage "especially interesting because most of the Senators who voted would not have the foggiest idea how to get on the Internet in the first place." Senate Committee on the Judiciary, *Cyberporn and Children: The Scope of the Problem, the State of the Technology, and the Need for Congressional Action: Hearing Before the Committee on the Judiciary* (Washington: GPO, 1996), 8.

41. *NYT*, 9 Nov. 1995; *Washington Post*, 5 Aug. 1995; *San Francisco Chronicle*, 8 Feb. 1996. On the convoluted legislative history of the CDA and Telecommunications Act see Robert Cannon, "The Legislative History of Senator Exon's Communications Decency Act: Regulating Barbarians on the Information Highway," *Federal Communications Law Journal* 49, no. 1 (1996): 52–94.

42. Marjorie Heins, *Not in Front of the Children: "Indecency," Censorship, and the Innocence of Youth* (New York: Hill and Wang, 2001), 169; *Reno v. ACLU*, 521 U.S. 844 (1997).

43. Bill Clinton, "Statement on the Supreme Court Decision on the Communications Decency Act," 26 June 1997, American Presidency Project, www.presidency.ucsb.edu.

44. *Cong. Rec.* 142 (30 Sept. 1996): 11840; *Washington Post*, 4 Oct. 1996.

45. COPA provisions included in *Ashcroft v. ACLU*, 535 U.S. 564 (2002); *Internet World*, 17 Nov. 1997; *Tampa Tribune*, 23 Oct. 1998; *Ashcroft v. Free Speech Coalition* 535 U.S. 234 (2002); *Los Angeles Times*, 22 Jan. 2009.

46. *NYT*, 9 Sept. 1995. See the memorandum sent to all U.S. Attorneys by Deputy Atty. Gen. Eric Holder, 10 June 1998, at www.usdoj.gov/dag/readingroom/obscen.htm.

47. *Kansas City Star*, 1 July 1997.

48. *Denver Post*, 30 Aug. 1997; *Washington Post*, 1 March 1998; *(New Orleans) Times-Picayune*, 21 Oct. 1997; *Atlanta Journal and Constitution*, 20 Dec. 1998; ibid., 21 Oct. 1998; *Birmingham News*, 11 Nov. 1999.

49. *Cleveland Plain Dealer*, 5 Feb. 2000; ibid., 11 Nov. 2000; *(Bergen County, NJ) Record*, 20 June 2001.

50. *Birmingham News*, 10 Feb. 1998; *Cincinnati Enquirer*, 25 Jan. 2001; *Kentucky Post*, 22 Feb. 2001.

51. On Bush see Ben Fritz, Brian Keefer, and Brendan Nyhan, *All the President's Spin: George W. Bush, the Media, and the Truth* (Boston: Touchstone, 2004); Charles Tiefer, *Veering Right: How the Bush Administration Subverts the Law for Conservative*

Causes (Berkeley: University of California Press, 2004); Sidney Blumenthal, *How Bush Rules: Chronicles of a Radical Regime* (Princeton, NJ: Princeton University Press, 2006); Jordan Paust, *Beyond the Law: The Bush Administration's Unlawful Responses to the "War" on Terror* (New York: Cambridge University Press, 2007).

52. Alan Crawford, *Thunder on the Right: The "New Right" and the Politics of Resentment* (New York: Pantheon, 1980), 268; Associated Press State & Local Wire, 21 May 1999.

53. On "hardcore art" films see Linda Williams, *Screening Sex* (Durham, NC: Duke University Press, 2008), 258–98.

54. On these and other ideological abuses of science see Esther Kaplan, *With God on Their Side: George W. Bush and the Christian Right* (New York: New Press, 2005).

55. *NYT*, 21 Oct. 2001; Pete Winn, "New Obscenity Chief Examined," *CitizenLink*, 20 Nov. 2001.

56. *XBiz*, 23 Dec. 2003; Jan LaRue, "Shock and Awful: DOJ Announces New Internet Bust," *Concerned Women for America*, 1 April 2003, www.cwfa.org.

57. George W. Bush, "Protection from Pornography Week, 2003," 25 Oct. 2003, www .whitehouse.gov; DOJ, "Former Dallas Police Officer and Wife Convicted on Obscenity Charges," 22 Oct. 2003, www.usdoj.com; Candi Cushman, "Why the Wait?" *Citizen*, Dec. 2003.

58. "Statement of John G. Malcolm, Deputy Assistant Attorney General . . . Before the Committee on the Judiciary, United States Senate," 15 Oct. 2003, http://judiciary .senate.gov/ testimony.cfm?id=961& wit_id=2559.

59. *Boston Globe*, 23 July 2006; *Los Angeles Times*, 14 Feb. 2004; Christian Wire Service, 6 May 2004.

60. *Los Angeles Times*, 25 June 2005; DOJ, "Justice Department to Appeal District Court Ruling," 15 Feb. 2005, www.usdoj.gov; "FRC Applauds Anti-Pornography Taskforce," 6 May 2005, www.frc.org; *Washington Post*, 20 Sept. 2005.

61. *Salt Lake City Tribune*, 26 Feb. 2007; ibid., 15 June 2007; *XBiz*, 29 Nov. 2006; AP Wire, 6 Sept. 2006; *Salt Lake City Tribune*, 21 March 2007.

62. *Cong. Rec.* 149 (10 June 2003): 5167; U.S. Attorney Kasey Warner, quoted in Dan Kapelovitz, "Girlspooping.com: The Feds Make Webmasters Eat Shit," *Hustler*, June 2004, available at www.kapelovitz.com/poop.htm.

63. Department of Justice, U.S. Attorney's Office, Western District of Texas, Press Release, "Eight Defendants Plead Guilty," 14 June 2004; "*U.S. v. Coil*, History Repeated," *DOJ Obscenity Prosecution News*, spring 2005; U.S. Department of Justice Press Releases: "Operator of Sexually Oriented Business Pleads Guilty," 28 June 2005; "National Operator of Sexually Oriented Business Pleads Guilty," 4 Nov. 2005; all at www.usdoj.gov/.

64. For examples see DOJ, "Three Indicted on Conspiracy and Obscenity Charges," 27 May 2004; U.S. Attorney's Office, Southern District of West Virginia, "Nitro Man Sentenced to 18 Months," 15 Nov. 2004; DOJ, "Ohio Couple Sentenced," 16 Nov. 2004; DOJ, "Montana Man Sentenced," 8 June 2005; DOJ, "Sanford Wasserman Sentenced," 2 Dec. 2005, all at www.usdoj.gov/.

65. Patrick Trueman, Statement Before Hearing on Obscenity Prosecution, Committee on the Judiciary, U.S. Senate, 16 March 2005, http://judiciary.senate.gov/.

66. Cushman, "Why the Wait?"; Daniel Weiss, "Talking Points: Why Obscenity Must Be Prosecuted," *Citizen*, Dec. 2003; "CWA Calls DOJ's New Obscenity Prosecution Task Force a Warning Sign to Pornographers," Christian Wire Service, 6 May 2004.

67. See LaRue, "Shock and Awful."

68. *U.S. v. Extreme Associates*, 352 F. Supp. 2d 578 (2005); *Washington Times*, 10 Feb. 2005; *NYT*, 17 Feb. 2005; *Lawrence v. Texas*, 539 U.S. 558 (2003).

69. *U.S. v. Extreme Associates*, 431 F.3d 150 (2005); *U.S. v. Gartman*, 2005 U.S. Dist. LEXIS 1501; *Pittsburgh Post-Gazette*, 11 March 2009.

70. *AVN*, 3 Oct. 2008; *AVN*, 8 April 2008.

71. *Austin American-Statesman*, 14 Feb. 2008.

72. *Williams v. Pryor*, 220 F. Supp. 2d 1257 (2002), *reversed*, 378 F.3d 1232 (2004); Associated Press, 3 Oct. 2007; *Houston Chronicle*, 3 Oct. 2006.

73. *PHE, Inc. v. State*, 877 So.2d 1244 (2004); *Salina Journal*, 8 Sept. 2005; *NYT*, 18 July 2004; *Fort Worth Star-Telegram*, 24 March 2006.

74. Danielle Lindemann, "Pathology Full Circle: A History of Anti-Vibrator Legislation in the United States," *Columbia Journal of Gender and Law* 15, no. 1 (2006): 326–46; *Topeka Capital-Journal*, 4 Jan. 2007; *Reliable Consultants v. Earle*, No. 06-51067, Fifth Circuit Court of Appeals (2008); *Austin American-Statesman*, 14 Feb. 2008.

75. *Ashcroft v. Free Speech Coalition*, 535 U.S. 234 (2002); *NYT*, 17 April 2002.

76. Office of the Press Secretary, "President Signs PROTECT Act," 30 April 2003, http://georgewbush-whitehouse.archives.gov.

77. *U.S. v. Williams*, No. 04–15128, Eleventh Circuit Court of Appeals (2006).

78. Ibid., *reversed*, No. 06-694, Supreme Court of the United States (2008).

79. *U.S. v. Whorley*, No. 06-4288, Fourth Circuit Court of Appeals (2008).

80. Ibid.

81. U.S. Attorney Press Release, "Protecting Our Children," 10 March 2006, http://fbi .gov.; *U.S. v. Handley*, No. 1:07-cr-00030-JEG, Order, U.S. District Court for Southeastern Iowa, 2 July 2008. Thanks to Bethany Murray for pointing me toward manga-related resources.

82. *U.S. v. Handley*; DOJ Press Release, 20 May 2009, www.usdoj.gov/.

83. *NYT*, 28 Sept. 2007; *XBiz*, 7 Aug. 2008; *The (Lakeland, FL) Ledger*, 10 July 2009.

84. *NYT*, 25 March 2009.

85. "The Cambria List," 18 Jan. 2001, www.pbs.org/wgbh/pages/frontline/shows/porn/prosecuting/cambria.html; Mubarak Dahir, "Defending Porn from Bush," *Houston Voice*, 16 April 2004; Missy Suicide, "SG Removing Pictures, You Can Thank Bush," 24 Sept. 2005, http://suicidegirls.com/boards/Everything+SG/81705/page1/.

86. Declan McCullagh, "Mass Deletion Sparks LiveJournal Revolt," CNet News, 30 May 2007; Abe Hassan (burr86), "More Clarifications," 19 July 2007, http://community.livejournal.com/lj_biz/241428.html.

87. "Be Alert to Pornography's Effects," *Chattanooga Times Free Press*, 22 Jan. 2006; Dagmar Herzog, *Sex in Crisis: The New Sexual Revolution and the Future of American Politics* (New York: Basic Books, 2008), 91.

88. Paul Abramson, Steven Pinkerton, and Mark Huppin, *Sexual Rights in America: The Ninth Amendment and the Pursuit of Happiness* (New York: New York University Press, 2003), 1.

89. "Obama Justice Nominee Used to Represent Playboy," FOXNews.com, 4 Feb. 2009.

ACKNOWLEDGMENTS

SO MUCH GRATITUDE, so little space to express it! This book began life as a history dissertation at UCLA, and without my incredible committee it could never have existed at all. Ruth Bloch is everything one could want in a dissertation chair: intense in her scrutiny but generous in her support, which has extended for several years past my filing now. I'm not sure we agree on all of my arguments, but I am sure they're stronger for having been reshaped under her guidance. Jan Reiff has also never faltered in her constructive criticism and generosity, and if I can someday be as astute in my margin comments as she is, I will consider myself quite the sharp scholar indeed. Finally, Kathleen McHugh brought the outside wisdom of literary and film studies, and I'm delighted by the ways her comments over the years have inspired me, perhaps more than she yet realizes. To Ruth, Jan, and Kathleen go my boundless appreciation and admiration.

I was lucky enough to share my grad school years with a wonderful cohort. Kyle Livie, Petula Iu, and Mehera Gerardo were and are great friends. Laura Gifford offered astute feedback on several chapters and has informed my understanding of the New Right with her own smart work on the topic. Ellie Hickerson offered thoughtful commentary and has been a charming host on several trips through Colorado.

Much of the research for this project was undertaken on a seemingly endless drive around the country, a geekier version of *Two-Lane Blacktop* where the currency was not engine horsepower but archival footnotes. To archivists everywhere, I thank you for your incredible kindness to a somewhat shaggy grad student with oft-bloodshot eyes; your ability to treat that befuddled young man with respect was more appreciated than you may have realized, and your efforts in preserving, organizing, and making available the raw materials of history are the lifeblood of this and every book in the discipline. In particular, Jeff Rankin, Octavio Olvera, and the entire UCLA Special Collections staff, and Dan Linke at Princeton's Seeley G.

Mudd Library, were of great value on this front, but please consider every archival citation herein as a note of thanks to the respective archivists.

The evolution of this project from dissertation to book transpired as I've navigated the choppy waters of a rapidly restructuring academic labor market. Robin Bachin and Richard Godbeer offered me a tremendous opportunity to first set sail on those waters at the University of Miami, and I'll always appreciate it. When things looked dire the next year, Jesse Battan at Cal-State Fullerton came through with work and a supportive presence, and for this, too, I stay thankful. I revised this manuscript while teaching at Temple University, where I was welcomed into the campus community with open arms by seemingly everyone, and I particularly thank Patricia Melzer, Bryant Simon, Rebecca Alpert, Laura Levitt, Beth Bailey, Seth Bruggeman, Kristi Brian, and Lisa Rhodes for going out of their way to help me make a big transition east. Finally, my new colleagues at Rutgers University, Newark, have already revealed their kindness and congeniality, and I am thrilled to join them. I look forward to the years ahead on our great campus.

I feel incredibly fortunate to have also received encouraging words from so many scholars whose work long inspired me, and a few bear mention. Leigh Ann Wheeler showed magnanimity in both her responses to my work and her willingness to lend a helping hand. Gillian Frank has become a valued friend, not to mention a significant new voice in the history of sexuality. Rick Perlstein, who somehow balances panoramic views of the New Right with analysis of breathtaking exactitude (not to mention some of the best prose around), read the entire manuscript and improved it greatly with his suggestions. Finally, Andrea Friedman: as a grad student, I held her *Prurient Interests* as the precise model of what I wanted to accomplish for the postwar years; while I would never claim to have achieved that, to have had her read the entire work and offer her incisive feedback is a genuine honor.

Various forms of institutional support have also literally afforded me the opportunity to write this book. Grants from the Lyndon Johnson Presidential Library and Museum, Princeton University, the Southern California Historical Society, and UCLA's Graduate Division, History Department, and Center for the Study of Women all kept me afloat at various points and are much appreciated. Columbia University Press, too, has been wonderful to me, with Kabir Dandona and Philip Leventhal providing helpful guidance en route to the book's materialization. Joe Abbott's copy-editing gave the text a valuable polishing; blame for remaining blemishes falls strictly on me.

As a teacher, I have been deeply influenced by the challenging, nur-turing mentorship I received from my professors as an undergraduate at the University of Wisconsin, La Crosse. I try to replicate this in my own pedagogy, and I have in turn been continuously inspired by my students at the University of Miami, UCLA, Cal State Fullerton, and Temple. That inspiration has undergirded this whole effort, so I thank all of you.

Finally, life outside the Ivory Tower.

The emotional sustenance provided by intimates of various sorts gave a sense of meaning to things like formatting footnotes. Matt "Lloyd" Elsen, Bart Bly, and Steve Kube have always been there when I've needed them, no questions asked. Emily Burnett's endless willingness to explore the nooks and crannies of Los Angeles' fascinating social geography always made for a refreshing break. Without Jill Crouther's companionship on the Great Archival Expedition of '04 I would never have seen the Georgia Ru-ral Telephone Museum; her critiques of my works in progress have never minced words, but they're always worth their weight in bruised ego. My brother Doug Strub is always up for a show or a game, and he will lose the next racquetball contest, mark my word; my brother Brian Strub con-tinuously reminds me that, for all the harsh analysis of liberalism contained here, there is much to admire and respect in the movement, and I com-mend his principled stands. Gabriela Lizama was there through successes and failures, revisions and resubmissions, and she handled those and much more with the grace and poise befitting a top-notch neurologist. Lucky for her patients, that's what she is. Mary Rizzo showed up at 5th and Chestnut in a giant fuzzy pink hat and turned my life into a panoply of pleasures. She's simply amazing, and I am grateful. And while I barely met him in his all-too-short life, Lance Hahn profoundly informed my politics and iden-tity, and he continues to inspire me.

Above all else, my parents, Kris Breza and Ron Strub, deserve my gratitude. I couldn't begin to convey how supportive they've been, or how much that's meant to me, but suffice it to say, as proud as they are of me, I am of them for everything they've done in their lives. It might be more fitting if I had a book on, say, good parenting to dedicate to them, but a book on the politics of porn is what I've got, so joke if you must, but this is for them.

Index